Global Media Studies

Global Media Studies

TOBY MILLER AND MARWAN M. KRAIDY

polity

This book has benefited from a publication subsidy from the Project for Advanced Research in Global Communication Press, Annenberg School for Communication, University of Pennsylvania.

First published in 2016 by Polity Press
Reprinted 2018

Polity Press
65 Bridge Street
Cambridge CB2 1UR, UK

Polity Press
350 Main Street
Malden, MA 02148, USA

ISBN-13: 978-0-7456-4431-8
ISBN-13: 978-0-7456-4432-5(pb)

Library of Congress Cataloging-in-Publication Data

Names: Miller, Toby, author. | Kraidy, Marwan M., 1972- author.
Title: Global media studies / Toby Miller, Marwan M. Kraidy.
Description: Malden, MA : Polity Press, 2016. | Includes bibliographical
   references and index.
Identifiers: LCCN 2016000784| ISBN 9780745644318 (hardback : alk. paper) |
   ISBN 9780745644325 (pbk. : alk. paper)
Subjects: LCSH: Communication, International. | Globalization.
Classification: LCC P96.I5 M55 2016 | DDC 302.2--dc23 LC record available at http://lccn.loc.
gov/2016000784

A catalogue record for this book is available from the British Library.

Typeset in 9.5 on 12 pt Utopia by
Servis Filmsetting Ltd, Stockport, Cheshire
Printed and bound in the United States by LSC Communications

The publisher has used its best endeavours to ensure that the URLs for external websites referred to in this book are correct and active at the time of going to press. However, the publisher has no responsibility for the websites and can make no guarantee that a site will remain live or that the content is or will remain appropriate.

Every effort has been made to trace all copyright holders, but if any have been inadvertently overlooked the publisher will be pleased to include any necessary credits in any subsequent reprint or edition.

For further information on Polity, visit our website:
politybooks.com

Contents

Abbreviations

AEJMC	Association for Education in Journalism and Mass Communication
API	American Petroleum Institute
ARABSAT	Arab Satellite Organization
ASBU	Arab States Broadcasting Union
ASTC	Arab Satellite Television Charter
ASU	Arizona State University
AVML	Audio-Visual Media Law
BEA	Broadcast Education Association
BRIC	Brazil, Russia, India, and China
DARPA	Defense Advanced Research Projects Agency
DMC	Dubai Media City
DVRs	Digital Video Recorders
FCTC	Framework Convention on Tobacco Control
GNI	Gross National Income
IAMCR	International Association for Media Communication and Research
ICA	International Communication Association
ICANN	Internet Corporation for Assigned Names and Numbers
ICTs	information and communication technologies
IGF	Internet Governance Forum
ISI	import substitution industrialization
MBC	Middle East Broadcasting Center
MeCCSA	Media, Communications and Cultural Studies Association
MERCOSUR/MERCOSUL	Mercado Comun del Sur/Mercado Comum do Sul
MSA	Master Settlement Agreement
NAFTA	North American Free Trade Agreement
NCAVM	National Council of Audio-Visual Media
NFL	National Football League
NICL	New International Division of Cultural Labor
NIDL	New International Division of Labor
NWICO	New World Information and Communication Order
OCIAA	Office of the Coordinator of Inter-American Affairs
PGA	Producers Guild of America
PR	public relations
PRC	People's Republic of China
RCA	Radio Corporation of America

SCA	Speech Communication Association
SCMS	Society for Cinema and Media Studies
TLCAN	Tratado de Libre Comercio de América del Norte
TSN	The Sports Network
U&G	uses and gratifications
UAE	United Arab Emirates
UDC	Union for Democratic Communications
UNESCO	United Nations Educational, Scientific and Cultural Organisation
WTO	World Trade Organization

Introduction

Mary-Kate and Ashley Olsen, twins in real life, starred as babies, toddlers, and 'tweens in the US ABC TV network situation comedy *Full House* from 1987 to 1995, sharing the role of Michelle Tanner. During those years, a merchandising company emerged to capitalize on the girls' prominence via music, books, and videos. By the time the teenaged twins launched a clothing line, *Hollywood Reporter* magazine nominated them as "the most powerful young women in Hollywood." At 18, each was worth over US$130 million, derived from US$1.4 billion in sales (Shade and Porter, 2008).

Numerous Bangladeshi women (whose names we do not know) made the clothing that was owned and endorsed by the cute-as-a-button Olsens, clothing that the *New York Times* acclaimed as "ashcan chic," "homeless masquerade," and "[d]umpster dressing" (La Ferla, 2005). These employees worked for between US$189.28 and US$436.80 a year, and were denied mandatory paid maternity leave until the third sector intervened and embarrassed the cuddly designers (Mensch, 2006).

A New International Division of Cultural Labor (NICL), of which more below, thus saw a fashion line neatly – and gruesomely – index the difference in choices between the Olsens and their employees. Meanwhile, pro-anorexia websites highlighted the twins as role models, and 2011 found the bubbly twosome releasing an alligator backpack retailing at US$39,000 (Shade and Porter, 2008; Lipczynska, 2007).[1] The *Times of India* praised their "sisterly bond" and the *Guardian* called 2015 the year when they became "the go-to brand for minimal chic" (Cochrane, 2015).[2]

The Olsens' careers have seen them move across shifting discourses of femininity, in a world where women may stand for domestic values, be high-profile actors in public life, or live as low-paid, exploited workers – sometimes next door, sometimes next continent. As part of that shift, from a very early age the Olsens were both embroiled in and representative of complex commodity and labor relations, for which they were held responsible. Their struggles with education, weight, and love made them subjects of identification for many others dealing with the impact of feminism – without its ideological, organizational, and interpersonal buttressing (Probyn, 2008). Their arms-length exploitation of others is less visually central to their image, but materially crucial to it.

The lesson of this anecdote is that the media engage a multitude of topics and sites and require multiple analytic approaches if they are to be understood, and that a purely media-centric approach, focused on, for example, the Olsens' renowned TV program, will be as inadequate as a US-centric approach would be. A more comprehensive and varied view is required, one that takes into account processes of production, distribution, text, and use, including how the media reproduce sociocultural norms, values, identities, and ideologies on a regional, national, and global scale. This necessitates consideration of the conditions that underpin the Olsens' world in order to draw attention to a dialectical struggle between their privileged, if sometimes traumatic, lives, which are routinely subject to public scrutiny, and the infinitely harsher, equally gendered, frequently invisible labor processes on which their affluence depends.

In keeping with that brief exemplar, understanding the media requires studying them up, down, and sideways. That means researching production and distribution, cross-subsidy and monopoly profit, national and international public policy, press coverage, meaning, audience interpretation, and environmental impact, *inter alia*. We must tease out the manifold complexities of media production, signification, and reception.

For that reason, this book covers a very wide terrain, and in varied forms. Each chapter is animated, either overtly or implicitly, by three elements that are at play in the Olsen twins' labor narrative:

- theories (in this instance, political economy, psychology, and feminism);
- genres (situation comedy, fashion, and celebrity); and
- places (the United States and Bangladesh).

Those three tendencies are heuristic rather than substantive divisions; theories use genres and articulate to places. But we find the distinction useful because it enables three key forms of media analysis:

- theorization, whether everyday understandings or academic norms;
- generic distinctions, based on themes and qualities; and
- places, or the locations in which theories and genres occur and are modified.

This book also engages some perennial questions that have been posed by and of media studies:

- who runs the media?
- who makes the media?
- what is on media platforms?
- what is the audience to them? and
- how do the media enter the public sphere and human consciousness as they circulate sounds, images, ideologies, and waste?

To engage such questions, the issues we address include policy, production, genre, audience, and environment. Our goal is to acknowledge the equal importance and achievements of work done in political economy, textual analysis, and reception, the principal fields that address such matters. We do so in a way that seeks to enlarge those fields both conceptually and geographically. We believe in mixing methods – connecting numbers to meanings (for instance, tying ratings analysis to textual analysis) and acknowledging that meaning matters when it is linked to numbers (such as discerning both the deep meaning of specific texts and how representative they are). We think the distinctions between qualitative and quantitative methods that underpin much of US social science need to be compromised.

Each section of the volume (i) presents relevant topics for debate, poses new questions, and opens new horizons; (ii) contextualizes theories, methods, and traditions of intellectual reflection and empirical research, giving recognition both to mainstream and marginal, established, and emergent voices and norms; and (iii) explains the historical, social, economic, and political conditions that have contributed to the inception, support, and decline of approaches, where appropriate. Our intellectual agenda is thematically internationalist, politically socialist, and methodologically promiscuous. It is equally influenced by feminism, postcolonialism, Marxism, and social movements. We seek a blend of market and non-market principles that derive from the French Revolutionary cry, *liberté, égalité, fraternité* (liberty, equality, solidarity) and the Argentine left's contemporary version, *ser ciudadano, tener trabajo, y ser alfabetizado* (citizenship, employment, and literacy). The first category concerns political rights; the second, material interests; and the third, cultural representation.

We are not the first to tread this path. One of our inspirations is Clare of Assisi, a teen runaway from the thirteenth century originally named Chiara Offreduccio. The first Franciscan nun, she is also the patron saint of television, having been canonized in 1957 for her prescient bedridden vision of images from a midnight mass cast upon a wall. Seven hundred years later, Pius XII decreed this to have been the first TV broadcast (Pius XII, 1958).[3] We are indebted to her example as the earliest media celebrity and theorist – a rare combination.

The need for most academic books to be written in English militates against complex cultural analysis. We originally planned to mitigate this limitation, at least in terms of research, by writing this volume with South Asian and Chinese co-authors, but that did not eventuate. As veterans of such arrangements will know, many collaborations do not take root as first envisaged, and tend to develop organically. Our linguistic limitations as scholars therefore condition much of what follows. We are most fluent in English, Arabic, French, and Spanish, which immediately limits the purview of a book called *Global Media Studies*. That said, we hope that our years spent living and working across the world, and learning from others who think, listen, watch, speak, write, read, and live differently, will make the project worth our readers' time.

Chapters 1 and 2 lay out the state of play. We begin with media studies – where it came from, what it does, and what it ought to do. This is followed by a contextualization of such work inside the shift in discourse from international communication to global media. Chapters 3 and 4 look at institutional methods for comprehending the global media. After explicating and illustrating how to undertake political economy, we examine global policymaking and rule. Chapters 5 and 6 look in depth at mobile telephony and the impact of the US media – two virtually universal phenomena. Chapters 7 and 8 are dedicated to textual analysis, once more offering both metacritical and applied commentary and exemplification, with a heightened focus on reality television. We conclude with an investigation of audiences.

This book has been a long time in the making. Other projects and life situations have intervened, as sometimes happens. But our collaboration has been stimulating and even fun, and we hope you enjoy its result. Many people around the world have contributed in ways small and big to our understanding of the global life of media. We especially wish to thank our collaborators and friends Richard Maxwell and Bill Grantham, whose insights and prose make them co-authors of chapters 5 and 6 respectively.

1 Media Studies

The word "media" is often used in a very limited fashion, to designate a small number of discrete communications technologies and platforms: newspapers, magazines, film, radio, and television.[1] But the wider field of communications, from cable to satellite to telephony, have become key sites for producing and receiving the media, and there is increasing overlap between such sectors, as black-box techniques and technologies, once set apart from audiences, become part of public experience and debate.

"Medium," the singular form of the word "media," has been in English usage since the seventeenth century. It refers to something that lies between two objects and links them. With that in mind, we use the term "media" as a *portmanteau* word to cover a multitude of cultural and communicative machines and processes that connect people, processes, institutions, meanings, and power in the material world.

The media constitute and are constituted by:

- technologies, which form their conditions of possibility;
- policies, which determine the field in which they operate;
- genres, which organize texts as drama, music, sport, information, and so on;
- workers, who make media texts through performances and recordings;
- audiences, who receive and interpret the ensuing content; and
- the environment, which is affected by the creation, use, and detritus of the media.

There is increasing convergence across the different media. In 1940s sociology and 1960s economics, the term "convergence" referred to capitalist societies that were becoming more centrally planned even as state-socialist ones grew more capitalist (Galbraith, 1967). In 1980s communication theory, convergence explained the processes whereby people and institutions share expressions and issues (Bormann, 1985).

Today, convergence is occurring across media platforms. Consumer electronics connect to information and communication technologies (ICTs) and vice versa: televisions resemble computers, books are read on telephones, newspapers are written through clouds, and so on. Genres, gadgets, and bodies that were once separate are now linked to produce what the US Television Advertising Bureau calls a "Great Circle of modern consumerism" – while audiences watch programs on TV, they use their tablets to buy the products that are being advertised.[2] Film, radio, newspapers, television, and so on can no longer be considered as individually autonomous media, isolated from the internet and mobile telephony. Convergence is at play and work through blogging, fan sites, ringtones, and music and video downloads and applications.

Throughout our investigations, we'll bear another core concept in mind: "culture."

It derives from the Latin *colere*, a verb to describe tending and developing agriculture. With the advent of capitalism's division of labor, culture came both to *embody* instrumentalism and to *abjure* it, via the industrialization of farming, on the one hand, and the development of individual taste, on the other (Adorno, 2009: 146; Benhabib, 2002: 2).

Eighteenth-century German, French, and Spanish dictionaries bear witness to a metaphorical shift during this period from agricultural cultivation to spiritual elevation. As the spread of literacy and printing saw customs and laws passed on, governed, and adjudicated through the written word, cultural texts supplemented and supplanted physical force as guarantors of authority. With the Industrial Revolution, populations urbanized, food was imported, and textual forms were exchanged. An emergent consumer society produced such events as horse racing, opera, art exhibits, and balls. The impact of this shift was indexed in cultural labor: *poligrafi* in fifteenth-century Venice and hacks in eighteenth-century London wrote popular and influential conduct books. These works of instruction on everyday life marked the textualization of custom and the development of new occupations. Anxieties about cultural imperialism also appeared, via debates over Western domination that occupied intellectuals, politicians, and moral guardians beyond the West, particularly in what is often referred to as "the Muslim world" (Briggs and Burke, 2003; Kraidy, 2010; Mowlana, 2000; Sabry, 2010). Welcome to the foundations of media studies.

In the eighteenth century, Immanuel Kant ideologized these commercial and imperial changes, arguing that culture ensured "conformity to laws without the law." Aesthetics could generate "morally practical precepts," schooling people to transcend particular interests via the development of a "*public* sense, *i.e.* a critical faculty which in its reflective act takes account (*a priori*) of the mode of representation . . . to weight its judgement with the collective reason of mankind" (1987; also see Hunter, 2008). Kant envisaged an "*emergence from . . . self-incurred immaturity,*" independent of religion, government, and commerce (1991: 54). In other words, if readers could interpret art, literature, and drama in logical, emotional, and social ways – and comprehend the difference between them – they could be relied upon to govern themselves.

The Beginning – Media Studies 1.0

The media have usually been understood in two quasi-Kantian registers, via the social sciences and the humanities. They emerged as secular alternatives to deistic knowledge (Schelling, 1914) focused on dual forms of "*self-realization*" (S. Weber, 2000) – truth and beauty.

A heuristic distinction in the sixteenth century, this bifurcation became substantive as time passed (Williams 1983: 38). The media came to be understood as markers of differences and similarities in taste and status within and between groups. These qualities were explored interpretatively or methodically, with the social sciences animated by empirical facts and the humanities exercised by aesthetic qualities.

Today's social sciences focus on the languages, religions, customs, times, spaces, and exchanges of the media, as explored ethnographically or statistically. The humanities analyze the media through textual criticism and institutional history.

So whereas the social sciences articulate differences within populations through social norms (for example, correlating media usage with health), the humanities do so through symbolic norms (for example, providing some of us with the cultural capital to appreciate high culture) (Wallerstein, 1989; Bourdieu, 1984).

The media's connection to collective and individual identity and conduct has produced some powerful reactions to emergent media technologies and genres. In the nineteenth century, theorists from both right and left argued that newly literate publics would be vulnerable to manipulation by demagogues. This Kantian concern has continued ever since. For its part, contemporary bourgeois economics may assume that rational consumers determine what is popular in the media, but its sacerdotes are equally concerned that people can be bamboozled by unscrupulously fluent media organizations. On the other side of politics, Marxism has often viewed the media as a route to false consciousness that diverts the working class from recognizing its economic oppression, but also as an opportunity for agitprop. Feminist approaches have moved between condemning the media as distractions from gendered consciousness and celebrating them as distinctive parts of women's culture; and cultural studies has regarded the media as key locations for symbolic resistance to class, race, and gender oppression (Smith, 1987; Hall and Jefferson, 1976).

From an array of political and epistemological perspectives, there has therefore been an emphasis on the origin, number, and conduct of media audiences: where they came from, how many there were, and what they did as a consequence of being present. Such concerns are coupled with a focus on content: *what* were audiences watching when they . . . . And so both audiences and texts are conceived as empirical entities that can be known, via research instruments derived from sociology, psychology, history, literary criticism, demography, linguistics, communications, anthropology, accountancy, economics, and marketing.

Perhaps the foremost early theorist of the media in critical thinking of the kind represented in this volume is the Italian Marxist Antonio Gramsci, whose opposition to fascism in the 1920s and '30s is an exemplar for progressive intellectuals. Gramsci maintained that each social group creates "organically, one or more strata of intellectuals which give it homogeneity and an awareness of its own function not only in the economic but also in the social and political fields" – the industrial technology, law, economy, and culture of such groups. The "'organic' intellectuals that every new class creates alongside itself and elaborates in the course of its development" assist in the emergence of that class, for example via military expertise. Media intellectuals operate in "[c]ivil society . . . the ensemble of organisms commonly called 'private,'" that of 'political society' or 'the State'." They comprise the "'hegemony' which the dominant group exercises throughout society" as well as the "'direct domination' or command exercised through the State and 'juridical' government." Ordinary people give "'spontaneous' consent" to the "general direction imposed on social life by the dominant fundamental group" (Gramsci, 1978: 5–7, 12). In other words, the media legitimize socioeconomic-political arrangements in the public mind. They can be sites of struggle as well as domination.

Gramsci's notion of hegemony has had global purchase. The Welsh cultural critic Raymond Williams (1977) developed the idea of residual, dominant, and emergent hegemonies to describe the process whereby class formations compete over media narratives that legitimize social control. At the time he wrote, in the 1970s, examples of these categories included the remains of empire (residual), a modern mixed economy (dominant), and neoliberal transformation (emergent). Extensive use has been made of hegemony theory beyond the Global North. In Latin America, Gramsci's notion of the national popular harnessing of class interests is common sense for both left and right (Massardo, 1999). The same applies in South Asia and segments of the Middle East and Africa (Patnaik, 2004; Dabashi, 2013; Marks and Engels, 1994).

While hegemony theory is alert to struggle rather than absolute domination, some critiques of the media suggest that its commercial manifestations "impress . . . the same stamp on everything" because their organizational form necessitates repetition rather than difference via the factory-like production of films, songs, news bulletins, radio formats, and programs – as if they were cars. This perspective derives from the Frankfurt School, a group of anti-Nazi scholars writing around the same time as Gramsci. The principals of that School, Theodor Adorno and Max Horkheimer (1977), saw consumers and citizens as manipulated from the social order's economic apex, with "domination" masquerading as choice in a "society alienated from itself." Consumers were not active agents engaging the media, but its objects, just as much as programming or poetry.

For Adorno and Horkheimer, the media are industrial products, ruled by dominant economic forces that diminish ideological and generic innovation in favor of industrial standardization – a blend of political and economic calculation. The result? Whereas they might have begun as reflections of reality, commodity signs on show in the media necessarily displace representations of the truth with false information. Then these two delineable phases of truth and lies become indistinct. Once underlying reality is lost, signs become self-referential, with no residual correspondence to the real: they have adopted the form of their own simulation (Baudrillard, 1988).

People are said to buy commodities to give meaning to their world because societies no longer make them feel as though they belong. This concatenating simulation has implications for the aesthetic and social hierarchies that "regulate and structure . . . individual and collective lives" (Parekh, 2000: 143) in competitive ways that harness the media to social and commercial purposes. For this reason, analysts discern close ties between industrial power and ideological impact.

A further transformation has occurred during the twenty-first century: the media are not just superstructural forces that provide ideological support to the real substructure of the economy. These days, they are at the heart *of* that economy. The inaugural President of the European Bank for Reconstruction and Development and noted music theorist Jacques Attali explains that a new "mercantile order forms wherever a creative class masters a key innovation from navigation to accounting or, in our own time, where services are most efficiently mass produced, thus generating enormous wealth" (2008: 31). He recognizes that a prosperous economic future lies in finance capital and ideology rather than agriculture and manufacturing – seeking revenue from innovation and intellectual property, not minerals or masses. It is no surprise, then, that the global trade in culture increased from US$559.5 billion in 2010 to US$624 billion in 2011 (United Nations, 2013).

As a consequence, the canons of aesthetic judgment and social distinction that once separated social science and humanities approaches to the popular – distinguishing aesthetic tropes, economic needs, and social norms – are collapsing in on each other. Positive discourses about the media say they can elevate people above ordinary life, transcending body, time, and place, or settle us into society through the wellsprings of community, as part of daily existence. A discourse about popularity idealizes media fun, promising secular transcendence (Frith, 1991: 106–7).

The media are now more than textual signs or everyday practices, more than objects of subcultural appropriation and re-signification. They offer important resources to markets and nations – reactions to the crisis of belonging and economic necessity occasioned by capitalist globalization. Crucial to advanced and developing economies alike, the media can also provide the legitimizing ground on which particular groups (e.g., African Americans, lesbians, the hearing-impaired, evangelical Protestants, women, or artists) claim resources and seek inclusion in national and international narratives (on Latin America, see Yúdice, 2002; Martín-Barbero, 2003; on the Arab world, see Colla, 2012; Kraidy, 2010; Kraidy and Khalil, 2008; Pahwa and Winegar, 2012; Sakr, 2004; on China, see Yang, 2009; on Ghana, see Boateng, 2008).

Some analysts argue that the media form a high stage of social and political development. Rather than encouraging alienation, they stand for the expansion of civil society, the moment in history when the state becomes receptive to, and part of, the general community. The entire population is now part of social development, rather than being excluded from the means and methods of political calculation. This coincides with other changes, such as a lessening of traditional authority, the promulgation of individual rights and respect, and a newly intense, interpersonal, large-scale human interaction. These transformations are necessitated by industrialization and aided by communication. The spread of advertising is taken as a model for the breakdown of social barriers, exemplified in the triumph of popular culture (Shils, 1966; Hartley, 1992). This was the fulcrum of founding BBC Director-General John Reith's famous broadcasting philosophy: "The best of everything to the greatest number of homes."[3]

Cultural studies has offered a productive, nuanced response to popular culture in general and the media in particular. Historical and contemporary analyses of slaves, crowds, pirates, bandits, minorities, women, and the working class have utilized archival, ethnographic, and statistical methods to emphasize day-to-day non-compliance with authority, via practices of consumption that frequently turn into practices of production. For example, UK research has lit upon Teddy Boys, Mods, bikers, skinheads, punks, school students, teen girls, Rastas, truants, drop-outs, and romance-fiction readers as its magical agents of history – groups who deviated from the norms of schooling and the transition to work by generating moral panics. Scholar-activists examine the structural underpinnings to collective style, investigating how *bricolage* subverts the achievement-oriented, materialistic values and appearance of the middle class. The working assumption has often been that subordinate groups adopt and adapt signs and objects from dominant media culture, reorganizing them to manufacture new meanings. The oppressed become producers of new fashions, inscribing alienation, difference, and powerlessness on their bodies (Leong, 1992).

There remains a paradox and possibly a contradiction in cultural studies' account of the media: corporations have learnt to respond, almost gratefully, to critical subcultures. For instance, even as the press and politicians in the Global North announced across the 1970s that punks were folk devils, setting in train various moral panics about their effect on society, the fashion and music industries were sending out spies to watch and listen to them as part of a restless search for new trends to market. John Fiske (1989) uses the example of blue jeans to illustrate this: as marginal groups "personalize" denim, for example happily displaying holes that result from normal wear and tear and limited economic resources to replace beat-up clothes, the industry begins selling brand new jeans with holes in them. Relatedly, whenever the politics of spectacle is used effectively by social movements, advertising agencies watch on and parrot what they see. Advertising executives were involved in branding Lebanon's 2005 independent intifada as "the Cedar Revolution" in Washington, DC, while the aesthetics of protest evident in downtown Beirut were later recycled on the advertising billboards that dominate Lebanese highways. Capitalism appropriates its appropriators.

The need for an awareness of this double-edged investment in commodities, as objects of resistance whose very appropriation can then be recommodified, makes socioeconomic analysis via critical political economy a good ally of representational analysis via close reading. A certain tendency on both sides has maintained that the two approaches are mutually exclusive: one is concerned with structures of the economy, the other with structures of meaning. But this need not be the case. Historically, the best critical political economy and the best close reading have worked through the imbrication of power and subjectivity at all points on the cultural continuum, bringing together the insights of Gramsci and Frankfurt in analyses that are attentive to local context. We seek to model this in the chapters to come.

A Brief History of Media Inquiry

As they have developed over time, the media have given rise to three related topics of scholarly inquiry:

- technology, ownership, and control – their political economy;
- textuality – their meaning; and
- audiences – their public.

Within these categories lie three further divisions. First, approaches to technology, ownership, and control vary between neoliberal endorsements of regulation by the state in order to protect property and guarantee market entry for new competitors, Marxist critiques of the bourgeois media for controlling the sociopolitical agenda, and environmental investigations of the impact of media gadgetry on energy use and electronic waste (e-waste). Second, approaches to textuality vary between hermeneutics – which unearths the meaning of individual programs and links them to broader social formations and problems, such as the way that social identities are represented – and content analysis, which establishes patterns across significant numbers of similar texts, rather than close readings of individual ones. Third, approaches to audiences vary between social-psychological attempts to validate correlations between television and social conduct, political-economic critiques of imported texts threatening national culture, and celebrations of spectators' interpretations.

These tasks articulate to particular academic disciplines, which in turn are tied to particular interests of state and capital:

- engineering, computing, public policy, journalism, and "film" schools create and run media production and reception via business, the military, the community, and the public service;

Table 1.1

Topics	Objects	Methods	Disciplines
Regulation, industry development, new technology	State, capital, labor	Political economy, neoliberalism	Engineering, computer science, economics, political science, law, communication studies
Genre	Text	Content analysis	Communication studies, sociology
Genre	Text	Textual analysis	Literary/cultural/media studies
Uses	Audience	Uses and gratifications	Communication studies, psychology, marketing
Uses	Audience	Ethnography	Anthropology, cultural/media studies, communication studies
Effects	Audience	Experimentation, questionnaire	Psychology, marketing, communication studies

- communication studies focuses on such social projects as propaganda, marketing, and citizenship;
- economics theorizes and polices doctrines of scarcity, as well as managing overproduction through overseas expansion;
- Marxism points to the impact of ownership and control and cultural imperialism on the media and consciousness; and
- cultural criticism evaluates representation, justifies protectionism, and calls for content provision.

Today, major engagements with the media come from the psy-function (psychology, psychiatry, and psychoanalysis), other social sciences (sociology, economics, communication studies, anthropology, political science, and law), and the humanities (literature, cinema studies, television studies, languages, and cultural studies).

This complex melange offers seven principal forms of inquiry, which (i) borrow ethnography from sociology and anthropology to investigate the experiences of audiences; (ii) use experimentation and testing methods from psychology to establish cause-and-effect relations between media use and subsequent conduct; (iii) adapt content analysis from sociology and communication studies to evaluate texts in terms of generic patterns; (iv) adopt textual analysis from literary theory and linguistics to identify the ideological tenor of content; (v) apply textual and audience interpretation from psychoanalysis to speculate on psychic processes; (vi) deploy political economy to examine ownership, control, regulation, and international exchange; and (vii) utilize archival, curatorial, and historiographic methods to give the media a record of their past. (See Table 1.1.)

So where did this hybrid creature come from? Media studies emerged from a complex blend of the social sciences and the humanities, from qualitative and quantitative sociology and communications, from language and literature departments, and various formations across these and other domains, such as area studies.

A key source has been speech communication, which was founded in the United States a century ago to assist with the assimilation of white, non-English-speaking migrants into the workforce. It became the first home of media education, because

Table 1.2

International Association for Media and Communication Research	Union for Democratic Communications
Broadcast Education Association	Association for Education in Journalism and Mass Communication
National Communication Association	International Communication Association
Society for Cinema and Media Studies	American Association for Public Opinion Research
American Journalism Historians Association	Asociación Latinoamericana de Investigadores de la Comunicacion
Association for Chinese Communication Studies	Association of Internet Researchers
	International Association for Media and History
Chinese Communication Association	European Consortium for Communications Research
European Society for Opinion and Marketing Research	Global Communication Research Association
International Association for Media History	Southern African Communication Association
Media, Communications & Cultural Studies Association	Canadian Communication Association

the engineering professors who founded radio stations in colleges during the 1920s needed program content, and drew volunteers from that area. These stations became laboratories, with research undertaken into technology, content, and reception (Kittross, 1999).

This was a period of massively complex urbanization and the spread of adult literacy, democratic rights, labor organization, and socialist ideas, which gave rise to a social science equivalent to the study of speech: mass communication. First cinema, then radio and TV were simultaneously prized and damned for their demagogic qualities, which it was hoped and feared could turn people into dutiful consumers or devious communists.

Universities across the United States also introduced degrees to prepare students for media work, whether through film and journalism schools or broadcast radio and television majors. In Britain, Granada TV endowed a research position into television at Leeds University in 1959. Then the Society for Education in Film and Television and the British Film Institute began sometimes separate, sometimes overlapping forms of stimulus in the 1960s and '70s, from seeding teaching posts to publishing critical dossiers. This ultimately fed into major formations of UK media studies influenced by continental Marxism and feminism, then by similar social movements as the US[4] (Bignell et al., 2000: 81; Bolas, 2009).

Some of the bodies listed in Table 1.2 see themselves as feeder groups and even advocates for the industry; some identify as purely scholarly entities; and others call for progressive change. Let's consider key instances, mostly from the Anglo world.

The Association for Education in Journalism and Mass Communication (AEJMC) describes itself as "a multicultural network of practitioners." Founded in 1912, AEJMC seeks to "advance education in journalism, cultivate better professional practice and promote the free flow of information, without boundaries," while the National Communication Association, formerly the Speech Communication Association (SCA, which began in 1914) says it is "[d]edicated to fostering and promoting free and ethical communication."[5]

The Broadcast Education Association (BEA) commenced in 1948 as an educational arm of the US radio then TV industry through the National Association of Broadcasters, which has provided it with resources to fund events and publications (Kittross, 1999). The BEA bears the lineaments of a heritage "preparing college students to enter the radio & TV business."[6]

The (US) Society for Cinema and Media Studies (SCMS) says it is "devoted to the study of the moving image." Founded in 1959, the Society aims to "promote all areas of media studies" and "advance multi-cultural awareness and interaction."[7] Attempts to bring other media into the former Society for Cinema Studies were roundly rejected in the 1990s by cinéphiles. It may be that the eventual expansion of their rubric to incorporate "media studies" derived from "the higher-prestige if loosely defined field of new media studies" (Boddy, 2005: 81): US universities "tend to value anything called new media" thanks to its applications to militarism, and its ability to draw hefty research money through governmental and commercial fetishes for new technology. The upshot is that "studying anything that comes over the Internet . . . has somehow become more legitimate than studying television itself" (Spigel, 2005: 84).

The International Communication Association (ICA), which started in 1950 as a breakaway from SCA focusing on mass communication, avows that it exists:

• to provide an international forum to enable the development, conduct, and critical evaluation of communication research;
• to sustain a program of high-quality scholarly publication and knowledge exchange;
• to facilitate inclusiveness and debate among scholars from diverse national and cultural backgrounds and from multi-disciplinary perspectives on communication-related issues; and
• to promote a wider public interest in, and visibility of, the theories, methods, findings and applications generated by research in communication and allied fields.[8]

Britain's Media, Communications and Cultural Studies Association (MeCCSA) is the newest of these bodies (it was established in 2007). MeCCSA presents itself as a service to students, rather alarmingly suggesting that "[m]any of the jobs you will go into once you have finished your degree have not yet been invented." The Association suggests that obtaining employment may flow from "the ability to produce high-quality research, to analyze sociological trends, to work effectively with people, to organize events, to think creatively and to write well."[9]

The International Association for Media Communication and Research (IAMCR) – started by the United Nations Educational, Scientific and Cultural Organisation (UNESCO) in 1957, and the only body discussed here that is not Anglo-dominated – says that it "aims to support and develop media and communication research throughout the world. It particularly encourages the participation of emerging scholars, women and those from economically disadvantaged regions."[10] In the 1970s,

ICA was known jocularly as the CIA and IAMCR as the KGB – a mutual alphabetic, acronymic parody.

By contrast with the jobs, legitimacy, and inclusivity emphases of these associations, and the aesthetico-historical goals of SCMS, the US Union for Democratic Communications (UDC, founded in 1981) sees itself as an organization of communication researchers, journalists, media producers, policy analysts, academics, and activists dedicated to:

- critical study of the communications establishment;
- production and distribution of democratically controlled and produced media;
- fostering alternative, oppositional, independent and experimental production;
- development of democratic communications systems locally, regionally and internationally.[11]

This is a transformative rather than a parthenogenetic project: UDC works toward a different world, as opposed to generating new cohorts of producers, scientists, rhetoricians, journalists, and aesthetes to populate the existing one.

Clearly, there is no single professional association to go to in order to see how academia makes sense of the media. And we could just as easily have listed relevant segments of professional bodies within the different disciplines.[12] There would be considerable overlap as well as many epistemological, methodological, focal, national, and political differences.

The same applies to journals. Table 1.3 lists a huge, diverse, yet only partial, list. Some of these journals are the organs of professional associations: authors may be obliged to join in order to publish there, and will be expected to cite the work of powerful fellow-members. Others are journals of tendency, which seek new and transformative work rather than the reiteration of normal science. Some are tied to particular regions or countries.

It should be clear from this schematic account of scholarly bodies and publications that media studies is fractured by objects of study, politics, nations, disciplines, theories, languages, and methods. This is hardly surprising, given that it derives from the spread of new media technologies over the past two centuries into the lives of urbanizing populations, and from the policing questions that both state and capital have had to face up to: what would be the effects of these developments, and how would they vary between those with a stake in maintaining society versus transforming it?

More than half a century ago, Dallas Smythe explained that audience attention – presumed or measured – is the commodity that TV and radio stations sell to advertisers (2004: 319–20). Texts are therefore not so much consumer items as "symbols for time" (Hartley, 1987: 133). Audiences participate in the most global (but local) communal (yet individual) and time-consuming practice of making meaning in the history of the world. The concept and the occasion of being an audience are links between society and person, yet viewing and listening may equally involve solitary interpretation.

Production executives invoke audiences to measure success and claim knowledge of what people want, regulators to organize administration, psychologists to produce proofs, and lobby groups to change content. Hence the link to panics about education, violence, and apathy supposedly engendered by the media and routinely

Table 1.3

International Journal of Cultural Policy, Entertainment Law Review, Transnational Television Studies, Global Media Journal, Television & New Media, Global Media and Communication, Poetics, Journal of Media Economics, Media International Australia, European Journal of Communication, Media Culture & Society, International Communication Gazette, Media Law and Practice, Feminist Media Studies, Comunicaço & Politica, International Journal of Communication, International Journal of Communications Law and Policy, Asian Journal of Communication, Games & Culture, Journal of Broadcasting & Electronic Media, Revista Electrónica Internacional de Economía Política de las Tecnologías de la Información y de la Comunicación, Entertainment and Sports Law Journal, Asian Media, Comunicaçao e Sociedade, Convergence, Loyola Entertainment Law Journal, Columbia VLA Journal of Law and the Arts, Loyola Entertainment Law Journal, Cultural Studies Review, Mediascape, Communication Review, Cultural Politics, Critical Studies in Media Communication, Quarterly Review of Film and Video, Cinema Journal, Journal of Media Sociology, Democratic Communiqué, Television Quarterly, Cultural Sociology, Journal of Arab and Muslim Media Research, Journal of Creative Communications, Media Development,	*Canadian Journal of Communication, Visual Anthropology, Visual Anthropology Review, NORDICOM Review of Nordic Research on Media and Communication, Journal of International Communication, Asian Journal of Communication, New Media & Society, Journalism & Mass Communication Quarterly, Journal of Communication Inquiry, Historical Journal of Radio, Film & Television, Journal of Communication, European Journal of Cultural Studies, Journalism History, Journalism: Theory, Practice and Criticism, Media History, Women's Studies in Communication, Public Opinion Quarterly, Political Communication, Gamasutra, Federal Communications Law Journal, Fordham Intellectual Property, International Journal of Press/ Politics, Popular Communication, Media & Entertainment Law Journal, Topia, Cultural Studies, Communications, International Journal of Cultural Studies, Journal of British Cinema & Television, Social Semiotics, Journal of E-Media Studies, Critical Studies in Television, Chinese Journal of Communication, Jump Cut, Screen Education, Screen, Velvet Light Trap, Flow, Journal of Film & Video, New Review of Film and Television Studies, Journal of Popular Film & Television, Middle East Journal of Culture and Communication, Political Communication, Media Psychology*

investigated by the state, psychology, Marxism, feminism, conservatism, religion, and others. The audience as consumer, student, felon, voter, sexist, heathen, progressive, and fool engages such groups. Media effects and ratings research wanders the world, traversing the industry, the state, and criticism. Academic, commercial, and regulatory approaches focus most expansively on audiences as citizens and consumers, far more than media technology, law, or even content.

Each new media innovation since the advent of print has brought an expanded horizon of texts to audiences. In keeping with this history, texts and viewers come to be defined in both market terms and through a regulatory morality of conscience and taste: "a new practice of piety" accompanies each "new communications technology" (Hunter, 1988: 220). As a consequence, moral panics are common amongst the denizens of communication studies, pediatrics, psychology, and education, who largely abjure cultural and political matters to do with the media in favor of experimenting on their viewers, listeners, players, and readers. This is the psy-function at work.

As we have seen, media studies also covers political economy, which focuses on ownership and control rather than audience responses. Because the demand for texts is dispersed but much of their supply is centralized, political economy as per the Frankfurt School argues that the media are diminished in quality and diversity by the search for standardized production. Far from reflecting already-established and -revealed preferences of consumers in reaction to tastes and desires, the media manipulate audiences from the economic apex of production, with coercion mistaken for free will. The only element that might stand against this leveling sameness is said to be individual consciousness. But that consciousness has itself been customized to the requirements of the economy and media production: maximization of sameness through repetition and minimization of innovation and newness, in order to diminish risk and cost (Adorno and Horkheimer, 1977).

There are significant ties between critical theory, which calls for a resistive consciousness through artisanal rather than industrially created texts, and political economy, which calls for diverse ownership and control of the industry. The first trend is philosophical and aesthetic in its desire to develop modernism and the avant-garde, the second policy-oriented and political in its focus on institutional power. But they began as one with lamentations for the loss of a self-critical philosophical address and the triumph of industrialized cultural production. The two approaches continue to be linked via a shared distaste for what is still often regarded as mass culture (Garnham, 1987).

From many perspectives, the media are said to force people to turn away from precious artistic and social traces of authentic intersubjectivity and lose control of their individual consciousness. This part of media studies is frequently functionalist, neglecting struggle, dissonance, and conflict in favor of a totalizing narrative in which the media dominate everyday life. Together, these theories and methods amount to Media Studies 1.0.

New Directions – Media Studies

Something happened in the mid-1960s to counter these two forms of knowledge: the advent of a more conflictual version of media studies, often influenced by Gramsci. The Italian medievalist, semiotician, columnist, and novelist Umberto Eco (1972) developed notions of encoding–decoding, open texts, and aberrant readings by audiences. He looked at differences between the way meanings were put into Italian TV programs by producers and how they were deciphered by viewers. Eco's insights were picked up by the English political sociologist Frank Parkin (1971) and the Jamaican-British cultural studies theorist Stuart Hall (1980).

There have been two principal methodological iterations of the encoding-decoding approach: uses and gratifications (U&G) and ethnography/cultural studies. Uses and gratifications operates from a psychological model of needs and pleasures, cultural studies from a political one of needs and pleasures. U&G focuses on what are regarded as fundamental psychological drives that define how people use the media to gratify themselves. Conversely, cultural studies' ethnographic work has shown some of the limitations to claims that viewers are stitched into certain perspectives by the interplay of narrative, dialogue, and image. Together, they have brought into question the notion that audiences are blank slates ready to be written on by media messages.

Drawing upon these findings, some denizens of media studies argue that today's new media represent the apex of modernity, the first moment in history when central political and commercial organs and agendas became receptive to the popular classes. This perspective differs from the idea that the apparatus is all-powerful. It maintains instead that the all-powerful agent is the audience: the public is so clever and able that it makes its own meanings, outwitting institutions of the state, academia, and capitalism that seek to measure and control it. In the case of children and the media, anxieties about turning Edenic innocents into rabid monsters or capitalist dupes are dismissed.[13] Welcome to media studies 2.0.

This tendency has reached its apogee in the era of the internet, when new technologies supposedly obliterate geography, sovereignty, and hierarchy in an alchemy of truth and beauty. Today's deregulated, individuated media world allegedly makes consumers into producers, frees the disabled from confinement, encourages new subjectivities, rewards intellect and competitiveness, links people across cultures, and allows billions of flowers to bloom in a post-political cornucopia.

Sometimes, faith in the active audience reaches cosmic proportions, such that the media are not held responsible for anything. Consumption is the key, with production discounted, work neglected, consumers sovereign, and research undertaken by observing one's own practices and those of one's friends and children. This is narcissography at work, with the critic's persona a guarantor of audience revelry and Dionysian joy (Morris, 1990). Welcome to "Readers Liberation Movement" media studies (Eagleton, 1982): everyone is creative and no one is a spectator. Internally divided – but happily so – each person is "a consumer on the one hand, but . . . also a producer" (Foucault, 2008: 226). We shall look into these competing notions again in chapter 9.

Media studies 1.0 buys into, while condemning, corporate fantasies of control – the political economist's arid nightmare of music, movies, television, and everything else converging under the sign of empowered firms. Media studies 2.0 incarnates individualist fantasies of reader, audience, consumer, or player autonomy – the libertarian intellectual's wet dream of music, movies, television, and everything else converging under the sign of empowered fans. Those antinomies shadow the fetish of innovation that informs much talk of media technology and consumerism, while ignoring the environmental destruction and centralized power that underpin them (Maxwell and Miller, 2012).

Media studies today thrives in the context of a reformist, even reactionary formation, which rejects the field's past in favor of hitching itself to the new surge in cultural industries represented by upbeat public policies and investment patterns. This has involved consultancies on behalf of the media, museums, copyright, pornography, schooling, and cultural precincts. Instrumental policy people and scholars argue for an efflorescence of creativity, cultural difference, import substitution, and national and regional pride and influence, thanks to new technologies and innovative firms – with capitalism an ally, not a foe (Hartley, 2005; Florida, 2002).

This position connects with a new model of consumer freedom that derives from subcultural politics. The two developments share little in terms of commitments to social justice. The working assumption they have in common is that corporate popular culture is being overrun by individual creativity in a Marxist/Godardian fantasy where people fish, film, fornicate, and finance from morning to midnight.

This new world supposedly destroys the inequalities and injustices personified by the Olsen twins and their nameless employees. The *Magna Carta for the Information Age*, for instance, proposes that political-economic transformations have been eclipsed by technological ones:

> The central event of the 20th century is the overthrow of matter. In technology, economics, and the politics of nations, wealth – in the form of physical resources – has been losing value and significance. The powers of mind are everywhere ascendant over the brute force of things. (Dyson et al., 1994)

Time magazine exemplified this love of a seemingly immaterial world when it chose "You" as 2006's "Person of the Year," because "You control the Information Age. Welcome to your world" (L. Grossman, 2006). The *Guardian* newspaper is prey to the same touching magic: someone called "You" headed its 2013 list of the hundred most important people in the media.[14]

Most media and some academic discourses on activism, during twenty-first-century Arab uprisings in particular, but other social movements as well, focus on media technologies rather than forces of history, labor, social inequality, cultural norms, and other factors that shape how activists used media.

Utopian media studies 2.0 discourse takes one or several of the following tacks:

- because of new technologies and inventive practices of consumption, concentration of media ownership and control no longer matters – information is finally free, thanks to multi-point distribution and destabilized hierarchies;
- consumers are sovereign and can transcend class and other categories;
- young people are liberated from media control;
- journalism is dying as everyone and their owl become sources of both news and reporting;
- creative destruction is an accurate and desirable description of economic innovation;
- when scholars observe media workers and audiences, they discover that ideology critique is inappropriate;
- Marxist political economy denies the power of audiences and users and the irrelevance of boundaries – it is pessimistic and hidebound;
- cultural imperialism critiques miss the creativity and resilience of national and subnational forms of life against industrial products; and
- media-effects studies are inconsequential – audiences outwit corporate plans and psy-function norms.

What is left out of these seemingly dynamic and innovative, but in fact tired and venerable lines? Here are areas with unanswered – in fact, unasked – questions that media studies 3.0 must pose and resolve:

- the ecological impact of the media;
- questions of labor and life in the cognitariat;
- the experiences of those who essentially live outside consumption, beyond multi-national markets – beyond an electricity grid and potable water, for example;
- citizenship;
- concentrated ownership and obedient regulation;
- cultural imperialism's resonance with populations and activists;
- the fact that the supposedly new vulnerability of media organizations to the power of the young, the rebelliousness of consumers, and the force of new technology is as old as these organizations themselves;
- the expansion of newspapers outside the Global North – people still line up in Barranquilla by the dozen each morning to place classified advertisements in the local paper, for instance; and
- the use of new technologies – for example, people citing one another's sexting or Facebook and Twitter activity in family courts to undermine claims to parental responsibility, leading to judgments that decide child-custody cases.[15]

In an exciting blend of 1.0 and 2.0, an emergent media studies 3.0 can be skeptical without being cynical, rigorous without losing optimism, and committed to popular democracy. It has seen analyses devoted to key issues that go beyond the psy-function, political economy, and active audiences, while drawing on their insights. A brief list might include:

- feminist concerns over the representation of women, both on- and off-screen;
- critics' desires to reach beyond bourgeois-individualistic accounts of creativity in favor of generic analyses;
- studies of postimperial social control in the Global South via domestic and global media dominance;
- Marxist aesthetics reading stories against ideologies; and
- voices from below, heard through participant observation of workers, audiences, and activists.

Foundational debates since 1990 have put leftist, queer, disabled, feminist, multi-cultural, and postcolonial formations in play. Such staples as cultural-imperialism critique and national media history have been supplemented by work on regional, global, diasporic, First Peoples, women's, and activist textuality. Ideology critique has been enriched by Gramscianism, racialization analysis, queer theory, and policy studies. This is in keeping with broader intellectual developments and political trends, such as social movements, the globalization and privatization of the media in the wake of the Cold War, and the rise of neoliberalism.

As higher education has grown and opened up to these critical tendencies within the human sciences, social movements, and more instrumental, conservatory-style training, media studies has often been deemed simultaneously too progressive and too applied by many traditionalists. Unlike, for instance, neoclassical economics or the psy-function, it has attracted intense opprobrium.

Within the bourgeois media, the *Village Voice* dubs us "the ultimate capitulation to the MTV mind . . . couchpotatodom writ large . . . just as Milton doesn't belong in the rave scene, sitcoms don't belong in the canon or the classroom" (Vincent, 2000).

For the *Times Literary Supplement*, media and cultural studies form the "politico-intellectual junkyard of the Western world" (Minogue, 1994: 27). The *Wall Street Journal* describes our work as "deeply threatening to traditional leftist views of commerce," because its notions of active consumption are close to those of the right: "cultural-studies mavens are betraying the leftist cause, lending support to the corporate enemy and even training graduate students who wind up doing market research" (Postrel, 1999). The *Observer* scornfully mocks via a parental parody: "what better way to have our little work-shy scholars rushing off to read an improving book than to enthuse loudly in their presence about how the omnibus edition of *EastEnders* [1985–] is the new double physics?" (Hogan, 2004). The *Telegraph* thunders that media studies is "quasi-academic" and delights whenever enrolments diminish (Lightfoot, 2005; Cairns, 2013), while the *Daily Express* deems it "worthless" (Douglas, 2011).

Alan Sugar, UK inquisitor for *The Apprentice* (2005–), worries that media studies "may be putting future scientific and medical innovation under threat" and "undermining the economy" (Paton, 2007). Britain's former Inspector of Schools denounced it as "a subject with little intellectual coherence and meager relevance to the world of work" (Woodhead, 2009). Chris Patten, the last Governor of Hong Kong, former Chair of the BBC Trust, and Chancellor of the University of Oxford, called us "Disneyland for the weaker minded" (quoted in Morley 2007: 17). The late *Guardian* newspaper columnist Simon Hoggart could be seen on British television in 2000 chiding local universities for wasting time on this nonsense when they should be in step with Harvard and MIT.[16] Similar criticisms come from Adam Gopnik in the *New Yorker*, who expresses alarm that so much "energy on the American left is in cultural studies, not health care" (1994: 96). National Public Radio places us among the "softer majors" whose alumni are fated to "pretty low salaries, and that's where the trouble really is" (Editor, 2014).

In 2014, the British government's Office of Qualifications and Examinations deemed media studies to be one of the country's high school subjects that must be made more "demanding" and subject to "reform" or be discontinued within four years, despite the fact that more than 55,000 pupils were enrolled (high numbers in comparison with most other areas, but heading downwards as the concerted attacks mentioned above gained traction) (Ofqal, 2014). Squeals of delight from the bourgeois press were immediate: the *Daily Mail* singled out media studies in welcoming a "crackdown on easy subjects" via a "bonfire" (Harris, 2014), the *Guardian* highlighted the drive to make our field "new, tougher" (Adams, 2014), and the *Telegraph* headlined the notion of being "dramatically toughened up" (Paton, 2014). The *Independent* also used this hyper-masculinist language, describing the reforms as directed at 'soft" subjects (Dugan, 2014).

Within academia, MeCCSA argues that media studies gets "negative publicity" because it "involves studying things which are generally seen as entertaining but trivial" or "by using complicated theoretical language."[17] Robert W. McChesney laments that we are "regarded by the pooh-bahs in history, political science, and sociology as having roughly the same intellectual merit as, say, driver's education" (2007: 16). Similar attitudes abound within the humanities (Hilmes, 2005: 113). *The Simpsons and Philosophy* (Irwin et al., 2001), probably the biggest-selling academic work ever on TV, sold a quarter of a million copies within six years without any relationship to work done in media studies (Asma, 2007).

The news is not all bad! It is worth recalling that new subject areas tend to cause controversy when they enter universities, as per the British experience with the introduction of the natural sciences in the nineteenth century, and politics, philosophy, English, and sociology in the twentieth. These innovations were practical responses to major socioeconomic transformations – industrialization, state schooling, class mobility, literacy, numeracy, and public welfare (Fox, 2003; Whittam Smith, 2008). They were far from welcome at the time of their advent, yet came to be key elements of a liberal education. As the *Scotsman* acknowledged in its defense of studying the media, "Mickey Mouse is no cow'rin, tim'rous beastie" (Instrell, 2014).

Moreover, within the industry, Greg Dyke, a leading British media and sports executive, says we are good for both citizenship and professional awareness (Burrell, 2008), and Britain's communications regulator Ofcom has a *Media Literacy E-Bulletin*, amongst other initiatives, while UK employment data show very positive signs for media studies graduates, albeit at low rates of pay (E. Anderson, 2013; Office for National Statistics, 2013: 19). And Mexican *telenovelas*, now seen in more than 100 countries, are researched and revised by TV Azteca via a blend of genre study and *análisis semántico basado en imagenes* (semantic analysis based on images). It uses viewer interviews to uncover cultural responses to stories as they unfold. In other words, data and analysis from media studies help to determine plot lines (Clifford, 2005; Slade and Beckenham, 2005: 341n.1).

Finally, whereas talk in the Global North of a "crisis" in journalism dominates, in the Global South, the media industries have expanded tremendously in the last couple of decades: Arab and Indian media, to take only a couple of examples, are, on the whole, vibrant industries and sizeable employers that are on the lookout for recent graduates. If you wander the corridors of journalism schools in Hong Kong or Colombia, you will encounter returning alumni lauding the critical education they received prior to entering the profession.

Away from debates about the value of studying the media, it is abundantly clear that they cause anxiety, whether about their own audiences or audiences to classes about them. Why? As Smythe said 60 years ago, the media channel an immense "flow of representations of the human condition" (1954: 143). John Hartley suggests that "the energy with which audiences are pursued in academic and industry research" is "larger and more powerful than the quest for mere data," because it seeks "knowledge of the *species*" (1992: 84; also see Ang, 1991).

The media have probably received more attention (and frequently demonization) than any other cultural field. Their opulence as a set of technologies is supposedly matched by a barrenness of civilization. Critics find them responsible for deficits in knowledge, concentration, and responsibility among populations. Aesthetically, they are said to appeal to base instincts and lowest-common denominators. Politically, the media are seen as instilling either quietude or hysteria. Criticisms come from both left and right that a surfeit of signage and a deficit of understanding thereby cheapen public culture: kitsch overruns quality (Martín-Barbero and Rey, 1999: 15–16, 22, 24).

Most of the media are dedicated to entertainment. That focus, along with their ease of use, have long produced embarrassment and even shame on the part of some audience members. Consider this Ivy League product recalling his New Haven follies of 1953:

> [A] Yale faculty member who owned a television set lived dangerously. In the midst of an academic community, he lived in sin. Nevertheless, in an act of defiance, we put our television set in the living room instead of the basement or the garage where most of the faculty kept theirs, and we weathered the disapprobation of colleagues who did not own or would not admit to owning this fascinating but forbidden instrument. (Silber, 1968: 113)

Communitarian US sociologists contrast an allegedly active public with a putatively passive audience:

> [W]e are not happy when we are watching television, even though most of us spend many hours a week doing so, because we feel we are "on hold" rather than really living during that time. We are happiest when we are successfully meeting challenges at work, in our private lives, and in our communities. (Bellah et al., 1992: 49)

US television producer and talk-show host David Susskind confided to 1950s readers of *Life* magazine that he was "mad at TV because I really love it and it's lousy. It's a very beautiful woman who looks abominable" (quoted in Schramm et al., 1961: 3). This sexist metaphor exemplifies the seemingly ineradicable fear of degradation through the media. Such gendered nightmares have not receded. Fifty years after Susskind, then-Fox Entertainment president and former NBC executive Kevin Reilly said: "NBC is like the crazy ex-wife I can't get away from" (quoted in Friedman, 2009b).[18]

That returns us to the Olsens. Remember the US$39,000 alligator backpack brought to you, and people like you, by the twins? May 2014 found Mary-Kate advising the *Wall Street Journal* that the loveable twosome had "spent a couple of years . . . retraining the customer that that's not the only product that's available."[19] Only by working across varying forms of knowledge and places of production, meaning, and reception can we hope to comprehend such complex phenomena as the Olsens. To do so, media studies must loosen some of the moorings we have outlined above and risk a more radically contingent way of seeing that destabilizes time and space to blend the discourses we have outlined into a new version, 3.0.

2 Global Studies

Many analysts of the media undertake research in purely national or solely English-language contexts. These professional norms have served them well in terms of publication and pedagogy. Technological, migratory, linguistic, and politico-economic changes now make it imperative that we study the media in their global context, and slough off monolingual disciplinary parthenogenesis. This does not mean that this book will cover every region of the world with the same level of depth and expertise. Rather, it means that we are guided by the conviction that the complexity of processes subsumed in the media makes linguistically, analytically, and geographically narrow approaches to the topic simply untenable.

Technologies like telecommunications satellites and the internet operate across borders as a matter of fact. Media conglomerates, transnational corporations *avant la lettre*, have long done exactly that, rarely restricting themselves to national frontiers. Media work, too, disobeys frontiers again and again. And mass migration and the spread of ideas make extrapolating from English-language work almost facetious. Anthropologists used to travel to faraway places and identify intermediaries who could speak local languages and interpret for them. That ceased to be acceptable practice decades ago in their field, and so it should be in ours.

At a moment when the Global North uses culture as a selling point for deindustrialized societies, and the Global South does so for never-industrialized ones, scholars must adopt a nimble, hybrid approach that is governed neither by the humanities or the social sciences, nor by the parent disciplines mentioned in chapter 1 – and assuredly not by one language – but by a critical agenda that inquires *cui bono*: who benefits and loses from governmental and corporate maneuvers, who complains about the fact, and how can we learn from them?

This also relates to a political project. Cosmopolitan commitments to social and cultural justice as well as academic theorization and research have proven magnetic to subordinate groups around the world who have entered academia for the first time over the last 50 years. Hence the appeal of studying the media not only at the conventional scholarly metropoles of the United States and the United Kingdom, but in Colombia, Brazil, Mexico, Turkey, India, and other important sites that are all too accustomed to being theorized and analyzed; and all too unfamiliar with being regarded as the *sources* of ideas, not merely places for their application.

"Global media studies" is an interdisciplinary rubric that emerged in the late 1990s to describe the convergence of areas of study traditionally known as "international communication" and "comparative media systems" (in the social sciences) or "national cinema" and "world cinema" (in the humanities). It reflects conceptual, disciplinary, and ideological changes that we discuss in this chapter and elaborate throughout the book.

Despite recent changes, and its name notwithstanding, the field remains dominated by English-language scholarship, especially publications originating and extrapolating from the United States (Graham, 2015).[1] After explaining this history and reactions against it, we look at the recent emergence of global media studies.

Imperial and Neocolonial Development

There is some history to an imperialistic attitude to culture and the globe. In nineteenth- and early twentieth-century Britain, the study of culture formed "the core of the educational system." It was "believed to have peculiar virtues in producing politicians, civil servants, Imperial administrators and legislators," incarnating and indexing "the arcane wisdom of the Establishment" (Plumb, 1964: 7). Culture was expected to produce and renovate what the Victorian poet, theorist, and schools administrator Matthew Arnold called "that powerful but at present somewhat narrow-toned organ, the modern Englishman" (1875: x), who must be readied to go forward and build empire.

Unsurprisingly, Spain's *conquista de América*, Portugal's *missão civilizadora*, Britain's civilizing mission, and France's *mission civilisatrice* created an anxiety about foreign cultural domination that has never subsided. The British Empire and its intellectuals, for instance, were more concerned to control colonial media than "civilize" people (one reason for the famines plaguing India was that information about food needs did not circulate freely because of colonial newspaper censorship) (Sen, 2009).

Over the last century, we have witnessed the continued hegemony of postcolonial powers in their former possessions, and the global entertainment demesne of the United States, thanks to the power of language, technology, habit, force, and wealth (Mowlana, 2000). Former US Secretary of State and master of the dark art of international relations Henry Kissinger (1999) says "globalization is really another name for the dominant role of the United States." His consulting firm advises that the United States must "win the battle of the world's information flows, dominating the airwaves as Great Britain once ruled the seas," not least because "Americans should not deny the fact that of all the nations in the history of the world, theirs is the most just, the most tolerant, the most willing to constantly reassess and improve itself, and the best model for the future" (Rothkopf, 1997).

In mainstream US international relations, the media serve as ideological underpinnings to material realities or threats. Nevertheless, their public policy significance waxes and wanes. Republicans nearly put an end to official propaganda when they took control of Congress in the mid-1990s, dramatically diminishing funding and staffing for culture as part of their dislike of artists and intellectuals and in response to the obsolescence of anti-Sovietism; but Cold War II was soon followed by September 11, 2001. The newly modish term "public diplomacy" suddenly appealed to the federal government, which sought an answer to the plaintive cry, "Why do they hate us?" The White House Office of Global Communications and a Policy Coordinating Committee on Strategic Communications were created to build trust of the United States overseas, stress common interests and ideologies, and influence elites. By 2003, the State Department's cultural budget was up to US$600 million (Advisory Committee on Cultural Diplomacy, 2005) and former National Intelligence Council chair Joseph Nye (2002-3) was promulgating the embarrassingly penile metaphor "soft power" to describe the use of US culture as propaganda.

Public diplomacy is supposed to transcend the material impact of US foreign policy and corporate expropriation by fostering communication at a civil society level, directly linking citizens across borders to "influence opinions and mobilize foreign publics" by "engaging, informing, and influencing key international audiences" (Council on Foreign Relations, 2003: 15; Gilboa, 1998; Brown, 2004). The idea is to work in the interest of the US government, but avoid that connotation. Related initiatives are under way across a wide array of governmental agencies: the State Department, the US Agency for International Development, the Broadcasting Board of Governors, the Pentagon, and the Open Source Center (Government Accountability Office, 2007). Today's State Department supports "regional media hubs" to forward its project of *Leading Through Civilian Power* (2010: 60–1).

The United States was not always a cultural exporter. In 1820, the noted British essayist Sydney Smith asked: "In the four quarters of the globe, who reads an American book? or goes to an American play? or looks at an American picture or statue?" (1844: 141). And three decades later, Herman Melville opposed the US literary establishment's devotion to all things English. He contrasted a Eurocentrically cringing import culture with a mission to "carry republicanism progressiveness into literature, as well as into Life" (1850; also see Newcomb, 1996).

Unsurprisingly, the United States became an early modern exponent of anticultural imperialist, pro-nation-building sentiment, using import substitution industrialization (ISI) to develop its communication capacities by rejecting intellectual property regimes. That dedication to ISI changed when its market position did, as decades of protectionism and an increasingly large and affluent domestic population created robust cultural industries by the turn of the twentieth century. Overseas expansion was soon necessary because of a saturated domestic market. And with the United States in a dominant economic and military position after World War II, it created a policy discourse in which Hollywood became the implicit price deflator of other countries' film industries, which were criticized for state subvention versus its supposedly laissez-faire system. Similarly, New York and Washington were held up as models of journalism in contrast to the supposed lack of "objectivity" elsewhere.

In both the social sciences and the humanities, these prejudices informed US foreign policy and vice versa. An "obsessional concern with the rivalry between the United States and the Soviet Union" (Hardt 1984: 134) led to mechanistic, polarized models of global media such as Fred Siebert et al.'s *Four Theories of the Press* (1963/ 1956), which divided the world into authoritarian, libertarian, socially responsible, and Soviet-totalitarian systems, clearly betraying what was as much a narcissistic, parthenogenetic, and political project as an intellectual one. The targets of these struggles-by-proxy were Latin America and new African and Asian states emerging from imperial control, which were seen as potentially drawn to Marxist-Leninist-Maoist ideas if they were not shown the one true path to life, liberty, and the pursuit of cornflakes.

Modernization theory had its heyday during this period, manifest in international communication research as "development communication." There were three distinct phases in the evolution of this paradigm (Fair and Shah, 1997). Daniel Lerner's *The Passing of Traditional Society: Modernizing the Middle East* (1958) emerged as an early master-text, followed by Schramm's *Mass Media and National Development: The Role of Information in the Developing Countries* (1964). These models adopted vertical modes of communication, psychologistic accounts of subjectivity, and functionalist views of the mass media. They conceptualized societies' backwardness as a function of irrational beliefs, attitudes, and behavior that could be rectified by expertly designed media campaigns. The media could also distribute vital information about health, agriculture, and weather, and urge upon citizens a national rather than a tribal form of identification. Diffusion from the example of the Global North was the order of the day.

Back in the Global North, appropriate developments in the media and associated technologies of knowledge were likened to a new Industrial Revolution or the Civil and Cold Wars – touted as a route to economic development as well as cultural and political expression. In the 1950s and '60s, futurists identified "knowledge workers" as vital to information-based industries that would generate productivity gains and competitive markets and expand the middle class (Bar with Simard, 2006). Cold Warriors like National Security Advisor and political scientist Zbigniew Brzezinski (1969), cultural-conservative sociologist Daniel Bell (1977), populist author and business consultant Alvin Toffler (1983), and professional anti-Marxist communications professor Ithiel de Sola Pool (1983) saw converged communications and information technologies removing grubby manufacturing from North to South and ramifying US textual and technical power, provided that the blandishments of socialism, and negativity toward global business, did not create class struggle. This was diffusion of dirt as much as development.

Initially, development advocates spoke of countries creating their own infrastructure, from telecommunications to television channels – ISI. But this soon turned to a notion of transfer, whereby wealthy nations sold gadgets and genres to less wealthy ones. By the 1950s, the successful export of media technologies and texts from the United States to the Global South was deemed to be critical for the development of populations said to be mired in backward, folkloric forms of thought and lacking the trust in national organizations required for modernization (Pye and Verba, 1965). Public investment was discouraged as a means of autonomy, displaced by a cosmic faith in market-driven power: the triumph of diffusion.

In the Global North, the post-Cold War era remains dominated by cultural issues, but of a quite different kind from these, thanks to the contributions of Ottoman historian and professional anti-Palestinian Bernard Lewis and Cold War political scientist and Vietnam War architect Samuel Huntington. In the wake of Sovietism, these two men turned from politics and economics to culture in search of geopolitical comprehension.

Lewis (1990) coined the expression "clash of civilizations" to capture the difference, as he saw it, between the separation of church and state that had generated US successes, versus their inter-calculation in Islamic nations, which had supposedly made those countries subordinate. Huntington appropriated the "clash of civilizations" to argue that future world-historical conflicts would not be "primarily ideological or primarily economic," but "cultural" (1993: 22).

This "cartoon-like world" (Said, 2001) has gained immense media and policy attention since September 11, 2001. Journalists in the Global North promote the notion of an apocalyptic struggle between good and evil as the bifurcation of the West and

Islam. Across the daily press and weekly and monthly magazines of ruling opinion, extra-state violence is attributed to Islam in opposition to freedom and technology, never as the act of subordinated groups against dominant ones.

The *New York Times* and *Newsweek* gave Huntington room to account for what had happened in terms of his "thesis," while others actively adopted it as a legitimate call for empire, from the supposed New Left through to leading communitarians and the neoliberal *Economist*. Arab leaders met to discuss the conceit, and Italian Prime Minister Silvio Berlusconi invoked it. When the US occupation of Iraq entered its third year, military commanders and senior noncommissioned officers were required to read the book (along with V. S. Naipaul and *Islam for Dummies*) (Rusciano, 2003; Said, 2001; Schmitt, 2005).

Not everyone was so taken with these ideas. UNESCO's Director General prefaced the Organization's worthy Declaration on Cultural Diversity with a rebuttal (Matsuura, 2001) and *El País*'s cartoonist Máximo traumatically constructed a dialog alongside the tumbling Towers: "Choque de ideas, de culturas, de civilizaciones" (clash of ideas, of cultures, of civilizations) drew the reply "choques de desesperados contra instalados" (the clash of the desperate against the establishment) (quoted in García Canclini, 2002: 16). Israel's *Ha-aretz* regarded Lewis and Huntington's "hegemonic hold" as "a major triumph" for al-Qaeda, and the *Arab News* aptly typified it as "Armageddon dressed up as social science" (quoted in Rusciano, 2003: 175).

Study after study has disproven Lewis's and Huntington's wild assertions about growing ethnic struggle since the Cold War and a unitary Islamic culture opposed to a unitary Western culture. Such claims neglect conflicts over money, property, and politics and cultural differences within the two blocs (Fox, 2002; Norris and Inglehart, 2003: 203; United Nations Development Program, 2004). The clash-of-civilizations thesis does not work if you apply it to Iran supporting Russia against Chechen rebels and India against Pakistan, for example (Abrahamian, 2003: 535). Yet, for all its absurdity and lack of scholarly credibility, we must engage this discourse, because it represents a powerful anxiety underpinning ideas of development and communication that is as fundamental as the concerns about Marxism-Leninism and Maoism of an earlier period.

We also need to look at economic changes. Latin Americans generated the theory of dependent development (*dependencia*) in the 1940s to explain how the industrial take-off experienced by Western Europe and the United States had not occurred elsewhere. It gained adherents across the Global South over the next three decades in reaction to the fact that rich societies at the world core had become so through their colonial and international experience, importing ideas, fashions, and people from the periphery, while exporting media texts (Prebisch, 1982; Cardoso, 2009).

By the 1970s, developing markets for labor and products, and the shift from the spatial *sen*sitivities of electrics to the spatial *in*sensitivities of electronics, pushed the Global North beyond treating the Global South as a supplier of raw materials to view them as shadow-setters of the price of work, competing amongst themselves and with the Global North for employment. Production became split across continents via a New International Division of Labor (NIDL) (Fröbel et al., 1980).

This presaged the NICL: labor market expansion and developments in global transportation and communications technology have diminished the need for co-location of management, work, and consumption. Just as manufacturing fled the

Global North, cultural production has also relocated: popular and high-cultural texts, computer-aided design and manufacture, sales, marketing, and information may now be created and exchanged globally as part of the NICL that was mentioned in our Introduction (Miller et al., 2001b; Miller et al., 2005).

There is a deep and rich alternative history within the Global South of theorizing development and communication that derives from these positions (Manyozo, 2006). And nineteenth-century US critiques of cultural imperialism as per Melville still resonate (elsewhere) in everyday talk, broadcast and telecommunications policy, unions, international organizations, nationalistic media and heritage, cultural diplomacy, anti-Americanism, and postindustrial service-sector planning. The contemporary Chinese desire to overcome negative images of its brutal antidemocratic ways through exported media is a clear instance (Sun, 2010).

The cultural-imperialism thesis turned Melville's original argument on its face. It said that the United States, which had become the globe's leading media exporter, was transferring its dominant value system to others, with a corresponding diminution in the vitality and standing of local languages, traditions, and national identities. Lesser, but still considerable, influence was attributed to older imperial powers, via their cultural, military, and corporate ties to newly independent countries. The theory attributed US cultural hegemony to its control of news agencies, advertising, market research, public opinion, screen trade, technology transfer, propaganda, telecommunications, and security (Primo 1999: 183).

US involvement in Southeast Asian wars, and its adherence to the Monroe Doctrine in the Americas, enunciated almost two centuries ago to keep British troops out of the region by declaring anything that went on there to be the domain of the United States, led to critiques of military interventions against struggles of national liberation. This argument targeted links between the military-industrial complex and the media, pointing to the ways that multinational communications and cultural corporations bolstered US foreign policy and military strategy, which in turn facilitated commerce.

Critiques of media imperialism have found significant uptake in the Global South, not least for their focus on the machinery of propaganda sold to ordinary people by powerful sovereign states. They have enjoyed a particular purchase in Latin America, because of the region's proximity to the United States, and in other postcolonial states whose traditions and languages tie them to texts exported from the metropole (Segoviana García, 2011; Dorfman and Mattelart, 1971).

The cultural-imperialism thesis argues that the United States and former colonial powers in Europe were the world's leading producers and exporters of journalism, music, and television and film drama. As Herbert I. Schiller expressed it, "the media-cultural component in a developed, corporate economy supports the economic objectives of the decisive industrial-financial sectors (i.e., the creation and extension of the consumer society)" (1991a: 14). Schiller penned this influential definition of cultural imperialism as "the sum of the processes by which a society is brought into the modern world system and how its dominating stratum is attracted, pressured, forced and sometimes bribed into shaping social institutions to correspond to, or even promote, the value and structures of the dominating center of the system" (1976: 9).

In the UK, Jeremy Tunstall referred to "authentic, traditional and local culture . . . being battered out of existence by the indiscriminate dumping of large quantities of slick commercial and media products, mainly from the United States" (1977: 57). Luis Ramiro Beltrán, a Bolivian scholar, described cultural imperialism as "a verifiable process of social influence by which a nation imposes on other countries its set of beliefs, values, knowledge, and behavioral norms as well as its overall style of life" (1978: 184).

This media-imperialism position attributed US and Western European political, military, and economic hegemony to dominance over news agencies, advertising, market research, public opinion, screen trade, technology, propaganda, and tele-communications. The long history of US participation in Latin American politics and involvement in Southeast Asian wars during the 1960s led to particular critiques of its military interventions against struggles of national liberation, which in turn targeted links between the military-industrial complex and the media.

During the 1960s and 1970s, cultural-imperialism discourse found a voice in public policy debates through the Non-Aligned Movement and UNESCO. The Global South (known then as the Group of 77, after the number of postcolonial states at the time) lobbied for a New World Information and Communication Order (NWICO). UNESCO set up an International Commission for the Study of Communication Problems to investigate North–South flows and power. It reported in 1980 on the need for equal distribution of the electronic spectrum, reduced postal rates for international texts, protection against satellites crossing borders, and media systems that would serve social justice rather than capitalist commerce (Mattelart and Mattelart, 1998: 94–7). The 1973 meeting of Heads of State of Non-Aligned Countries spoke of a "need to reaffirm national cultural identity" (quoted in Sinclair, 1982: 8), mirroring calls for a New International Economic Order and a revised North–South dialogue in general.

Such arguments have long resonated in everyday talk, broadcast and telecom-munications policy, unions, international organizations, nationalistic media and heritage, cultural diplomacy, anti-Americanism, social movements, and postindus-trial service sector planning (see Schiller, 1976 and 1989; Beltrán and Fox de Cardona, 1980; Dorfman and Mattelart, 1971). They are exemplified by the Belgian/Latin American Armand Mattelart's stinging denunciation of external cultural influence on the Global South:

> In order to camouflage the counter-revolutionary function which it has assigned to communications technology and, in the final analysis, to all the messages of mass culture, imperialism has elevated the mass media to the status of revolutionary agents, and the modern phenomenon of communications to that of revolution itself. (1980: 17)

Dependency theory, and its offshoot in international communication studies, the media/cultural imperialism paradigm, mounted a radical critique of development, emerging as "a healthy antidote to the mindless optimism of the orthodox 'modernization' theory of economic growth and development" (Hardt, 1984: 136). Various scholars attacked modernization as simplistic (Hardt, 1984), ethnocentric (Golding, 1974), and propagandistic (Halloran, 1997), and for glossing over the history of colonialism, imperialism, and global inequality. Grounded in a radical political economy tradition, media-imperialism researchers focused on capital, infrastructure control, and structures of ownership, distribution, and regulation as determinants of dependency that helped maintain political, economic, and cultural inequities between nations and regions.[2]

Numerous studies showed that international media flows favored rich Western nations, exporting to developing nations, which also received limited and negative news coverage in Western media (Varis, 1974; 1984). Work deriving from cultural-imperialism critique looked at the role of international press agencies, the flow of film and television, village versus corporate values, distribution systems, and the dominance of international communications technology and infrastructure. Another major area of research deconstructed the rhetoric of development via commercialism, particularly in advertising, which was found to distort the allocation of resources.

This development polarized UNESCO into two groups. The first group, comprising the United States and the United Kingdom, insisted on the "free flow of information." It advocated unfettered market processes in information and media programs. The second group, a coalition of Western, state-socialist, and developing countries, perceived the free-flow-of-information ideology as a justification for continued Anglo-American economic and cultural domination, what Mattelart retrospectively derided as "the free fox in the free chicken house" (1994: 236). The latter group argued instead for a "free and balanced flow" of information (Kraidy, 2005; Masmoudi, 1979; Schiller, 1974; Zassoursky and Losev, 1981).

Under the presidency of Ronald Reagan, the US government led a charge against NWICO, calling on UNESCO to cease its attempts to "control press freedom." Some in the US administration even advocated the First Amendment to the US Constitution as a framework for global media flows (Kleinwachter, 1994). As is customary in foreign affairs (until US casualties mount) the US prestige press echoed foreign policy: "If it turns out to be impossible to reject this attempt to tamper with our basic principles," thundered an editorial in the *New York Times*, "there is always the alternative of rejecting UNESCO itself" (quoted in Gerbner, 1994: 114).

The United States and the United Kingdom indeed withdrew from the Organization in 1985 because it did not toe the line of the rising global neoliberal regime spearheaded by Reagan in the United States and Margaret Thatcher in the United Kingdom: UNESCO was still advocating state intervention against private capital's hegemony over the media. In addition, the Organization denounced Zionism as racist and supported balanced global media and cultural flows. The next three decades saw UNESCrats distance themselves from NWICO in the hope of attracting these countries back to the fold (Gerbner, 1994: 112-13; Gerbner et al., 1994: xi–xii). In NWICO's aftermath, instead of noting lopsided global media flows in need of redress, UNESCO publications were pervaded by a discourse of diversity and hybridity (for example, Portella, 2000). UNESCO's ideological outlook changed radically. This became clear when George W. Bush announced in his infamous "Axis of Evil" speech in 2002 that the United States was rejoining the Organization it had noisily quit 20 years earlier (Kraidy, 2005). When Hillary Clinton visited UNESCO headquarters in 2011, a page had been turned; but then the Organization recognized Palestine, and the United States again refused to pay its dues (State Department, 2011).

The Canadians have long had a unique purchase on anxieties about US media domination. Even before the inception of television there in 1952, affection for Yanqui culture was officially derided as unpatriotic. This slightly improbable struggle by the state dates back even before it began – there were 150,000 TV sets in Canada tuned to US signals prior to the advent of local broadcasting. There has been over half a century of battling what is perceived as "an ideological misrecognition whereby Canadians mistake American television for what they really like while simultaneously neglecting the Canadian television that they ought to like." But by contrast with these overwhelming Anglo anxieties, French Canadian media were avowedly populist and commercially successful (Attallah, 2007: 334, 331, 338, 344).

As per that story, a media survey by *The Economist* in 1994 remarked that cultural politics is always so localized in its first and last instances that the "electronic bonds" of exported texts are "threadbare" (Heilemann, 1994: SURVEY 4). Rather than simply selling its own stories to others, Hollywood has long justified the exclusion of black actors from leading roles as necessary because of what it argued was global – i.e., non-American – audiences' rejection of such actors and their urban, basketball, and rap-saturated environments (Kraidy, 2005).

Cultural-imperialism theory also lost its cachet among many progressive academics, who criticized the paradigm made famous by Schiller and his colleagues as part of the turn to media studies 2.0. These criticisms concerned cultural imperialism's conception of culture as a holistic, organic entity closely associated with nation-states, which gave birth to visions of cultural authenticity that neglected internal difference within countries. Critics also argued that the notion of cultural domination was reminiscent of early mass society theories and subsequent "magic bullet" and "hypodermic needle" models of powerful media effects, which ignored active processes of reception, and that there was a lack of empirical data supporting the claims of cultural-imperialism research. NWICO was also vulnerable because of its inadequate theorization of capitalism, postcolonialism, class relations, the state, and indigenous culture, in addition to its complex *frottage*: UNESCO's advocacy of pluralism insisted on the relativistic equivalence of all cultures and defied chauvinism, but rubbed up against a powerful equation of national identities with cultural forms (Salwen, 1991; Sreberny-Mohammadi, 1997; Straubhaar, 1991; Schlesinger, 1991: 145).

This concentration on national culture also denied the potentially liberatory and pleasurable nature of different takes on the popular, forgot the internal differentiation of publics, valorized frequently oppressive and/or unrepresentative local bourgeoisies in the name of maintaining and developing national cultures, and ignored the demographic realities of its "own" terrain. For example, alternatives to Hollywood funded under the sign of opposition to cultural imperialism frequently favored exclusionary, art-house-centered hegemons that privileged "talent" over labor, and centralized authority over open decision-making. All too often, this led to public subvention of indolent national bourgeoisies or oleaginous Gringos using proxy locals to fund offshore production (Miller et al., 2005).

Titles of publications in this revisionist wave of research speak for themselves: "media imperialism reconsidered" (Lee, 1980), "decentering cultural imperialism" (Sinclair, 1992), "beyond media imperialism" (Golding and Harris, 1997; Straubhaar, 1991), "media imperialism reformulated" (Boyd-Barrett, 1998), and "media imperialism revisited" (Chadha and Kavoori, 2000).

In summary, between the 1970s and the 1990s, criticisms by dependency theorists led to a re-evaluation of US development studies and launched a second phase (Rogers, 1976). This second wave was characterized by a tripartite fragmentation: US futurists proclaiming an end to ideology and class conflict; the emergence of nations driven by education and technology to become information societies; and the NWICO debate against the backdrop of Cold War geopolitics and an emerging Third Cinema.

Then we saw the advent of poststructuralism, postmodernism, and postcolonialism in the social sciences and humanities, raising questions about the grand narratives of liberalism and Marxism, seemingly natural political orders, and unitary social identities. Related to this emergence of constructivist and critical approaches to development, gender arose as a central category in the development communication literature (Wilkins, 1998).

This has been part of the rise of globalization as a framework for international communication research and the eventual emergence of global media studies. It also reflected a more developed appreciation of culture within the political economy tradition (Mosco and Schiller, 2001) and the emergence of a literature about the media and ICTs that mixed the theories and methods of political economy and cultural studies (Miller *et al.*, 2005; Kraidy, 2005; Zhao and Chakravartty, 2007).

Several factors stand behind the push to replace "cultural imperialism" with "cultural globalization." They are not all progressive or compelling, even when efficacious. The end of the Cold War as a shaper of ideological, geopolitical, and economic competition encouraged a rethinking of analytic approaches and categories. The emergence of the United States as the lone superpower also left the world politically fragmented; as the post-Cold War era unleashed tensions between global forces of cohesion and local reactions of dispersal.

Advocates of "cultural globalization" as an analytical paradigmatic substitute for "cultural imperialism" argued that the former better reflects the multiplicity and complexity of global dynamics that were weakening the cultural unity of *all* nation-states, including powerful industrialized Western nations (Tomlinson, 1991). In addition, the field of international communication opened its doors to approaches beyond social psychology and political economy, a second force pushing in favor of the switch from imperialism to globalization. The entrance of cultural sociology, anthropology, literary criticism, semiotics, and Marxist cultural interpretation shaped the relatively contained field of international communication into a more explicitly interdisciplinary configuration of approaches that became known as global media studies (Kraidy, 2002). On the cinema studies side, interest expanded beyond film to television and digital media, in a diasporic and postcolonial frame (Stam and Miller, 2000). The diffusion model was supplemented by a participatory one that was less ethnocentric and saw development defined and delivered by recipients of aid as well as their donors (Morris, 2003).

Global media studies also arose as part of a multidisciplinary frenzy over globalization that took the social sciences and humanities by storm in the 1990s. Though the term "global" is at least 400 years old, in 1961 *Webster's* was the first dictionary to define "globalization" (Waters, 1995). Like cultural imperialism in the 1970s and postmodernism in the 1980s, globalization is an elastic notion, "a maddeningly euphemistic term laden with desire, fantasy, fear, attraction – and intellectual imprecision about what it is supposed to describe" (Miller et al., 2001b: 18).

Globalization's early master definitions emerged in sociology: Anthony Giddens famously described it as the "intensification of world-wide social relations which link distant localities in such a way that local happenings are shaped by events occurring

many miles away and vice versa" (1990: 64). Roland Robertson defined globalization as "the compression of the world and the intensification of consciousness of the
world as a whole" (1992: 8). In short order, globalization drew anthropologists such
as Ulf Hannerz, who wrote about a global "ecumene" as a "region of persistent culture
interaction and exchange" (1989: 66), and Arjun Appadurai (1994), who described
disjunctive flows and "scapes" of people, capital, technology, images, and ideologies.
    Néstor García Canclini argued that:

> The fusion of multimedia and concentrated media ownership in cultural produc-
> tion correlate[s] with changes in cultural consumption. Therefore macrosociological
> approaches, which seek to understand the integration of radio, television, music,
> news, books, and the internet in the fusion of multimedia and business, also need an
> anthropological gaze, a more qualitative perspective, to comprehend how modes of
> access, cultural goods, and forms of communication are being reorganized. (2008:
> 390)

The humanities generated a series of books and special journal issues dedicated to
globalization throughout the mid- to late 1990s. In one of the resulting volumes,
Fredric Jameson terms globalization "a communicational concept, which alternately
masks and transmits cultural or economic meanings. . . . But the communicational
focus of the concept of globalization is essentially incomplete: I defy anyone to try
to think it in exclusively media or communicational terms" (1998: 55). Jameson's
assertion underscores the centrality of media, communication, and information to
globalization, and, at the same time, the inability of media studies alone to understand the phenomenon, given the importance of the mobility of war, environment,
labor, capital, religion, and refugees.
    The designation "global media studies" first emerged in the early 2000s (Kraidy,
2002; Murphy and Kraidy, 2003) to reflect a variety of interdisciplinary theories that
have widened the scope of research on global media and activated a consideration of
the linkages between production, texts, and consumption, a task that the traditional
international communication canon failed to accomplish. Different traditions have
tended to focus on one out of three stages of the communication process. Cultural
imperialism, grounded in critical political economy, focused on production and distribution. In contrast, media criticism, derived from literary and rhetorical criticism,
examined the layers of meaning embedded in media texts. Reception studies, rooted
in cultural anthropology and sociology, semiotics, and reader-response theories,
emphasized the creative abilities of active media audiences.
    Global media studies also encompasses diasporic media research, an area tradi-
tionally not included in the international communication canon (Cunningham and
Sinclair, 2000; Gillespie, 1995; Kolar-Panov, 1996; Naficy, 1993). García Canclini's
notions of hybrid identity and interculturalism (1995, 2004; García Canclini, 2014)
were helpful. He noted three paradoxes in his account of contemporary hybridity. First,
globalization also deglobalizes, because its dynamic and impact are not only about
transport and exchange, but also disconnectedness and exclusion. Second, minority
communities no longer primarily exist within countries – they emerge at transnational levels, due to massive migration by people who share languages, through which
they continue to communicate, work, and consume, albeit often thanks to innovative
code-switching or familial forms. Third, distinct demographic groups within sovereign

states may not form new and local cultural identities if they largely consume imports from their places of origin dispatched through the culture industries. An example would be China's fairly poor record of exporting media texts, which is largely restricted to people of Chinese origin living in Southeast Asia (Feifei, 2014).

Integrating these different aspects can improve our understanding of the links between media culture and broader social processes in a comparative context. Finally, global media studies is less television- and film-centric than international communication, including in its purview a wide gamut of digital media, from mobile phones to social networking sites.

What are the implications of the debates we have outlined above? Whereas the media-imperialism paradigm regards powerful Western states as complicit with global capital and its exploitation of developing nations, whose people are seen as low-cost labor, some cultural globalization scholars either dismiss the importance of the state or bemoan what they see as the state's protectionist or authoritarian tendencies: "cultural globalization is viewed as positive precisely because it is thought to weaken the nation" (Curran and Park, 2000: 11).

Replacing "international" with "global," however, does not mean doing away with the state as a governing entity or a conceptual issue, nor its role in capital accumulation and the expropriation of surplus value. Rather than relegating the state to the margins of history, globalization and neoliberalism have redefined its role. Thus the shift from international communication to global media studies reflects a widening scope as much as an ideological move. There is a major problem with teleological metanarratives of "linear development in which those mired in the error of media imperialism theory have been corrected by the sages of cultural globalization" (Curran and Park, 2000: 8). The continued relevance of the state, or at least of some states, in global communication, cannot be denied (Braman, 2002; Miller et al., 2001a, 2001b; Morris and Waisbord, 2001). Global media studies recognizes that the role of the state has changed in important ways under neoliberalism, and that powerful countries like the United States subsidize their cultural industries while asking others to open their own media and cultural spheres to unfettered economic access. In addition, global media studies acknowledges that regions such as North America (Mosco and Schiller, 2001), Central and South America (Straubhaar, 2007), Eastern Europe (Imre, 2009), Greater China (Curtin, 2007), and the Arab world (Kraidy, 2010) have emerged as important analytical sites that complicate relations between both nation-states and local-to-global forces.

The new paradigm must engage the fact that we are in the midst of the greatest global economic crisis in seven decades, one that exceeds the 1930s and 1970s versions in both its reach and impact, and a global environmental crisis that is entirely without precedent. Orthodox policies and programs have failed to comprehend or ameliorate these situations. Radical critics continue to problematize dominant discourses of development, globalization, and communication. Although today's neo-modernization models are more sensitive than their forebears to unequal wealth, influence, and status, they do not measure up to critical theories of dependent development, underdevelopment, unequal exchange, world-systems history, center–periphery relations, cultural imperialism, postcolonialism, and environmental impact (Kavoori and Chadha, 2009; McPhail, 2009; Miller, 2012c).

Conclusion

The future domination of English as the major language of international diplomacy, business, and education seems assured. Safely positioned in the top three internet languages and the top two Twitter languages, it is the preferred mode of communication for international airline pilots, corporate engineers, university physicists, global organizations, and medical researchers, *inter alia*. In academia, the social sciences and humanities remain partial holdouts, perhaps because of the spread of the two other principal imperial languages, French and Spanish, the wealth of their sponsoring nations, and the localism of their discourse. But even these areas are changing; for example, Latin American universities clearly favor work published in English over the languages of their own countries (Miller, 2013b).

At the same time, English-language countries are now engaged in an unseemly rush for East Asian money in the social sciences and humanities. (We have great universities! You have great finance! We welcome you!) The curriculum will largely remain as it was, of course. (We built it that way, it's about us, you want it.)

"We" might engage in partnerships with Korean or Chinese universities to add Asia and stir, but our discourse, our theories, and our points of departure will continue. This means we can go on teaching our own country's students as before, with the costs to them kept somewhat under control by income from "the other." It all sounds very neat. But it's flawed and stupid.

First, the Asian wave may be changing direction toward local education with the rapid rise of its own universities. Second, many forecasters think that the rise of the BRIC countries (Brazil, Russia, India, and China) as economic powerhouses may be coming to an end, as a result of factors ranging from rising wage expectations and class struggle, to state corruption, inefficiency, and shifts in patterns of consumption: the *Financial Times* runs a "Beyond the Brics" series highlighting the potential of countries such as Indonesia and Mexico.[3] There have been false dawns for these countries before. But betting against them now would be ill-advised, given their strategic position in the international political economy and their blend of natural resources and human capital.

As media academics, we must remake ourselves in ways that transcend the limits of managerial and bureaucratic imaginations and undertake an immediate revolution in how we hire faculty, train graduate students, and undertake research. We should conceive of our teaching and research on a collaborative basis. That means, depending on the topic, working in teams. Those teams should involve people who are fluent in all the major world languages (Putonghua, English, French, Arabic, and Spanish); who mix academic backgrounds across the human sciences; and who are prepared to rewrite the rules of what counts as knowledge and where they should publish it.

The effortless extrapolation from Anglocentric/Eurocentric literary criticism or social theorization undertaken from stained and worn armchairs and breathlessly reinvigorated over sleek, youthful laptops will no longer do. To remain as we are, in our methodological nationalism and monolingualism, is impractical, given the new needs and orientations of our political economy, and also anti-intellectual, given the new opportunities for knowledge that such a revision promises. The future is not English.[4]

In addition, counter-discourses of the kind produced across the Global South pro-vide vigorous and inventive tactics and strategies countering labor exploitation and occupational health and safety risks, offer environmental alternatives, and mount vibrant critiques of structured domination in communications (Bycroft, 2011; Kapur and Wagner, 2011; Bolaño, 2012).

They can remind us of the value as well as the limitations of utopianism, which has been an ongoing feature of the discourse on new media and international relations. The interwar League of Nations sought to use film as an international *lingua franca* toward both national cultural self-expression and international peace. Henry Ford, patriarch of the motorcar, wrote in 1929: "The airplane and radio know no boundary. They pass over the dotted lines on the map without heed or hindrance. They are bind-ing the world together. . . . Thus may we vision a United States of the World" (1929: 18–19). The Italian inventor Guglielmo Marconi, who pioneered radio transmission, said broadcasting could "make a material contribution towards greater understand-ing and amity between Nations, the cementing of home life and the happiness of the individual" (1924: vii). The German psychologist Rudolf Arnheim's 1935 "Forecast of Television" predicted that the new device would offer viewers simultaneous global experiences, transmitting railway disasters, professorial addresses, town meetings, boxing title fights, dance bands, carnivals, and aerial mountain views – a spectacu-lar montage of Broadway and Vesuvius. A common vision would surpass linguistic competence and interpretation: "the wide world itself enter[ing] ... our room" via TV might even bring global peace with it, by showing spectators that "we are located as one among many" (Arnheim, 1969: 160–3). Three years later, the noted children's writer and essayist E. B. White argued that television, the new "peephole of science," would transport us "beyond the range of our vision," to reveal "either a new and unbearable disturbance of our general peace or a saving radiance in the sky: We shall stand or fall by television – of that I am quite sure" (1997: 2). The Radio Corporation of America's (RCA) David Sarnoff hoped for "the greatest opportunity ever given us for creating close ties of understanding among the peoples of the world" (2004: 310).

Communication technology's binding and unbinding of time and space, and the visibility and audibility of signs from elsewhere, has long stimulated discussion of this kind about the possibility of a new world order, brought on by the spread of knowl-edge to all, which would transcend the chauvinism of sovereign states (Marvin, 1988: 192–3). Today, the touchingly old-fashioned Facebook predictably features "Peace on Facebook" that will "decrease world conflict" through intercultural communica-tion. Twitter modestly announces itself to be "a triumph of humanity."[5] But there is another side that global media studies must also inherit and process.

George Orwell (1944) dissected the antecedents of today's deterritorializing, apolitical media rhetoric 70 years ago. His critique resonates with us:

> Reading recently a batch of rather shallowly optimistic "progressive" books, I was struck by the automatic way in which people go on repeating certain phrases which were fashionable before 1914. Two great favourites are "the abolition of distance" and "the disappearance of frontiers". I do not know how often I have met with the statements that "the aeroplane and the radio have abolished distance" and "all parts of the world are now interdependent."

Technological determinists' lack of originality and tendency to repeat exploded myths as if they were new and true refuses to lie down and die. Today's social media are one more cliché dalliance with new technology's supposedly innate capacity to endow users with transcendence, but no less powerful (for all its undoubted banality) because of the interests it serves and the cult of newness it subscribes to (Ogan et al., 2009).

Utopian hopes should be part of our deliberations – but couched as citizenship rights rather than technological gifts. The UN's definition of communication for development calls for: "two-way communication systems that enable dialogue and that allow communities to speak out, express their aspirations and concerns and participate in the decisions that relate to their development" (quoted in United Nations Development Program, 2009). And the World Congress on Communication for Development seeks: "a social process based on dialogue using a broad range of tools and methods. It is also about seeking change at different levels including listening, building trust, sharing knowledge and skills, building policies, debating and learning for sustained and meaningful change" (quoted in United Nations Development Program, 2009).

How can these aims be achieved? A clear-headed analysis of unequal exchange of cultural textuality, technology, environment, and labor should be our starting-point – not fantasies about development models or technological transformations. The supple openness of global media studies allows us to follow these tendencies without the nationalistic presuppositions of the past.

3 Political Economy

This chapter lays out one of the foundational methods we use throughout the book: the critical political economy of the media.[1] Political economy is one of the oldest theories and methods available to understand the intersections of politics and economics – as we have seen, it is a venerable part of media studies 1.0. Despite its age, the paradigm continues to produce vibrant and relevant work that is crucial to 3.0.

We practice a critical political economy of communication, which poses the following questions of media infrastructures, institutions, images, stories, and sounds: who controls, owns, regulates, and benefits materially from them, and who and what suffers? Such an analysis draws on many sources, including laws and legal cases, business magazines, corporate reports, regulatory discourse, union actions, policy discourse, accounting, social movements, environmental science, industrial sociology, and lived experience. It examines both powerful structures and the complex struggles that go on within them. We give extended examples below of such analyses to examine the world of work in Hollywood and the global export of its texts. But first, to give some detail and flavor of how political economy works, consider the capsule study of the world's dominant player in public relations (PR), presented in Box 3.1.

The idea of a choice between economic and cultural analysis of the media has rightly been problematized (Caldwell, 2013). Work done in communication, film, cultural, and media studies often ignores research by sociologists, management scholars, geographers, psychologists, and others, especially within critical political economy.[2] The dichotomy often claimed to exist between economic and cultural analysis is therefore a false one.

Political economy's blend of a concern with justice and a commitment to knowledge is in keeping with its origins as an Enlightenment project dedicated to bettering the lives of ordinary people in a democratic and secular way that rejects sectarian tendentiousness other than on behalf of the socio-economically disenfranchised. Political economy mixes social struggle and social science, with an abiding concern for class interests and other forms of inequality. It focuses on material power, the capacity to mobilize resources, the warp and woof of history, and the correlation of meanings with economic and political interests. It sees culture as created through struggle, with an emphasis on social power as a determinant, examining the relationships between political consciousness and industrial organization, state and citizen, and government, labor, and capital.[3]

In this book we try to blend the traditions of critical political economy with the best of the rest of media studies, to erase what Roger Chartier calls "the tenacious division that for so long separated sciences of description and sciences of interpretation, morphological studies and hermeneutical analysis." The goal is to recognize that the "'world of text' . . . [is] a world of objects and performances" (2005a: 38–9).

Box 3.1

Edelman is one of the world's biggest PR corporations. Caught out when other major PR concerns announced in 2014 that they would no longer work for climate change deniers (Goldenberg, 2014), the group responded with the same guarantee. But a year later, word spread that it had advised the American Petroleum Institute (API) through a subsidiary, Blue Advertising. Tax filings disclose that API paid Edelman US$327.4 million between 2008 and 2012 (Quinn and Young, 2015). In return for this largesse, Edelman schooled API in award-winning campaigns[4] designed to avoid the charge of climate-change denial.

API's website offers the following: "While the world relies on oil and gas for most of its energy and is likely to do so for years to come, emissions from their production and use have raised concerns. These emissions may be helping to warm our planet by enhancing the natural greenhouse effect of our atmosphere."[5] Here's our tendentious translation: "We keep you warm, cool, connected, and mobile – so don't regulate us. We, too, worry about the environment and will fix it before we ruin it."

In responding to the controversy, Edelman did what it might advise a client to do: claimed to be misunderstood, sacrificed an executive, announced that it believed in climate change, and divested from Blue Advertising (Gunther, 2014; Elliott, 2014).[6]

Let's get real: Greenpeace's *Dealing in Doubt* reports are remarkable indictments of PR firms like Edelman that facilitate climate change denial.[7] The industry routinely funds astroturf organizations (faux grassroots activism) and coin-operated think-wankery (failed academics) that appeal to everyday experience and junk science and against democratic regulation underpinned by scholarly advice (Schäfer, 2012; Schlichting, 2013).

Edelman oleaginously refers to astroturfing as "third party technique" (Burton and Rowell, 2003) and is the author of a "Grassroots Advocacy Vision Document" that incarnates civil society mimesis on behalf of corporate distortion.[8]

Such conduct runs contrary to the US PR industry's code of ethics. Its list of "improper conduct" includes "'grass roots' campaigns or letter-writing campaigns to legislators on behalf of undisclosed interest groups" and "employing people to pose as volunteers to speak at public hearings and participate in 'grass roots' campaigns."[9] The bizarrely titled Word of Mouth Marketing Association (truly) promises that its members will "make meaningful disclosures of their relationships or identities with consumers in relation to the marketing initiatives that could influence a consumer's purchasing decisions."[10] Note that the word "citizen," which should apply given the attempt to forestall the democratic regulation of industries, is invisible.

Edelman has form in this regard, across many industries. In tobacco, it dedicated decades to combating medical science, encouraging simpleton smokers to continue their deluded indulgence.[11] In pharmaceuticals, it spruiked spurious studies guaranteeing hair regrowth to gullible guys (Moynihan et al., 2002). In chemicals, it set up supposedly grassroots campaigns for Monsanto contra critiques of genetically modified food (Beder, 1998). In retail, it paid operatives masquerading as cross-country campers to blog favorably about Wal-Mart car parks and store managers (Frazier, 2006). And in the extractive sector, its collaboration with Trans Canada sought to discredit anyone questioning the Energy East pipeline.[12]

Edelman registered record profits in 2014: US$812 million, up 8.2 percent on the previous year. The company noted in particular that it helped universities deal with the impact on public opinion of sexual violence on campus (Barrett, 2015). Right. In 2015, the firm launched its latest "Trust Barometer Survey," which disclosed that "half of the global informed public believe that the pace of development and change in business today is too fast, that business innovation is driven by greed and money rather than a desire to improve people's lives and that there is not enough government regulation of many industry sectors."[13]

Doesn't this make the case for subjecting its own segment of society to democratic scrutiny, as a quasi-clandestine element of the media that operates under the radar and is immune to significant critical appraisal? PR gets a bad press because it does PR: legitimizing the illegitimate will do that to a body of knowledge or profession. Hence the industry's paradoxical obsession with ethics: "We are faithful to those we represent, while honoring our obligation to serve the public interest."[14]

Thirty years ago, Edelman's founder proudly announced a company and industry mission for the twenty-first century: "We have to prove by our performance that public relations is not a devious kind of work, a covering up, a cosmeticizing or distortion of reality" (Edelman, 1983). His legacy makes the very case its patriarch hoped to disprove. The Edelman–API romance may be over, but it's difficult to know what the promised divestment signifies in terms of personnel and money. Perhaps we found an answer in a Hong Kong bar as we finished a draft of this chapter: a white expat announced to a waitrand: "You're listening to two, three professional bullshitters." Indeed. Critical political economy is the best means we know of exposing such antics.

Unlike bourgeois or neoclassical economics, which is dominant in economics and political science, political economy does not take as its lodestone the individual rationality of consumers and firms. Rather, it starts from an historical understanding of how power operates in everyday work and domestic life, stressing that value is generated by workers, who rarely gain due benefit from it – unlike the owners of capital. Political economy concentrates, in the words of the physicist-novelist C. P. Snow, on people "lost in the great anonymous sludge of history" (1987: 26–7, 42), occupying a world described by Thomas Hobbes as one of "continual fear and danger of violent death, and the life of man solitary, poor, nasty, brutish, and short" (n.d.: ch. XIII).

And whereas orthodox economics assumes that supply and demand determine price, political economy examines the role of the state and capital in controlling labor and pleasing and ideologizing consumers and citizens (hence its media orientation). In other words, the orthodox approach looks to the role of markets, regarding them as jewels of human behavior. The heterodox approach challenges this focus on consumption and looks instead to production, regarding it as a site of value and tool of power.

So political economy notes with alarm that, in 2011, the cost of broadband in the Global South was 40.3 percent of average individual Gross National Income (GNI). Across the Global North, by comparison, the price was less than 5 percent of GNI per capita (International Telecommunication Union, 2012: 4). Within Latin America, for example, there are major disparities in pricing. One megabit a second in Mexico costs US$9, or 1 percent of average monthly income; in Bolivia, it is US$63, or 31 percent. Access is also structured unequally in terms of race, occupation, and region: "indigenous people represent a third of rural workers in Latin America and over half in some countries are essentially disconnected. The digital divide between indigenous people and the rest of the population in Mexico is 0.3, in Panama 0.7, and Venezuela 0.6" (Bianchi, 2015). If these numbers are functions of market life, then it is clearly producing and reinforcing inequality. This inequality is not only about consumer and citizen access to the media. It also concerns the exploitation of labor, as per the NICL, which we'll explain below and in chapter 5.

This latter method argues that objects and services accrete value through corporate exploitation of the people who make them. The power of capital includes both authority over the conditions and possibilities of the workplace and surplus value, realized as profit. The division of labor links productivity, exploitation, and social control. As capital subdivides, multiplies, and spreads geographically, it hides the labor that constitutes it (Marx, 1906: 49, 83).

In the late 1970s, former colonial powers still dominated the Global South, exercising power over client states to extract surplus value. But in some instances, domestic bourgeoisies were emerging. This was spectacularly true of Taiwan, South Korea, Hong Kong, and Singapore, known then as "Newly Industrialized Countries" or "Asian Tigers/Dragons." They benefited from US, Japanese, and West European investment in and control of transport and communications and investment, undertaken because they were capitalist states rather than Maoist or Marxist-Leninist ones in a region that Cold Warrior Yanquis feared might "turn Red." But they were not mere pawns of foreign governments and multinational corporations exploiting cheap labor and repatriating profit: domestic wealth creation did occur, albeit in a way that constructed profound inequalities. Consider South Korea's rapid transformation from a very poor, essentially peasant economy to a vibrant manufacturing one (Park, 1997).

As the global value chain grew more diverse, those of us who were influenced by *dependencia* and critics of cultural imperialism had to confront the fact that core–periphery relations were not uniform. This necessitated a partial break with *dependencia* as an explanatory mechanism. In its place – or perhaps supplementing it, given that such asymmetries continued to characterize much of the world – came the idea of the NIDL (Fröbel et al., 1980; Higgott, 1993).

Theorists of the NIDL identified an increasingly global competition for working-class labor as manufacturers looked to invest in places where employees were capable, cheap, and compliant – the ultimate realization of a worldwide reserve army of workers. So the production of cars, boats, refrigerators, and televisions might still be funded from Tokyo or New York, but it could be undertaken in Seoul or Guadalajara (Higgott and Robison, 1985).

The NIDL would supposedly not impoverish the West, because the latter would embark on structural adjustment by retraining blue-collar workers away from assembly and toward services. This was in accordance with the neoclassical economist Fritz Machlup's (1962) bedside essential for true believers in doctrines of human capital. The party line was that the middle class would continue its merry investment in human capital through higher education as manufacturing left the Global

North. There would be four, largely painless, changes from production to services: the preeminence of professionalism and technique, the importance of theory to innovate and generate public policies, the formation of a discourse of the future, and new intellectual technologies to help make decisions (Mattelart 2003: 77–8).

This technocratic vision promised a world of modernity, of rationality, of the ability to apply reason to problems and seek salvation in the secular. As we have seen, futurists like Brzezinski, Bell, Toffler, and de Sola Pool championed this position. Their ideas were at least partially as amenable to the center-left as the right, fulfilling Keynes's idea of a 15-hour work week enabled through technology and compound interest as well as Machlup's model of investment in the self (Keynes, 1963: 358–73).

The fantasy has suited policymakers and think-tanks ever since, for reasons of ideology as much as efficiency. Reagan launched his successful 1966 campaign for the governorship of California in this context, saying: "I propose . . . "A Creative Society" . . . to discover, enlist and mobilize the incredibly rich human resources of California [through] innumerable people of creative talent." That rhetoric publicly birthed today's idea of technology unlocking the creativity that is allegedly lurking, unbidden, in individuals, thereby permitting them to become happy, productive – and without secure full-time employment.

Then an even more spectacular change in the market for labor occurred in the five years after 1989. The collapse of state socialism saw people from the former Soviet empire enter the capitalist world *tout court*, followed more importantly by the People's Republic of China and India opening up to international competition. Virtually overnight, the global pool of workers doubled, as massive reserve armies of labor were unleashed (Shepherd and Stone, 2013).

In China's case, this was achieved under the tight control of semi-state corporations and the first police state dedicated to export-oriented industrialization. Footloose capital could rejoice as billions of mostly unskilled workers lined up for obedience school. For its part, India benefited from decades of centralized technocratic planning that had produced huge cohorts of educated people who also spoke English, the world's *lingua franca*. It garnered a great deal of skilled work in the services sector, from software to sales.

At the same time, the spread of the internet permitted unprecedented surveillance of inventory and labor. "Cool stuff" abounded, made by pliant employees. This development immediately cut into the lives of unskilled First World labor (Fuchs, 2014). The new wave of workers in the NICL was not just doing traditional manufacturing, but, rather, cultural manufacturing: assembling vast numbers of machines dedicated to making meaning, such as photocopiers, printers, laptops, tablets, and phones. They became the invisible background of cultural work, and frequently in the informal as well as the formal sectors of the economy. The NICL was exerting its hold across the globe and across the media industries.

As part of the NICL urged on by the futurists, new "jobs" have emerged in the Global North, for example in surveillance. Audience members spy on fellow-spectators in theaters to see how they respond to coming attractions. Opportunities to vote in the Eurovision Song Contest or reality programs disclose the profiles and practices of viewers, who can be monitored and wooed by marketers. Twitter and Facebook sell information about users' past and present lives and likes, monitoring their every move. End-user licensing agreements ensure that players of corporate games online sign over their cultural moves and perspectives to the companies they are paying in order to participate (T. Miller, 2007).[15] The labor of consumers becomes the property of the companies they are patronizing; a neat corporate trick – an unpaid NICL.

The amount of information about people online, the speed with which it is collected and analyzed, and the way it is articulated by marketers to corporations have all dramatically increased in both reach and effect as part of what the futurists called an information society. The US Federal Trade Commission (2012) has alerted citizens to how much surveillance they are subject to in the name of consumer sovereignty. But it claims that if consumers give companies information about themselves, their desires will be met more easily and rapidly.

The Commission acknowledges concerns about the use of such data by firms, but fails to point out that beyond privacy lies the question of the ownership and use of ordinary people's intellectual property: their ideas and identities should be theirs to share or not, for monetary gain or not. So it's not just that they must be allowed to keep things private – they should be *paid* by corporations that wish to collect, analyze, exploit, and sell information about them.

Dividing lines between labor and play are being redrawn, simultaneously before our eyes and behind our backs. The comparatively cheap and easy access to making and distributing meaning afforded by internet media and genres is thought to have eroded the one-way hold on culture that saw a small segment of the world as producers and the larger segment as consumers. New technologies supposedly allow us all to become simultaneously cultural consumers and producers (prosumers) without the say-so of media gatekeepers. The result is said to be a democratized media, higher skill levels, and powerful challenges to old patterns of expertise and institutional authority – hence the term "disintermediation" (Graham, 2008; Ritzer and Jurgenson, 2010).

In this cybertarian world free of intermediaries, everyone and no one is a producer in the traditional, quasi-institutional sense, just as everyone is simultaneously an unpaid worker and a paying customer. Fans write zines that end up on screens. Interning graduate students in New York and Los Angeles read scripts for producers then pronounce on whether they tap into audience interests. Precariously employed part-timers spy on fellow-spectators in theaters to see how they respond to coming attractions, and report back to moguls (T. Miller, 2007).

Facebook and academia work in step, rejoicing in proving the uncanny accuracy of prosumer control through the use of big data (Kosinski et al., 2013). Target was rightly embarrassed by the revelation in 2012 that it analyzed purchasing patterns by women to determine whether they were pregnant, then proceeded to advertise pregnancy and baby products through direct mailing to their homes. That risked disclosing their situation to people from whom they might wish to keep such matters private, be they parents, grandparents, children, lovers, or lodgers (Duhig, 2012). Despite such outrages, the paucity of citizen knowledge of the extent and impact of corporate surveillance and manipulation remains striking (Madden et al., 2013).

The information society has disempowered the very people around whom it was built – the educated middle class. This has been achieved by drawing on the example of fringe intellectuals, from jazz musicians to street artists, cultural workers who have long labored without regular compensation and security. Now they model the expectations we are *all* supposed to have, as opposed to our parents' or grandparents' assumptions about life-long, or at least steady, employment. Cultural production shows that workers can move from security to insecurity, certainty to uncertainty, salary to wage, firm to project, and profession to precarity – with obligatory smiles on their faces (Ross, 2009). The NICL distributes that systematic insecurity across industries and places. Contemporary business leeches luxuriate in flexibility over the people they employ, the technologies they use, the places where they do business, and the amounts they pay – and *in*flexibility of ownership and control (Mosco, 2014: 155–74).

Consider entities such as Mindworks Global Media, a company outside New Delhi that provides US and European newspapers with Indian-based journalists and copyeditors who work long-distance and offers 35–40 percent cost savings on employing local reporters (Lakshman, 2008).[16] Or the advertising agency/broker Philadelphia/Dana Point's former company Poptent, which undercut big competitors in sales to major advertisers by exploiting prosumers' labor in the name of "empowerment." That empowerment took the following form: the creators of homemade commercials made US$7500; Poptent received a management fee of US$40,000; and the buyer saved about US$300,000 on the usual price (Chmielewski, 2012).[17] The slogan says it all:

Accelerate your video career
Access the biggest brands. Build your network. Get paid.

The NICL doesn't conclude once gadgets or programs are made. When old and obsolete media technologies are junked, they become e-waste, the fastest-growing component of municipal cleanups around the Global North. E-waste salvage yards have generated serious threats to worker health and safety wherever plastics and wires are burnt, monitors smashed and dismantled, and circuit boards grilled or leached with acid, while the toxic chemicals and heavy metals that flow from such practices have perilous implications for local and downstream residents, soil and water (Maxwell and Miller, 2012; E. Grossman, 2006: 18–20, 44–5; and chapter 5 *passim*).

Most electronic salvage and recycling is done in the Global South by pre-teen girls, who work with discarded television sets and computers to find precious metals and dump the remains in landfills. The e-waste ends up there after export and import by "recyclers," who eschew landfills and labor in the Global North in order to avoid the higher costs and regulatory oversight of recycling in countries that prohibit such destruction to environment and workers. And businesses that forbid dumping in local landfills as part of their corporate policies merrily mail it elsewhere (Hardell et al., 2009; Crosby, 2007; Rydh, 2003; Sadetzki et al., 2007).

Clearly, we need to transcend the beguiling simplicity of dominant economics. Political economy offers a way out. While there is a deep and rich history within the Global South of theorizing the political economy of the media, going at least as far back as 1970s Chile (Dorfman and Mattelart, 1971) and continuing today (Manyozo, 2006; Bolaño, 2009, 2012; Aguilar et al., 2009), the dominant paradigm in policy terms and influence originated in the North and often obscures potential and actual South–South communication and theorization.

We concentrate below on two themes from a political-economic analysis of the media that bring together questions of consciousness and industry and are relevant to places beyond the wealthy nations: Hollywood actors and TV drama trade. These topics are familiar to us all. They address the human figures that dominate our screens, and the experience of hearing and watching them. Two classic questions recur for our students: how are stars made, and why is US television popular in other countries? The next two sections use political-economic approaches to answer these queries and engage two core themes of human knowledge: the conduct of institutions and populations.

Not all the research summarized below was undertaken by people calling themselves political economists. Their methods include participant observation, critical analysis of monopoly capitalism, regression, content and textual analysis, archival research, questionnaires, and interviews. Binding these forms together with an eye to social justice permits political economy to assess the issues with which we began, of control, impact, and benefit.

Hollywood Work

A factory-like studio system of production known as Fordism applied in Hollywood between about 1920 and 1970. It began to erode by the late 1940s due to vertical disintegration (studios that blended production, distribution, and exhibition were forced to cease this through anti-trust action), suburbanization (white people left city centers with government aid to start new families and new suburbs), and televisualization (the rapid uptake of TV militated against routine film-going). The US film industry adapted to those shocks. In the process, it became a pioneer of the NICL (Kavoori and Chadha, 2009; McPhail, 2009; Miller, 2012a; Miller et al., 2005).

The NICL today sees workers and capitalists strike complex, transitory arrangements on a project basis to create temporary organizations. Small numbers of divers hands are involved at each stage other than production, when sizeable crews operate both together and semi-autonomously. Places and networks matter in terms of textual cues, policy incentives, educational support, financing, and skills. Time matters because of cost and marketing. Work may be subject to local, national, regional, and international fetishization of each component, matching the way that the labor undertaken is largely hidden in the final text, such that it becomes invisible to viewers. Conventional organization charts are inadequate explanations, especially if one seeks to elude the conventions of hierarchy through capital while recognizing the eternal presence of managerial surveillance.

Hollywood may therefore be more complex than the Frankfurt School's Fordist analysis allows, and closer to Gramsci's conflict-based account. With jobs constantly ending, starting, and moving, it exemplifies "flexible specialization" – a shift from life-long employment to casual labor. Hollywood has an economic commitment to "permanent innovation," and a political commitment to control its environment (Piore and Sabel 1984: 17).

This explains the appeal of the NICL to other segments of the media. The power and logic of domination by a small number of vast entities is achieved via a huge globalizing network of subcontracted firms and individuals, in turn mediated through unions, employer associations, education, and the state.

Many of the people working in the media have highly educated, middle-class backgrounds, as per a concept that Toffler (1983) invented three decades ago: the cognitariat. His idea has since been taken up and redisposed for political economy by Antonio Negri (2007). Negri applies the term to people who are mired in contingent media work but have educational qualifications and a facility with cultural technologies and genres. This cognitariat plays key roles in the production and circulation of goods and services, through both creation and coordination. As per Gramsci, the *"culturalization of production"* increases the importance of intellectuals, because it places them at the center of world economies. But it simultaneously disables them, thanks to flexible production underwritten by the ideology of "freedom."

What used to be the fate of artists and musicians – where "making cool stuff" and working with relative autonomy was meant to outweigh ongoing employment – has become a norm. The outcome is contingent labor as a way of life that is no longer defined in terms of location (factories), tasks (manufacturing), or politics (moderation of ruling-class power and ideology) and comprises people whose immediate forebears, with similar or less cultural capital, were confident of secure health care and retirement income. It lacks both the organization of the traditional working class and the political *entrée* of the old middle class.

As noted earlier, most of this work is invisible to viewers of Hollywood. The people we see and remember are stars, i.e. celebrities. Their history predates film; celebrities have been around since the first portraits of writers and painters in twelfth-century Europe, which marketed their painters and subjects alike to potential patrons. In the seventeenth century, portraits transformed into methods of instruction, as depictions of daily life at court became model rituals for courtiers. Then, democracy and capitalism invented the idea of publicity, transferring esteem and legitimacy from royalty and religion to upwardly mobile businessmen. Hence today's debates over stars' trans-historical as opposed to ephemeral value, their authentic versus manufactured images, and their public and private lives – in other words, the full catastrophe (and pleasure) of forming a nouveau riche and providing popular methods for measuring bodies, families, and lifestyles (Briggs and Burke 2003: 11, 41).

The result is big business. In 2005, the cost of celebrity endorsements in advertising exceeded a billion dollars. This expenditure is predicated on a conceptual tie-in between commodities and stars, such that the lifestyle of celebrities can be purchased along with the products they favor (Spears et al., 2013; Becker, 2013).

As audiences, we may know less about stars than we imagine – for instance, the public probably agrees with Hollywood that the key to the industry's financial success is stardom, despite the evidence of regression analysis, which highlights genres, corporations, and directors (De Vany, 2003). It is also common to negate the centrality of institutions to stars. In many popular and academic analyses, the dominant thesis is that actors become popular because of their individual abilities and characteristics. Four qualities associated with them encourage this view: beauty, age, skill, and screen image, as evident in their characters in films, their private selves, and their public personae (Clark, 1995; Dyer, 1986).

But rather than the culmination of emotional interiority or thespian skill, stars are complex mixtures of marketing methods, social signs, nationalism, capitalism, individualism, and consumption. Each element imbricates the public with the private. Actors transmogrify into stars when their social and private lives become more important than their professional qualities, when the public wants to emulate them.

They feed into and generate stereotypes of success, power, and beauty, incarnating dramatic roles or fashions and indexing the limitations and the promises of the age. Each star "es una imagen; pero no una imagen natural" (is an image; but not a natural image). Their crucial transformation is from an "icono ideográfico en icono normativo" (ideographic icon into a normative one) (Bueno, 2002).

This is neither magical nor a reflection of some naturally occurring *Zeitgeist* determined by audiences. It is a result of corporate agility and the "emotional labor" (Hochschild, 1983) undertaken by the "smiling professions" (Hartley, 1992) of PR, publicity, advertising, literary and artistic representation, and brand consultancy.

For example, the major talent agencies in Los Angeles identify causes for their celebrity clients to endorse, based on visibility, subjectivity, interest, availability, and other pragmatic factors. Consider cause marketing, whereby stars associate themselves with social movements, perhaps most notably environmental activism. It is not clear how well this works, given research that suggests minimal media attention to these efforts, audience skepticism, and credibility that lessens with the contentiousness of the issues discussed (Spears et al., 2013; Becker, 2013).

Apart from the tenuous impact of such activism, it fails to disclose the ecological realities of Hollywood itself. The major scholarly study on the topic names the motion-picture industry as the biggest producer of conventional pollutants in Los Angeles, because it uses so much electricity and petroleum and releases hundreds of thousands of tons of deadly emissions each year. In the state of California overall, screen drama's energy consumption and greenhouse-gas emissions are akin to those of the aerospace and semiconductor industries (Corbett and Turco, 2006). But we don't see cause marketing by A-, B-, or C-list celebrities that brings into question their own industry.

Nevertheless, we can connect celebrity eco-activism and Hollywood ecological damage via political economy. Take the example of Leonardo DiCaprio, who announced a 2013 sabbatical from filmmaking to "fly around the world doing good for the environment." As part of this paradox, DiCaprio helped launch World Wildlife Fund's "Hands Off My Pants" campaign. With compelling solipsism, his accompanying press release focused on a country that had incurred the great man's particular displeasure, "calling on Thailand's government to show leadership on elephant conservation by shutting down its ivory market."[18]

Of course, some of the money DiCaprio uses to "fly around the world doing good for the environment" comes from his films, and political economy directs us to consider how those activities sit with his activism. Consider *The Beach* (2000), shot in Thailand and directed by Danny Boyle, whose nationalism suffused the opening ceremony of the 2012 Olympic Games, encouraging the *Guardian* newspaper to ennoble him as a "champion of the people" and "the ultimate idealist" (Freedland, 2013). Like his star DiCaprio, Boyle feels strongly about ecology. He claimed *The Beach* was "raising environmental consciousness" among the Thai population, whose appreciation of these things he deemed to lag "behind" US "awareness." Boyle elected to "give something back to Thailand" by hiring local apprentices, even though this meant "[w]e were hauling 300 fucking people around wherever we went. And you know how hard it is to learn Thai names. Every lunchtime was like a prime minister's reception." Before the film was released – but no doubt having had their consciousness raised – environmental groups sued the studio and local officialdom for contravening the

National Parks Act and the Environmental Protection Act. It took seven years, but the Thai Supreme Court found in their favor in 2006 (Maxwell and Miller, 2012; Forsyth, 2002).[19]

Despite these instances, environmental celebrity does not have to be so deliriously self-regarding and chauvinistic. The key is unpacking the political-economic realities of such activism, especially the extent to which stars endeavor to be consistent across private and public spheres. For example, Darryl Hannah travels by train, even across the United States, and was arrested after chaining herself to the gates of the White House in protest at a proposed oil pipeline. This forms part of a serious engagement with issues that often sees her face media opprobrium and state violence (Rowlatt, 2009; Wood, 2009; Goldenberg, 2013). Such actions produce press coverage, photos, and popular discourse in a reflexive way that takes account of one's own complicity, as opposed to a hypocritical Messianic wish fulfillment fueled by the very actions it purports to change. When we examine Hollywood from this perspective, the tools of political economy unveil both its industry-wide exploitation of labor and natural resources and the gaps that its struggle for hegemony opens up.

TV Trade

The United States remains the world's dominant media actor, forming a power triad alongside Japan and Western Europe. None of that has changed or been even mildly imperiled by the newer media or anything else. China and India are finally becoming the economic powers that their population numbers should ensure. Although the latter have many leading software engineers in addition to a huge army of labor, they lack the domestic venture capitalists, the military underpinnings to computing innovation, and the historic cross-cultural textual power that characterize Sony, the BBC, Hollywood, and the Bay Area. India, for instance, is the globe's biggest newspaper market, second Facebook community and telecommunications sector, and third largest TV zone, but it remains a fairly minor player in the export of media texts (Mehta, 2015).

It comes as no surprise that the triad still accounts for 80 percent of the globe's TV programming market (Best et al., 2011; Boyd-Barrett, 2006),[20] or that the US children's channel Nickelodeon is available in well over 150 countries, and 80 percent of shows for children outside the white-settler colonies and China come from the United States (Osei-Hwere and Pecora, 2008: 16, 19; Götz et al., 2008).

The United States continues to be the major source of news and current affairs around the world, while Britain has about a fifth of global exports. This power is exerted via CNN and the BBC, on the one hand, and news agencies – Associated Press Television News and Reuters Television – on the other. CNN broadcasts to more than 130 nations across the principal world languages, with globally generated as well as regionally specific content a key to its prominence. Germany has two major networks across Asia, received by more than 1,000 satellite systems. Three-quarters of its programming is in German and a quarter in English.[21] Such inequality in the source and ideology of stories about the Global South, reported both elsewhere and back to them, has led to ongoing calls for a contra flow of news (Thussu, 2004). Politics in its most formal sense also sees the impact of lopsided transnational networks – the United States absolutely bombards Iran with satellite TV in Farsi (25 networks in 2005, many of which focused on politics), generated by "Persian" expatriates in southern California who define themselves against the Islamic Republic (Semati, 2007: 151–2).

Hollywood's route into the trade in TV drama is not simply via direct exports – it also engages in franchising via format sales in order to localize product. In the 1960s, Disney television in Australia consisted of rebroadcast US programs on local stations; by the 1990s, these shows were seemingly if superficially localized, via young, cute, and stupid Australian presenters. And General Motors translated its "hot dogs, baseball, apple pie, and Chevrolet" jingle into "meat pies, football, kangaroos, and Holden cars" for the Australian market. Sony, Time Warner, and Disney all produce thousands of hours of television texts in foreign markets each year, designed for local audiences. In Italy, *The Nanny* (1993–9) was dubbed to make Fran Drescher's character Sicilian rather than Jewish, thereby connoting someone adjacent yet still marginal to the dominant culture. In South Africa, former African National Congress Communist Party leader Tokyo Sexwale, now a billionaire, played the business leech in the localized version of *The Apprentice* (Miller, 2010a; Glenn, 2008).

"The West" finally won over a key segment of the Indian market with a localized *Who Wants to be a Millionaire?* (1998–), memorable for its "role" in *Slum Dog Millionaire* (Danny Boyle, 2008). While the original program was British, it met many Yanqui stylistic and ideological criteria of game-show consumerism and sexual objectification, and may have "softened up the general public for the 'knowledge economy'" (Hartley 2008: 244; for the fullest version of such claims, see Ott, 2007). The program was sold to 107 countries by 2009. In the Middle East, it was adapted as a pan-Arab game show (Bielby and Harrington, 2008: 113; Kraidy, 2010). The managing director of Celador, which sold the format, says: "It's a bit like the old days of the British empire. We've got a map of the world in the office colored in pink where we've placed the show" (quoted in Freedman, 2008: 213). Of course you do, old thing.

Textual formats are traded in both regulated and pirated ways, with multinational firms moving easily between high moralism about ownership and exceedingly sharp practice. The Format Recognition and Protection Association represents more than 100 TV companies worldwide and tries to protect, i.e. charge for, their intellectual property. It exists to systematize monetary exchange for drawing on others' creativity.[22]

Agile format firms are all too aware of how local-content regulations are designed to stymie TV imports, so they point out to companies based in small nations that protect their local industries and culture through quotas that buying a format and making a version of it can often satisfy such policies (Moran with Malbon, 2006: 9).

Not all format exchanges go easily. A famous case concerns the 1999 Mexican program *TeleChobis*, an unauthorized TV Azteca version of the BBC children's program *Teletubbies* (1997–2001, 2015–), which was screening on its rival, Televisa. TV Azteca's copycat introduced many national signifiers, and live children – but was ultimately stymied through intellectual property regimes (Kraidy, 2005: 104–14). Such edgy conduct is not the unique province of the Third World, of course. Along with the English Premier League, the Scottish Premier League, and Rodgers & Hammerstein, MTV's owner, Viacom, has sued YouTube for copyright infringement; but MTV arranged with MySpace to overlay advertising on clips that it owned.[23] And a leaked memo within ABC, copied below, shows how high up within the delightful "family-

 **studios**

Memorandum

To: ABS Studios Term Deal Executive Producers   Date: June 24, 2008

From: Howard M. Davine   Extension: 0050

Subject: **Foreign Formats**

As I'm sure you're all aware, foreign formats have increased in popularity as the basis for US television development and production. What is often overlooked, or not fully appreciated, are the complexities associated with negotiating format deals, coupled with the fact that often-times what is appealing in the format may be nothing more than a general underlying premise, which, in and of itself, may be no reason to license the underlying property.

There are a multitude of business reasons to carefully scrutinize entering into a transaction based on an underlying format. The most common are:

(a) The format rightsholders will typically seek executive producer credit and a degree of creative control/involvement, typically to be rendered from a foreign location, adding perhaps an unnecessary layer to the creative process.

(b) Between format rights fees and executive producer fees, there are significant costs added to your production budget that will impact what you can put on the screen.

(c) A large chunk of the backend will go to the format rightsholder.

(d) Depending on the stature of the underlying property or the stature of the rightsholder, we may find ourselves freezing or being unable to acquire rights that limit our abilities to fully develop and exploit derivative uses of your show – be it on stage, as a feature, or in format sales of our own US production.

(e) Deals regularly get bogged down or sometimes break down entirely on issues relating to our ability to sell the US series without restriction internationally and issues relating to the desire of the foreign rightsholder to sell episodes of their underlying series in the US market. Here, it is not a symmetrical two-way street. Whereas the economics of producing a foreign series are not dependent on a vibrant US marketplace for the product, the economics of US network production do indeed depend on our ability to sell our series internationally without restriction.

I am aware that quite often you are first exposed to the idea of creating a project based on a property developed in a foreign country by your agents who send you submission material to review. The purpose of this communication is to ask your cooperation in the following manner:

1. Do not accept any submission based on a foreign TV property (be it a script, pilot or series episodes) without first discussing the nature of the property with ABCS Creative Affairs. I would like us to make our own independent evaluation whether the license of the property is necessary or appropriate.

2. If you on your own have come across an existing foreign TV project that you feel is something you'd like to explore adapting for the US market, again, please first discuss the opportunity with ABCS Creative Affairs to give us the same opportunity to independently evaluate whether a license of the underlying property is warranted.

Let me assure you that we continue to be actively, competitively and aggressively engaged in developing product based on foreign formats and our decision whether or not to get into negotiations will be premised purely on creative need and our legal analysis as to whether underlying rights are required.

Please feel free to contact me if you'd like to discuss this matter in greater detail.

Figure 3.1

Source: http://www.deadlinehollywooddaily.com/bombshell-abc-studios-memo-a-blueprint-to-rip-off-foreign-tv-series/

values" domain of Disney lurked executives who were content to pick and choose their adherence to law and lore (Holmwood, 2008).

Then there is the question of entire channels undergoing localization. Since the 1980s, smaller nations have experienced global TV channels as well as exported programs: CNN and MTV symbolize the ways that truth and fun are sold as ways of life – and not just as shows, but as entire networks. While criticisms were long made of MTV internationally for a preponderance of US material, in some ways it quickly became regional rather than local or Yanqui in its programming. By 2008, the network was in 162 countries across 33 languages, with revenue not only from the sale of texts but from massive merchandising tie-ins as well – toys, clothes, and, of course, *Rock Band* (2007–), the video game that has sold millions of copies in its various iterations. MTV's customization to local markets never prevented the egregious Sumner Redstone, its owner, from boasting about his universal influence. Meanwhile, deregulatory policies saw massive markets such as India open up to overseas ownership. Viacom entered the fray with its network Colors in 2008 and quickly achieved second place in national ratings among Hindi channels (Miller et al., 2005; Bignell and Fickers, 2008: 41; Fung, 2008: 85).[24]

And when it comes to cinema on television, US exports remain extremely powerful. In 1995, 89 percent of films screened on Brazil's cable channels were US imports, which also occupied 61 percent of time dedicated to cinema on Mexican TV. When cable and satellite opened up in the Arab world across the 1990s, there was a scramble both to "secure access to Western content" and to "Arabize." US film channels were potent contributors, including a special Arab-dedicated Disney channel. By 1999, the latter was selling US$100 million a month, and in 2002, Showtime offered 10 new channels through Nilesat. From its earliest days in the 1960s, Malaysian television relied on US films for content. The trend has never let up and dominates prime time along with Bollywood, while local productions are under pressure to conform to narrative and stylistic norms from LA. The same is true in Sri Lanka and the Philippines, where local films are rarely seen on television. Eurodata TV's 1999 analysis of films on television found that 14 Hollywood pictures drew the highest audiences in 27 nations across all continents (Miller et al., 2005; Ishak, 2011).

In 1974, the Soviet Union imported 5 percent of its programming and in 1984, 8 percent; but Russia imported 60 percent of its TV in 1997, much of it from the United States. This was associated with a comprehensive rearticulation of views of the United States on television, from demonization under the USSR to sanctification in the early post-state socialist period of the '90s, when Yanqui programs, propaganda, and products proliferated and US style became ultra-fashionable (Mickiewicz, 1999: 21). The USSR had been a major exporter of television to East Germany and Bulgaria. Once state socialism was displaced by authoritarian capitalism, the picture changed dramatically. By 1997, the United States had completely displaced Soviet exports to Eastern and Central Europe. The de-Sovietization process of privatizing TV stations from the early 1990s rapidly decimated the screening of local films – previously the most significant genre on TV in terms of time – in favor of imported drama (Rantanen, 2002: 86, 97). Almost all commercials consisted of imported US material dubbed into Russian (Morris, 2007: 1390–1). Though many commercials are now localized, their promises remain marked with US diacritics.

Television drama more generally shows the same trend. In 1983, the United States was estimated to have 60 percent of global TV sales. By 1999, that figure had grown to 68 percent, thanks to 85 percent of exported children's programming and 81 percent of TV movies. The only sizeable trade the other way was Britain's paltry export figure of US$85 million; the following year, its share of world television exchange stood at 9 percent, France's and Australia's at 3 percent. The British went from a small TV trade surplus in 1989 to a deficit of £272 million in 1997 and £403 million in 2000 – the difference arising from fashions in public policy, because the proliferation of channels following deregulation created new opportunities for English-language text from Hollywood's archive. Meanwhile, British TV exports dropped by 10 percent in 1999 and 11 percent in 2000, victims of the tendency to buy British formats rather than programs, thereby minimizing price and maximizing local signification. The nation's Channel Five is meant to turn a profit but stress UK programming. In 2006, its six most popular programs included two Hollywood movies and three versions of *CSI: Crime Scene Investigation* (2000–15) and its spin-offs, *CSI: Miami* (2002–12) and *CSI: NY* (2004–13) (Ofcom, 2007: 107).

The *CSI* franchises were the most popular TV shows in the world for five of the years between 2007 and 2012. In 2015, an episode of the original was simulcast in 171 countries (Ben Block, 2015).[25] In 2014, the world's most popular drama programs came from the United States. A third were police procedurals, a fifth general drama, *telenovelas*/soap operas and situation comedies 15 percent each, and action-adventure 10 percent (Ben Block and Roxborough, 2014).

A key to Hollywood's success has been its capacity to set export prices that are cheaper for importing nations than the cost of making their own programs, since initial expenditures can largely be recouped in advance of overseas sales via the sizeable US domestic market. To give a sense of how differential pricing can aid in entering other countries, let's consider the key world television market, MIPCOM. Prices are on a sliding scale that reflects wealth, gullibility, and domestic competition rather than audience desire (see tables 3.1 and 3.2).

Even when the volume of US television exports *de*creases, revenue from sales frequently *in*creases. In 2000, receipts from US programming in Europe grew by 15.9 percent although the amount of programs sold diminished from 223,000 hours to 214,000. The audiovisual imbalance of trade stood at US$8.2 billion, up 14 percent on 1999. In 2001, volume diminished again, by 1 percent. Co-productions may account for the change in imported hours. Many such texts are made in concert with the United States, but count as European for the purposes of public subsidies. The few competitors for the European market have fallen away recently, notably New Zealand/Aotearoan and Australian soap operas, which were once successful. By the late 1990s, Indonesia's five commercial stations were importing 7,000 shows annually, mostly from the United States (Boellstorff, 2003: 37). Kenyan television remains over 70 percent dominated by material from the Global North, across the gamut from international news to drama and reality (Evusa, 2008: 209–10).

Dedicated genre channels (sometimes known as thematic channels) rely massively on US imports. They are mostly excluded from official statistics, which tend to focus on broadcast stations. An exception can be seen in numbers from Australia (table 3.3), which show a massive jump in imported TV with the advent of genre channels.

Although prime time on broadcast TV worldwide is usually occupied by local shows, a vast amount of potential investment in the European industry goes in

Table 3.1 Sites, genres and US$ prices for US texts in television market, 2002 (drama per hour, others per half-hour)

Genre	Feature	Tvmovie	Drama	Comedy	Documentary	Child
SITE						
Australia	1 million	30,000	10,000	5,000	4,000	3,000
Brazil	60,000	16,000	9,000	2,500	3,000	2,250
Canada	125,000	100,000	50,000	35,000	5,000	25,000
Czech Rep	30,000	3,500	3,000	800	800	500
France	2 million	90,000	55,000	25,000	12,000	10,000
Germany	5 million	200,000	75,000	20,000	18,000	14,000
Italy	1 million	100,000	30,000	10,000	7,000	7,000
Japan	1.4 million	30,000	23,000	7,000	16,000	5,000
Mexico	40,000	15,000	8,000	6,000	2,000	2,000
Nordic	200,000	18,000	7,000	4,500	3,500	2,500
Spain	1 million	50,000	20,000	6,000	5,000	3,000
Britain	2 million	35,000	50,000	25,000	20,000	22,500

Source: Miller et al., 2005

Table 3.2 Sites, genres and US$ prices for US texts in television market, 2008

Genre	Documentary	Drama	Format	Animation
SITE				
US	100,000–1m	300,000–1m	20,000–50,000	5,000–100,000
UK	10,000–200,000	20,000–120,000	15,000–40,000	12,000–34,000
Australia	3,000–10,000	16,000–50,000	7,500–35,000	1,000–4,500
Mexico	1,000–3,0000	2,500–10,000	2,000–10,000	1,500–4,000
Japan	6,000–50,000	16,000–35,000	10,000–30,000	8,300–20,000
China	1,000–2,000	1,000–2,500	1,000–3,500	1,200

Source: Television Business International (October/November 2008). Programme Prices Guide

buying Hollywood programs. In 2007, the dominant drama series were *CSI: Miami*, *Desperate Housewives* (2004–12), *Lost* (2004–10), *Without a Trace* (2002–9), and the longest-running series in US prime time history, *The Simpsons* (1989–) (Bignell and Fickers, 2008: 8). In Asia, Sony's AXN satellite network had 25 million fans watching the three *CSI* shows (Cohan 2008: 4; Goode, 2007). US influence continues to apply under new technology: when TV commercials are displaced by the internet – in Britain, revenue for the two media are close to equal at £3 billion annually – the majority goes to US companies (Duncan, 2009). When it comes to video on demand, the United States dominates (see table 3.4). In 2014, Netflix and HBO had two-thirds of the world market. Netflix was available in 46 countries and HBO in 61 across Latin America, Asia, and Europe. iTunes is the leader in download sales, with 65 percent of film downloads and 67 percent of TV series in 2012 (Le Borgne, 2014).

Table 3.3

Year	Exports	Imports	Deficit (A$millions)
1991/92	36	−240	−204
1992/93	39	−242	−203
1993/94	62	−268	−206
1994/95	79	−272	−193
1995/96	101	−312	−211
1996/97	134	−272	−138
1997/98	115	−357	−242
1998/99	134	−432	−298
1999/00	182	−449	−267
2000/01	1,209	−471	738
2001/02	124	−538	−414
2002/03	158	−489	−331
2003/04	179	−529	−350
2004/05	140	−616	−476
2005/06	204	−552	−348

Source: Australian Bureau of Statistics (ABS), Balance of Payments and International Investment Position; includes some Australian Film Commission estimates of unpublished data. Data revised by the ABS December 2006. The only year of net exports (2000/01) was due to the Sydney Olympics.

The main element of difference within these globalizing yet centralizing tendencies is the Latin American *telenovela*. *Telenovelas* began when US companies looked to sell the same cleaning products to women they had sold domestically through soap opera. The genre quickly underwent local customization from the 1950s (Straubhaar, 2007: 9). By 2002 the foreign trade in these *novelas* amounted to US$300 million in overseas sales (Havens, 2005: 271, 275). Televisa, the Mexican network, has been able to export both across Latin America and to Spanish-language stations in the United States. Encouraged by the wealth of the Latin@ audience north of the border, Mexico launched a satellite in 1984 and was selling *telenovelas* to nearly 100 countries within 15 years. TV Globo exported such shows from Brazil to Europe from the 1970s. By 2001, it reached 130 nations. In 2009, Brazil produced a 200-episode *novela* shot and set in India (Protzel, 2005; Havens 2005: 275; Cajueiro, 2009).

In the United States, the most popular programs on the Spanish-language network Univision are Latin American imports, such as *Las Tontas no Van al Cielo* (2008) (*Stupid Girls Don't Go to Heaven*) and *Sin Tetas no Hay Paraíso* (2006) (*There's No Paradise Without Breasts*). They are also the most-pirated downloads on YouTube of any TV programs, which led to a gigantic legal battle with Mexican suppliers (Goodwin, 2009; Wentz, 2009; James, 2009).

Colombia's *Yo soy Betty, la fea* (1999–2001) was remade as *Ugly Betty* (2006–10) for the United States following focus-group research on behalf of the US producer and network. The firm undertaking the work (one psychologist = "the firm") was *anglo parlante*, and the program drew negative reactions from trial viewers. But the

Table 3.4   Geographical origins of television fiction programmed by major networks (sample week March 12–18, 2000)

		Domestic	US	European	Other
United Kingdom	Whole day	47%	43%	0%	10%
	Prime time only	51%	49%	0%	0%
Germany	Whole day	36%	57%	5%	2%
	Prime time only	56%	44%	0%	0%
France	Whole day	25%	56%	15%	5%
	Prime time only	75%	25%	0%	0%
Italy	Whole day	19%	64%	4%	13%
	Prime time only	43%	51%	6%	0%
Spain	Whole day	20%	56%	7%	17%
	Prime time only	51%	37%	12%	0%

Source: Miller, 2010a: 77

network proceeded anyway, probably due to executive producer Salma Hayek's power and the mythology then surrounding NBC's Ben Silverman. No wonder many Latin critics bemoan the pressure to standardize that has come with international sales, resulting in a loss of specificity, localism, and cutting-edge critique of social relations (Mazziotti, 1996: 113).

Despite this notable exception of the *telenovela*, the overall weight of evidence on globalization is clear. The volume of US exports may be unstable, but their relative significance if anything increases, and their symbolism continues to resonate as both an index and a cause of the power of that country to bewilder, horrify, and enchant people everywhere. And TV's capacity to travel and sell is undimmed. In 2008, the trade in television programs across the Americas, the Asia-Pacific region, and Europe was worth €271.6 billion, up 5 percent on the previous year.[26] In 2012, the United States sold close to US$25 billion of film and TV internationally out of a total of US$36 billion (Siwek, 2013).

There is, of course, resistance to this hegemony, in keeping with cultural/media-imperialism critique. Consider a 2014 tweet from Delcy Rodríguez, who at the time was Venezuela's People's Power Minister for Communication and Information. She accused Hollywood of producing scripts that take "imperialistic actions against legitimate governments."[27] Rodríguez was complaining about a 19-second sequence in "Lords of War," the third episode of *Legends*, a serial on the mid-tier US cable TV network TNT that first aired on August 27, 2014. The program stars Sean Bean as a quasi-vigilante working for the FBI who is ready to do anything to keep the country safe.[28] In the segment in question, Bean tortures a man suspected of trading in poisonous gas, sneering that "there are more nerve endings in the lower back than the genitals," before jamming a hot iron on his back. Bean's captive reveals that he is working for "Maduro" because the "PSUV is worried about civil unrest in Venezuela." "Maduro" is of course President Nicolás Maduro, and the acronym stands for the Partido Socialista Unido de Venezuela, Hugo Chávez's legacy.

The rest of the episode veers away from Venezuela. But for Rodríguez, the damage was done. She complained and ordered the nation's telecommunications regulator, CONATEL, to investigate. The Venezuelan media, which increasingly do the state's bidding, denounced the sequence, including it in on-line coverage as video or screen shots, complete with Spanish subtitling and accusations about "US trans-nationals" and the power of Time Warner, TNT's owner. Fox21, which produced the show, issued a formal apology. This wasn't enough for the Communications Minister, who insisted the offending material be removed from future screenings.[29] Her reaction related not only to the US government's formal support for political opposition groups, but numerous other slights toward the Venezuelan state from Hollywood: the show *Homeland* (2011-) had a 2013 sequence in which its repugnant, drug-addicted, male protagonist resided in La Torre de David (Centro Confinanzas), a notorious, incomplete tower block in Caracas that has been squatted in real life by violent supporters of the state/heroic anarchists (depending on your view). Other programs, including *NCIS Los Angeles* (2009-), *The Good Wife* (2009-), *Saturday Night Live* (1975-), and *Parks and Recreation* (2009-15), have drawn the ire of *Chavistas* for representing Venezuela as an illegitimate state, as did the films *We Bought a Zoo* (Cameron Crowe, 2011) and *Captain America: The Winter Soldier* (Anthony and Joe Russo, 2014) (De Santis, 2014).

It's easy to dismiss such anxieties over dramatic representation as trivial. We can argue that by fetishizing the 19 seconds of offending code, Caracas is drawing more attention than would otherwise apply to a passing moment, in an unpopular show, on an insignificant network. We could say that audiences are active, competent interpreters who ably distinguish between ideology and pleasure, between current affairs and fiction. And we might criticize the critics for being unduly affected by latter-day obsessions with things being ideologically sound or politically correct.

That said, casual denunciations, as per the episode of *Legends*, which liken a democratically elected head of state to those seeking to kill thousands of innocent people, are narratively improbable, politically unwise, and fundamentally unfair. Most US viewers will have no idea who Maduro is and what he represents – the sequence amounts to an in-joke for the right wing, a way for a Hollywood often portrayed domestically as too liberal to display its nationalistic credentials.

But without in any way endorsing *Chavismo*, the issue needs to be understood in the context of two long histories. The first is the Monroe Doctrine (see chapter 2). The second is Hollywood's frequently clumsy and bigoted view of the "other" Americas. In 1922, Mexico embargoed film imports from Hollywood because of the "greaser" genre, and was supported by other Latin American countries; and there have been 90 years since of either denial or stereotyping (Miller *et al.*, 2005). An agile, materialist political economy is a crucial way to disclose these problems. In chapter 4, we seek to apply it to some of the global regimes that govern the media.

4 Policy and Governance

The previous chapter made a case for the value of political economy, which is uniquely positioned to help us track, map, and understand the interplay of political, economic, and cultural influence. In this chapter, we turn to one of the most important domains governing the media's institutions and infrastructures: policy and governance.[1] These discourses and practices are central to understanding the global media, because they represent each "epoch's consciousness of itself" – how it wishes to be seen (Althusser, 1969: 108). As a consequence, audiences, creators, governments, and corporations make extraordinary investments in media policy at national, regional, and global levels. Think of media policy as a blueprint negotiated by a wide variety of "stakeholders." In this sense, media policy often reflects power relations between different social players within a policy sphere that is no longer exclusively national; it can be transnational and even global.

With the advent of numerous media forms over the last century and a half, from telegraphy to cinema to radio to television to cable to satellite to the internet, nation-states have confronted the risks and hopes associated with instantaneous and powerful forms of communication. For the majority of the twentieth century, most responded with great caution, reserving radio and TV, for example, for state forms of broadcasting, whether propagandistic or at arm's length from governments.

From the mid-nineteenth century onwards, travelers arriving in any reasonably wealthy country could orient themselves by spotting large testimonies to efficient socialism: post offices and telephone exchanges. These sizeable buildings were ostentatious monuments to public service. Whether beautiful or ugly, grandiose or functional, they seemed to be solid and permanent, like their socialization of ownership. Other media were regarded similarly. The ruling assumption was that, on the one hand, the media should promote "good" conduct: learning and self-control, training and the superego, and preparation and responsibility. On the other, they might induce the diametric opposite of each "positive" effect: respectively, ignorance and self-indulgence, guesswork and the id, or lassitude and selfishness.

Above all, the question has been whether they will promote nationalistic feeling and international solidarity. For instance, the BBC was designed to be a bulwark against both rampant commercialism (e.g., the United States and its successful cinema exports) and political extremism (e.g., the Soviet Union and Italy and their successful ideological exports) (McGuigan 1996: 56). In 1936, the League of Nations created an International Convention Concerning the Use of Broadcasting in the Cause of Peace that was designed to prohibit messages sent from one national radio system to another, lest they foment social struggle or operate "in a manner prejudicial to good international understanding" (quoted in McDonald, 1999). The media were basically thought of as public goods that should serve the public interest as practiced by seasoned professionals and nudged along by readers and listeners.

But there have always been those seeking to profit from the media, whether directly through sales or indirectly through advertising, so in addition to state-dominated media systems, such as in Northern Europe, there have been commercially dominant ones, as per the Western hemisphere. Since the 1980s, neoliberal shifts toward deregulation assume that the media are no more deserving of public intervention than other industries. As a consequence, we have seen the triumph of private concerns in most countries, or at least shifting power bases between traditional media models and new ones. Because the media trade in culture, this is necessarily a contentious and partial change rather than a wholesale one. Whether we are speaking of maniacal religionists terrified by pleasure, or political powerbrokers hopeful of propaganda, there is always an oscillation between regulatory and deregulatory norms.

Policymaking about the media displays many of the tendencies of public policy more generally, however, and the models that have been developed to account for policy shifts more broadly are good starting points. The liberal democratic understanding of public policy assumes a pluralistic world in which certain key, settled, if opposed players with differing interests compete for policy outcomes. This roughly assumes that there are interests predominantly of capital versus labor, of the wealthy versus the popular classes, and that these contests take place at least partly in the political sphere with parliamentary representatives of each bloc.

This claim held up for decades in the conventions of political science until it became blindingly clear even to some former advocates that capital kept winning because it bought votes. When a former chorine, Charles E. Lindblom (1977), turned against his true love to acknowledge that pluralism was a nonsense and labor kept getting a poor deal, the madmen at Mobil Oil denounced him in the *New York Times* (Mobil Oil, 1978).

Although today the idea of labor versus the market would be displaced by a distinction of society versus the market, the opposition and how it is resolved by governments continues to be relevant in policymaking. This applies to other important social groupings, such as age, religion, race, gender, immigrant status, and so on. Assertions of openness and an eventual equilibrium, where different interest groups both get an equal hearing and frequently succeed, remain the presumptive claim against which democracies and other nation-states are often evaluated.

The term "policy" refers to a regularized set of actions based on a principle. Its authority depends on transparent rationality rather than kindship, tradition or individual charisma. All entities make policies, in the sense of regularized plans of action and norms that they follow, whether these organizations are private or public. Policies are developed and implemented by businesses as often – if less publicly – as governments. Business participates in the media through a desire to profit by selling advertising time on air and subscriptions on satellite, as well as aiding its specific and class-based political-economic interests via populist programming that both underwrites and is underwritten by nationalism and capitalism.

The media live hybrid lives as creatures of the state, commerce, and voluntarism. As noted above, the tendency is toward deregulation, privatization, and a notion that the market can competently allocate access, rather than there being a duty of care to ensure all citizens have equal rights to communication (Murdock, 2005; Becker et al.,

2010). It follows that different countries' media systems have particular emphases in their coverage of, for instance, what are superficially the same sporting events, without this necessarily resulting from government policy. For example, NBC adopts policies that mean the summer Olympics on US TV amount to little more than swimming, gymnastics, and track and field, with a focus on national success. Other nations are more catholic. And policy decisions on coverage across a wider array of sports see the British media respond to poor Olympic results with retribution, the Chinese with forgiveness, and the Russians with analysis (Project for Excellence in Journalism, 2008). Most Israeli media insist that local Arab footballers speak Hebrew, suppress alternative identities and politics, and shun independent nationhood (Shor, 2010).

These are not state policies of censorship and propaganda. They are policies adopted in newsrooms and based on nationalism, everyday practice, and audience research. As H. G. Wells put it: "The sport-loving Englishman, the sociable Frenchman, the vehement American will each diffuse his own great city in his own way" (1902: 57).

This is not to suggest that such policies lack a wider geopolitics, of course. Consider Edward Said's reflections on US talk radio:

> The American consciousness of sports, with its scores and history and technique and all the rest of it, is at the level of sophistication that is almost terrifying, especially if you compare it with the lack of awareness of what's going on in the world. That's where you get the sense that the investment is being made in those things that distract you from realities that are too complicated. (1993: 23)

This attention is neither accidental nor driven by a natural interest. Rather, as Herbert I. Schiller explains:

> The child, the teenager, and the adult now encounter in their daily routines, in the home, at school, on television, in the movies, at sports events, in museums and concerts, and at recreational parks, messages and images that celebrate and promote consumption. In these communications, democracy comes to be defined as the act of choosing . . . goods. (1991b: 58)

The state mostly participates in the media via two intersecting models: indirect control, through the regulation of ownership and textuality; and direct and indirect production, through government-run media, as per state socialism, or quasi-independence, as per public broadcasting. State media policy is frequently unstable: an adage has it that, in the United States, when Democrats are in power, media policy focuses on violence; when Republicans are on top, policy emphasizes sex. In contrast, in Saudi Arabia, violent media content usually raises no hackles, but sexual content launches vitriolic moral panics.

Then there is the matter of technological change. From the eighteenth century through the 1940s, the media generally originated from a central node, whether public or private, governmental or commercial, that sent out material to readers and audiences within circumscribed political, physical, and demographic terrain. It was not person-to-person, and only newspapers were conventionally available by subscription.

The media have unfurled from this centralist concentration into a diverse, multidirectional system of both embedded and explicit policies, interests, and knowledges.

For example, with the advent of transistors, radio developed genres and themes for stations to organize listeners; increased its capacity for transmission and reproduction; and mobilized new spaces of reception, such as the beach, car, and workplace. It displaced the newspaper's monopoly over time – but limited spatial reach – by temporal continuity and a less measurable and contained dominion over space. In today's era of digital technology, consumer sovereignty, and antidemocratic deregulation, niche programming and channels proliferate. The internet and cell phone are really extensions of the transistor radio's reach and adaptability.

In addition to state and corporate policies, because media infrastructure, such as cables and satellites, often transcend both state boundaries and commercial rents, they may be managed by international organizations. This phenomenon is neither new nor entirely dissociated from national citizenship. The affairs of such organizations are sometimes conducted at a state level, sometimes through civil society, and sometimes both. In almost every case, they encounter or enact legal and political doctrines that make them accountable in certain ways to the popular will of sovereign-states, at least in name. While that popular will may frequently be overdetermined or overrun – by technocratic mandarinism, superstitious god-bothering, or corporate shill – it remains a key site of change via representative government.

While the media have been transformed technologically, much of their essence remains – information is sent out from a point and takes root elsewhere. Consider sports again. Tensions have long existed between the notion of sport as part of a pre-existing cultural environment and the use of intellectual property and ownership by the media to capitalize on its popularity then charge the public. When US, European, or Chinese legislation identifies copyrighted elements or territorial rights of television, internet, or radio coverage, this has implications for audience pleasure and price, state participation, team ownership, and media profit (Evens et al., 2011; Song, 2011; Court of Justice of the European Union, 2011). Many sports, such as football, cricket, and basketball, owe their popularity in part to free-to-air transmission that was then turned into a commodity by cable or satellite for which audiences had to pay. Policies are sometimes in place to mitigate this exclusivity when it is felt that particular events, such as the men's World Cup or the Olympics, are of national significance and should be protected from capitalist predation.

The field of global media policy and governance studies is always already a work-in-progress because it has to play catch-up with technological, political, cultural, legal, and regulatory issues as they unfold across the world. In the past half century, media policy has mostly been studied within a framework of nationally comparative research, and focused on laws and regulations. It is only within the last decade that a sustained literature has emerged seeking to address the question: "What is global media policy?" Spurred by the global growth of the internet and the agendas of the global enforcers of neoliberalism seeking to adapt corporate management practices to nation-states, the notion of governance emerged in tandem with attempts to come to terms with the global scale of media policy But scholarly attention to global media policy still largely ignores the transnational scale. The advent of transnational media policy regimes warrants a re-examination of regional/transnational media policy as an integral part of global media policy and governance.

After a brief discussion of media policy within a comparative systems framework, we examine the emergence and growing definitional pains of global media policy and global media governance, then consider transnational systems. Our case study is the commercial pan-Arab media industry and the emerging transnational policy regime exemplified by the 2008 Arab Satellite Television Charter (ASTC). We compare it to the 1989 EU *Television Without Frontiers* directive, which advocated a continental TV system in part to protect against the influence of Hollywood. Standing two decades apart, the Arab and European cases compel us to think of transnational/regional media policy as an integral part of global media policy.

Comparative Media Systems

The comparative media-systems approach is an extension of the field of comparative politics, in which political scientists worked on understanding what were known as "press–politics relations" in the Lerner and Schramm diffusion models described earlier. Such research has relied to a large extent on normative theorizing about journalism, especially *Four Theories of the Press* (Siebert et al., 1963/1956). As we saw earlier, this Cold War scholarly and political manifesto classified media systems as libertarian (the United States), social responsibility (Western Europe's public broadcasters), authoritarian (their view of the developing world), and Soviet totalitarian (self-explanatory) (Siebert et al., 1963/1956). Decades later, Dan Hallin and Paolo Mancini correctly argued that *"Four Theories of the Press* has stalked the landscape of media studies like a horror-movie zombie for decades beyond its natural lifetime ... it is time to give it a decent burial and move on to the development of more sophisticated models based on real comparative analysis" (2004: 10). In its stead, they identify four principal dimensions of comparative media analysis:

- the development of media markets;
- political parallelism, i.e. the degree to which a media system parallels its national political system;
- journalistic professionalization; and
- the role of the state.

Media policy chiefly resides in the fourth dimension. Dutiful Weberians that they are, the authors distinguish between what they call "rational-legal authority" – that is, the rule of law – and clientelism, or playing favorites, as important aspects of media policy and shapers of the different ways in which the media and politics relate. They deploy three models:

- Mediterranean polarized pluralism;
- North/Central European democratic corporatism; and
- North Atlantic liberalism.

The first has an elite-oriented press, high political tension, economically dependent media, low professionalization, and significant clientelism. The second has partisan party newspapers, high to moderate political tension, high professionalization, economically independent media, and strong state intervention. In the third model, commercial newspapers predominate, political tension is low, there is considerable internal pluralism, professionalization levels are high, political instrumentalization is low, and commercial influence strong (Hallin and Mancini, 2004: 75). The three models focus on the press, do not account for media systems outside the "West"

(North America, Europe, and Australia), and do not address the rise of communication across national borders.

The intensification of international communication and the growth of global media corporations, structures, and flows and the advent of the NICL pose a challenge to comparative media systems' focus on the nation-state as the locus of media-political relations and policy. As we shall see in our exploration of transnational media systems and policy, the rise of pan-Arab media as a transnational system raises questions about the universal applicability of the nation-state as the locus of media policy.

The Emergence of Global Media Policy

As indicated above, global media policy is a new area, an "embryonic field . . . [with] no systematic articulation of concepts and approaches." A theory is required to explain "the diversity, dynamics and complexity that characterize its governance landscape; one that acknowledges existing definitional attempts and yet contributes to the elaboration of a holistic approach able to transcend different terminologies and theoretical assumptions" (Raboy and Padovani, 2010: 150–1).

Sandra Braman proposes a definition of media policy that is comprehensive, theoretically based, methodologically operationalizable, and transferrable into law (this betrays a very US orientation, as, in the vast majority of countries, public policies and programs are largely independent of law other than in terms of enabling legislation). She also argues that media policy is coextant with information policy, defined as all law and regulation across an information production chain that includes creation, processing, flows, and use (2004a: 153). In similar vein, Marc Raboy (2007) defines media policy as attempts by state and nonstate actors to influence the media.

This breadth of scope poses analytical and definitional challenges. One analytic difficulty is the ability to "develop tools for making micro-level observations of patterns without losing sight of the macro-level of realities of experience" (Chakravartty and Sarikakis, 2006: 3). Indeed, media policy encompasses multiple forces engaged in various interactions. Hence the phenomenon of media precession, which "occurs when two systems interact such that a decision or event in one changes the axis along which decisions or actions in the other can take place" – for example, the interaction between patent and anti-trust laws or coproduction film treaties and the NICL. To comprehend this complexity, Braman advocates "linking analysis of several types of decisions in order to understand the implications of their interactions" (2004a: 167).

This complexity is compounded at the global level, when policy interdependence, which reflects the emergence of networked forms of organization, increases. For many countries, international organizations are as important as national governments in shaping media policy. For instance, Europe's Economic Commission has applied competition law to member states in the area of information infrastructure. North–South relations also create interdependence and complications (Braman, 2004b; Chakravartty and Sarikakis, 2006). Such complexity necessitates the multi-sited political economy and ethnography described in chapter 3.

Global media policy has undergone several shifts since World War II, driven by the changing role of the nation-state in formulating policy, the evolution of "North–South relations," and the "material and symbolic dimensions of the reregulation of global communication policy" in the light of the rise of the market, international/

multilateral organizations, and civil society – often at the expense of national sovereignty (Chakravartty and Sarikakis, 2006). As a consequence "there is constant innovation, genres are blurred, players have multiplied, and policy subjects are now often networked rather than autonomous entities" (Braman, 2004a: 161). A definition of global media policy should take account of corporate globalization, multilateral politics, the changing role of the nation-state, and the emergence of civil society (Raboy, 2007: 344).

Marc Raboy and Cecilia Padovani understand global media policy in this way:

> The multiplicity of configurations or interdependent but operationally autonomous actors, that are involved, with different degrees of autonomy and power, in processes of formal or informal character, at different and sometimes overlapping levels – for the local to the transnational and global – in policy-oriented processes in the domain of media and communication, including infrastructural, content, usage, normative and governing aspects. Through their interactions, actors may (re)define their interests and pursue different goals; contribute in framing policy-relevant issues and produce relevant knowledge and cultural practices; promote the recognition of principles and the evolution of norms that inform state-based policy-making, as well as non-state based standard setting and self-governing arrangements. Ultimately, they may engage in political negotiation while trying to influence or determine the outcome of decision-making. (2010: 162–3)

Global Media Governance

The above definition reflects some of the factors that facilitated the emergence of "global media governance" as an approach to media policy. This notion of governance developed in new institutional economics, where it initially referred to "rules that help to reduce transaction costs" (Puppis, 2010: 135). In international relations, global governance described the work of international organizations and agreements that are not centrally controlled. As James N. Rosenau put it, "governance without government presumes the absence of some overarching governmental authority at the international level" (1992: 6). This notion of a nonhierarchical, interactive, adaptive sphere resonates with neoliberal hostility to strong states and centralized economies. Thus a distinction is born between "'bad' government and 'good' governance" (Puppis, 2010: 137). This tendency is sometimes referred to as a "New Medievalism," because it weakens central state control in favor of a patchwork of associations, localities, and internationalisms (Strange, 1995: 56). It often favors light regulation because powerful interests putatively run themselves ethically. Lindblom, as well as hard-core Marxists, would laugh morosely and futurists and neoliberals smile contentedly at such fabulations.

In this scenario, the role of the state is to facilitate social, political, and economic relations, with the latter occupying a privileged position. A "promotional state" is dedicated to "infrastructure regulation and the new forms of intervention created to act upon media content in a space of global flows" (Abramson, 2001: 301), not to redistribution of resources on a socially equal basis. Using the example of Canada, Bram Dov Abramson argues that media policies leading to the globalization of media industries are direct consequences of (national) government action. In such an environment, "rerouted through the market, regulation was dispersed, not eliminated or shunted aside. Regulatory reform in the telecommunications and media sector is the fragmentation of regulation itself, such that the moves which structure media globalization become harder and harder to track" (2001: 316).

In a sense, then, global media governance means global media deregulation and deepening public ignorance of how media capitalism does its business. The Commission for Global Governance in 1995 defined global governance as:

> the sum of the many ways individuals and institutions, public and private, manage their common affairs. It is a continuing process through which conflicting or diverse interests may be accommodated and cooperative action may be taken. It includes formal institutions and regimes empowered to enforce compliance, as well as informal arrangements that people and institutions either have agreed to or perceive to be in their interest (Ó Siocrú and Girard, with Mahan, 2002: 15)

As Paula Chakravartty and Katherina Sarikakis put it, global governance occurs "where the object and actors that define state intervention have changed from centralized state bodies focusing on domestic performance of the national economy to 'partnerships' between private actors, non-governmental organizations . . . and state bodies to coordinate the delivery of social goods and services at the local level" (2006: 38).

Media governance therefore includes "the entirety of forms of collective rules in the media sector" (Puppis, 2010: 138) – a "framework of practices, rules, and institutions that set limits and give incentives for the performance of the media" (Hamelink and Nordenstreng, 2007: 232). In addition to transnational corporations and the myriad nongovernmental organizations commonly known under the sobriquet "global civil society," key institutions involved in global media governance include the International Telecommunication Union, World Trade Organization, UNESCO, the World Intellectual Property Organization, and the Internet Corporation for Assigned Names and Numbers (ICANN).

Because media governance includes a variety of state and nonstate norms, practices, and centers of power, global media governance gives transnational corporations and global civil society influential roles in policy-making at the national and transnational levels. Seán Ó Siochrú and Bruce Girard (with Amy Mahan) put forward two possible scenarios for global media governance. One is a dominant trade and liberalization paradigm, which "envisages current dominant trends proceeding several steps forward." The second, "multilateral cooperation reborn," sees the democratic core of media and communications governance structures reinvigorated, drawing on the example of NWICO (2002: 172, 176).

Governance appeals to many scholars and practitioners dealing with the global internet. In fact, "internet governance" has been in use for longer than "media governance," probably because it resonates analytically and ideologically with the global, networked, multifaceted, neoliberal, and relatively nonhierarchical mythology of the internet. William H. Dutton and Malcolm Peltu divide internet governance into three issues: internet-centric, internet-user centric, and non-internet centric development (2007: 64). The internet-user centric category concerns use or misuse of the internet by individuals, groups, or organizations for legal, illegal, appropriate, and inappropriate actions. The non-internet-centric category concerns policies anchored in bodies and jurisdictions that include but transcend the internet, for example political expression, copyright, and intellectual property rights.

Global internet governance has been chiefly concerned with two issues. The first is collaboration over legal issues that cross national boundaries among state, corporate, and civil society stakeholders. The second focuses on access and inequality – the digital divide – especially in poorer countries around the world. One recurring issue in global internet-governance debates is concern over the US government's control of root servers, which gives it a dominant role in the technical operation of the global internet (Dutton and Peltu, 2007: 67–8).

Internet infrastructure in the Global South is growing, but inequalities remain sharp, as we noted in chapter 3. The Internet Governance Forum (IGF) for multi-stakeholder dialogue on policy was created during the 2005 Tunis round of the World Summit on the Information Society. It aimed to "foster internet's sustainability, robustness, security, stability and development" in response to the increasing deployment of internet infrastructure in developing countries and the new regime of ICANN (Rasmussen, 2007: 16). The IGF is emblematic of organizations involved in global internet governance. According to Terje Rasmussen, they enjoy three types of legitimacy:

- representative legitimacy, reflecting the global political system of nation-states;
- interest legitimacy, as in the case of non-state interested parties; and
- market legitimacy, based on the business sector.

Finally, net neutrality has emerged as a contentious issue in global and internet governance. In the United States, it is highly publicized and politicized. Sacha D. Meinrath and Victor Pickard define the concept as:

> non-discriminatory interconnectedness among data communication networks that allow[s] users to access the content and run the services, applications and devices of their choice. In essence, network neutrality forbids preferential treatment of specific content, services, applications, and devices that can be integrated into the network infrastructure. (2008: 1)

This crystallizes a longstanding debate about control and access. Global media policy has grappled for years with the neutrality of technologies in terms of access to information. During the internet's formative years, the prevailing technical, political, and cultural assumptions were that it was "essentially open and therefore neutral and non-political" (Rasmussen 2007: 3). Today, however, with the growth of a commercial agenda and advocacy groups committed to fighting corporate control, the issue of internet neutrality continues to be salient.

The Rise of Transnational Policy/Governance

The advent of regional-transnational policy regimes, covering groups of countries whose geographical contiguity, linguistic affinities, and infrastructural integration make them in effect one realm of policy and governance, has still not received adequate attention in the literature. The issue emerged in Europe in the late 1980s with *Television Without Frontiers* (Miller, 1993; Wheeler, 2004). It sought to make internal boundaries among European countries more flexible, while hardening Europe's external media borders to keep at bay that historical Other, the United States, and its commercial media fare.

In some cases, neighboring countries develop parallel or similar patterns of governance, such as France and Italy when they completed transitions from public broadcasting systems to neoliberal regimes. This spawned what Pierre Musso called "*sarcoberlusconisme*" (a grotesque hybrid of Nicholas Sarkozy and Silvio Berlusconi) "a new Euromediterranean neoliberal political model, of a Bonapartiste type, combining the authority of the State, reverence to Catholicism, and reference to Business" (2009: 9). This is perhaps symptomatic of what Hallin and Mancini acknowledged may be a global convergence of their liberal model of media and politics, and increasingly close links between media ownership and political power under neoliberalism, as exemplified in the US Telecommunications Act of 1996, Mexico's so-called Ley Televisa (2006), which gave rights to the digital spectrum in Mexico to a duopoly of Televisa and TV Azteca, or Lebanon's 1994 Audio-Visual Media Law, which distributed television broadcasting licenses to an assortment of business tycoons and political bosses.

Regional-transnational media spheres emerge and operate differently in various parts of the globe. The 1994 North American Free Trade Agreement (NAFTA)/Tratado de Libre Comercio de América del Norte (TLCAN) (McAnany and Wilkinson, 1996; Mosco and Schiller, 2001; Gómez, 2007), the EU (Miller, 1993; Collins, 1994), and the Mercado Comun del Sur/Mercado Comum do Sul (MERCOSUR/MERCOSUL) represent "three distinct ways to reconcile the tension between economics and culture intrinsic to cross-border trade in audio-visual products" (Galperin, 1999: 627).

According to Hernán Galperin (1999), regional policy and media trade regimes differ across three dimensions. The first is their "industrial profile," or the distribution of political-economic resources to media industries among countries that are made by regional pacts. National cultural and communication policies, including media and telecommunications, are the second factor. The third refers to obstacles raised by cultural and linguistic variations among different countries in one regional trade sphere. The governing imperatives are that commodities, capital, and companies have comparatively free access to each country, even though a desire for national self-expression remains strong. We'll briefly look at these three examples before focusing on the Arab world as our core case study.

NAFTA/TLCAN is an overarching agreement about trade between Canada, Mexico, and the United States, including the media. The accord has favored the Mexican firms Grupo Televisa and TV Azteca, which import large quantities of licenses, shows, and Hollywood films, and sell licenses and content in the United States (Gómez, 2007). It is controversial in all the countries involved because of manufacturing, agriculture, pollution, and immigration rather than media policy.

Although the relationship between Televisa in Mexico and Univision in the United States is the most intense in Latin@ and Mexican media history, other strategic alliances have emerged in the last two decades that are unconnected to NAFTA/TLCAN. Before Azteca America was launched, TV Azteca, Argos, and the Colombian network RTI had important ties with Telemundo (Piñón, 2011). There are strategic alliances such as the one between Sony and Colombia's Caracol, which signed a three-year coproduction agreement in 2011 to create television series, in the same way that Univision is in partnership with Venezuela's Venevision. Other examples include the participation of Spain's Grupo Prisa in VMe and News Corp and Colombia's RCN launching of MundoFox (now MundoMax) in 2012. MundoMax targets young people and a notion of "living on the hyphen" between social and national identities – hence its tagline, "Americano como tú."[2] MundoMax embodied new media–business relations between the United States and Colombia, suggesting a cultural turn that will leaven the Mexican character of much Spanish-language US television. Meanwhile, Telmex, a dominant economic actor across Latin America in telecommunications and pay-TV, is also expected to take a role in the United States. In Mexico, it operates the internet TV channel UNOTV Noticias. Most of these arrangements operate outside the accord. It has had media effects, but is trilateral and very broad in its economic purview, if limited in terms of citizenship rights by contrast with, most notably, the EU.

The European instance covers many more countries. They have a massive binding link through new ideas of sovereignty. It also has specific media policies, conceived in terms of protection from the popularity of Hollywood and stimulation of industries in their own right. Those issues apply across the EU, but they derive from a particular bilateral struggle. Its history helps to inform the ongoing attempt to create a European audiovisual bloc against US screen power.

When candidates take the test to become a US citizen, one of the 100 questions they must prepare to answer asks which three countries won World War II. The "correct" answer is: the United States, England [sic], and France. As for those 20 million-and-counting Soviet citizens who gave their lives in Stalingrad and elsewhere – they were presumably off playing tiddlywinks. And the United States considers the Statue of Liberty its most powerful symbol of welcome and freedom – a gift from the people of France.

Despite those mythologies, a profound mistrust runs through the Franco-American relationship, exemplified in the unpleasant epithets that were part of everyday talk under George W Bush in response to France's opposition to the invasion of Iraq ("surrender monkeys" and congressional menus renaming "French fries" as "Freedom fries" were personal favorites of ours).

This cosmic ambivalence is regularly reinforced by conflicts over media policy. The short version is that France favors exempting culture from free trade agreements, whereas the United States wants a pure market. France says culture is akin to the environment or the military – it isn't something that can or should be alienated through international competition, because culture has a special quality, a unique meaning that helps hold a people together. But the post-Herman Melville US argues that culture is one more commodity, like sugar or transport.

Two decades ago, Bill Grantham called France and Hollywood

> the feuding hillbilly dynasties of world culture . . . it appears impossible for more than a few months to go past without some person who should know better declaiming about the God-given right of the people of France to view some forgettable special effects extravaganza, or of the urgent need to protect the gossamer-fragile civilization of Racine, Flaubert, and Proust from the cultural depredations of Bruce Willis and Leonardo DiCaprio. (1998)

The feud derives in part from the French belief that their invention of film technology a century and more ago was denied its full reward because of dirty US tricks over patents. In addition, the French have long argued that their way of life could be compromised by the US fetish for technology and accounting. This anxiety's venerable, decadent, and distinguished heritage arches back even further, to the libertine poet Charles Baudelaire. In the mid-nineteenth century, he feared that "[t]he world is coming to an end" because "[t]he mechanical will so have Americanized us, progress will so have atrophied all our spiritual side."[3] In other words, the French think they have been cheated financially by the United States *and* their spirituality is threatened.

The latest struggle has emerged over film and music subsidies during negotiations for an EU–US trade treaty (Elliott, 2013). Reaction to French wishes for a clause exempting culture from these negotiations has been virulent: José Manuel Barroso, then President of the European Commission, derided Paris's position as "culturally reactionary" and showing "no understanding of the benefits that globalization brings . . . from a cultural point of view" (quoted in Parker and Houlder, 2013).

The rhetoric of each side of this latest debate is suspect. On the Hollywood side, the notion that the successful export of film and TV drama is simply to do with skillful management and innovation rather than state action is a very tall tale indeed. The reality is that the US industry relies on vast public subsidies from inside and outside the country. A network of hundreds of domestic and international film commissions offers tax breaks and pliant workforces to attract Los Angeles-based studios to produce elsewhere; the Pentagon gifts technology, locations, and extras; and the state and commerce departments feverishly deliver plenipotentiary services. Hollywood is not laissez-faire (Miller et al., 2005). We shall investigate this further in chapter 6. On the French side, claims for a cultural exemption from international trade are similarly flimsy. The bourgeoisie of its film industry is protected from market forces without really delivering a truly representative product: the argument that it reflects the nation back to itself falls down in terms of the race, gender, and region of the major players and the stories they tell (Grantham, 2000).

When the French government protests over culture, however, it is not just speaking for itself. Many smaller nations feel the same way about Hollywood in terms of language, themes, and influence, but dare not speak the truth to power (or are not heeded). France may be just as hypocritical as the United States, but it presents an alternative to the commodification of all and sundry and the entrenchment of English as a dominant world language. So even as we question French motives, we should think very deeply about their critiques, and query Hollywood's claims. Capital loves subsidies, regardless of whether it is French or American – and the resulting investments need to be evaluated in both industrial and textual terms against their claims to represent the public interest. Today's trade arguments are not merely to do with culture as something outside commodification, though that is certainly relevant. They are also to do with a long-held belief that Hollywood stole the treasure. This is a potent example of the need to study the media in political-economic, textual, and global ways to tease out realities and contradictions. Policy is always about power, meaning, identity, and money – first, second, last, and all points in-between.

The EU's media initiatives have developed very much under the French sign, as both industrial subsidy and cultural protection. The Union has attempted to balance the notion of building Europeanness and industry through TV drama, while acknowledging the medium's national specificity and the difficulties of dealing with so many languages.

The default international language of much television is English, which has enabled and in turn *been* enabled by the popularity of US material, a further cause of concern to many nations in the Union. EU agencies have been torn between the notion of an unfettered regional market for the exchange of programs that will appeal across 465 million people, the wealthiest TV market in the world; the desire to generate a continental sense of belonging; and the complexities of so many member states with so many different languages, few of which have strong, embedded television systems. Its neoliberal elements are opposed to public service broadcasting, as are parts of the World Trade Organization (WTO). But there can be a *rapprochement* between these drives, via the notion of viewers as consumers with rights to quality, just as they have over appliances, food, or open debate (Open Society Institute, 2005; Celot and Gualtieri, 2007).

Television Without Frontiers attempted to dismantle obstacles to the travel of television programs across the EU, while strengthening the walls that protected European industries from the onslaught of US imports. This "signaled a conflict between the economic priorities of industrial competitiveness on the one hand and the desire to maintain the principles of European cultural identity on the other" (Wheeler, 2004: 350).

The *Television Without Frontiers* Directive brings to the fore the rising power of transnational bodies in media policy. Article 2 "abolished EU member states' sovereignty over their national systems, thereby facilitating the free movement of television broadcasting services across frontiers within the Union." To make that work, the EU relied on a previous legal text about transnational authority, the Maastricht Treaty. Its notion of "mutual recognition" held that, "as long as minimal regulatory rulings were met by the provisions of the originating member state, the legal justifications for another member state to impede the reception or retransmission of broadcasts were removed" (Collins, 1994: 59–60). But the Directive also attempted to weaken national policies designed to support television production, underlying its broadly neoliberal ethos based on market competition.

As such, *Television Without Frontiers* was "a victory for commercial forces and those who favoured anti-protectionist policies" (Negrine and Papathanassopoulos, 1990). This led to the proliferation of format television, though there is some evidence that the Directive has also overcome divergences among national media laws and policies and stimulated an increase in the volume of European productions shown in the EU (Burri-Nenova, 2007; Besio et al., 2008).

MERCOSUR's policies, which cover the Southern Cone of Argentina, Brazil, Paraguay, Uruguay, and Venezuela, are very much based on this model (Crusafon, 2009). They demonstrate both neoliberal ideas about open markets and nationalistic ones about the patrimony of the audiovisual sphere, describing their relative linguistic similarity in comparison with the EU (Moguillanksy, 2009). There continue to be endeavors to harmonize digital TV policy across the pact (de Carvalho and de Carvalho, 2014). So, on the one hand, there is stimulus to counter the influence of cultural imperialism; on the other, stimulus to counter the influence of closed borders (Sarikakis and Ganter, 2014).

These brief accounts indicate the tensions that arise from attempts to generate collective identity, sustain industries, and free markets. In the extended example that follows, we add to this mixture a powerful blend of geographic, linguistic, and religious consanguinity that is also about intense and frequently contumacious differentiation, resource politics, masculinity, and imperial religious desire.

A Pan-Arab Model?

In 2008, Arab information ministers adopted what became known as the ASTC during an emergency meeting in Cairo that was dedicated to reigning in the burgeoning satellite television industry. As the first Arab League-sponsored policy document addressing transnational television, the Charter reflects the anxieties of Arab governments over their dwindling control of television. Since the 1990s, the advent of a vibrant transnational commercial industry had posed difficult challenges to Arab states. In the early 1990s, offshore London-based Arab satellite channels hosted various Arab dissidents on their programs. Since 1996, guests on al-Jazeera talk shows have skewered leaders of the Arab status quo for corruption, authoritarianism, and dependence on the United States, while the Lebanese channels LBC and Future TV regale the public and spawn controversies with bold talk, variety, and reality shows. In 2003, the invasion of Iraq compelled Saudi interests to launch al-Arabiya, a pro-Saudi, pro-US rival to al-Jazeera, at the same time as it unleashed the unbridled growth of an anarchic Iraqi television scene. The pan-Arab satellite TV industry has increased since then to include approximately 500 channels dedicated to women, youth, music, religion, finance, and real estate, most of which lie beyond the direct control of Arab states (Kraidy and Khalil, 2009).

With the ASTC, Arab governments appeared to be finally catching up with the industry, after decades of reactive, slow-moving, inconsistent, and limited policymaking. Besides regular meetings of Arab information ministers, which resulted in rhetorical pronouncements about the need to develop Arab media, regional (i.e. pan-Arab) policy developments concerning television were, until recently, restricted to the establishment of the Arab Satellite Organization (ARABSAT), headquartered in Saudi Arabia, and the Arab States Broadcasting Union (ASBU), based in Egypt. ARABSAT was established to create a satellite infrastructure for the telecommunications needs of Arab states, and ASBU to facilitate program exchanges and organize training workshops for employees of national broadcasting sectors. Designed as instruments for *international* cooperation between Arab states, the two organizations in effect prepared the ground for a *transnational* commercial satellite television industry. Given that the commercial satellite sector arose in 1991 and developed with breakneck speed, the fact that it took Arab governments nearly 20 years to react reflects the dearth of transnational pan-Arab policymaking. Transnational media policy in the Arab world is in its initial phase. Unlike global media policy's institutional "placelessness" and use of English as a *lingua franca*, this emergent sphere primarily appears during meetings (and ensuing exchanges) of Arab information ministers under the auspices of the League of Arab States.

The formation of the ASTC is best understood as an attempt by dominant Arab states like Saudi Arabia and Egypt to project their national media policies onto the pan-Arab arena. National media policies in Saudi Arabia, Lebanon, and the United Arab Emirates (UAE) have also played a disproportionate role in shaping the pan-Arab media environment. Saudi Arabia, a country with vast resources and the cradle of Islam, developed media policies to ensure internal control and the transnational projection of influence, blending religious proselytizing and a foreign policy aligned with US priorities. The Saudi royal family enabled sympathetic Saudi moguls to invest petrodollars in the then-nascent satellite TV industry during the early 1990s, setting the ground for businesses that are privately-owned but friendly to governments. In addition, the prime importance of the Saudi advertising market meant that pan-Arab satellite producers and programmers assiduously catered to Saudi viewers.

Lebanon, a small country with a weak state, witnessed the development of a vibrant and anarchic media scene during the 1975–90 war, out of which a few advertising-supported channels emerged as pan-Arab leaders in entertainment television. Lebanese media workers fleeing the war pursued lucrative employment opportunities in the growing Saudi media. For its part, through the development of Dubai Media City (DMC), the UAE provided a space where Saudi capital and institutions employed numerous Lebanese workers, directors, producers, and programmers, resulting in a "Saudi-Lebanese connection" (Kraidy, 2009). This is not to deny the contributions of other national sectors to the emergent pan-Arab policy landscape, but to highlight the importance of this Saudi–Lebanese–UAE role.

Challenges to National Media Policy

Comprehending the shift to transnational policymaking requires an understanding of central issues that have historically animated media policymaking at the national level in the Arab world. At the top of the list is maintaining regimes. In a region with few rulers who enjoy popular legitimacy, kings and presidents have long regarded media institutions as key instruments for holding on to power. Since the late 1950s, royal families, ruling parties, and political dynasties have monopolized television broadcasting, banning critical coverage of themselves, the armed forces, and other components of the apparatus of power.

In addition to political calculations, putative moral values and sociocultural concerns motivate many Arab media policies. Television is especially susceptible to censorship, based on anxiety about its impact on national and cultural identity, relations between men and women, young people, and prevailing moral values. These concerns are full of religious discourse, as governments seek to justify policies or Islamist opponents decry their lack of legitimacy. In this context, opponents of Westernized television content assert themselves as moral guardians against a "cultural conquest" that they claim endangers Arab and Islamic values. Another concern has been that as newly independent Arab states struggled to solidify national unity and foment socioeconomic growth, television policies in many Arab countries focused on promoting development and preventing negative coverage of financial and economic issues.

A couple of recent challenges have compounded customary policy concerns. One is the decline of state broadcasters and the rise of the commercial satellite industry, which compelled states to embark on liberalization – understood in the narrow sense of allowing privately owned satellite (but rarely terrestrial) channels to operate within strict political constraints – with the twin goals of reaching their own national viewers and projecting transnational influence. "Media cities" were established in Egypt, the UAE, Jordan, and Syria with attractive terms and laws that permit commercial media to operate as per the NICL.

Another challenge is that Arab opposition movements have exploited the emerging media environment to solidify national bases and forge transnational links. Saudi dissidents attack the Saudi royal family over al-Jazeera from London, bloggers affiliated with the Muslim Brotherhood in Egypt post videos of police abuse that end up on satellite television, and Hezbollah uses the TV channel al-Manar to mobilize its Lebanese base against the pro-Western ruling coalition in Beirut and influence pan-Arab public opinion.

In the 1960s and early 1970s, Beirut hosted Arab dissidents – exiled politicians, fiery intellectuals, and threatened journalists – who spoke and wrote critically. Nowadays, London, Paris, and various Arab capitals host dissidents against other Arab regimes and wage rhetorical wars via television. Arab states have scrambled to address such challenges through national regulatory frameworks focused on preserving the political status quo.

Beyond the preservation of regimes, national media policies differ in some respects, as reflected in the cases of Saudi Arabia, Lebanon, and the UAE, to which we turn next.

Saudi Media Policy

Saudi Arabia is the most important national advertising market in the Arab world; it also has a peculiar philosophy concerning the role of the media in society, as reflected in the country's media-ownership structure, policies, and regulations. In the 1960s, Saudi rulers launched a television service to promote national unity and move forward with modernization. Saudi media resembled other mid-century systems in the Global South that focused on socioeconomic development and national unity. In a sparsely populated country marked by resilient local identities, TV in particular was to play a crucial role (Kraidy, 2007).

First, television was a vital instrument of modernization that catered to a growing Saudi professional class with experience of TV in Egypt and Lebanon. Second, there was a need to counter hostile propaganda from Egypt that reached Saudis through radio. Third, television was an educational and developmental tool. Finally, it would foster national unity (Boyd, 1999). This was serious business: when militants marched on the Saudi television building to shut it down in 1965, the police shot dead a prince whose brother took revenge 10 years later when he assassinated King Faisal.

In other aspects, the Saudi Arabian media have a unique history, characterized by clerical hostility to "new" media. An historical alliance between the al-Saud (the rulers) and the al-Sheikh (the establishment clerics) gave the former supremacy in politics, while awarding the latter leadership in religion, education, and culture, including media policy; Wahhabi clerics hold sway (Kraidy, 2006).

As the Saudi media grew more integrated with the larger, pan-Arab media sphere across the 1990s, clerics lost control over what Saudis watched. As a result, a parallel policy space developed. Clerics made numerous public pronouncements and religious rulings about television beyond the purview of state institutions that were mandated to undertake media regulation like the Ministry of Culture and Information, which was established in 1962, shortly before King Faisal announced a plan to launch television by the following year (Kraidy, 2009).

Television served the royal family well in 1979, by demonstrating, after days of conflicting accounts, that armed militants who had stormed the Grand Mosque were in the custody of Saudi security services. To tighten control on the media, a 1981 royal decree reshuffled the Saudi Higher Media Council and placed the Interior Minister and royal prince Nayef at the head of a new media committee that controlled information policy in the kingdom. During the years that followed, Saudi princes and business moguls expanded their stakes in pan-Arab television industries, beginning with the Middle East Broadcasting Center in 1991, leading to the 2003 launch of al-Arabiya and growing Saudi influence over Lebanese satellite stations (Kraidy, 2009).

This transnational expansion went hand in hand with continued government ownership and operation of all channels (terrestrial and satellite) on Saudi territory. There are currently five stations, including the all-news channel al-Ekhbariya, which was launched in 2004 within a media-reform plan that included revamping existing stations and launching a sports channel. It was designed to lure Saudi viewers back to state television in the wake of their migration to commercial satellite offerings.

Since the 1960s, media regulation has prohibited women from wearing revealing clothing or dancing, scenes that "show overt acts of love," drinking alcohol, betting, gambling, attacks on any of the "heavenly religions," criticism or mockery of other countries and their rulers, criticism of the House of Saud, references to Zionism, and excessive violence (Shobaili, 1971, quoted in Boyd, 1999: 164). In the case of Egyptian movies shown on Saudi television, unmarried actors portraying a married couple are prohibited from sitting on the same bed at the same time with the door closed. No women should appear on screen during the Holy Month of Ramadan, which is also the peak viewing season, and parents cannot be seen kissing their children of the opposite sex (*Index on Censorship*, 1992, quoted in Boyd 1999: 165). Though some of these guidelines have changed (women are now seen on the screen during Ramadan), contemporary standards remain similar.

As mentioned earlier, television policy is not the exclusive realm of the Ministry of Culture Information. Whenever they feel sidelined in public debates, Saudi clerics make pronouncements about TV. During Ramadan, they are vocally critical of programming (Kraidy and Khalil, 2009). In 2008, they were especially frightened of a Turkish series, *Gümüş* (2005–7), dubbed into Arabic as *Noor* (*Light*). It featured a romantic, egalitarian relationship between a young married couple that allegedly led women to neglect their professional and familial duties. After King Abdallah reshuffled his cabinet in early 2009, 35 clerics issued a call to the new Information Minister to ban the appearance of women on Saudi television and in the press.[4] The king did not acquiesce. During Ramadan 2009, the Saudi Mufti renewed attacks on *Tash ma Tash* (1992–), a popular Saudi comedy that skewers social norms. Similar negotiations between hardline clerics and more liberal real audiences are undertaken by TV producers in other Islamic contexts, such as Indonesia (Barkin, 2014).

Lebanese Media Policy

In comparison to Saudi Arabia, Lebanese television is underregulated. After three decades of a government–private sector shared service, the 1975–90 civil war unleashed chaos on the airwaves as assorted militias and warring parties launched unlicensed television channels (Boyd, 1991; Kraidy, 1998). The situation was not regulated until the 1990s, when the postwar reassertion of state authority led to an Audio-Visual Media Law (AVML) in 1994, the first Arab legislation to address privately owned radio and television. AVML revoked Télé-Liban's exclusive rights to broadcasting, reaffirmed constitutional guarantees of media freedom, and gave the

Council of Ministers media licensing power. It also created the National Council of Audio-Visual Media (NCAVM) to set technical standards, monitor media performance, and recommend sanctions to the Minister of Information. The powers of the minister were enhanced to include the right of auditing all financial records, since the law prohibited stations from operating in deficit for a protracted period. AVML affirmed core prohibitions against stirring sectarian conflict, insulting the head of state or those of friendly countries, and endangering public order and national security (Kraidy, 1998).

From dozens of applicants, all four stations licensed in 1996 had close connections to leading politicians, including the prime minister and the President of the Council of Deputies. They reflected the country's consociational division of resources, despite the legal stipulation of multisectarian boards: the ownership of LBC was Maronite Christian, of Future TV Sunni Muslim, of MurrTV Greek Orthodox, and of NBN Shi'i Muslim. By licensing only a few privately owned television stations and establishing a regulatory framework, the AVML set the ground for commercial competition to operate in tandem with political and sectarian considerations (Kraidy, 1998).

In the first few years thereafter, the government exercised direct and indirect media control (Kraidy, 1999). Several major political crises over media policy ensued. The last two of these, the closure of Murr Television in 2000 and the forced disconnection of New TV in 2002, reveal political instrumentalization and overlapping jurisdictions in media policy formulation and implementation, in addition to the customary twin concerns of Lebanese media policy – preserving internal stability and projecting a positive external image.

The raid by security forces on MurrTV and the decision to close the channel stunned the country, publicizing contradictions in policy. First and foremost was the strong condemnation of the raid by the Minister of Information, Ghazi Aridi. He criticized the shutdown as "purely political" and affirmed his lack of knowledge of the decision, raising questions about who was running media policy in the country. Second, the way in which the Beirut Court of Publications reached a verdict, without the station having the right to appeal, raised questions about due process and overlapping jurisdictions. This is an important issue, because under the AVML, the Minister of Interior is charged with monitoring and sanctioning the media. Third, the way the action was carried out smacked of repression, with security forces pushing, beating, and hurling obscenities at the station's employees and others who worked in the building. Finally, the shutdown set an alarming precedent: it was the first time in Lebanon's history that a television channel was shuttered by the authorities (Kraidy, 2003). (After fundamental changes in the Lebanese political landscape that began in 2005 when Syrian troops withdrew from Lebanon, MurrTV reopened in 2009.)

Beirut's Court of Publications had ordered the closure under Article 68 of the Elections Law, which prohibits radio and television stations from airing electoral advertising. This law had been passed before Lebanon's first postwar elections, in 1992. It was designed to prevent the country's then-unregulated, anarchic 60-station television sector from becoming a propaganda nightmare. The legislation called for the "complete suspension of violators, without right of appeal before the order is executed." When MurrTV was shut down, appeals to various courts revealed that the government had interpreted "complete" to mean "permanent." The other troubling issue is that the 1992 Election Law was superseded by the AVML, which charges the

Information Minister (in consultation with the NCAVM) with sanctioning stations (Kraidy, 1998). More than any other incident, the shutdown exposed Lebanon's convoluted regulatory environment, which is prone to overlapping jurisdictions and crippling political interference.

Though MurrTV technically violated the law by airing political communication during the 2000 elections, so did virtually every other television station, including Future TV and Télé-Liban. MurrTV, however, had become the voice of the anti-regime, anti-Syrian, predominantly Christian opposition. As information that became available after the 2005 Syrian withdrawal made clear, MurrTV was shut down by order of Syrian military intelligence. Because of the politicization of media regulations and the seemingly overlapping jurisdictions, 2002 ended with calls to revise and update media laws, in addition to renewed demands to reform the judiciary and grant it more independence. However, under Syria's suffocating control of public affairs in Lebanon, these calls went unheeded. Some observers worried that the traditionally vibrant Lebanese media sector was falling under authoritarian control.

UAE Media Policy

Media policy in the UAE gives considerable independence to each Emirate. DMC is the crown jewel of a system designed to create dynamic clusters of media activity. They enjoy considerable economic freedom but limited editorial autonomy. With scarce natural resources since 1979, Dubai has aimed to become a major commercial hub between Southeast Asia and Europe, capitalizing on its geographic location with the establishment of free zones such as the Jebel Ali Port. DMC reflects an advanced stage of Dubai's transition to a NICL and the growing importance of economic growth and diversification as a shaper of media policy in the Arab world. It opened in 2001 at an estimated cost of more than US$800 million (Arab Advisors Group, 2004). The timing was opportune, as Dubai benefited from the repatriation of Arab money from the West after the events of 9/11, in addition to a spike in Iranian and Saudi oil revenues. With its motto "Freedom to Create," DMC has also provided an ostensibly "safe" but in fact highly self-censored haven for creative talent escaping difficult or dangerous working conditions in Lebanon, Egypt, Palestine, Iraq, and Syria.

The number of users of DMC increased from 880 in 2004 to more than 1,200 in 2008 and 2,000 in 2013.[5] The area is a significant hub of the NICL marketing, broadcasting, new media, publishing, music, film, and events services. DMC has transformed Dubai into a competitor with the historical media production centers of Beirut and Cairo. In 2005 alone, 20 new television channels were introduced, and by 2009, DMC was home to more than 60 satellite broadcasters operating some 150 stations. By relocating to DMC, pan-Arab and international broadcasters (MBC and BBC World) and news agencies like Reuters and CNN provide concrete recognition of new parameters for media autonomy, albeit relative ones.

Despite this growth, Beirut and Cairo remain important: in 2005 the trade magazine *Arab Ad* estimated that only 20 percent of Arab television output was produced in Dubai.[6] As a result, US$110 million was spent in building Dubai Studio City to increase film and television production. DMC also sponsors the Dubai International Film Festival, which has become a gathering for Arab, Hollywood, and Bollywood producers and stars, in addition to the Ibda' (creativity) Media Student Awards, designed to capitalize on emerging creative talent.

With this widening gamut of activities, DMC's organizational structure has evolved from a government project to a private subsidiary of TECOM Investments, the parent company of Dubai Internet City, Knowledge Village, Dubai Studio City, and the International Media Production Zone. TECOM is one of seven companies under the umbrella of Dubai Holding, which handles "large-scale infrastructure and investment projects."[7] Although Dubai Holding is a private company, Sheikh Mohammad bin Rashed al-Maktoum, Dubai's ruler and the UAE's prime minister, controls it. He is credited with coming up with the idea of media-focused free zones as "symbols of the potential of the knowledge economy in the region."[8] The government builds infrastructure and subsidizes its use by private ventures, attracting finance from companies operating in DMC and private investors who develop buildings on DMC-owned land. The city manages properties and takes care of immigration and labor paperwork for its NICL customers.

This centralization of media activity in DMC has affected the development of media cities in the UAE and across the region. It was only when DMC was unable to meet demands for space and facilities that broadcasters started looking for alternatives. So DMC provided an economic impetus for the deregulation of media industries across the region, with governments hoping to benefit from much-needed direct foreign investment. The Jordanian and Bahraini governments, for example, were able to lure, respectively, Arab Radio & Television to fund the establishment of Jordan's Media City in 2001 and Orbit to relocate its headquarters to Bahrain in 2003.

In addition to boosting regional television industries, Dubai's grounding of media policy in economic policy, which has included generous subsidies and lease terms at DMC, exposes these industries to other changes. The future growth of DMC is challenged by factors peculiar to Dubai, such as the soaring cost of living, and external pressures such as competition from other parts of the Arab world, and global economic recessions. The recent expansion of TECOM has focused on developing local talent and investing in Indian production centers to maintain DMC's market lead, a diversification that focuses on the local (Dubai and UAE) and the global (Bollywood), instead of just the pan-Arab sphere (Kraidy and Khali, 2009).

Even in DMC, media policy remains inconsistent. One challenging area has been the regulation of the NICL. After CNBC Arabiya, a pan-Arab satellite franchise of the US financial cable channel, laid off some people in 2006, the fired workers started a media campaign claiming ill-treatment by management. According to a former CNBC Arabiya employee and spokesperson for the dismissed employees, DMC pushed CNBC Arabiya to settle the matter promptly and quietly (Kraidy and Khalil, 2009).

Another problem has been editorial content, for which DMC established a Broadcasting and Publication Standards Tribunal in 2003. The Tribunal's singular achievement was devising a media code that covers religious sensibilities, alcohol, smoking, and sex (Addington, 2006). When the first issue of *Focus On* magazine hit the stands with a pullout of Miss May, a semi-naked model, DMC shut it down for not adhering to its "business plan" (Addington, 2005). Geo, a DMC-based Pakistani satellite channel, was closed by DMC because it claimed that Geo interfered with Pakistani politics.[9]

A third challenge came from the global economic crisis, which hit Dubai particularly hard. As frequent Western press stories shifted from lauding Dubai as the new El Dorado to focusing on the flight of suddenly unemployed workers and bankrupt business owners and their mistreatment by local authorities, the government sought to preempt negative reporting about Dubai and the UAE in general. The result was its controversial Media Law, passed by the Federal National Council in 2009. Though the law was an advance on previous legislation, notably in terms of not subjecting journalists to imprisonment, it renewed concerns about self-censorship and government intervention. Several watchdog groups, most notably Human Rights Watch (2009), criticized, *inter alia*, "content-based restrictions . . . stymieing criticism of the government" and "ambiguous, overbroad provisions" against reporting about the national economy and disparaging government figures.

The director-general of the UAE National Media Council, Ibrahim Al Abed (2009), argued that the law distinguished between criticism of government officials and "insults to the person." He emphasized that allegations against the media of harming the national economy had to be proven in court before any sanctions could be applied. Al Abed also denied that the changes came about in response to negative reporting after the global economic crisis, claiming that work on it had begun two years earlier, with extensive vetting by several groups, including the UAE Journalists Association.

Emergent Transnational Media Policy

The preceding examples show that Arab states have become adept at developing abuse-prone regulatory and policy environments and instrumentalizing the changing media landscape. Ambiguous catch-all provisions pertaining to "national unity" and "the national economy" are used to repress opposition; royal decrees and presidential fiats trample over regulatory bodies; overlapping jurisdictions lead to inconsistency and arbitrariness, with various ministries (of information, of the interior, of telecommunications, or of religious affairs), in addition to clerics in the case of Saudi Arabia, laying claim to media policy and regulation; and dated press and publication laws apply to television and the emerging media environment.

The boundary between state-owned and privately owned media has become increasingly porous, with states enabling private and politically sympathetic satellite channels, while clamping down on institutions expressing dissent. To regain viewers who deserted state TV for commercial competitors, Arab governments have facilitated the production of entertainment programs.

By attempting to preserve both the state's capacity for repression and the commercial interests of major media players, the ASTC brought into view multiple contradictions within and between Arab states, reflecting confusion and an inability to confront challenges posed by new permutations of delivery platforms, programs, and viewers. In addition to being shaped by media convergence, Arab television programs are characterized by a blurring of genres that puzzles policymakers long used to a single and rigid distinction between "political" and "non-political" programs: religion mixes with personal finance or sexuality, reality shows dabble in politics, infomercials blend news and advertising, talk shows blur politics and entertainment, and drama discusses public affairs such as disease and terrorism. To reign in this media anarchy, states have used both direct repression and laws and regulations that co-opt TV.

In this respect, the ASTC represents an attempt to expand the national policy regimes of key Arab states into the transnational realm. The main motivation for passing the Charter was political, even if Arab governments paid lip service to perennial concerns about morality and social change and took influential commercial interests into account. In the weeks leading to the Cairo meeting, the Saudi and Egyptian information ministers lobbied their Arab counterparts to support the Charter, a draft of which had been prepared by a "committee of experts." Work on the document started following the summer 2006 war in Lebanon, when the Israeli military devastated Lebanese infrastructure after Hezbollah captured two Israeli soldiers in a cross-border operation. When hostilities broke out, Egyptian and Saudi leaders first condemned Hezbollah's actions as reckless, but changed the tenor of their discourse in the light of Hezbollah's better-than-expected military performance and mounting civilian casualties from Israel's onslaught. In the meantime, Hezbollah's television station al-Manar climbed to the top 10 in pan-Arab ratings, and live talk-show hosts struggled to prevent callers from heaping verbal abuse on pro-US Arab states.

Though not criticized as intensely as Saudi government leaders, Hosni Mubarak's regime contended with a growingly sophisticated Muslim Brotherhood whose voice could be heard through a variety of platforms, from al-Jazeera to Hamas' al-Aqsa television to the Arabic-language blogosphere. In that context, a regulatory document that would place "political restrictions" on Arab airwaves reflected shared Saudi-Egyptian interests.

The ASTC is a broad-ranging document, covering news, political shows, entertainment, and sports. It recognizes the broad diversity of the pan-Arab television scene, which has come to include, in addition to general news and entertainment channels, niche outlets dedicated to religion, real estate, music, and fashion. At the same time, the Charter is restrictive, giving Arab governments tools to sanction satellite broadcasters who attack leaders, harm national reputation, or air socially unacceptable content. The ASTC hits several birds with one stone. By penalizing content that allegedly promotes sexual activity or alcohol consumption, it placates socially conservative Islamists, including Egypt's Brotherhood, who for years have advocated such restrictions. By purporting to protect "Arab identity from the harmful effects of globalization," it resonates with Arab nationalist and Islamist ideologies. And by prohibiting content that would "damage social harmony, national unity, public order, or traditional values" – notice how all-encompassing these terms are – it justifies authoritarian rule. Finally, the Charter has a populist provision, stipulating Arab viewers' information rights, including watching sports on free-to-air government channels even when commercial stations have purchased exclusivity. In addition to reasserting the rights of state television channels, this gives the Charter some credibility with Arab publics (Kraidy, 2008).

ASTC also reflects the double standards of the emerging policy landscape. The controversial UAE draft Media Law, for instance, "does not apply to the media Free Zones, in Abu Dhabi, Dubai and elsewhere, which is where offices of foreign publications, television channels and news agencies are based" (Al Abed, 2009). This essentially creates two classes of media institutions, one predominantly local and subject to the law, the other predominantly foreign and outside it.

Arab countries are largely willing and able to apply the ASTC to the half-dozen Arabic-language television channels operated by non-Arab states: al-Hurra (The Free One), funded by the US Congress, Rusya al-Yawm (Russia Today), bankrolled by the Kremlin, al-'Alam (The World), owned by the Iranian state, the resuscitated BBC Arabic, Deutsche Welle World TV, France 24, a French channel broadcasting in various languages including Arabic, and Arabic TRT, a Turkish Arabic-language channel. Applying the ASTC to these channels risks complicating relations between Arab states and great powers. Not applying it exposes them to domestic accusations of double standards and of succumbing to foreign, and in the case of Egypt and Saudi Arabia, US pressure. Reflecting post-9/11 anxieties in the capitals of great and regional powers and the resurgence of the Arab world as a geopolitical flashpoint, these channels operate in a regulatory vacuum at the intersection of global, regional, transnational, and national realms.

Arab media and journalism circles felt that the ASTC dashed hopes that the pan-Arab media sphere would continue to offer more editorial autonomy than national TV. A pan-Arab framework may be needed to regulate hundreds of stations peddling fortune-tellers, alternative medicines, Jihadi ideas, titillating bodies, stock market schemes, and more mainstream news and entertainment. But besides the daunting challenges inherent in establishing a transnational policy regime, Arab governments' record on media autonomy is dismal. Even Syria, which at the time was engaged in a media struggle with Saudi Arabia over Lebanon, signed off on the Charter. Arab journalists, intellectuals, and dissidents are now worried that, while regimes disagree on many things, information ministers agree about muzzling speech.

The ASTC is a telling document, less because it has been effectively implemented – it has not – than because it makes visible the actors contending to shape media policy, unmasks their agendas, and brings into focus industry and related social and political developments that lead to and shape the emerging Arab policy regime. As the first formal pan-Arab regulatory text, the Charter reflects the desire of Arab governments to reassert control over an unwieldy transnational media scene that, in addition to television, is witnessing an explosion of "small media" like mobile telephones, blogs, and social networking sites such as Facebook and their local versions (these include Naqa Tube, a Saudi alternative to YouTube that is compliant with "Islamic principles"). With the growing harassment and arrest of bloggers in Egypt, Saudi Arabia, and elsewhere, a more sweeping charter regulating the Arab internet is now to be expected, and a document concerning mobile telephony may follow.

The current Charter poses dilemmas concerning the relationship between the national and the transnational. It reflects a strong regulatory approach by Arab states, synchronized with a global post-9/11 emphasis on security and control. This represents an extension into the transnational sphere of national Arab media laws, virtually all of which have ambiguous language that prohibits libel, slander, and criticism of leaders and their families. It also affirms current practice: several Arab states have revoked Arab satellite channels' licenses to report from their territories.

The ominous catch-all provision against harming "national reputation" enables a wide range of repressive measures. In this respect, ASTC extends to the pan-Arab sphere provisions already in effect within nation-states. In doing so, it essentially contradicts itself when it asserts the "country of origin principle," which stipulates that media outlets be regulated by the laws in effect in the country from which they transmit, while emphasizing individual states' prerogatives to regulate incoming satellite signals.

ASTC differs sharply from *Television Without Frontiers*. In Europe, the country-of-origin principle was instrumental for constructing a pan-European sphere, based on the notion of mutual recognition enshrined in the Maastricht Treaty (Wheeler, 2004). It simplifies media law and reinforces competition among states, motivated by their ability to influence media content (Price, 2008). A second major difference between the European and Arab documents is that the former expresses concerns about media consolidation, while the latter ignores the issue altogether – a logical outcome when one considers that pan-Arab media ownership is concentrated in the hands of Saudi moguls close to the royal family. A third contrast lies in *Television Without Frontiers'* affirmation of pluralism, cultural diversity, and the "enhancement of citizen choice" (Wheeler, 2004: 252), versus the Arab Charter's reassertion of concerns about national unity, public order, and putative (Arab-Islamic) social values.

The Charter represents de facto recognition by Arab states that satellite TV has achieved a level of social relevance, cultural resonance, and political influence that matches or exceeds the capacities of national media systems. Satellite television has become a professional benchmark for national broadcasters' programming strategies, production values, and institutional practices. As a consequence, ASTC reflects the convergence of previously separate national systems, a trend also visible in post-Soviet developments in Eastern Europe (Price, 2009). The national scale is receding as a locus of analysis in favor of the regional–transnational, where policymaking has long been more grounded and concrete than at the global level, but not traditionally in comparison to the nation-state (Miller, 1981; 1984).

This does not mean that the nation-state has become a less powerful actor. Rather, the Arab sphere reflects the transnational rise of some dominant nation-states, specifically Saudi Arabia, while others see their cross-border influence dwindling. Though a few similarities exist between ASTC and *Television Without Frontiers* – including their transnational scale, regulatory challenges posed by the rise of powerful commercial media institutions, national broadcasters' rights to air sports events of national relevance, etc. – the models are different.

The two accords reflect fundamentally different interstate relations in radically different political contexts: liberal democracy in the EU and authoritarianism in the Arab world. This explains additional differences between the two documents. Whereas *Television Without Frontiers* called for assistance to European countries with weak production capacities, ASTC affirmed the agendas of powerful Arab states. That distinction is exacerbated by the breadth and depth of the institutionalization of media policy in Europe, where a variety of bodies, commissions, and bureaucracies conduct policymaking and implementation, compared with the absence of such specialized institutions in the Arab world.

A further fundamental difference between the Arab world and Europe is the comparative linguistic unity of the former and diversity of the latter. In this respect, the Arab world resembles Spanish-speaking Latin America more than the EU. Consisting of 22 geographically contiguous countries that share the Arabic language, the region is a "geo-linguistic market" (Straubhaar, 2007), a sphere within which media texts face relatively weak cultural obstacles. This does not mean that the boundaries of the Arab sphere are impermeable to outside influence. But unlike *Television Without*

Frontiers, which focused on strengthening continental TV by softening borders within Europe while hardening boundaries to Hollywood, ASTC was motivated less by concerns about US programming, which is virtually absent from the leading Arab and pan-Arab channels in prime time, than by anxieties about Iranian influence through Arabic-language channels like al-Aqsa (Hamas), al-Manar (Hezbollah), and Iran's al-'Alam.

After a 2009 meeting of select information ministers and media moguls in the Saudi capital, a decision was made to suspend al-'Alam's satcasts from the Saudi-control ARABSAT and Egypt-owned NILESAT satellites. In addition, the rise of Turkey as a regional political and economic powerhouse, coupled with the wide success of dubbed Turkish soap operas in the Arab world, has alarmed authorities in countries like Saudi Arabia. These developments have diminished fears of an exogenous Western (read US) "cultural invasion" and built up concerns about endogenous politico-cultural influence emanating from non-Arabic speaking but Islamic nations in the region. The rise of Iranian and Turkish influence, both diplomatic and cultural, poses new challenges while affirming the importance of the regional-transnational realm both for media policy and its academic study.

Conclusion

Global media policy and governance have to take into account a dizzying complexity of nations, actors, institutions, technologies, and interactions. As a result, there are many conceptual, analytical, and definitional challenges. Scalar issues, which concern how the transnational, international, and national domains interact with the global as shapers and loci of media policy and governance, continue to animate debate. We see intellectual, political, and economic investments in cities and regions as centers of media activity. The rise of Asia is said to compromise both national and media-imperialism discourses, and the triumph of neoliberalism and consumerism sometimes appears to make criticism of corporate capitalism all but unsayable in global media policy (Chadha and Kavoori, 2015).

Two issues are important to keep in mind. First, although the nation-state has been relegated to secondary importance in the literature on global media studies for much of the past two decades, the role of the state has not disappeared. Rather, it has shifted in many regions from being largely a protector, regulator, and enforcer to being a mediator, facilitator, and promoter of media institutions (Braman, 2002; Curran and Park, 2000; Morris and Waisbord, 2001).

Second, the transnational subglobal realm is distinct from both national and global policy in linguistic, political, and regulatory terms. It complicates the neat opposition between the national and the global that is often taken for granted in global media studies. In chapter 5, we examine one of the principal fields where national policies, individual consumption, the NICL, and global governance intersect – mobile telephony.

5 Mobile Telephony

(with Richard Maxwell)

The first four chapters presented foundational building blocks – historical, conceptual, and methodological. From now on, we zero in on specific media technologies, sites, and genres to offer a textured portrait of the field by focusing on areas that we believe best reflect the developing global media landscape. This chapter examines mobile telephony, which brings together issues of political economy and policy/governance at a personal level that can resonate with us all – after all, our cells ring inside our jackets and handbags as we touch, view, and hear them each day. Mobile telephony combines broad policy and structural issues with moving, media-using bodies. As some analysts have argued, mobile devices' "permeation into 'everyday life'" warrants that we call them media (May and Hearn, 2005), and, we would add, their saturation of most corners of the planet earns mobile telephony entry to *global* media-hood.

Just a few years ago, if you introduced the subject of telephony at a party or in a lecture, you'd be met with blank looks followed by empty rooms. Now, hipster dinners reverberate not just with the noise of cell phones, but discussion of them: the topic seems to be not about a singular part of daily life, but almost life itself. Cell phones are ubiquitous: they are utilized by 78 percent of the world's population. Current estimates put the number of mobile subscriptions on a par with the entire population – nearly seven billion. Combined users of mobile and landline broadband – the high-speed network at the heart of digital mobile living – make up about half that. Subscriptions rose from 145 million in 1996 to more than 6.9 billion in 2014. By the end of 2013, over three-quarters of the world's roughly 5.4 billion cell phone accounts were held in the Global South.[1]

At this rate, mobile traffic will grow 89 times between 2010 and 2020. And, according to Bell Labs, "[b]y 2017 more than 5 zettabytes of data will pass through the network every year. That is the equivalent of everyone in the world tweeting non-stop for more than 100 years."[2] Given this extraordinary success story, perhaps it is no wonder that the claims made for both the value and the peril of cell phones are so extraordinary. Let's look at four of them:

> Mobile phones have become affective technologies. That is, objects which mediate the expression, display, experience and communication of feelings and emotions. . . . They are an extension of the human body . . . building and maintaining . . . groups and communities. (Lasén, 2004)
>
> G[race] K[hunou]: A cell phone is the best accessory ever. Those without disposable income find ways of owning one and having airtime. A lot of the hip guys do not leave their cell phones in their cars or put them in their pockets. They hold them in their hands. . . . Another thing they have to be seen as having are the smallest cell phones.

You lose points if you are seen with a heavy and big cell phone. . . . Cell phones are also very much a female accessory. For some women, having accessories such as these are a reason for having multiple boyfriends, whom they refer to as "ministers" – that is, different boyfriends to provide for their different needs.

N[sizwa] D[lamini]: It is considered degrading to give someone a landline phone number, as it suggests that one does not have a cell phone. Even those who have one are not off the hook, as their phones have to be tiny, lighter, and look good. . . . Bigger ones are given names such as a "brick" (Mbembe et al., 2004)

The increasingly faster and more versatile computers, appealing mobile phones, high-definition TVs, Internet, tiny music players, ingenious photo cameras, entertaining games consoles and even electronic pets give us the idea of a developed, pioneering and modern world. It is indeed a new era for many; but the dark side of this prosperous world reveals a very different reality, that far from taking us to the future, takes us back to a darker past. (Centro de Reflexión y Acción Laboral, 2006)

[T]he woman came back carrying a small cardboard box. She went directly to Bosch and handed it to him, then bowed as she backed away. Harry opened it and found the remains of a melted and burnt cell phone. While the woman gave Sun an explanation, Bosch pulled his own cell phone and compared it to the burned phone. Despite the damage, it was clear the phone the woman retrieved from her ash can was a match. "She said Peng was burning that," Sun said. "It made a very foul smell that would be displeasing to the ghosts so she removed it." (Connelly, 2009: 243)

The first two epigrams above are comforting. One speaks in universal terms about the phenomenology of the cell phone: everyone is embraced by and embracing what seems to be a natural extension of their very selves. The cell phone is soothing, helpful, special – an elemental force that has become part of us. The second quotation is more localized. It refers to life in Soweto after liberation from Apartheid, where the cell phone's gift of commercial freedom has adapted to local gendered circumstances and mores. At the same time, this epigram, too, is universal in claiming the phone's centrality to everyday life.

By contrast with the nurturing common sense of their predecessors, the third and fourth epigrams are quite shocking. The first is an account of the putrid, dangerous creation of cell phones in the electronics industry, which delivers the products that Sowetans and the rest of us own. The second references Hong Kong customs and the putrid, dangerous afterlife of cell phones once their cuddly qualities have become obsolete and they must be exterminated.

These differences should come as no surprise, given the provenance of the epigrams. The first derives from scholarship and publication funded by Vodafone, a major supplier of the objects that are so thoroughly humanized by its "academic staff." The second is written by professors who focus on the life they see around them and ignore the fact that raw materials for cell phones are tearing huge swathes of their continent apart. By contrast, the third epigram was generated by a nongovernmental organization that seeks to protect and expand workers' rights in Mexican *maquiladoras*. And the source of the fourth is crime fiction, hard-boiled, code-driven detection that observes horror wherever it is found, almost without commentary.

The key to bridging the gap between these quotations is a materialist one. A recent contribution from archaeology offers some contextualization:

The phone has much in common with the portable artifacts of a more traditional archaeology, like flint hand-axes or pottery vessels. . . . an object scaled to fit the human world. . . . shaped to fit the hand and fingers, and has action capabilities . . . orientated towards other parts of the body. (Edgeworth 2010: 143)

Drawing on this materialist perspective in its search for media studies 3.0, global media studies must hold utopic and dystopic accounts of the cell phone in tension.

Optimistic descriptions anchor the cell phone to a high capitalist consumerism that is said to deliver happiness, development, and revolution. Such tales pay attention to personal and social rather than psychological and biological aspects. They love cell phones. Pessimistic descriptions, by contrast, see the cell phone era as one of social fragmentation, as managerial and administrative control lead workers and others on a frantic, alienated search for connectedness that leaves little time or inclination to ponder prevailing political-economic arrangements and potential alternatives. This dystopian perspective criticizes the quasi-religious nature of utopian discourse. It emphasizes protests and studies that expose the harms that cell phones cause in the service of profit and bureaucracy – most significantly to workers and environment.

To enact that tension, this chapter starts with a positive case for welcoming the cell phone as a transformative, even revolutionary, technology, then examines its sordid history of surveillance, labor exploitation, and environmental destruction.

Utopia: Cell Phones Make You Free

94% of cell users ages 12–17 agree that cell phones give them more freedom because they can reach their parents no matter where they are. . . .
Teens who have multi-purpose phones are avid users of those extra features. The most popular are taking and sharing pictures and playing music:

- 83% use their phones to take pictures.
- 64% share pictures with others.
- 60% play music on their phones.
- 46% play games on their phones.
- 32% exchange videos on their phones.
- 31% exchange instant messages on their phones.
- 27% go online for general purposes on their phones.
- 23% access social network sites on their phones.
- 21% use email on their phones.
- 11% purchase things via their phones. (Lenhart et al., 2010: 5)

The figures above come from the United States. And of the 83 percent of US adults who own cells, three-quarters use text messaging, 41.5 times on a typical day. In Kenya, cell phone banking accounts for US$1 billion of transactions a month. In China, 73 percent of people aged 15–24 regularly access the internet by phone, compared with under 50 percent in the United States and the United Kingdom and less than 25 percent across Europe. The use of messaging is almost universally feminized, apart from in Italy, Saudi Arabia, and China (NielsenWire, 2011; Pew Research Center, 2011; Voigt, 2011; Smith, 2010).

Cybertarians – true believers in technological determinism and consumerism and opponents of socialized communications as per post offices – adore these data. Such cathexis dates back to Marshall McLuhan's 1970s pre-cell phone fantasies of telephony. He spoke of a long-distance call as a complete phenomenological transformation of space: "The spirit leaves immediately to Tokyo. There is no longer a body hardware. There is only software";[3] while, for Edgar Morin (1999), the instantaneity of phone communication means that our "world is made more and more whole."

Cybertarian discourse buys into fantasies of reader, audience, consumer, player, and activist autonomy, where music, movies, television, and politics converge under the sign of empowered fans and rebels holding neither swords nor ploughshares, but telephones. True believers invest with unparalleled gusto in Schumpeterian entrepreneurs, evolutionary economics, creative industries, and revolution. They've never seen an "app" they didn't like, or a socialist party they did. Faith in devolved, mobile media-making via telephony amounts to a secular religion, offering transcendence in the here and now. This "literature of the eighth day, the day after Genesis" (Carey, 2005), seems to end the era of the gatekeeper and restore the media to culture's original, organic qualities as the property of ordinary people. Customs override consumption, capitalism is no longer corporate, and citizens govern suzerains.

Manuel Castells, a renowned lapsed Marxist whose work has shifted from critical European urbanism to mainstream US communication studies, is one of the leading scholars forwarding utopian ideas about cell phones. In a 2007 study, his research team cited many positive features: they broaden channels of communication, secure personal safety, integrate family life, improve peer groups, speed up rendezvous, and allow users to produce content, create their own language, and forge personal statements in their choice of exterior design – in other words, they make users feel important (Castells et al., 2007: 246–58). Castells claims these devices are politically transformative:

> The spread of instant political mobilizations by using mobile phones, supported by the Internet, is changing the landscape of politics. It becomes increasingly difficult for governments to hide or manipulate information. The manipulation plots are immediately picked up and challenged by a myriad of "eye balls," as debate and mobilization are called upon by thousands of people, without central coordination, but with a shared purpose, often focusing on asking or forcing the resignation of governments or government officials. (2007: 251)

In a similar vein, Ulrich Beck, noted for his work on risk society, says that the cell phone has altered "sociological categories of time, space, place, proximity and distance" as it "makes those who are absent present, always and everywhere" (2002: 31). Such observations reinforce Castells's theories of "timeless time" and a "space of flows."

Using the same discourse, neoclassical economists and their bourgeois masters in business form a vanguard of institutional boosters. They promote cell phones as crucial to democracy, efficiency, pleasure, and development in the Global South (International Telecommunication Union, 2008: 67–84; 2009: 2, 5; Jones, 2008; Hanna and Qiang, 2010; Prahalad and Hart, 2008; Sachs, 2008). Industry magazines such as *Advertising Age* positively salivate over the spread of cell phones, as the absence of conventional telecommunications and financial infrastructure is supposedly overcome thanks to digital wallets and micro-payment systems (Shapiro, 2010). This happy state of affairs finds the world's leading media ratings company, Nielsen, publishing an unimaginably crass account that begins: "Africa is in the midst of a technological revolution, and nothing illustrates that fact [more] than the proliferation of mobile phones." It then notes casually that "more Africans have access to mobile phones than to clean drinking water" (Hutton, 2011).[4]

Bourgeois economists argue that cell phones have streamlined hitherto inefficient markets in remote areas of the Global South, enriching people in zones where banking services and commercial information are scarce due to distance and terrain. Exaggerated claims for the magic of mobile telephony in places that lack electricity, plumbing, fresh water, hospital care, and the like include "the complete elimination of waste" and massive reductions of poverty and corruption through the empowerment of individuals (Jensen, 2007).

Such scholarly devotees of the cell phone are captivated by a Schumpeterian wet dream in which cell phone consumers rise up as one and rebel against capital, even as they renew it. They form an imaginary, bizarre alliance with entrepreneurs against corporate domination and closed markets:

> Our case studies range over several emergent industries based about consumer cocreation in digital media. Each has been made possible by new digital information and communication technologies centred about the Internet as a universal platform for social networks and business models, and about new digital consumer goods and services. . . . the value-creation proposition about which business models are adopted and adapted is premised on the provision of content emanating from a distributed network of consumers or users operating in partnership with producers and, equally importantly, from the self-organization of the community protocols that coordinate such flows. This cultural and technological dynamic is both inducing new creative activities (e.g. MMOGs, video and photo-sharing) as well as displacing and disrupting extant industries (e.g. media journalism and music). (Potts et al., 2008: 465)

Nowhere were celebrations of the emancipatory magic of digital communication more manifest than in predominant media and academic representations of the popular uprisings and civil wars captured by the rubric of "the Arab Spring." Debates between otherwise sensible people for a while revolved around whether these were "Facebook revolutions" or "Twitter Revolutions." Talk of "digitally enabled" activists overshadowed the reality of long, arduous, material, and ideological struggles that made the Arab popular rebellions possible. Expecting Anglo-only analysts to revisit how "media" operated in the 1919 Egyptian revolution against the British or the 1979 Iranian revolution against the Shah may be asking too much. But they might at least acknowledge the important antecedents of Tunisia's 1984 Bread Riots and the 2008 miners' strikes in Gafsa, or Egypt's 2008 Mahalla al-Kubra's textile workers, to mention recent examples. Doing so would locate politico-economic concerns of inequality, poverty, and deprivation at the center of revolutionary action, rather than the ability to manipulate digital gadgetry. Excesses of market fundamentalism chaperoned by the erstwhile dictators Ben Ali of Tunisia and Mubarak of Egypt, and the havoc they wrought on people's livelihoods, were foundational to the revolts that ousted them – not wireless communication (Armbrust, 2011; Zuraik, 2011).

Dystopia: Cell Phones Make Others Unfree

> [I]t is now necessary to impose silence in restaurants and places of worship or concert halls. One day, following the example of the campaign to combat nicotine addiction, it may well be necessary to put up signs of the "Silence Hospital" variety at the entrance to museums and exhibition halls to get all those "communication machines" to shut up and put an end to the all too numerous cultural exercises in SOUND and LIGHT. (Virilio, 2004: 76)

It is tempting to regard cell phones as *sui generis*, because of their supposedly unique role as makers and un-makers of consciousness. But in addition to acknowledging that mobile telephony facilitates a certain autonomy of communication and self-presentation as well as economic exchange, we must go beyond the appeal of pleasure and "efficiency," of consumerism and business, to examine what lies before, within, around, and after the cell phone. We must appreciate its entire life as a commodity sign, as per the Chartier model described earlier, and note that its advent has coincided with increasing inequality of wealth across much of the world and the rise of a new middle class in others (Shepherd and Stone, 2013).

Almost a century ago, Max Weber underlined the role of the phone in fictive capital:

> The "arbitrager" seeks a profit in that he simultaneously sells a good at a place where it is, at that moment, able to be sold at a higher price, while he buys it at a place where it is to be had more cheaply. His business is therefore a pure example of calculating the numbers. He sits at a telephone . . . and, as soon as he notices the possibility of, for example, making a profit from buying Russian notes or notes of exchange drawn on Russia available in London and then selling them in Paris, he places his orders. (2000: 344)

And consider the other side to de Sola Pool's historical celebration of landlines' potential for managerial control of work:

> The company president located himself at the place where most of his most critical communications took place. Before the telephone, he had to be near the production line to give his instructions about the quantities, pace, and process of production. Once the telephone network existed, however, he could convey those authoritative commands to his employees at the plant and could locate himself at the place where the much more uncertain bargaining with customers, bankers, and suppliers took place. (1980: 2)

Bearing these warnings in mind, some circumspection is called for. As we have seen, it's tempting to view cell phones as magical agents that can induce "leapfrogging" over stages of socioeconomic development to produce market equilibrium and hence individual and collective happiness. But the new freedoms associated with cell phone usage have created new nightmares for denizens of the planet, workers, public health professionals, and environmentalists.

Critical analyses point out that cell phones are surveillance tools of state control and corporate management. Jack Qiu (2007) offers telling examples from Malaysia, Britain, Australia, and China, where "an industrial complex has emerged since 2000 to serve the control needs of the power elite" via cell monitoring (also see Turow, 2005; Andrejevic, 2006; Baruh, 2004). The World Privacy Forum proposes that we are inhabiting a *One-Way Mirror Society*, where power accretes to corporations through the supposedly even-handed tool of interactivity (Dixon, 2010).

Surveillance has long been a central strut of modernity, supposedly to make populations secure, content, and productive. With the expansion of state authority into the everyday, into all corners of life, the quid pro quo for the security afforded by governments became knowing everyone's identities and practices. The equivalent expansion of corporations into those everyday corners had as its quid pro quo for the provision of goods and services that they, too, know more and more about us. The telephone's real owners – the corporations that possess its networks and track its users – share data with states and companies at will (Murdock, 2014). This is in keeping with classic dystopian assessments of communication, command, and control, famously fictionalized in Yevgeny Zamyatin's *We* (1924), Aldous Huxley's *Brave New World* (1932), and George Orwell's *Nineteen Eighty-Four* (1949), where freedom is just another word for loss of privacy.

Andrew Keen, a lapsarian prophet of the internet, argues that the new landscape is abuzz with noise and ignorance rather than subtlety and knowledge (2007: 12). He sees a dreary world where constant clatter and frenzied imagery denature aesthetics in favor of uninterrupted stimulus. For their part, hitherto true-believing editors of *Wired* magazine see the internet undone by the corporatization of knowledge and sealed-set model of phone applications (Anderson and Wolff, 2010).

And when we get adequately empirical about how successive new technologies have supposedly liberated consumers, we see that established technologies and corporations always respond ably. In the 1980s, video-cassette recorders and premium cable television channels threatened to take control of the US audience away from capital. These concerns were reawakened when Digital Video Recorders (DVRs) permitted viewers to elude commercials in real time. DVRs were even advertised for these qualities, supposedly transforming audiences into schedulers. There was a brief but dramatic loss of confidence in TV's efficacy amongst major advertisers, despite this additional intelligence about viewers, out of fear that "[l]e pouvoir de programmer passe des mains de l'éditeur à celles du téléspectateur" (the power to program is shifting from editors to spectators) (Cristiani and Missika, 2007; also see Carlson, 2006). By 2009, almost a third of US homes had DVRs. But just 5 percent of TV was being time shifted, and people skipped a mere 3 percent of commercials.[5] Time shifting grew in 2010, with the average resident watching nearly 10.5 hours more that way by the end of the year. The biggest annual increase was in the third quarter, which was 17.9 percent over the same period in 2009.[6] But these increases came from a small base. Furthermore, the first popular versions of these devices only worked when subscribers connected them to the internet, thereby allowing service providers, TiVo and ReplayTV, to collect information about them, which disclosed that no fewer than a third of US sports audiences who communicate electronically at the same time as viewing refer to the commercials they have seen, and almost two-thirds have greater recognition of them than those who simply watch TV without reaching out in these other ways to friends and fellow-spectators (J. Lewis, 2001: 40; Rose, 2001; Attallah, 2007: 330; Loechner, 2007).[7] Liberation from capital? Autonomy from traditional media? Not so much.

Dan Schiller (2007) challenges cell phone enthusiasts by demonstrating that social stresses fuel consumer needs, as people rush to buy inferior phone services at high cost. Schiller describes the displacement and deracination of modern life into a mode of sociality in which individuation (separateness and privacy) combines with mobility (transport and access). He argues that political-economic arrangements allow mobile telephony to emerge in a form befitting divided societies. This is particularly so in the United States, where a decline in governmental oversight of the telecommunication industries since World War II has diminished the quality and regulation of competition.

US residents check their smartphones for messages 150 times a day – that's about once every six and a half minutes.[8] What are they looking for, and what is otherwise lacking in their world? The psy-function calls this fear of separation from one's smart phone "nomophobia" (fear of no mobile). A concept invented by the UK Post Office, it is now part of widespread investigations into the sense of isolation – and even fear – induced by being without a cell phone, to the point where there is agitation for it to be included in the instruments that diagnose mental illness (Yildirim and Correia, 2015; Bragazzi and Del Puente, 2014).

In Wagga Wagga, pride of Australia's western New South Wales, a study of 616 women on Facebook found that "more 'lonely' people disclosed their Personal Information, Relationship Information, and Address than 'connected' people and more 'connected' people disclosed their Views and their Wall than 'lonely' people" (Al-Saggaf and Nielsen, 2014). We also know that Facebook use correlates with feeling miserable (Kross et al., 2013). It may be that these sites are better suited to learning about people's pleasure and displeasure than anything else, as per the hedonometer developed at the University of Vermont, which uses Tweets to establish levels of happiness.[9] Facebook and Twitter operate with certain assumptions about the desire for connectedness that may not apply. We don't have to "Like" news stories to deem them worth sharing with others. Our "friends" may be professional or activist colleagues rather than intimates. The lexicon of social media may require revisiting.

And consider some distinctly anti-social media successes of recent times: http://gottasplit.com/, which promises to help users "avoid unwanted encounters," and http://usecloak.com/, the "incognito mode for real life" application for smart phones: "avoid exes, co-workers, that guy who likes to stop and chat – anyone you'd rather not run into." Cloak, for instance, warns users if Instagram, Facebook, Twitter, or Foursquare suggest that people they don't want to see are nearby.

The European Union's Court of Justice has ruled that Google must give its citizens a "right to be forgotten," to remove themselves from scrutiny through search engines when the information that emerges about them is spurious.[10] So the happy utopia promised by social media and celebrated by media studies 2.0 is running into some serious resistance.

We must attend to Walter Benjamin's Proustian lament for the loss of authentic interpersonal collective or individual aura (1992: 184) caused by a technology that looks back at us and carries our images and statements in a reciprocal loop. How ironic that the supposed depersonalization of modern Parisian life was both exemplified and countered by the advent of the telephone as a commercial apparatus in the 1870s, simultaneously rendering the public private and the private public (Innis, 1991: 60; Attali and Stourdze, 1977: 97–8). The cell phone is a very odd thing when seen in this light – built upon the stressful fragmentation of social life, corporate control, division between rich and poor, and the false promise of consumerism.

Phone-based mobility is also necessarily implicated with the interests of large firms that control the infrastructure on which it relies. For instance, the US phone company AT&T's second-quarter profits for 2014 were US$3.82 billion from revenues of US$32 billion (Gryta and Stynes, 2014). That same year, AT&T was busy settling with the Federal Communications Commission, agreeing to US$105 million in reparations to customers because of unauthorized subscriptions and premium text-messaging services.[11] A month later, it was required to pay the state of California close to US$52 million because of environmental violations – the fruits of almost a decade merrily spent in the illegal disposal of e-waste. No fewer than 235 AT&T facilities across the state had dispatched batteries, aerosols, and everything in-between to landfills in a lawless quest for profit.[12] And in December, the National Association of African American Owned Media Firms filed a US$10 billion lawsuit against AT&T and numerous subsidiaries, including DirecTV, for allegedly contravening the Civil Rights Act by paying black cable TV stations negligible amounts.[13]

Or consider a little place called Knocknaheeny, a suburb of Cork in Ireland where Apple's European headquarters are located. In 2014, Joaquín Almunia, then an EU Vice-President, delivered a report from the European Commission that accused Apple of cleansing profits in Ireland by avoiding taxation that would be due in other member states of the Union where its manufacturing, sales, and stockholders happen. The company had apparently been receiving a massive state subsidy from the Irish, which the report suggests involved the illegal payment of millions from taxpayers to bloat Apple's already wondrous profits and diminish its risks (European Commission, 2014). In the US Senate, a supposedly high priest of private enterprise, Rand Paul, waded in to defend Apple, while Carl Levin and John McCain mounted a powerful case querying the tiny percentages that the corporation pays in taxes and noting that US citizens are the poorer for it (Volz, 2014). A strong case has been made that Apple should return its stupendous profits and assets (over a hundred billion in liquid form) not to shareholders, but to taxpayers (Lazonick et al., 2013).

Those stories connect to a dilemma that confronts media studies 2.0 and cell phone fans alike – namely, who invented their phones? One answer might be to name the companies whose trademark gives cultural and commercial meaning to these appliances. Another would be to dig a little deeper than trademarks. Metaphorically, of course. The first kind of answer is likely to mention Samsung or Apple, with other possibilities including LG, HTC, Motorola, Nokia, or Blackberry. Look at your phone and you have a pat response. The second kind of answer will probably be more abstract and ideological, but equally pat. It goes something like this: "Laissez-faire entrepreneurialism meeting consumer demand has been the basis for the new digital economy." If we expand on that thinking, a clear path opens up, along the following lines: "As both inventors and consumers, we need to stop the inevitable tendency for government to get involved in regulating, which discourages innovation in this crucial sector of our economy and social and cultural life."

Lifting their lids and examining these devices, we see that their variety and quality are imposing. A quick list would probably feature click wheels, multi-touch screens, global positioning systems, lithium-ion batteries, signal compression, hypertext markup language, liquid-crystal displays, Siri, cellular technology, microprocessors – and the internet itself.

In wondering who or what invented, synthesized – and paid for – these things, the popular answers can again be guessed pretty easily. We should thank Apple, Microsoft, Dell or someone like them – or perhaps a nerdy guy with a straggly beard in a shed, badly in need of better personal hygiene – or maybe a giddy entrepreneur burnishing credentials from business school. Right? Media studies 2.0 knows.

In which case, it should think again: these donations to our daily digital lives came from the US Defense Advanced Research Projects Agency (DARPA), the European Organization for Nuclear Research, the US Department of Energy, the CIA, the National Science Foundation, the US Navy, the US Army Research Office, the National Institutes of Health, the US Department of Defense – and research universities like the one you are probably attending (Mazzucato, 2015).

In addition to such questions eluding cell phone celebrants, these devices have created a new nightmare for public health professionals, because sex workers at risk of sexually transmitted diseases increasingly communicate with clients by phone and travel to a variety of places to ply their trade. This makes them less easy to educate and assist than when they work at regular venues. Illegal gambling is also facilitated, putting chronic users at risk (Mahapatra et al., 2012; Agur, 2015).

These matters of political economy and public safety and health might seem quite foreign to our daily experiences of these pocket-sized devices. Such controversy is like a distant land where rare species of politicians and policy wonks natter on about Apple's tax mischief or prostitution. We are probably more concerned with paying for a new iPhone, sharing videos that show it bend, or demonstrating a fancy new application.

But this political economy is, in reality, very close to home. Apple's shenanigans should matter to us as consumers who want to pay a price based on competition between providers rather than distortion through governmental clientelism. It should also matter to us as citizens and workers. We all play different and sometimes contradictory roles, as parents, cooks, coaches, failures, professors, retirees, authors, Marxists, Luddites, and so on. These various positions both arise from and encourage a commensurately wide array of beliefs, commitments, and experiences. Cultural theorists sometimes call this feature of modern life "multiple subject positions." And helping to demarcate these positions are things like phones – fashion choices that become integral to who we are.

So when we occupy the position of an iPhone customer, it's easy to forget a worker's or citizen's perspective on its industrial origin, manufacture, legal status, and environmental impact. We forget those links to our lives as we pursue the magic and pleasure of consumption. And in that forgetting, large parts of our history are left out.

The noted playwright, dramaturg, and poet Bertolt Brecht, who wrote the lyrics to "Mack the Knife," "The Alabama Song," and "Surabaya-Jonny," produced a moving paean to worker creativity, "Questions from a Worker who Reads," on just this topic (1935). Brecht's question concerned people who work to shape history but are left out of its chronicles, excluded from written records. He juxtaposes leading figures of conventional history with a query about those who enabled their successes but are forgotten. He asks: "Every 10 years a great man. Who paid the bill?" What, we wonder, would "Questions from a Consumer who Texts" reveal about what happens beyond the subject position of the consummate consumer of iThings? Perhaps it might be: "Every two years a new model. Who paid the bill?"

Materiality: Cell Phones and the Environment

> I work like a machine and my brain is rusted – 19-year-old female worker from Guangxi at the Compeq printed circuit board factory in Huizhou City, China. (quoted in Chan and Ho, 2008: 22)

Cell phone design, production, and distribution have significantly augmented toxic elements in the biosphere through lead, mercury, chromium, nickel, beryllium, antimony, and arsenic, as well as such valuable metals as gold, silver, palladium and platinum, tantalum, and flame retardants made of polybrominated diphenyl ethers. *Mother Jones* magazine offers an account of what was inside the iPhone 3GS: where it came from, who made it, and at what cost and risk. The tin used to solder circuit boards netted armed groups in the Democratic Republic of the Congo over US$90 million annually, and the gadget relied on Chinese tungsten mining, Bolivian salt-flats excavation – and monumental exploitation of assembly workers.[14]

Congo has a third of the world's columbite-tantalite (coltan). Over 90 percent of its eastern mines are controlled by militias. They use threats, intimidation, murder, rape, and mutilation to enslave women and children, and buy weapons with the profits. Since the 2000s, more than five million people have perished in the country's civil war. Congolese "conflict" metals and minerals, such as coltan, are exported for smelting in China then mixed with the overall global supply and sold on the international commodities market as tantalum, a core component in capacitors that end up in phones and other electronic equipment (Global Witness, 2009; Montague, 2002; Cox, 2009: 21; Ma, 2009; United Nations Panel of Experts, 2002). Two remarkable documentaries illuminate these horrors: *Blood Coltan* (Patrick Forestier, 2008) and *Blood in the Mobile* (Frank Piasecki Poulsen, 2010), in addition to a video report on cell phones and coltan.[15]

All mobile phones need batteries, which contain poisonous components. As one environmental health scientist warned: "In a phone that you hold in the palm of your hand, you now have more than 200 chemical compounds. To try to separate them out and study what health effects may be associated with burning or sinking it in water – that's a lifetime of work for a toxicologist" (quoted in Mooallem, 2008: 42).

The companies whose names appear on cell phones subcontract their dirty work to miners, cottage assemblers, and manufacturers. The latter undertake approximately 60 percent of cell phone production (GoodElectronics et al., 2009: 19–20). Both the environment and workers are vulnerable to harm throughout the chain. Investigations into Apple's Taiwanese suppliers, Foxconn, found children in China assembling its gadgets, workers exposed to chemical poisoning, and 17 suicides in the first eight months of 2010. Similar conditions exist in India, Mexico, and other offshore assembly sites. When the iPad was launched outside the United States, protestors in Hong Kong responded to the deaths by ritually burning photographs of iPhones (Chan, 2010; Moore, 2010a and 2010b; Barboza, 2011; Balfour and Culpan, 2010; Students & Scholars Against Corporate Misbehaviour, 2010; Kumar and Kumar, 2010; Ribeiro, 2010).[16]

Apple's supplier audits have been notoriously thin on facts about labor violations, including n-hexane poisonings of 137 workers at the factories of Lianjian Technology Group, which manufactures iPhone touch screens. N-hexane poisoning causes damage to the peripheral nervous system, which is extremely painful and leads to numbness in the limbs, chronic weakness, fatigue, and hypersensitivity to heat and cold. In 2010, workers were poisoned while degreasing the Apple logo with n-hexane at the Yuhan Lab Technology Company and the Yun Heng Hardware & Electrical factory. Both subcontractors were among dozens of "suspected Apple suppliers" poisoning workers and polluting surrounding communities in China, according to the Beijing-based Institute of Public and Environmental Affairs (2011).

When 许立志 (Xu Lizhi), a Foxconn employee, committed suicide in 2014 after four years working the line to produce cell phones and other media devices, his friends collected his poetry for publication in a newspaper. The alienation, disappointment, and boredom of making Apple's treasures resonated with young workers across the country (Dou, 2014; Nao, 2014).[17] The parent firm has generated intense annoyance because of its secret ways, to the point where 贾跃亭 (Jia Yueting), billionaire head of the Leshi online video site, tastelessly likens Apple to Hitler.[18]

The semiconductor, the heart of all electronic equipment, is produced by hundreds of companies around the world for a market dominated by Intel, Samsung Electronics, Toshiba Electronics, Texas Instruments, Qualcomm, and ADM. A single semiconductor facility may require 832 million cubic feet of bulk gases, 5.72 million cubic feet of hazardous gases, 591 million gallons of deionized water, 5.2 million pounds of chemicals, including acids and solvents, and 8.8 million kilowatt hours of electrical power. Semiconductor workers are potentially exposed to skin irritants, acids that harm mucous and pulmonary tissue, and chemicals that can cause cancer, reproductive complications, and debilitating illnesses. The durable half-life of toxic waste emitted into the soil from semiconductor plants leaves groundwater and land unusable or highly dangerous for populations who live atop them long after culpable firms have departed. Entire communities like Endicott, New York – the original home of IBM – have seen their aquifer and soil cursed with such carcinogenic compounds as trichloroethylene (a solvent) that will remain active for decades (Silicon Valley Toxics Coalition, n.d.; E. Grossman 2006: 109–11).

The extraction and processing of raw materials – the chemicals and minerals in cell phones – are responsible for lasting biophysical harm. Data from the Norwegian silicon-carbide industry's smelters indicate elevated risks of stomach and lung cancer by contrast with the wider population as a consequence of exposure to crystalline silica, dust fibers, and silicon carbide particles (Romundstad et al., 2001).

Phone mobility is also responsible for rising energy consumption. A recent study estimates that 90 percent of the total energy consumed by mobile connections is attributable to wireless access providers – not counting the energy used by the devices themselves. Another 9 percent can be linked to data-center energy use (Centre for Energy-Efficient Telecommunications et al., 2013). That may not seem like a lot, but the aggregated electricity consumed globally by data centers – the core of today's cloud computing – is somewhere between the total amount of energy that India and Japan use annually (Greenpeace, 2012). One hour of video streaming to an individual mobile device via the cloud requires more electricity than two new refrigerators (Mills, 2013), and the International Energy Agency (2014) estimates that US$80 billion was wasted on powering mobile devices in 2014 when in standby mode – more than Canada's annual energy use. All told, the energy used by consumer electronics worldwide reached 15 percent of the residential electricity load in 2009. It is on target to reach 30 percent of global energy demand by 2022 and 45 percent by 2030. So mobile connectivity is one of the fastest growing contributors to atmospheric climate change (Smith, 2010; Mouawad and Galbraith, 2009; International Energy Agency, 2009: 5, 21; Climate Group, 2008: 18–23; Hancock, 2009; Organisation for Economic Co-Operation and Development, 2010: 19; Greenpeace, 2012).

Telecommunications companies have built an inefficient infrastructure that cannot be easily, or cheaply, replaced. And public policy has been rigged to relieve corporations from the obligation to make that infrastructure greener and more affordable. The big telecommunications multinationals certainly understand that this level of energy consumption is a threat to both the environment and their continuing market domination. Their response has focused so far on technical fixes, with some deceptively playful interactive tools, but little concern for the wider public interest.[19] These companies concentrate on raising demand, working against environmental regulation, and keeping their place in the growing market for green-branded, 'smart" technologies.[20]

Such short-sightedness is in keeping with the strange status of clouds by contrast with their predecessors, the telephone exchanges and post offices that we referred to earlier. Unlike those very public spaces, the cloud hides its private ownership – in fact its very existence – behind a metaphor of ephemerality. Clouds come and go, like private investment. You could blink and miss them. How many of us know where our nearest data centers are, let alone their environmental impact? They are in huge buildings, just like the old post offices and telephone exchanges, but they don't say what they are. Instead, they appear metaphorically as a crucial natural form floating above us, ready to bring needed water to our world or sustain our Google searches.

Then there is the thorny issue of the health impact of cell phone use. Mobile phones report their location to cell towers every 900 milliseconds in modulated bursts of radiation. In that moment, whether people are using their phones or not, the radiation becomes critical. If it's close to their bodies, they are absorbing it. Most independent research looking into this problem – i.e., studies that do not receive funding from the telecommunications or electronics industries – has linked this exposure to cancer, reproductive difficulties, brain and nervous system problems, and sleep disruption (Jacobson, 2013).

Unsurprisingly, research that finds few or no negative health effects tends to be the product of corporate-financed studies – part of a global "doubt industry" that disputes the legitimacy of research showing evidence of harm. Hired skeptics work to muddy public thinking with the claim that there are two sides to the story. The "war-gaming" of mobile phone science – attacking any evidence of harm – worked well for the tobacco corporations for many years, until industry hacks and the hacking coughers they cultivated could no longer deny that these products caused sickness and death (Davis, 2013).

The Italian Supreme Court was the first to challenge the mobile industry's war-gaming tactic. In 2012, it ordered Italian authorities to pay workers' compensation to a former businessman who developed a tumor in his head because of heavy, long-term use of his cell phone. The court threw out industry-funded studies on the grounds that they were tainted by conflict of interest. It accepted independent research that found a causal link between mobile phone use and cancer (Giuliani et al., 2012).[21]

European health agencies have issued many warnings about cell phone radiation exposure. Regulators in several countries have recommended caution to adult users and extreme caution for children, pending ongoing research. The French Senate has proposed legislation to ban cell phone use by children under the age of 6 and advertising directed to children under the age of 12 (Sénat français, 2009). The European Parliament's resolution on health concerns associated with electromagnetic fields (INI/2008/2211) affirms potential risks from a range of wireless electronic devices, including Wi-Fi/WiMAX, Bluetooth, and cordless landline phones. It calls for campaigns to educate citizens in the safe use of electronics and avoidance of transmission towers and high-voltage power lines.

The International Commission on Non-Ionizing Radiation Protection has appealed for public policy to set limits on "simultaneous exposure" to multiple electronic devices. The European Environment Agency followed up a major scientific review by the Bioinitiative Working Group on radiation from wi-fi, cell phones, and their masts in 2007 by announcing that action was needed lest the latest fad end up as damned for its health impact as lead and tobacco in the previous century (Lean, 2008; Organisation for Economic Co-Operation and Development, 2007; Environmental Working Group, 2009: 3–4, 18–22, 28,).

The WHO's International Agency for Research on Cancer advises that the family of frequencies that includes cell phone emissions "is possibly carcinogenic to humans." The US National Cancer Institute adds that, while studies have not proven that cell phones can cause cancer, additional research is needed because these technologies are changing so quickly. And the American Academy of Pediatrics has called on the US government's Federal Communications Commission and Food and Drug Administration to revise electromagnetic frequency standards to account for different peoples' vulnerability to cancer from cell phones, notably pregnant women and children (McInerney, 2013).

There are further risks to consider. In 2013, 25 percent of automobile accidents in the United States were caused by cell phone distraction, and 52 percent of fatal crashes were related. These are the reported figures; the actual number may be much higher, according to safety experts. Similarly, over the past 10 years, there has been an exponential increase of injuries credited to pedestrians using cell phones walking distractedly into traffic, lampposts, and other people (Copeland, 2013; Nasar and Troyer, 2013). We've all dodged them; we've all been one of them.

About 130 million cell phones are trashed each year in the United States alone, where people purchase replacements annually. And when old and obsolete cell phones are junked, just like other communication technologies, they become e-waste. E-waste recyclers are exposed to heavy metals (lead, cadmium, and mercury, among others) dioxin emitted by burning wires insulated with polyvinylchloride, flame retardants in circuit boards and plastic casings containing polychlorinated biphenyls or newer brominated compounds, and poisonous fumes emitted while melting electronic parts for precious metals such as copper and gold. Cell phones can be found in this dangerous discarded state throughout the traditional sites selected by the wealthy to dispose of their detritus: Latin America, Africa, and Asia (Leung et al., 2008; Wong et al., 2007; Ray et al., 2004; Ha et al., 2010; Secretaría Federal de Asuntos Económicos, 2008; Inform, 2008). These issues are graphically illustrated in the BBC *Panorama* program on illegal e-waste recycling in West Africa, where 77 percent of British e-waste goes and the US current-affairs show *60 Minutes*' harrowing account from China.[22]

Table 5.1 Global personal computer market by territory, second quarter 2011 and forecast 2011 and 2012

Territory	2Q11% share	2011% share	2012% share
China	22.0	20.3	21.8
US	21.0	20.6	19.6
Others	57.1	59.1	58.5

Source: http://www.idc.com

This North–South asymmetry is changing as India and China generate their own detritus. In terms of computer purchase, for example, the trends at mid-2011 are shown in table 5.1.

So-called emergent markets have startling e-waste implications in their mimesis and expansion of Yanqui excess; India, for instance, rings in its newfound wealth with 8–10 million new cell phone subscriptions a month, drawing on diesel-fueled power sources to compensate for the absence of a functioning national grid.[23] The other major change under way is that intensive use of the internet by phones means they are increasingly responsible for destruction of the climate through the multiple powerful energy sources needed for such access (Suckling and Lee, 2015).

Cell phones are also perilous to wildlife. Phone masts kill tens of millions birds annually in the United States, affecting more than 200 species, and erode animals' natural defenses, health, reproduction norms, and habitat. Between 1990 and 2000, the number of cell towers and antennae in the United States grew to 130,000; 40,000 towers were 200 feet tall, and many reached 1,000 feet (United States Fish and Wildlife Service, 1999; Wikle, 2002: 46; Broad, 2007; Schoenfeld, 2007; Krasnow and Solomon, 2008: 50, 62–3; Balmori, 2009; Pourlis, 2009; Eilperin, 2013).[24]

Conclusion

> She hung up before he could say goodbye. Stood there with her arm cocked, phone at ear-level, suddenly aware of the iconic nature of her unconscious pose. Some very considerable part of the gestural language of public places, that had once belonged to cigarettes, now belonged to phones. Human figures, a block down the street, in postures utterly familiar, were no longer smoking. (Gibson, 2010: 103)

The cell phone generates affect, money, detritus, and disease. It appears to consumers as a discrete object of material culture, but through its life causes harm to far-flung natural and biophysical environments as its by-products travel the earth via a NICL comprising slaves, miners, smelters, assembly and transport workers, consumers, salvagers, and recyclers. Human and nonhuman organisms endure similar burdens to those that were caused by older industrial products and processes – from smokestacks and chemico-mechanical methods dependent on abundant sources of electrical energy to the spreading sediment of poisonous waste.

Cell phones clearly exercise a special hold on much of the public imagination. But there is a wider question here about the new and enduring freedom, pleasure, and – above all – faith that accompany digital gadgetry, particularly via mobile privatization. That faith makes it especially difficult to find a secular view of technology, one that refutes the totemic, quasi-sacred power that industrial societies have all too frequently ascribed to modern machinery.

In the nineteenth century, people were supposedly governed by electrical impulses. Telegraphy was conceived of as a physical manifestation of intellect that linked the essence of humanity to communicative labor. In the early twentieth century, radio waves were said to move across the ether, a mystical substance that could contact the dead and cure cancer. During the interwar period, it was claimed that the human sensorium had been retrained by technology. By the 1950s and 1960s, machines were thought to embody and even control consciousness.

This mad mixture of science and magic continues into our own digital culture: cyber-enthusiasts fetishize each new "upgrade" as if it could reboot their identity into a perpetual now-ness. Two decades ago, this frenzy was captured on video as people lined up to buy the Windows 95 operating system, amid Microsoft's advertising futurism.[25] Today, the excitement gathers around a different firm's wizardry; tomorrow it will be yet another . . .

Tim Cook, Apple's CEO since 2011, decrees "we are in business to empower and enrich our customers' lives" (2015). He's right. An improbable blend of the awesome with the aesthetic, the sublime, and the beautiful, has made the firm's commodities unprecedentedly successful since the early 2000s, as its targeted consumers have transmogrified from geeks and artists to middlebrow wannabe hipsters. And, as the screenwriter Aaron Sorkin said, "if you've got a factory full of children in China assembling phones for 17 cents an hour, you've got a lot of nerve" (quoted in Ritman, 2015).

The built-in obsolescence carved out by those workers is just as central to these triumphs as any notion of meeting customer needs. iPod batteries are made to last a year, iPhones can be recharged a finite number of times, and most established iPod sleeves and holders do not fit new versions, because the built-in obsolescence mandated for and by Apple designers requires that customers keep buying replacement technology. The sleek, minimalist design of smart phones appears to offer a world of wonder within, like the police box in the long-running TV series *Dr Who* (1963-89, 2005-) that opens up to disclose a huge machine capable of transporting people across time and space.

Before we get carried away with the metaphor, consider its more potent meaning: this bit of magic is precisely how corporations merchandise consumer media technologies – they promise transcendence from both our daily lives and the technology's dirty industrial origins. The supply of new designs from phone companies seems unlimited, along with their ability to stimulate demand and overproduction through imitation as the supposedly "virtuous circle" sees expensive prototypes copied more cheaply once a market has been established (Arrighi, 2007). New models arrive in packages of wonder that offer to transport people across time and space. Repetitive purchasing is seemingly undertaken each time as a novelty, governed by what Benjamin called, in his awkward but occasionally illuminating prose, "the ever-always-the-same" of "mass-production," cloaked in "a hitherto unheard-of significance" (1985: 48).

We can shake off such media studies 2.0 magic if we treat innovation skeptically, questioning the planned obsolescence that confuses an abundance of i-Things with wellbeing and creativity. We gain something in return: a connection to the present where we can comprehend the deplorable working conditions that bring these media-technology wonders into the world, and their ecological impact.

To assist in achieving that end, this chapter has sought to follow the life of the cell phone. Due to the heavy, heady environmental implications of this deadly yet playful apparatus, political-economic method has been inflected with environmental studies. The record exposes contradictory interpretations of the cell phone's meaning and value. The utopian love affair with this latest wonder of communication technology evokes ancestral cries for community, progress, and freedom. Dystopian perspectives resonate with past techno-critical skepticism and research, focusing on the dangers of social fragmentation and intensified command-and-control functions created by machines that have become emblematic of twenty-first-century modernity.

Recognizing the multifaceted material paradoxes and contradictions posed by these newest of toys is a crucial task for our present and future. Having looked at what used to be of minimal interest to many – how telephones work – but has been transformed into a dangerous international love affair *of* all and *for* all, in chapter 6, we look at perhaps the longest-standing and most fraught love affair of all – the United States and the world.

6 The United States of America as Global Media Behemoth

(with Bill Grantham)

If mobile telephony, discussed in the previous chapter, appears to put technological power in the hands, ears, and mouths of the multitude, this chapter grapples with what for many remains the principal quandary of much global media – the textual and technological power of the United States to enter those same bodies.[1] This power is far from a supposedly neutral mechanism like a phone (though we have seen that the mobile phone is far from a benign transmitter). It is a signifier of Yanqui entertainment and propaganda on a truly global scale that necessitates revisiting issues of cultural imperialism and the trade in screen drama, along with the NICL.

We are endlessly being told that the era of US dominance is over. But while we acknowledge the rise of other powerful countries – China, India, Brazil, Turkey, etc. – and the expansion of their media footprints, the data endlessly show that the twenty-first century is as American as the one preceding it.

For example, China has been moved effortlessly into the center of Hollywood's overseas sales as its reserve army of productive labor becomes matched by a reserve army of audience labor. In the words of *The Economist*, "more middle-class movie-goers are being minted every day."[2] The Motion Picture Association of America (2014), the peak body representing the major studios, notes that Hollywood receipts around the world "reached $36.4 billion in 2014." Chinese box office increased by 34 percent, "the first international market to exceed $4 billion in box office."[3] The People's Republic of China (PRC) accounted for 16 percent of Hollywood's international receipts in 2015 (Cain, 2015). By contrast, TV sales from China to the United States in 2013 were worth well under five million dollars.[4]

The intimate interpenetration of nation, state, ideology, and capital via the culture industries swirls around such success. It is perhaps best expressed in the anecdote with which Ed Halter (2006) begins his journalistic history of computer games – the moment in 2003 when Los Angeles was occupied by US Special Forces. Just two months after the start of their ill-starred imperialist venture in Iraq had begun, these troops invaded LA's Convention Center as part of Electronic Entertainment Exposition, the annual showcase of video games. Their mission was to promote *America's Army* (2002), an electronic game designed to recruit young people to the service of the state via simulated first-person shooting. The game included notes to parents that stressed the importance of substituting "virtual experiences for vicarious insights" (quoted in Halter, 2006: viii–ix) – an exciting euphemism for "cyber-boot camp" (Lenoir, 2003: 175).

The Special Forces were enacting a marketing triumph in LA rather than a military one; but they symbolized a malignant amalgam of state violence and commercial entertainment. For the media have become part of perpetual virtual war by mixing hyper-masculinist action-adventure ideology, supinely celebratory military news

Table 6.1 Hollywood films that have earned $1 billion in global box office

Rank	Title	Studio	Release Year	Box Office ($mm)			
				Worldwide ($)	Domestic ($)	China ($)	China % of WW
1	Avatar	Fox	2009*	2,788	761	204	7.3
2	Titanic	Paramount	1997*	2,187	659	199	9.1
3	Marvel's The Avengers	Disney	2012	1,519	623	86	5.7
4	Furious 7**	Universal	2015	1,469	341	389	26.5
5	Harry Potter and the Deathly Hallows Part 2	WB	2011	1,342	381	61	4.5
6	Frozen	Disney	2013	1,274	401	48	3.8
7	Iron Man 3	Disney	2013	1,215	409	121	10.0
8	§ Transformers: Dark of the Moon	Paramount	2011	1,124	352	165	14.7
9	The Lord of the Rings: The Return of the King	New Line	2003*	1,120	378	10	0.9
10	Skyfall	Sony	2012	1,109	304	59	5.3
11	§ Transformers: Age of Extinction	Paramount	2014	1,104	245	320	29.0
12	The Dark Knight Rises	WB	2012	1,084	448	53	4.9
13	† Pirates of the Caribbean: Dead Man's Chest	Disney	2006	1,066	423	0	0.0
14	Toy Story 3	Disney	2010	1,063	415	17	1.6
15	§ Pirates of the Caribbean: On Stranger Tides	Disney	2011	1,046	241	70	6.7
16	§ Jurassic Park	Universal	1993*	1,029	403	57	5.6
17	† Star Wars: Episode 1 – The Phantom Menace	Fox	1999*	1,027	475	0	0.0
18	† Alice in Wonderland (2010)	Disney	2010	1,026	334	0	0.0
19	§ The Hobbit: An Unexpected Journey	WB	2012	1,017	303	50	4.9
20	† The Dark Knight	WB	2008*	1,005	535	0	0.0
21	§ Avengers: Age of Ultron**	Disney	2015	1,000	343	150	15.0

Source: Boxofficemojo.com, Pacific Bridge Advisors research
* Indicates moves that earned their box office gross over multiple releases
** Indicates moves still in release
§ Films that needed China to reach $1 billion
† Films not released in China

coverage, and complicit new media (Deck, 2004). Their method is at once collective – we are the United States and we're here to intimidate and destroy – and individual, thanks to the immersive interpellation of narrative film, current affairs, and gaming. They are crucial components of the necessarily ongoing, incomplete project of constructing the nation as natural, a project undertaken through the diurnal and the cinematic, the banal and the spectacular (Puri, 2004).

This chapter begins by considering how the imperial agenda of the United States is enabled and legitimized through cinema, news and current affairs, and electronic games. Second, we go beyond that very ideological textual analysis to examine the who, what, when, where, and how of Hollywood producing – the NICL at play, as it were. Our hope is that this will give readers a material study of these phenomena that can engage the political dimension (and dementia) of texts and the mundanity of production – an example of media studies 3.0 at work.

Cinema

Cinema may well be the model for the propagandistic simulation of US culture and nationalism in general. The government has a long history of direct participation in production and control (Hearon, 1938). The notorious racist epic, *Birth of a Nation* (D. W. Griffith, 1915), was given official military support by order of the Secretary of War, while the so-called Western genre is a triumphalist enactment of racialization and genocide (Shapiro, 2004). From the moment the United States entered World War I, theaters across the country featured speakers and movies that purported to testify to German atrocities, while films from the Central Powers were banned (Turse, 2008: 104; Andersen, 2006: 7).

Immediately afterwards, the Department of the Interior recruited the industry to its policy of "Americanization" of immigrants (Walsh, 1997: 10), screening Hollywood movies on ships bringing migrants (Hays, 1927: 50). Paramount-Famous-Lasky studio executive Sidney R. Kent proudly referred to cinema as "silent propaganda" (1927: 208).

In the 1920s and '30s, Hollywood lobbyists regarded the US Departments of State and Commerce as its "message boys": the State Department undertook market research and shared business intelligence, while the Commerce Department pressured other countries to permit cinema free access and favorable terms of trade. In the 1940s, the United States opened an Office of the Coordinator of Inter-American Affairs (OCIAA) to gain solidarity in Latin America for World War II. Its most visible program was the Motion Picture Division, headed by John Hay Whitney, recently co-producer of *Gone with the Wind* (Victor Fleming, 1939) and future secret agent and front man for the CIA's news service, Forum World Features (Stonor Saunders, 1999: 311–12). The OCIAA had at least one Hollywood film reshot because it showed Mexican children shoeless in the street, and was responsible for getting Hollywood to distribute *Simón Bolívar* (Miguel Contreras Torres, 1942) and produce *Saludos Amigos* (Wilfred Jackson, Jack Kinney, Hamilton Luske, and Bill Roberts, 1943) and *The Three Caballeros* (Norman Ferguson, Clyde Geronimi, Jack Kinney, Bill Roberts, and Harold Young, 1944). Some production costs were borne by the OCIAA in exchange for free prints being distributed in US embassies and consulates across the region; Whitney even accompanied Walt Disney and Donald Duck to Rio de Janeiro (Powdermaker, 1950: 71; Kahn, 1981: 145).

During the invasion of Europe in 1944 and 1945, the military closed Axis films, shuttered the industry, and insisted on the release of US movies. The quid pro quo for the Marshall Plan was the abolition of customs restrictions, amongst which were limits on film imports (Trumpbour, 2002: 3–4, 62, 63, 98; Pauwels and Loisen, 2003: 293). In the case of Japan, the occupation immediately changed the face of cinema. When theaters reopened after the United States dropped its atomic bombs, all films and posters with war themes were gone. The occupying troops established an Information Dissemination Section in their Psychological Warfare Branch to imbue the local population with guilt and "teach American values." Previously censored Hollywood texts dominated screens (High 2003: 503–4).

The film industry's peak association at this time referred to itself as "the little State Department," so isomorphic were its methods and ideology with US policy and politics. This was also the era when Hollywood's self-censoring Production Code appended to its bizarre litany of sexual and narcotic prohibitions and requirements two items requested by the "other" State Department: selling the American way of life around the world, and avoiding negative representations of "a foreign country with which we have cordial relations" (Powdermaker, 1950: 36).

Meanwhile, with the Cold War under way, the CIA's Psychological Warfare Workshop employed future Watergate criminal E. Howard Hunt, who clandestinely funded the rights purchase and film production of Orwell's anti-Soviet novels *Animal Farm* (Joy Batchelor and Jon Halas, 1954) and *1984* (Michael Andersen, 1956) (Cohen, 2003). Producer Walter Wanger trumpeted this meshing of what he called "Donald Duck and Diplomacy" as "a Marshall Plan for ideas ... a veritable celluloid Athens," because the state needed Hollywood "more than ... the H bomb" (1950: 444, 446). Industry head Eric Johnston, fresh from his prior post as Secretary of Commerce, saw himself dispatching "messengers from a free country." President Harry Truman agreed, referring to movies as "ambassadors of goodwill" (quoted in Johnston, 1950; also see Hozic, 2001: 77).

The US Information Service spread its lending library of films across the globe as part of Cold War expansion. President John F. Kennedy instructed the Service to use film and television to propagandize, and his administration funded 226 film centers in 106 countries, equipped with 7,541 projectors. The title of a Congressional Legislative Research Service 1964 report made the point bluntly: *The US Ideological Effort: Government Agencies and Programs* (Lazarsfeld 1950: xi; Legislative Research Service 1964: 9, 19). That impulse has been renewed: four decades later, union officials soberly intoned that "[a]lthough the Cold War is no longer a reason to protect cultural identity, today US-produced pictures are still a conduit through which our values, such as democracy and freedom, are promoted" (Ulrich and Simmers 2001: 365).

Then there is the Defense Department. Since World War II, the Pentagon has provided technology, soldiers, and settings in return for a jealously guarded right to veto assistance to any Hollywood story that offends its sensibilities (Robb, 2004). Today's hybrid of SiliWood (Silicon Valley and Hollywood) blends northern Californian technology, Hollywood methods, and military funding. The interactivity underpinning this hybrid has evolved through the articulation since the mid-1980s of southern and northern California semiconductor and computer manufacture and systems and software development (a massively military-inflected and -supported industry until after Cold War II) to Hollywood screen content, as disused aircraft-production hangars became entertainment sites. The links are as much about technology, personnel, and collaboration on ancillary projects as they are about storylines. Stephen Spielberg is a recipient of the Pentagon's Medal for Distinguished Public Service; Silicon Graphics feverishly designs material for use by the empire in both its military and cultural aspects; and virtual reality research veers between soldierly and audience applications, much of it subsidized by the Federal Technology Reinvestment Project and Advanced Technology Program. This has further submerged killing machines from public scrutiny, even as they surface superficially, doubling as Hollywood props (Directors Guild of America, 2000; Hozic, 2001: 140–1, 148–51). Nye's soft power distinction that we encountered in chapter 2 seems problematic – Hollywood is both soft and hard.

Simplistic textual reflectionism, which argues that cowboy-style heroes have not appeared in Hollywood since 2001 as unproblematic message boys of imperialism (Douthat, 2008) misses the point. The film industry sprang into militaristic action in concert with state preferences after September 11, 2001, and even became a consultant on possible attacks. And with the National Aeronautics and Space Administration keen to renovate its image, who better to invite to lunch than Hollywood producers, in the hope that their next releases would portray it as benign and exciting? Why not form a "White House–Hollywood Committee" while you're at it, to ensure coordination between the nations we bomb and the messages we export? The CIA set up formal liaison with Hollywood in 1995. Because it has few spectacular assets by contrast with the Defense Department's ships, guns, and planes, the Agency encourages the writing and selection of scripts that portray it favorably (Jenkins, 2009). The very week before the 2001 attacks on the United States, the *New York Times* previewed the coming fall TV drama schedule with the headline "Hardest-Working Actor of the Season: The CIA" (Bernstein, 2001; also see Cohen, 2001) because three prime time shows were made under the aegis of the Agency. In the process, profound contradictions between pursuing profit and violence versus civility get washed away, their instrumentalism erased in favor of dramatic re-enchantment as a supposedly higher moral purpose expressed in nation and valor (Behnke, 2006).

Television

In this context, it comes as no surprise that nationalistic militarism also colors the way that US television covers news and current affairs, since the private media are in step with more formal, state-based propaganda. Consider the coverage of civilian casualties in imperialist conflicts since 2001.

Lawrence Eagleburger, a former Secretary of State, who was called in to comment by CNN after the September 2001 attacks on the United States, said: "There is only one way to begin to deal with people like this, and that is you have to kill some of them even if they are not immediately directly involved," while Republican Party house intellectual Ann Coulter called on the government to identify the nations where terrorists lived, "invade their countries, kill their leaders and convert them to Christianity."[5] Coulter was also the author of the notorious rebuke on TV to a disabled Vietnam veteran: "People like you caused us to lose that war." She proceeded to propose that the right "physically intimidate liberals, by making them realize that they can be killed too" as well as informing Fox News watchers and magazine readers that liberals desire "lots of 9/11s" and "Arabs lie" (quoted in Alterman, 2003: 3–5). Coulter's reward for such hyperbolic ignorance was frequent appearances on NBC, CNN, MSNBC, ABC, and HBO, *inter alia* (Alterman, 2003: 5; FAIR, 2005).

When the assault commenced, desperate Afghans in refugee camps were filmed by the BBC, which sold the footage to ABC. The soundtrack to the two versions that were broadcast had incompatible meanings:

> British media presented the camps as consisting of refugees from US bombing who said that fear of the daily bombing attacks had driven them out of the city, whereas US media presented the camps as containing refugees from Taliban oppression and the dangers of civil war. (Kellner, 2003: 125)

CNN instructed presenters to mention September 11 each time Afghan suffering was discussed, and Walter Isaacson, the network's president, decreed that it was "perverse to focus too much on the casualties or hardship" (quoted in Kellner, 2003: 107, 66).

As the 2003 invasion of Iraq loomed, Rupert Murdoch said: "there is going to be collateral damage . . . if you really want to be brutal about it, better we get it done now" (quoted in Pilger, 2003). The human impact of the invasion was dismissed by Public Broadcasting Service *News Hour* executive producer Lester Crystal as not "central at the moment" (quoted in Sharkey, 2003). Fox News managing editor Brit Hume said civilian casualties may not belong on television, as they are "historically, by definition, a part of war." In the fortnight prior to the invasion, none of the three major commercial networks examined the humanitarian impact of such an action. Human Rights Watch's briefing paper, and a UN Undersecretary-General's warning on the topic, lay uncovered (FAIR, 2003a).

US viewers were treated to a carnival of *matériel* that oscillated between glorifying and denying death that privileged the technological sublime. In all, 38 percent of CNN's coverage of the bombardment emphasized technology, while 62 percent focused on military activity, without referring to history or politics. In the rest of the world's media coverage of the Afghan and Iraqi crises, invasions, and occupations, such military maneuvers and odes took second place to civilian suffering. Al-Jazeera, for example, dedicated only a third of its stories to war footage, emphasizing human distress over electronic effectiveness, vernacular reportage rather than patriotic euphemism. But thousands of civilian Afghan and Iraqi deaths reported by it and South Asian, Southeast Asian, Western European, and other Arab world news services went essentially unnoticed in the United States (Lewis *et al.* 2004: 14; Rich, 2003; Jasperson and El-Kikhia 2003: 119, 126-27; Herold, 2001; Flanders, 2001; Kellner 2004: 334; della Cava, 2003; Greenberg, 2003).

More than half the US TV studio guests talking about the impending action in Iraq in 2003 were superannuated white male war pundits (FAIR, 2003b), "ex-military men, terrorism experts, and Middle Eastern policy analysts who know none of the relevant languages, may never have seen any part of the Middle East, and are too poorly educated to be expert at anything" (Said, 2003). During the war, news effectively diminished the dominant discourse to technical efficiency and state propaganda. Of 319 people giving "analysis" on ABC, CBS, and NBC in October 2003, 76 percent were current or previous officials. Of the civilians, 79 percent were Republican Party mavens. In all, 81 percent of sources were Yanquis (Whiten, 2004; Rendall and Butterworth, 2004; Grand Rapids Institute for Information Democracy, 2005).

The *New York Times* refers to these has-been and never-were interviewees like this: "[p]art experts and part reporters, they're marketing tools, as well" (Jensen, 2003). But their virtually universal links to arms-trading were rarely divulged, and never discussed as relevant. Retired Lieutenant General Barry McCaffrey, employed in this capacity by NBC News, pointed to the *cadre*'s "lifetime of experience and objectivity." In his case, this involved membership of the Committee for the Liberation of Iraq, a lobby group dedicated to influencing the media, and the boards of three munitions companies that make ordnance he had praised on MSNBC. Even among the thoroughly ideologized US public, 36 percent believed the media overemphasized the opinions of these retirees (Roy, 2004; Benaim at al., 2003; Pew Research Center for the People and the Press 2004: 15).[6] Perhaps the most relevant number to consider is that the company that owned MSNBC and NBC at the time, General Electric, is one of the largest defense contractors in the world. It receives billions of dollars from the Pentagon each year. Disney (which owns ABC) is also a beneficiary of largesse from the Department of Defense (Turse, 2008: 3).

In addition to these complex domestic imbrications of the private and public sectors, the US government attempts to limit the expression of alternative positions on world television. To hide the carnage of its 2001 invasion, the Pentagon bought exclusive rights to satellite photos of Afghanistan (Solomon, 2001; Magder, 2003: 38). And consider its treatment of al-Jazeera. The US State Department tried to disrupt the network by putting pressure on Qatar's Emir Sheikh Hamid bin Khalifa al-Thaniof, and the channel's Washington correspondent was "detained" en route to a US-Russia summit in November 2001 (International Federation of Journalists, 2001: 20; Hafez, 2002; el-Nawawy and Gher, 2003; Miladi, 2003: 159). Al-Jazeera offices were assaulted by US munitions in Afghanistan in 2001 (where it was the sole broadcast news outlet in Kabul) and in Iraq in 2003, and the network was subject to then-Secretary of Defense Donald Rumsfeld's denunciation of it as "Iraqi propaganda" and the Bush regime's ignorant and insulting moniker: "All Osama All the Time." Throughout the US occupation of Iraq, al-Jazeera workers were subject to violent assaults by US soldiers, culminating in murders. Rear Admiral Craig Quigley, then US Deputy Assistant Defense Secretary for Public Affairs but soon to be one of the legion of superannuated officers working for the arms industry, justified the attack on the network's Kabul operations with the claim that al-Qaeda interests were being aided by activities going on there. Quigley's nutty proof was that al-Jazeera was using a satellite uplink and was in contact with Taliban officials – pretty normal activities for a news service (T. Miller, 2007).

The US government selected Grace Digital Media to beam an Arabic-language satellite television news service into post-invasion Iraq in direct opposition to al-Jazeera. A fundamentalist Christian company, Grace described itself as "dedicated to transmitting the evidence of God's presence in the world today" via "secular news, along with aggressive proclamations that will 'change the news' to reflect the Kingdom of God" (quoted in Mokhiber and Weissman, 2003). It fell apart in controversial circumstances, swallowed up by God TV.

Alternative voices in Iraq were discouraged. The Associated Press managing editors sent an open letter of protest to the Pentagon, noting that "journalists have been harassed, have had their lives endangered and have had digital camera disks, videotape and other equipment confiscated" by the US military.[7]

Many observers of US media coverage of the Afghan and Iraq wars argued that "we got our media back" after the chaos wrought on the US Gulf Coast by Hurricane Katrina in 2005 – that the catastrophe marked a recognition by the mainstream press corps that the administration was mendacious and incompetent, having sacrificed objective technocracy at the font of post-secular enchantment. That may be so – but the real test will come the next time the United States is invading somewhere, and pre-textual alibis are scant and spurious. The omens remain poor. For at this moment of putative rediscovery of truth and reason, the media continue to deliver falsehoods that have a huge impact on the public.

In 2008, CBS conducted a high-profile interview with the man who had been a US military interrogator of Saddam Hussein prior to the fallen dictator's execution. The segment was predicated on Hussein's alleged failure to admit that there were no weapons of mass destruction in Iraq prior to the 2003 invasion, which was explained as a puzzling error that had led to war. But Hussein had been interviewed on that very network five years earlier, days before the struggle began, assuring viewers that there were no such weapons. Quite clearly, CBS was seeking to give the US government a free pass after the event, rewriting its own archival history. And on the issue of Iraqis killed in the war, the valid statistical work done by top epidemiologists continues to be suppressed across TV news and current affairs. Hundreds of thousands of Iraqis have died, according to these estimates. But as at February 2007, in the eyes of the credulous US public, the Iraqi casualty figure was below 10,000 (FAIR, 2008; McElwee, 2008; Roberts et al., 2004).

Games

In addition to punditry, the Iraq war offered other money-making opportunities to superannuated veterans of imperialistic nationalism. Visitors to the Fox News site on May 31, 2004 encountered a "grey zone." On one side of the page, a US soldier in battle gear prowled the streets of Baghdad. On the other, a *Terror Handbook* promised to facilitate "Understanding and facing the threat to America," under the banner: "*WAR ON TERROR sponsored by* KUMA WAR" (a major gaming company). The *Kuma: War* game includes online missions entitled "Fallujah: Operation al Fajr," "Battle in Sadr City," and "Uday and Qusay's Last Stand." The legitimacy and realism are underwritten by the fact that the firm is run by retired military officers, and used as a recruiting tool by their former colleagues. Both sides benefit from the company's website, which invites soldiers to pen their battlefield experiences – a neat way of getting intellectual property gratis in the name of the nation (Deck, 2004; Power, 2007: 272; Turse, 2008: 137). The site boasts that: "Kuma War is a series of playable recreations of real events in the War on Terror. Nearly 100 playable missions bring our soldiers' heroic stories to life, and you can get them all right now, for free. Stop watching the news and get in the game!" Once again, a technological sublime that fetishizes *matériel* is doing dread work (Andersen, 2006: 296).

Many critics have expressed shock that US journalists embedded with the US military for the Iraq invasion said the experience was "like a video game" (quoted in Power, 2007: 271). They shouldn't have been so taken aback, because gaming is crucial to war and vice versa. War games became systematic training practices in the late nineteenth century at the US Naval War College, as simulations of Prussian and French field tactics. Such methods gained popularity after remarkable success in predicting the Japanese campaign in the Pacific from 1942. By the late 1950s, computers were utilized to theorize and simulate battles (Der Derian, 2003: 38–9). Game theory in 1960s and '70s political science and warcraft sought to scientize the study and practice of crisis decision-making, founded on a rational actor model of maximizing utility that was reapplied to the conduct of states, soldiers, and diplomats to construct nuclear war prospects and counters. Then, with the decline of Keynesianism, game theory's ideal-typical monadic subject came to dominate economics and political science more generally. Utility maximization even overtook parts of Marxism, which had tended to favor collective rather than selfish models of choice. Games were in, everywhere you looked.

And many electronic games were invented for the US military by defense contractors. The Pentagon worked with Atari to develop *Battlezone* (1980), an arcade game, for use by fighter pilots, at the same time as it established a gaming center within the National Defense University (Power, 2007: 276). In the early 1990s, the end of Cold War II wrought economic havoc on many corporations involved in the US defense industry. They turned to gaming as a natural supplement to their principal customer, the military. Today's new geopolitical crisis sees numerous firms (Quantum 3-D, Martin Marietta, and so on) conducting half their games business with the private market and half with the Pentagon (Hall, 2006).

The US military, that mismanaged, misdirected, but masterful behemoth that underpins globalization, calculates that it needs 80,000 recruits a year to maintain world dominance. The military-diplomatic-fiscal disasters of the 2001–7 period jeopardized the steady supply of new troops, imperiling the army's stature as the nation's premier employer of 17–24-year-old workers. At the same time as neophytes were hard to attract to the military due to the risks of war, recruits to militaristic game design stepped forward – nationalistic designers volunteered their services. Their mission, which they appeared to accept with alacrity, was to interpellate the country's youth by situating their bodies and minds to fire the same weapons and face the same issues as on the battlefield. TV commercials depicted soldiers directly addressing gamers, urging them to show their manliness by volunteering for the real thing and serving abroad to secure US power (Verklin and Kanner, 2007; Thompson, 2004; Power, 2007: 282).[8]

Players of the commercial game *Doom II: Hell on Earth* (1994) can download *Marine Doom* (1996), a Marine Corps modification of the original that was developed after the Corps commandant issued a directive that games would improve tactics. And Sony's *SOCOM: US Navy SEALs* (2002) website links directly to the Corps' own page. For the scholarly advocates of corporate culture who proliferate in game studies, this doesn't appear to be a problem: "games serve the national interest by entertaining consumer-citizens and creating a consumer-based demand for military technology" that is allegedly unrelated to actual violence (Hall, 2006; Power, 2007: 277).

Let's return to *America's Army*. The Naval Postgraduate School's Modeling, Virtual Environments and Simulation Academic Program first developed the game, which was farmed out to George Lucas's companies, *inter alia*. It was launched with due symbolism on July 4, 2002 – dually symbolic, in that Independence Day doubles as a key date in the film industry's summer roll-out of features. The military had to bring additional servers into play to handle 400,000 downloads of the game that first day. *Gamespot PC Reviews* awarded it a high textual rating, and was equally impressed by the "business model." Five years after its release, *America's Army* was one of the 10 most-played games on line. As of 2013, it had 13 million registered users. Civilian developers regularly refreshed it by consulting with veterans and participating in physical wargames. Paratexts provided additional forms of promotional renewal, taking full advantage of the usual array of cybertarian fantasies about the new media as civil society, across the gamut of community forums, internet chat, fan sites, and virtual competition. And the game is formally commodified through privatization – bought by Ubisoft to be repurposed for games consoles, arcades, and cell phones, and turned into figurines by the allegedly edgy independent company Radioactive Clown. Tournaments are convened, replete with hundreds of thousands of dollars of prize money, along with smaller events at military recruiting sites. With more than 40 million downloads, and websites by the thousand, its message has traveled far and wide – an excellent return on the initial public investment of US$19 million and US$5 million annually for updates. Studies of young people who have positive attitudes to the US military indicate that 30 percent of them formed that view through playing the game – a game that forbids role reversal via modifications, preventing players from experiencing the pain of the other, and sports a Teen rating. It is officially ranked first among the Army's recruiting tools (Power, 2007: 279–80; Lenoir 2003: 175; Gaudiosi, 2005; J Anderson, 2013; Nieborg, 2004; Turse, 2008: 117, 118, 123–4, 157; Craig, 2006; Shachtman, 2002; Thompson, 2004).[9] The invasion of Los Angeles by Special Forces in 2003 had worked – and it was an invasion by capitalism as much as nationalism.

America's Army is variously said within media studies 2.0 to be "primarily a ludo-logical construct" (Nieborg, 2004), or stimulus to a vibrant counter-public sphere in which veterans dispute the bona fides of nonmilitary players. It is allegedly a con-tested site where what began as a recruitment device has transmogrified into "a place where civilians and service folk . . . discuss the serious experience of real-life war" (Jenkins, 2006: 214–15).

These sanguine outlooks on militaristic recruiting games have their own material history in the sordid links of research schools, cybertarians, and the military. In 1996, the National Academy of Sciences held a workshop for academia, Hollywood, and the Pentagon on simulation and games. The next year, the National Research Council announced a collaborative research agenda in popular culture and militarism. It convened meetings to streamline such cooperation, from special effects to training simulations, from immersive technologies to simulated networks (Lenoir, 2003: 190; Macedonia, 2002).

Since that time, untold numbers of academic journals and institutes on games have become closely tied to the Pentagon. They generate research designed to test and augment the recruiting and training potential of games to ideologize, hire, and instruct the population. The Center for Computational Analysis of Social and Organizational Systems at Carnegie-Mellon University in Pittsburgh promul-gates studies underwritten by the Office of Naval Research and DARPA. DARPA is blissfully happy to use its US$2 billion annual budget to examine how social net-working uncovers "top America's Army players' distinct behaviors, the optimum size of an America's Army team, the importance of fire volume toward opponent, the recommendable communication structure and content, and the contribution of the unity among team members" (Carley et al., 2005). And it refers to Orlando as "Team Orlando" because the city houses Disney's research-and-development "imagineers," the University of Central Florida's Institute for Simulation and Training, Lockheed Martin – the nation's biggest military contractor – and the Pentagon's Institute for Simulation and Training.

In Los Angeles, the University of Southern California's Institute for Creative Technologies was set up as a means of articulating scholars, film and television producers, and game designers. It was formally opened by the Secretary of the Army and the head of the Motion Picture Association of America, and started with US$45 million of the military's budget in 1998, a figure that was doubled in its 2004 renewal and trebled to US$135 million in 2011. By the end of 2010, its products were available on 65 military bases. The Institute uses military money and Hollywood muscle to test out homicidal technologies and narrative scenarios – under the aegis of faculty from film, engineering, and communications. In 2016, this reached its logical extension when 70 officers were stationed there (Deck, 2004; Silver and Marwick 2006: 50; Turse 2008: 120; Hennigan, 2010; Dave, 2015).[10]

Companies such as Pandemic (part-owned by that high-corporate moralist, Bono) invest. The Institute also collaborates on major motion pictures, such as *Spider-Man 2* (Sam Raimi, 2004), and its workspace was thought up by the set designer for the *Star Trek* franchise (Robert Wise, Nicholas Meyer, Leonard Nimoy, William Shatner, David Carson, Jonathan Frakes, Stuart Baird, J. J. Abrams, Justin Lim, 1979–2016). It produces Pentagon recruitment tools such as *Full Spectrum Warrior* (2004) that double as "training devices for military operations in urban terrain": what's good for the Xbox is good for the combat simulator. The utility of these innovations continues in combat. The Pentagon is aware that off-duty soldiers play games. The idea is to invade their supposed leisure time, weaning them from skater games and toward what are essentially training manuals. It even boasts that *Full Spectrum Warrior* was the "game that captured Saddam," because the men who dug Hussein out had been trained with it. These games have become crucial tools because fewer and fewer nations now allow the United States to play live war games on their terrain (Burston, 2003; Stockwell and Muir, 2003; Andersen, 2007; Turse, 2008: 122, 119; Harmon, 2003; Kundnani, 2004).

But virtual blowback was under way, with al-Qaeda reportedly learning tactics by playing these games and developing counters of their own (Power, 2007: 283) and the artist Joseph DeLappe creating countertexts online by typing the details of dead soldiers into the game under the moniker "dead-in-Iraq."[11] For years, Hezbollah had created video games that flipped the good guy–bad guy dichotomy of Western games, where the "Arab" or "Muslim" was typically the evil actor to be blown out of existence (Sisler, 2008). Perhaps the unholy Trinity of media, Pentagon, and screen unwittingly stimulates opponents.

One thing is certain: its techniques of nationalism, from secreted state subvention to immense immersive interpellation, will continue for some time in the service of "the disappearance of the body, the aestheticising of violence, [and] the sanitisation of war" (Der Derian, 2005: 30). For war, profits, and economic restructuring are all too often obscured by the complex, multipoint nature of corporate, military, and entertainment interests and funds, working in the mutual interest of *raison Hollywood* and *raison d'état* under the brutal sign of "violent cartographies" (Shapiro, 2007: 293). Virtual or otherwise, their record of death, disablement, and destruction must be catalogued and criticized.

In addition to looking at the meanings and funding that characterize such projects, we also need to understand the wider Hollywood context and how it works. Our next section transports us into the industry's labor process.

Producers

As per cell phone manufacture and recycling, it is very important to address proletarian work in the media (Mazumdar, 2015). But here, we want to consider people at the apex of Hollywood: men in suits and women who power-dress – producers.

The Producers Guild of America (PGA)'s official history of contemporary Hollywood references important developments in labor, race, gender, technology, and genres.[12] The chronology is also revealing for what it excludes. Taking our touchstone from stakeholders as diverse as medical academia, animal liberation, neoclassical economics, political economy, and environmentalism, we'll plumb other areas with the same fervor as developments signposted by the Guild.

The PGA's history of the century begins with its 2001 merger with the American Association of Producers, which had covered associate producers of TV for the previous two decades. This indicates both the weakening of boundaries between old, middle-aged, and new media, and the sense that the various categories of producer, which range wildly and widely between the powerful and moneyed and the desperate and novitiate, can be accommodated within the same interest group. The PGA calls this "the most radical shift in the Guild's membership and direction since the 1960s." Why? Because of the desire to lob all producers into the same ownership class, and the recognition that Hollywood is principally about television in terms of production hours, commercials, overseas sales, and the actual profits eventually coming from cinema. The following year, technological challenges confronting the Guild saw the formation of a New Media Council. Once more, the development marked class consolidation but also a minimization of the barriers between genres and formats that nevertheless continue to dominate public rhetoric and academic disciplinarity.

In 2005, the PGA trumpeted a decision by the Motion Picture Academy of Arts and Sciences to use its standards of eligibility and arbitration process as a means of nominating Best Pictures. The following year, its Diversity Committee introduced workshops for "aspiring producers of diverse films and television programs." This references decades of critique because Hollywood powerbrokers were almost all white men. In 2007, the Guild intervened "on behalf of producing team members working under illegal conditions at E! Entertainment Television, negotiating a settlement with the network that restores overtime pay." The history concludes two years later with a new annual conference.

The PGA's timeline is a useful starting point as the official version of the period. But it doesn't get at the question: why produce films in the twenty-first century?

> For the cost of "Men in Black 3" . . . the studio [Sony] could have become one of the world's largest venture-capital funds, thereby owning a piece of hundreds of promising start-ups. Instead, it purchased the rights to a piece of intellectual property, paid a fortune for a big star and has no definitive idea why its movie didn't make a huge profit. Why is anyone in the film industry? (Davidson, 2012)

One answer could be that the film's worldwide film theater receipts were over US$550 million – that's before we factor in TV sales, digital video discs, Blu-Ray, and streaming (McClintock, 2012). But another answer might stress that those involved loved what they did; or, more prosaically, that the vast production costs were offset by product placement and merchandising[13] and helped Sony cope with massive losses in its technology business;[14] or that political economy has shown us for 70 years that bottom-line logics are often tied to the exercise of power.

What *are* the costs to a producer of making a Hollywood movie today? In 2005, average expenditure on a fiction feature film made by a major studio was US$96 million – a fourfold increase in two decades – and US$39 million for pictures produced by smaller project-based firms affiliated with them. These figures covered production, duplication, promotion, and distribution (Organisation for Economic Co-operation and Development, 2008: 16).[15]

Producers must meet two principal accounting categories: negative costs, which cover production, studio use, negatives, and capitalized interest; and print and advertising (P&A), which include duplication, distribution, and publicity. Taken together, these items comprise theatrical costs. They have shifted in importance over time. In 1985, negative costs averaged 72 percent of overall theatrical costs. By contrast, in 2005, P&A had risen sharply but negative costs had diminished to 62 percent of the total: promotion is spiraling in an inflationary direction (Organisation for Economic Co-operation and Development, 2008: 17). Now studios are talking, in rather hushed tones, about not releasing movies on film stock in the United States, cutting the price of duplication. Film prints can cost US $2,000, while digital discs are under $100, with satellite possibilities ahead (Verrier, 2014a; 2014b).

Over the last 30 years, sources of film financing have shifted from retained earnings and bank loans (Morawetz et al., 2007):

> [I]n the past third of a century, [the industry] has been increasingly reliant on dispersed and external financing, particularly bank financing, to spread risk and minimize the possibility of losing "everything" on any one production. Large studios often maintain revolving lines of credit with banks, usually based on a guarantee that the studio will market and distribute each film. (Miller, 2011: 1018)

In keeping with the NICL, many pictures are now co-productions between affiliated or independent production companies and major studios. The company that is the titular head of a movie may only exist for the life of that project, in keeping with the nature of its labor force and the quasi-entrepreneurial character of production (Organisation for Economic Co-operation and Development, 2008: 52–4).

> [I]ndependent contractors coalesce for a relatively short period of time around one-off projects to contribute the organizational, creative, and technical talents that go into the production of a film. The inherent transience of this production system results in a high rate of tie formation and dissolution, and a continuous rewiring of the network . . . Producers first identify and secure the rights for a story (script) with some potential and then hire the creative team (director, cinematographer, etc.) whose task is to bring the story to the screen. Filming begins once these individuals have signed onto the project and the team has secured the required financing. (Ferriani et al., 2009: 1548)

[M]ost production companies are now in effect system coordinators, focusing upon the planning and finance of films and taking advantage of large pools of freelance labour and specialized suppliers for actual production of them. Mass market film producers in the USA, India and European countries such as France and Denmark share this history of early horizontal integration and later disintegration of production processes. (Lorenzen, 2007: 350)

Prior to principal photography, quite small amounts are spent in order to obtain an option on both script and workers. Then talent has to be paid and equipment rented. Before "physical production" commences, producers running the relevant ad hoc company and their financial backers decide whether to proceed: the Green Light. Very few producers take such decisions on their own; they propose projects to executive boards by nominating, evaluating, and promising to minimize monetary risks (von Rimscha, 2009: 77).

The concept of the Green Light is predicated on the sticky concept of risk. According to Ulrich Beck, industrialized democratic societies are characterized by "institutions of monitoring and protection" that protect people from "social, political, economic and individual risks" and service the time discipline required by capitalism. Risk society "organizes what cannot be organized." If early modernity was about producing and distributing goods in a search and struggle for the most effective and efficient forms of industrialization, without thought for safety or the environment, risk society enumerates and manages such dangers. Rather than being occasional, risk is now a constitutive component of private and public life that can be sold, pooled, and reconfigured. This second modernity is characterized by ever more sophisticated mechanisms for measuring risk, even as the range and impact of risks grow less controllable (Beck et al., 1994: 5; Beck 1999: 135).

In Robert Wilson's neo-noir novel *The Vanished Hands*, Inspector Jefe Javier Falcón of Sevilla suggests to expatriate Yanquis Maddy and Marty Krugman that US society has been driven by fear since September 11, 2001. He is quickly rebuked: "It's *always* been fear" (2004: 41). The United States is *the* risk society, with 50 percent of the population participating in stock market investments. Risk is brought into the home as an everyday ritual, an almost blind faith (sometimes disappointed) in mutual funds patrolling retirement income. In 2005, US residents spent US$1.1 trillion on insurance – more than they paid for food, and over a third of the world's total insurance expenditure (Miller, 2008).

Hollywood talks about risk all the time. When one of us attended a 2003 conference on the economics of Hollywood at "a large university in the mid-West," every paper from business and economics faculty focused on a single topic – how firms could increase their revenues and diminish their risks. He felt like a fossil that had been invited to walk the earth one more time among these very contemporary handservants of capital.

Despite the fact that overall insecurity is borne by producers, people in US film and television drama seem haunted by risk. This is because they operate as part of the cognitariat and precariat, depending on their position above or below the line of accounting for labor skills and costs (Miller, 2010b; Maxwell and Miller, 2013). The increasing opportunity to draw on the NICL is at play here, as subsidies, skills, and pliancy spread across the globe (Hjort, 2013). Risk is factored, almost fetishized, as a core component of working life:

> Relative to all other media products, cinema and television entertainment requires by far the highest amount of initial investment per unit, most of which is high risk. Investors often adopt a venture capital model, financing a portfolio of productions, of which only a few are expected to be successful. (Organisation for Economic Co-operation and Development, 2008: 7)

The figure attracting the greatest calumny as the *locus* of uncertainty and risk is frequently the producer, who is of course subject to similar pressures. This represents continuity with an earlier era, when producers represented the full power of the studio system.

Why this carry-over across such different moments in employment history? Because the word "producer" signifies control and money via the dreaded bureaucratic "suit," whether that refers to female power dressing or male power dross, 1940s executives or noughties independents, stately studio statues or boutique effects houses. Consider the venerable history of scriptwriters complaining about the category, something that Raymond Chandler (1945, 2001) both derided and expressed in his remorselessly dialectical way: "[P]ersonal qualities of a producer are rather beside the point. Some are able and humane men and some are low-grade individuals with the morals of a goat, the artistic integrity of a slot machine, and the manners of a floorwalker with delusions of grandeur" (1945). He said: "A writer has no real chance in pictures unless he is willing to become a producer, and that is too tough for me. The last picture I worked on was just one long row" (2001). But today, the showrunner phenomenon sees writers *as* producers and *vice versa* (Phalen and Osellame, 2012).

Producers straddle more clearly than most workers the relationship between art and commerce, proletarian and bourgeois, bourgeois and petit bourgeois. They are marginalized by the *auteur* discourse of artistry as well as the studio discourse of finance, even as they enable all elements and sometimes achieve an alchemic personal apogee in the combinatory *mestizo* figures of Lucas and Spielberg. Producers can be entrepreneurs, managers, and artists all at once, and are frequently the only people heavily involved in pre- and postproduction as well as production (Pardo, 2010).

The next section looks at how the developments mentioned above, and others, ramify certain traditional producer logics and transform others. It focuses on a new market-driven and state-dependent production process that is tied, in ever more complex and complete ways, to global capital.[16] We'll examine blockbusters and co-productions, technology, public subvention, and citizenship.

Blockbusters and Co-Productions

> [A]verage costs have soared over the past 20 years, driven largely by the "blockbuster" phenomenon, where a large share of capital is invested in a small number of productions. Average costs have risen across the board, but much of the increase is in advertising and distribution, which now account for 30–40% of total costs for major studios. (Organisation for Economic Co-operation and Development, 2008: 7)

> Banks are more likely to feel comfortable funding large budget productions with higher blockbuster potential, while smaller budget movies that take more artistic

risks – the kind that may lead to awards and praise – find bank funding more difficult, as potential profits are judged to be smaller. (Miller, 2011: 1018)

Blockbusters generally draw on already-popular, ensemble, multigeneric formats with built-in, tested appeal: "Eighteen of the all-time 100 top-grossing movies (adjusted for inflation) were sequels, and more than half of those were released since 2000" (Davidson, 2012).

The process begins with serious investment. Rights to a best-selling book, for example, vary between US$500,000 and $2 million. Adaptation is equally expensive: leading screenwriters can cost as much as $2 million per project. Top directors may command $10 million per film and a percentage of profits. Actors in the front rank expect a sign-on fee of between $10 and $20 million dollars, in addition to a percentage of the box office. Computer-generated imagery can double the cost of a film, amounting to a $100 million alone. In terms of music, a leading rock star may only charge $1 million per new song. Producers also pay themselves, of course – modest altruists that they are. At the leading edge of the industry, they receive much less than leading actors, but sometimes over $5 million per film. Once a blockbuster is made, the largest single expense remains – marketing, sometimes amounting to half the original budget (Morris, 2012).

Blockbusters minimize character development, narrative complexity, and dialogue. They are driven by the global *lingua franca* of spectacle, testosterone, adventure, and multiculturalism: "[F]ilms that require no obvious connection with an identifiable actor or with a specific language or cultural context (e.g. special effects or animated films) may be more accessible to a global audience and offer more direct links to subsidiary markets for computer games, merchandising and so forth" (Organisation for Economic Co-operation and Development, 2008: 26). A blockbuster's media coverage and subsequent marketing depend a great deal on its opening weekend. Audiences for that period are dominated by male teens. Producers calculate, and studies back this up, that young men do not read press reviews but are very susceptible to marketing (Hennig-Thurau et al., 2012).

> [P]ersonal income, the comedy-drama genre, and the PG 13 ratings are the important positive factors in the financial success of a film when moviegoers know relatively little about a picture . . . [E]x post regressions demonstrate that peak screens, the quadratic of stardom, film award nominations and positive word-of-mouth information sharing are all positive and significant determinants of film performance. The impacts of production budget, the gross of a prequel, positive critical reviews, and release dates during the summer and Thanksgiving/Christmas seasons are robust across the models. The action-adventure and comedy genres were also consistently positive and statistically significant across the models. (Brewer et al., 2009: 589)

The desire to spread the risk of blockbusters is understandable. "Smaller" pictures, too, need a variety of funders, frequently as co-productions:

> Begun as a tool of resistance to the dominance of US films, [European] film funds were initially designed to support "high quality" movies that provided an artistic voice for domestic auteurs, an outlet that could not be supported by the mass market. . . . this system in which only the films that could not be supported in the mass market win funds encouraged the development of a film industry in many of these countries that could never become self-sufficient, as the system values art films over

> those that could appeal to the mass market, and as it values "quality" and artistic expression over development of a sustainable domestic mass market industry. . . . In the past two decades, discourse has begun to support public film policy that, instead of supporting individual local auteurs, favors the grooming of a local film industry workforce and foreign direct investment into local facilities. . . . In this way, public film support, particularly in Europe, shifted to encourage foreign productions to shoot on location domestically and to partner with local production companies. (Miller, 2011: 1019)

The system is now in full flight in search of the monetary aspects of the NICL:

> [F]inance in the US and international film industry [i]s filled with soft money from Europe[:] co-producing (co-financing) US pictures directly (as happened in Germany), or by bringing US or international production to Europe by using the co-production structure in the case of the UK model. In both cases the extent of money diversion was considerable. In 2000 alone . . . approximately $3 billion or 20 per cent of the entire US expenditure in film and video production was sourced from media companies and private equity film funds listed on the German "'new economy'" stock exchange Neuer Markt. ... Even after the Neuer Markt's collapse in 2000/2001, German private equity continued to flow into the US industry, with German film funds raising EUR 2.3 billion in 2002, EUR 1.76 billion in 2003 and EUR 1.5 billion in 2004. . . . The German government reacted to the abuse of the tax scheme at first with restrictions and finally closed it in 2005 (Morawetz et al., 2007: 436)

Co-production is a new part of the restless quest for the Asian market (meaning China and India). Co-productions work with "local production houses that know the culture and taste of the people" (Rasul and Proffitt, 2012: 567). In 2009, Spielberg received over US$800 million from Reliance Big Pictures, an Indian-based venture (Ganti, 2012: 344).

Then there is the question of revenue. Studios get about half of blockbusters' theatrical receipts, frequently based on a high percentage for the opening week, with exhibitors benefiting more as time passes. DVD revenue has been declining since its peak in 2004, but remains significant. Studios generally take 40 percent of DVD and other rental sales – over US$650 million for *Avatar* (James Cameron, 2009), an "event" film of the kind that people still want to "own." Merchandising brings in money through licensed toys, games, and posters, *inter alia*, amounting to 10 percent of income. Then comes television. This works through a range of venues chronologically: video on demand, followed by premium cable, then broadcast. Costs are based on theatrical success or failure and bring in approximately 11 percent of revenue (Morris, 2012).

Public Subvention

Up to now, the assumption in this chapter has mirrored that of the dominant discourse on Hollywood: namely, that the risks encountered in producing motion pictures are private. Let's analyze what Hollywood looks like in this version of the truth, where a market operates unfettered by governmental control or participation.

Table 6.2 invokes ideal-types from the discourse of neoclassical economics.[17] The state is magically airbrushed from view. We will redraw this grid at the chapter's conclusion, because we saw in chapter 3 that the risk is actually socialized across society.

Table 6.2

LAISSEZ-FAIRE HOLLYWOOD
No state investment in training, production, distribution, or exhibition
No governmental content
Copyright protection
Monopoly restrictions
Export orientation
Market model
Avowed ideology of pleasure before nation

Source: Maxwell and Miller, 2011

If it's German money funding a Hollywood film in the early twenty-first century, the chances are that it came from tax breaks available to lawyers, doctors, and dentists. French money might have come from firms with state subvention in other areas of investment, such as cable or plumbing, that subsidized US studios. TV shows shot in Canada relied on welfare to attract US producers.

Accommodation and sales-tax rebates are available to Hollywood producers almost universally across the United States. State, regional, and municipal commissions offer producers reduced local taxes, free provision of police services, and the blocking of putatively public wayfares. Such services even extend in some cases to constructing studio sites, as in North Carolina. The California Film Commission reimburses public personnel costs and permit and equipment fees, while the state government's "Film California First Program" covered everything from free services through to wage tax credits. If a movie or TV show is made in any particular state of the United States or other countries, the credits generally thank film commissions for subsidies of everything from hotels to hamburgers. This is in keeping with the emergence of the NICL, which has seen a vast expansion of Hollywood's production locations from Southern California to across the world (Kavoori and Chadha, 2009; McPhail, 2009; Miller, 2012a; Miller et al., 2005).

The primary goal of neoclassical media economics, as noted in chapter 3, is to organize resources in order to create capitalist goods. In this view, there are three principal economic actors: consumers, companies, and the state. This is not helpful for those of us on the left, who are concerned with workers, justice, and equity. That said, because neoclassical economists meticulously hunt for subsidies that prop up lazy members of the bourgeoisie, they are good at ferreting out state film policies that attract Hollywood – i.e., provide producers with "free money." Free money is the term producers use to describe their holy grail – how to find investors or bankers who won't claim equity or seek either interest or returns of any kind.

So public funding of Hollywood is one of those spheres of life where critical political economy and neoclassical economics can agree on a target and a way of attaining it: uncovering and problematizing state subsidies that enable allegedly laissez-faire bourgeoisies to survive and thrive (Tannenwald, 2010; Miller, 2005). For example, the Heartland Institute disparages such subvention as welfare for "some of America's most affluent businessmen at the expense of taxpayers" (Northdurft, 2008). The Tax Foundation rails at "corporate welfare" that guarantees investors 15–20 percent

Table 6.3 State tax incentives for Oscar-nominated motion pictures (2014)

Movie	Budget (millions)	State incentives	Location
American Hustle	$40	25% production and payroll credits; sales tax exemption	Massachusetts
Captain Phillips	$55	$300k Grant	Virginia
Dallas Buyers Club	$5.5	30% credit on expenditures; 5% payroll credit	Louisiana
Gravity	$100	25% credit on first $38m expenditures, 20% credit thereafter	United Kingdom
Her	$25	20% tax credit	California
Nebraska	$13	Eligible for funds from participating local economic development offices	Nebraska
Philomena	$5	25% credit on first $38m expenditures, 20% credit thereafter	United Kingdom
12 Years a Slave	$20	30% credit on expenditures; 5% payroll credit	Louisiana
Wolf of Wall Street	$100	30% tax credit	New York

Source: Budget estimates from IMDB and moveiboxoffice. State incentives from various government film offices.

returns on their investments and stimulates competition between states to provide more and more subsidies that are lapped up then forgotten by Hollywood once alternatives beckon, leaving minimal if any ongoing benefit (Henchman, 2008). Complaints are made that claims for economic development do not stand up because film and TV are not as sizeable as automobile manufacturing, and the preponderance of revenue from them lands in Californian pockets anyway (McHugh and Hohman, 2008).

The impeccably reactionary Manhattan Institute issued a neat diagram when the Academy of Motion Picture Arts and Sciences announced its 2014 Oscar nominees. Table 6.3 highlights Academy selections for Best Picture that made the most use of public subvention. *The Wolf of Wall Street* (Martin Scorsese, 2013) won, thanks to receiving a third of its US$100 million production cost from the taxpayers, as opposed to the gangs, of New York.[18] The left is similarly shocked: "The system of tax credits is like every other bloated financial system in the United States, moving capital between elites while workers live with exaggerated job insecurity, declining market value, and uncertain futures that make up the rest of the workforce" (Mayer and Goldman, 2010). Such issues duel in the bourgeois media with arguments about the glamour, tourism, and jobs that supposedly go with films as positive externalities (Sullivan, 2007).

Less tendentious researchers than right-wing think-tankers or progressive intellectuals, such as those at the Federal Reserve Bank of Boston (Rollins Saas, 2006), support skepticism about the benefits versus the costs of tax breaks for movies as opposed to other forms of longer-lasting job creation that do not have adverse effects on tax receipts or run the risk that filmmakers who would have come to particular locations anyway suddenly enjoy windfalls at ordinary citizens' expense.

In 2010, 43 US states alone sought to "attract" Hollywood. The overall cost was US$1.5 billion. On average, producers received 25 cents for each dollar of these sub-sidies, no matter the success or otherwise of their films and whether they intended to work somewhere anyway. Regardless of where projects are shot, most of the labor force is imported from the north-east and south-west, specifically New York, the traditional home of network TV, and Los Angeles, the traditional home of film. So the plum jobs go to people who spend most of their income and are levied most of their taxes outside the places where they briefly work. Locals get distinctly below-the-line positions, as caterers and hairdressers – frequently non-unionized jobs that hardly build careers. The 43 gullible states that engaged in this largesse did so for a variety of reasons – creating jobs during film or TV shoots, engendering public awareness of their locales to boost tourism, cleaving glamor to sponsoring politicians, fulfill-ing the remits of culturecrats, and satisfying the needs of powerful businesspeople. There is no evidence that the subsidies paid for themselves in terms of private sector expenditure during production and the establishment of secure, ongoing infrastruc-ture of filmmaking. Such prospects are jeopardized by both the big two locations and constant bidding contests between states as they ratchet up the terms they offer Hollywood to become temporary whatevers (Tannenwald, 2010; Foster et al., 2013).

This decade has seen a massive increase in subsidies, stimulated by Louisiana and New Mexico upping the ante. They have moved from traditional subvention, such as minimal credits against income tax, deductions based on losses, loan guarantees, free access to public services, and exemptions from hotel taxes, to much more expan-sive tax credits. Other states have followed suit, stimulating a new business in trading such credits. Transferability takes tax credits afforded by governments to producers and sells them to wealthy people who don't feel like paying their share of tax. This way producers get their money faster than via refunds. What began in 2009 is already a multimillion dollar business (Verrier, 2013).

The impact on actual shooting in LA has been profound, even if above-the-line labor still mostly lives and pays taxes there:

> In 1997, the majority of large-budget studio features were produced in California, with many in LA. By 2013, most high-value feature projects were made elsewhere; just two of the year's live-action movies with budgets above $100 million were filmed in LA. Today, most local Feature production is for small, independent projects that offer reduced employment and spending benefits. (Film L.A. Research, 2014)

> Entertainment media jobs in the Los Angeles metropolitan region declined by 7.7% between 2005 and 2010, manifesting the impact of the financial crisis. However, for Los Angeles, which has consistently maintained at least a 45% share of the US national film and television employment and is the single most important centre of film and television production in the USA (with a 10.71 location quotient for the industry code defining the motion picture- and video-recording industry), the crisis punctuated a longer-term decline in employment and production capacity . . . on-location shooting of feature films reached a high of 13,980 days in 1996; by 2009, it was only 4976 days . . . location activity for television productions reached a high of 25,277 days in 2008, reflecting the expansion of low-cost reality and dramatic productions for cable television. Demonstrating the impact of the recession, on-location television production days in Los Angeles dropped by almost 17% in 2009. So, the more-lucrative film production jobs were replaced during the decade

> by less-lucrative television jobs. These jobs then decreased as the recession took hold ... the number of workers employed in films, television programmes and commercials in 2010 in Los Angeles County was lower than that in any year since 2001. In addition, because of the supply chains that are connected to project-based production, California state employment numbers actually undercount employment losses in the entertainment industry agglomeration in Los Angeles: they do not include unemployment of part-time workers (nearly a quarter of the industry workforce) nor unemployment in ancillary business services such as property, houses and equipment rental shops, which depend on Los Angeles productions for their employment and profits. (Christopherson, 2013: 142)

Given these *caveats*, public programs have sometimes generated ongoing investment in new infrastructure – sound stages and skilled workers, for example – that provide ongoing attractions beyond temporary direct subvention,[19] and are claimed as part of encouraging "a 'clean' or 'environmentally friendly' industry" (Rollins Saas, 2006: 3; but see Maxwell and Miller, 2012).

Finally, it is worth seeing how closely the fiscal fortunes of Hollywood are linked to the complexion of the federal government. This is not about subvention per se, but rather the wider political economy. After the 2000 general election, Wall Street transferred money away from the media in general and toward manufacturing and defense as punishments and rewards for these industries' respective attitudes during the election and subsequent *coup*. Energy, tobacco, and military companies, 80 percent of whose campaign contributions had gone to George W. Bush in the presidential election, received unparalleled transfers of confidence. Money fled the cultural sector, where 66 percent of campaign contributions had gone to Al Gore – a victory for oil, cigarettes, and guns over film, music, and wires. The former saw their market value rise by an average of 80 percent in a year, while the latter's declined by between 12 and 80 percent (Schwartz and Hozic, 2001).

Citizenship

All of this raises the question of citizenship. Quite apart from the questions of economic efficiency that are raised by subvention, and issues of imperialism raised by Pentagon and CIA "distortions" of the market, how might social justice be addressed in the context of taxpayer support, as *quae pro quibus*?

The twenty-first century has seen a critique of Hollywood based on the fact that the industry imperils living creatures and the environment (Caplan-Bricker, 2013; Maxwell and Miller, 2012). Box 6.1 draws on public-health experts in their own words to make the case in terms of what these subsidies mean for their work. Its evidence is compelling and appalling.

Box 6.1

[A]n an estimated 1.1 million current adolescent smokers in the United States were recruited to smoke by tobacco imagery in films about 350,000 of whom will ultimately die from tobacco induced diseases. . . . two thirds of US developed, youth-rated film projects with tobacco imagery were filmed in the United States, a rate typical of all films released by US studios over the past decade. Filmed in a dozen states now offering subsidies, these 35 movies contributed 71 percent of the 11.4 billion tobacco impressions delivered to US theater audiences by youth-rated films in 2008. . . . states awarded an estimated $830 million in public subsidies to films with tobacco, including $500 million to youth-rated films with tobacco. For comparison, the states budgeted $719 million for all tobacco control in 2009. . . . An estimated 62 percent ($830 million/$1.3 billion) of state film subsidies go to smoking films. (Polansky and Glantz, 2009)

Voluntary agreements with the tobacco industry to limit smoking in movies have not and cannot work because the fiduciary interests of the tobacco industry are opposite to those of the public health community. In the United States, the Master Settlement Agreement (MSA) between states' Attorneys General and the major domestic tobacco manufacturers included a provision in which the manufacturers agreed to a prohibition on paid tobacco product placement in movies. . . .. However, evidence shows that smoking incidents increased in movies released subsequent to the MSA's 1998 implementation, peaking in 2005. (World Health Organization, 2011: 1)

An analysis of more than 1300 feature films accounting for 96% of all ticket sales in the United States between 2002 and 2010 found that tobacco imagery permeated both youth-rated (G/PG/PG–13) and adult-rated (R) movies, with 62% of top-grossing films featuring tobacco imagery. More specifically, 81% of all R-rated movies included smoking, while smoking appeared in 66% of movies rated PG-13 and 27% of movies rated G or PG. Altogether, top-grossing movies of all ratings distributed in the United States between 2002 and 2010 contained approximately 7500 tobacco incidents. (World Health Organization, 2011: 3)

From 2008 to 2010, 14 nations or their sub-units awarded an estimated US$2.4 billion to producers of 93% of the 428 films, mainly developed by companies based in the United States, which achieved top box office status in Canada and the United States. Half of these films featured tobacco imagery. Over three years, subsidized with US$1.1 billion in tax credits, these films delivered an estimated total of 130 billion tobacco impressions to theatre audiences worldwide. (World Health Organization 2011: 8)

Film industry representatives sometimes assert the need for smoking imagery in a movie to tell a story. The WHO [Framework Convention on Tobacco Control] FCTC certainly asserts that the implementation of a comprehensive ban on tobacco advertising, promotion and sponsorship should not prevent legitimate expression. However, the presentation of smoking on screen is rarely realistic, generally showing images more consistent with cigarette advertising than with authentic representations of the dire health consequences of tobacco use. (World Health Organization, 2011: 9)

[T]obacco incidents . . . per youth-rated movie fell from 20 in 2005 to seven in 2010, a 66% reduction; the degree of improvement, however, varied substantially by movie studio. The three companies with published policies designed to reduce smoking in their films (Disney, Time Warner and Comcast's Universal) reduced tobacco incidents per youth-rated (G/PG/PG-13) movie by more than 90%, to an average of fewer than two incidents per movie by 2010. The other companies (Sony, News Corporation's Fox, Viacom's Paramount, and independent film companies considered as a group) had 26–63% reductions and six to 14 tobacco incidents per youth-rated movie in 2010. . . . Published company policies, adopted between 2004 and 2007, provide for review of scripts, story boards, daily footage, rough cuts, editing decisions and the final edited film by managers in each studio with authority for implementing the policies. As of June 2011, none of the studios had blanket policies against including smoking or other tobacco imagery in youth-rated films that they produced or distributed. (World Health Organization, 2011: 25)

Human-rights issues also emerge in terms of gender in Hollywood:

> I think women make wonderful producers, because they're very nurturing, but at the same time, they feel things more. In this business, that's not necessarily a great thing, because you have to always say "Next." We tend to internalize things, so that's not good. I think in the long run it's not a bad business for women. It's not Wall Street. Creative instincts are rewarded. We have great women studio heads and role models and networking organizations. You can have a meeting with five women in it. There's not a lot of businesses you can say that about. (Lynda Obst, quoted in D'Addario, 2013)

Over 80 percent of the top-20 grossing Hollywood pictures between 1985 and 2005 were produced by men. Such tendencies are common in project-based industries as opposed to those that are governed by uniform organizational policies animated by the discourse of equal opportunity or affirmative action, because of a tendency toward parthenogenesis. Where female producers *are* involved, the likelihood of women directors increases (Skilton, 2008: 1749). In 2012, women made up just 18 percent of producers and other key above-the-line, off-camera participants in Hollywood's top-grossing 250 motion pictures, an increase of 1 percent on 1998. Women comprised 17 percent of executive producers and 25 percent of all producers, higher numbers than in other occupations; but their prominence decreased in prestigious producing positions – 40 percent of associate producers are women (Lauzen, 2013; Klos, 2013).

This is of course only part of the exploitative tradition of Hollywood filmmaking. We have already seen the environmental damage done by the industry, outlined in chapter 3. In addition, Hollywood has a horrendous history of the abuse of animals, through to the present, which discloses systematic barbarism. People for the Ethical Treatment of Animals has guidelines to producers that are very important.[20] Such issues of public health, gender, the environment, and our fellow-animals' rights are

Table 6.4

WELFARE HOLLYWOOD
Massive state investment in training via film schools and production commissions, major diplomatic negotiations over distribution and exhibition arrangements, and Pentagon budgets
Copyright protection as a key service to capital along with anti-piracy deals
Monopoly restrictions minimized to permit cross-ownership and unprecedented concentration domestically and oligopolies internationally
Export orientation aided by plenipotentiaries
Market model but mixed-economy practice through state subvention
Ideology of pleasure, nation, and export of *Américanité* as imperial power

all relevant matters of citizenship – just as much as the violence of gaming and the bigotry of news. Even when their targets are US viewers, their ideological and material effects are experienced elsewhere, with little or no recourse to state action.

Conclusion

> The economics of the film industry revolve around the need to protect large investments by managing risk. This involves aggregation, marketing and production strategies. The conventional way to control and co-ordinate production risks has been to aggregate production activities in one location. Thus, the US industry is clustered in Los Angeles, the UK industry in London and the French industry in Paris. But positive effects from clustering are now mostly confined to project development, financial, marketing and distribution. Many "Hollywood" films are no longer filmed in Hollywood – often taking advantage of location shooting incentives (tax breaks and subsidies), often in other countries. But arguably the markets for these films are still created in the Hollywood cluster. (Organisation for Economic Co-operation and Development, 2008: 28)

It is time to redraw the grid of laissez-faire Hollywood – see Table 6.4.

We can see from the above that the state is a crucial component in this avowedly private–sector jewel and that while Hollywood hegemons have undergone extensive changes in their working environments over the decades, three appetites have remained constant: for risk, for public money, and for "efficiencies" without due regard to human, animal, and environmental rights. More generally, we have seen that US media power is far from a simple outcome based on textual popularity. Rather, it both indexes and enables the awesome military, commercial, and environmental destructiveness of the nation. In chapter 7, we look at how to understand texts that result from such activities.

7 Textual Analysis

The world of global media encompasses a variety of structures – political, economic, regulatory – but it also includes what is often described by the banal term "content." That refers to the programs, songs, performances, films, words, images, and sounds that cultural scholars refer to as "texts." That can mean any media form, segment, episode, or utterance from newspaper, film, radio, television, the internet or elsewhere. Given our emphasis thus far on political-economic and policy approaches to global media studies, where does the meaning of a particular media text fit in?

This chapter lays out the foundations textual analysis. The singular importance of this approach is that by dissecting how media texts convey various meanings through numerous stylistic devices, we can comprehend how the global media articulate power and meaning. While its origins lie in media studies 1.0 and 2.0, textual analysis can be drawn upon and refined for 3.0.

We apply several methods to a genre and an exemplar, then investigate case studies, highlighting gender, violence, and the environment. In the process, we cross media forms to examine film, television, documentary, journalism, the internet, sports, war, politics, sexuality, *telenovelas*, and activism.

This focus on texts does not signify the abandonment of the institutional analyses undertaken so far. It seeks to illustrate how they can and should be blended with hermeneutic interpretation. We acknowledge the importance of the form and style of texts – how they make meaning – their semiosis. But we insist that significant texts transcend the words, images, and sounds that have been encoded at their point of production. So understanding them involves going beyond them as texts and into their careers.

Chartier seeks to establish and comprehend the always-contingent meanings of texts in three ways:

- a reconstruction of "the diversity of older readings from their sparse and multiple traces";
- a focus on "the text itself, the object that conveys it, and the act that grasps it"; and
- an identification of "the strategies by which authors and publishers tried to impose an orthodoxy or a prescribed reading on the text" (1989: 157, 161–3, 66).

Following in his stead, we seek to track both what happens *in* media texts and what happens *to* them as they travel, attenuating and developing links and discourses across their careers – in other words, we trace the complex, open, malleable, and polyphonic qualities of their "different and successive materialities" (Chartier, 2005a: 40; 2005b).

This orientation turns away from reflectionism, which argues that a text's key meaning lies in its overt or covert capacity to capture the *Zeitgeist*; rejects formalism's claim that a close reading of sound and image cues can secure a definitive meaning; and eschews the use of the psy-function to unlock people's heads. Instead, Chartier looks at the passage of texts through space and time, noting how they gain and lose meanings on their travels as they rub up against, trope, and are themselves troped by other fictional and social texts. Pierre Macherey's work (1977, 2007) on the materiality of meaning provides further inspiration, along with Alec McHoul and Tom O'Regan's "discursive analysis of particular actor networks, technologies of textual exchange, circuits of communicational and textual effectivity, traditions of exegesis, [and] commentary and critical practice" (1992: 5–6).

Latour (1993, 2004) offers valuable additional tools for media interpretation that connect to social and environmental questions. In examining the necessarily hybrid nature of communication, he allocates equal and overlapping significance to natural phenomena, social forces, and textual production. So just as objects of knowledge come to us in hybrid forms that are coevally affected by society and culture, the latter two domains are themselves affected by the natural world. Latour notes that "every type of politics has been defined by its relation to nature, whose every feature, property, and function depends on the polemical will to limit, reform, establish, short-circuit, or enlighten public life." From plutocracy to patriarchy, appeals to channel or protect nature, to govern it, are crucial to political hegemony (2004: 1, 33).

Engagements with texts must therefore be supplemented, or perhaps supplanted, by an account of the conditions under which they are made, circulated, received, interpreted, and criticized. The life of any popular text is a passage across space and time, a life remade again and again by institutions, discourses, and practices of distribution and reception – in short, all the shifts and shocks of a commodity, as per Tony Bennett and Janet Woollacott's (1987) exploration of James Bond's different incarnations and Toby Miller's (1997) research into the career of *The Avengers* television series.

Put another way, the media are not just a series of texts to be read, coefficients of political and economic power to be exposed, or industrial objects to be analyzed. Rather, they are all these things: a hybrid monster, coevally subject to rhetoric, status, and technology – to meaning, power, and science (Latour, 1993) – operating under the sign of intercultural globalization.

Texts deserve scrutiny within the broader media structure that they populate because they shape discourse in the public sphere. As Michael Warner (2002) has argued, people may both coalesce and separate around meaning. Martin Scorsese's film *The Last Temptation of Christ* (1988) mobilized publics who attacked it in the name of its misrepresentation of a revered religious figure, in turn prompting another public to react in the name of liberal values of freedom of speech and pluralism. In a later chapter, we shall see how audiences constitute themselves around highly popular texts.

As one example of this approach to the career of media productions, consider the afterlife of Alfred Hitchcock's 1938 movie, *The Lady Vanishes*. It has traveled a long way since its first voyage (the film is largely set on a train), leaving a mark on everything from twenty-first-century politics to contemporary transportation. To understand the film's meaning, we need to go well beyond the sounds and images of the original, because the eight decades since its release have reconditioned the text, given it new life and depth, motion and meaning. We must look at its intertexts, following the life of the commodity sign years after all its creators passed into history. *The Lady Vanishes* marks the commencement of an agreement whereby MGM engaged in co-productions with Gaumont-British and Gainsborough, which allowed Metro to distribute the picture in the United Kingdom – a key moment in Hollywood's use of the NICL to exploit resources and schemes across the globe.[1] Production was disrupted when the Electrical Trades Union went on strike.[2] So the text was dripping with ideological issues before it was even made: US cultural imperialism meets UK industrial action.

The London *Times* in 1938 reported that audiences responded with "'Mr. Hitchcock is right. We must shoot down these foreign blighters'."[3] There had to be a certain subtlety in handling such issues at the time. Prior to the outbreak of war in September 1939, the British Board of Film Censors was ill-disposed to films that deviated from appeasement or criticized the Nazis (Webster, 2009). Clearly, *The Lady Vanishes* has a storied history in the fantasy of espionage, the role of gender and Britishness between the wars, the fantasy of train travel and wealth, and a renowned auteur's filmmaking style.[4]

Remade in 1979, it also provided an obvious inspiration to *Flightplan* (Robert Schwentke, 2005). When new Virgin Trains rail franchises across Britain were promoted in 2005, the campaign was called "The Return of the Train," deploying what it called "the golden era of British cinema" as a marketing tool whereby stars of yesterday were digitally manipulated to marvel at the company's 125mph tilting Pendolino train rocketing across country. *The Lady Vanishes* figured prominently. The *Independent on Sunday* troped "The Lady Vanishes" to describe former French First Lady Cécilia Sarkozy's mysterious absences from state functions (Poirier, 2007), the *Independent* to ask what happened to the actress Fenella Fielding (Chalmers, 2008), *The Sun* to attack Margaret Thatcher for inaction during her first days as leader of the Conservative opposition in 1975,[5] and the *Guardian* to mark the (supposed) end of Thatcherite neoliberalism and authoritarian populism 20 years later (Rawnsley, 1999). For the *New Yorker*, it referred to the impenetrability of Hillary Rodham Clinton's character (Kolbert, 2007). When Clinton became Secretary of State, *Slate* insisted she watch the film in order to master the art of diplomacy (Kaplan, 2009). *The Scotsman* trivialized the country's then-Education Secretary Fiona Hyslop with the same referent (Maddox, 2009), the *Monterey County Herald* used it to account for the unexpected arrival of painted lady butterflies that resemble monarchs and confuse northern California residents (Agha, 2009), *Newsweek* to engage the films of Roman Polanski and Peter Yates (Kroll, 1988), the *New York Times* to explain fashion trends (Spindler, 2001), *O: The Oprah Magazine* to describe what it feels like for women when they cease to draw the male gaze ("Other People's," 2009), *The Age* to uncover racist Australian immigration policy (Marr, 2005), *The Economist* to write about Myanmar/Burma's detention of Aung San Suu Kyi,[6] and *The Wrap* to account for Rachel Uchitel canceling a press conference slated to detail her links to Tiger Woods (Mikulan, 2009).

For the *Journal of Bioethical Inquiry*, *The Lady Vanishes* encapsulated the absence of women from debates about somatic-cell nuclear transfer and embryonic stem-cell technologies (Dickenson, 2006), while the *Journal of Organizational Change Management* troped it to account for obstacles to women becoming leaders (Höpfl and Matilal, 2007), the *Journal of Lesbian Studies* to specify the complexity of identifying who is a lesbian (Weston, 2009), the *Australian Law Journal* to note the gendered workings of the law (Chatterjee, 2008), the *International Journal of Work Organisation and Emotion* to examine affective labor (Bolton, 2009), the *Australian Journal of International Affairs* to explain the subjectivity of the noted international relations scholar Coral Bell (Taylor, 2005), *Contemporary South Asia* to describe the Marxist historiography of India (Mitra, 2000), *Church History* to discern the impact of semiotics and poststructuralism on feminist scholarship (Clark, 1998), and *Film Quarterly* and *camera obscura* to identify a deep-seated fear of women (Fischer, 1979; Beckman, 2003).

Clearly, the very words of the film's title conjure up connotations of mystery: the richness of "vanishes" and the formality of "lady" in their syntagmatic state provide images suitable for dozens of tropes. The title also touches on the double-sided nature of femininity: the desire for visibility in a patriarchal world that denies women full membership of society and frequently engages in symbolic annihilation, glass ceilings, religious discrimination, and domestic violence, versus the desire for invisibility as opposed to the requirements of emphasized femininity to satisfy the norms of hegemonic masculinity and appear beautiful and appealing at all times (Connell, 2014). Such issues are played out in two of our case studies. We commence with the notion of genre, and the field within which *The Lady Vanishes* is generally categorized: espionage.

Genre

Genre derives from the same root form as gender, and it refers to classificatory methods of categorizing texts collectively: westerns, science fiction, romance comedy, punk, rhythm and blues, opera, and so on. Genre is therefore a tool of analysis and promotion alike, used by critics, merchandisers, audiences, and theorists when reviewing, selling, choosing, and analyzing media texts. It can be descriptive or evaluative and divide people by gender, age, and race (such as "chick flick," youth film, or black show). Genres are simultaneously textual, economic, and social. They involve the interplay of repetition and difference and their organization and interpretation during cultural production, scheduling, regulation, and interpretation. There is enough in common within a set of texts that are thought of as, for instance, action adventure, to classify them together and diminish the risk of investing in them, but enough that is distinctive about each one to make them individual and appealing (Miller, 1998).

Consider espionage. It involves surreptitiously conveying information about a country, company, or union to its enemy or rival. Much of this information is "official"; it has national security significance or economic value. Along with the glamor and romance of undercover work, a blend of fabrication and fact has long characterized espionage in a complex interplay of art and life. For example, Nicholas Hiley argues that the period up to the 1930s saw "most British intelligence officers [take] the greater part of their ideas of secret service directly from fictional sources" (1991: 57).

At an ideological level, espionage fiction's nexus of "spectacular violence and social vacuousness" has led to Marxist accusations that it models antisocial conduct, heroizes the capitalist state, and delights in basc consumerism (Westlake, 1980: 37; Kerr, 1981: 2; Morrison, 1990: 21). But the genre also has its champions. Reactionaries argue that espionage models struggle between bad and good and display democratic values, demonstrating that citizen-readers approve of their governments acting covertly in the interest of state security. Other critics find a romance of citizenship in this type of fiction, a drama where readers and viewers test and enjoy the limit cases that are regularly presented by the comparative anarchy of international relations. Loyalty, patriotism, and even the mundanity of public employment are entertainingly rehearsed as plays with death and doom (Der Derian 1992: 53–4, 57–8). It is worth interrogating the genre's history in some detail in order to consider these claims and situate Hitchcock's contributions alongside them.

Espionage fiction took off in the decade following *L'Affaire Dreyfus* in late-nineteenth-century France, when a Jewish military officer was falsely accused of espionage in what became a racially charged case that pitted an emergent group of progressive intellectuals against the state and the right. Wesley K. Wark traces connections at that time in Britain between cheap popular fiction, journalistic and governmental xenophobia, shifts in class formation and the division of labor, and the emergence of moral panics about foreigners and spying:

> The enemy could be the Jew, the foreigner, the not-quite gentleman, the corrupted, the bomb-throwers, the women. Why the day needed to be saved was very much a product of national insecurities that began to mount at the turn of the century. At their heart were fears about the pace of technological and societal change caused by the impact of the industrial revolution. In the wake of its manifold upheavals, traditional measures of the international balance of power were threatened and the domestic structures of government upset. (1993: 275)

Ernest Mandel's compelling sociohistorical account of such fiction describes the period between the two world wars, when *The Lady Vanishes* was made, as an epistemological watershed. Crime fiction was transformed to allow for a new force, directed against the sovereign state rather than property or individuals. These were crimes by one state against another, with governments personified by shadowy, undercover figures. Since that time, the element of mystery in espionage fiction has derived from identifying and sabotaging an enemy's alliances, supporters, methods, and reasons. Mandel explains that espionage plots usually concern a plan that has been devised and executed by an opponent of the state and is foiled in the lonely hour of the last instance by a lone operative working inside the enemy's own sphere of action. The operative's success is guaranteed by superior beauty, physique, and technology. Mandel ties these developments to the split subjectivity and increased alienation produced by consumer capitalism. Super-heroes must be raised to a higher level with the general development of bourgeois society: mechanization and diversification of commodity production, hyperconsumerism, and alienation of the individual (1984: 61–2, 65).

The appealing quality of many early espionage protagonists was their accidental, almost ironic emergence. Rather than hardened professionals, they were gifted amateurs thrust into a role as protagonists of history. Such figures have a long lineage. The "diminished claim of affective ties on the heroic adventurer" dates back to the world's foundational Anglo novel by the ex-spy Daniel Defoe. *Robinson Crusoe*'s 1707 anomic male subject must forage alone and govern himself until his historic destiny to control others is reactivated by the appearance of Friday. This trope also relates to the utilitarianism of sovereign consumers and the alibi for empire that sees gallant adventurers happening upon "possessions" while looking for their authentic selves (Thompson, 1993: 74).

In nineteenth- and twentieth-century espionage, this amateurism had exclusive economic and social preconditions. A clubbish male atmosphere was evoked by the nicknames that early members of the British secret service used to refer to one another: "Woolly, Buster, Biffy, Bubbles, Blinker, Barmy, [and] Tin-Eye" head one list (Porter, 1989: 169). Apart from attesting to the claim that English public schools produce children rather than develop them, this roll call signifies *joie de vivre*, not taking things too seriously, and never losing a sense of self that can transcend its environment – the stereotype of the phlegmatic all-rounder, accompanied by a flippant righteousness implicitly informed by race, class, and gender. Think of the moment when Nigel Havers clears hurdles adorned with champagne glasses in *Chariots of Fire* (Hugh Hudson, 1981).

We hope that this engagement with ideas of genre, and specifically a fictional one with close ties to international politics, gives an idea of how questions of form and style but also geopolitical economy are necessarily mixed together. The case studies that follow start with an example from the genre just described, then broaden the purview.

Case Studies

24

Our first case study is *24*. This most enduring and internationally successful US TV espionage show, it ran from 2001 to 2010 and was revived in 2014 as *24: Live Another Day*. *24* has all the arrogant vigilantism of the British spy from the classical period, but with a rough-and-tumble component at odds with how an English gentleman would comport himself.[7]

The program began in the fateful fall of the Northern Hemisphere, just after airplane missiles had struck the northeast of the United States. By 2009, a hundred million people were watching it across the world on 236 channels. The series bound together two senses of realism in a classic dual verisimilitude that drew both on faithfulness to a genre (espionage) and on narrative cues, images, sounds, and editing that are frequently associated with documentaries or news programs. This is in keeping with its central conceit of the action taking place over the 24 hours it takes to watch each season of episodes.

24 was welcomed as a return of high-quality drama to the US broadcast networks that ran counter to the hegemony of reality television. It was even celebrated as a grand piece of existential philosophy – a solitary figure standing against an array of untrustworthy institutions, upholding an obscure code in which he is police, jury, and judge rolled into one vigilante. Yet the program clearly borrows devices and storylines from more critically derided genres, such as soap opera, reality, and action adventure, thanks to its cliff-hanger episodic stories and macho violence – in addition to pirating the avant-garde, courtesy of fractured storylines and points of view. Of course, this is all underwritten by corporate messages; the first episode of 2003 began and ended with a six-minute film promoting a Ford car. And *24*'s uniqueness itself briefly became a formula when CBS announced *Harper's Island* (2008–9), an overtly self-destructing series in which viewers were guaranteed that a central character would die each week (Attallah, 2006; Lotz, 2008: 173; McMahon, 2008; McPherson, 2008; Miklos, 2008; Aitkenhead, 2009; Steinberg, 2009; Shimpach, 2010).

Then there is the question of *24*'s politics. Produced by Republicans – the show's creator, Joel Surnow, boasts of being a "rightwing nut job" (quoted in Aitkenhead, 2009) – it has featured cameos by their ideological *confrères* in Congress (John McCain) and the news media (Laura Ingraham and Larry Elder) and was endorsed by such intellectual lackeys of the George W. Bush regime as the *ur*-disgraced-academic John Woo, who wrote legal justifications of inhumane brutality. The Heritage Foundation, a reactionary, coin-operated think-tank, held a press conference in 2006 in celebration of the series that featured Michael Chertoff, the Secretary of Homeland Security, and talk radio host Rush Limbaugh, who announced that then-Vice-President Dick Cheney and Defense Secretary Donald Rumsfeld were fans of the program (Lithwick, 2008).

24 clearly endorses torture as a means of extracting information from terrorists – there were 67 instances of torture in the series. For some critics, it represents "la suma de los miedos americanos" (the sum of American fears) (Miklos, 2008: 79). *24* can be seen as "the most extended televisual reflection to date on the implications of 9/11" and an egregious argument in favor of the "need" for immediate and illegal action in the "public interest" (Downing, 2007: 62). It's fine for the hero, Jack Bauer, "a man never at a loss for something to do with an electrode," to deny medical assistance to a terrorist whom he has wounded, shoot another's wife in the leg, then threaten a second shot to the knee unless her husband confides in him; and fine for the US President to subject a Cabinet member to electric shocks to interrogate him (Downing, 2007: 72, 77; Lithwick, 2008) as Bauer endlessly intones "Whatever it takes." This is what Slavoj Žižek (2006) derides as "the lie of *24*: that it is not only possible to retain human dignity in performing acts of terror, but that if an honest person performs such an act as a grave duty, it confers on him a tragic-ethical grandeur."

A delegation from the major US officer training site, West Point, visited *24*'s producers in 2007 to express anxiety that many military recruits had adopted illegal, immoral attitudes to torture based on their interpellation by the series, while interrogators reported a direct mimesis between the show and actual practices in Iraqi prisons by US forces inspired by it. Human Rights Watch also weighed in. And when the program returned in 2014, Amnesty International noted its popularity in African nations that have not outlawed torture, claiming that glamorization of the activity desensitized viewers internationally. But the star and executive producer Kiefer Sutherland, the highest-paid TV actor in the world, who is liberal in his politics, disavows the notion that the program works ideologically at all: "It's good drama. And I love this drama!" And he made public service announcements in conjunction with the Council on American–Islamic Relations against stereotyping Muslims (Sutherland, quoted in Aitkenhead, 2009; Halse, 2015).

24 has been hailed for its images of African Americans and the sense of everyday bewilderment at chaos and danger it conveys that are said to characterize much of black life in a racist society (2015; Boney, 2015).[8] And it became the first carbon-neutral US TV fiction show in 2009, with offsets calculated against the impact of car chases, air travel, and coal-generated electricity, in addition to favoring wind and solar power (M. Miller, 2007; Kaufman, 2009; Glez, 2014; Toomer, 2014).[9] It's worth noting that in the United States, *24*'s staple audience was highly educated and affluent (Sconce, 2004: 99) – not people usually associated with the violence and anti-intellectualism of the program's far right producers and public supporters. *24* is an immensely rich, vulgar, polysemic, contradictory, educational, misguided, misguiding text. It is laden with imperialistic, messianic, vigilante messages – and underwritten by progressive ecology, reactionary producers, and a liberal star. Thank heavens for Stella Artois's Godardian spoof that reimagines the program as something from the *Nouvelle Vague*.[10]

India's Daughter

We turn now to a similarly violent television program, this time a BBC documentary, and one laden with even more complicated imperial and gender ideologies – *India's Daughter* (Leslee Udwin, 2015). It concerns sexual violence, specifically the rape and murder of a young woman by a group of men on a bus in Delhi in 2012 (Lodhia, 2015).

Rape is an endemic, systemic, systematic, global, and trans-historical phenomenon of gendered power. Across different laws and customs, varying forms of religion and government, and shifting coordinates of space and time, rape is a tragic constant, enabled by numerous patriarchal norms, from jurisdictions that allow rape within marriage to male violence and attitudes of superiority. The number of rapes varies across nations, because of anomalies in the definition and collection of statistics, and differences in the legal and cultural possibilities for women to seek redress. But the tendency is undeniably universal. Rape is often attributed to the biology of male sexuality, as if it were an inevitable consequence of physiological destiny. But rape is more accurately regarded as a method of male control, used to dominate women. It is about social power, not physical need. Although rape is traumatic in physical, psychological, and political ways, and recognized as such in most countries (frequently alongside ambivalent or negative attitudes to women's autonomy), its perpetrators are rarely charged or convicted (Edwards *et al.*, 2015).

The struggle over women's bodies is also an imperial and colonial question. It is embedded in global history, and anti-rape discourses sometimes show that lineage. For example, a haunting resonance accompanied the US–UK invasion of Afghanistan in 2001. As per Britain's involvement there a century and a half earlier, the US–UK military action and occupation were partially justified by a claim that the invading powers were driven by the desire to protect women and improve their lives. Colonialism would allegedly save women in 1838, in 1878 – and in 2001 (Cloud, 2004; Khalili, 2011; McClintock, 1995).

That complex background may help us understand the bitter controversy that swirled around *India's Daughter*. The Indian government imposed a ban on the film to prevent a local screening on NDTV. The state also demanded that the BBC remove the documentary from websites. Such drastic action was justified on the grounds that the filmmakers failed to obtain approval from prison authorities for their interview with one of the convicted rapists, they made it for profit, and they demeaned women, thus failing to comply with agreements struck at the time of original approval for filming (Sen, 2015).

While chary of censorship, many South Asian feminists reacted with understandable rage at the patronizing notion of having this story told to them by a white Anglo feminist; consider Paromita Vohra's open letter on the topic (2015). More than 3,000 people from India sent WhatsApp messages to the BBC within three minutes of the film's English broadcast, animated by the controversy.[11]

There are elements to this debate that concern the independence of the media from governmental control versus the responsibility of the state to protect vulnerable viewers. Then there is the difficulty of web censorship in comparatively open societies.[12] And swirling above all this, the reactionary nature of Prime Minister Narendra Modi's hard-right Hindu administration and what Arvind Rajagopal has termed "the reinvention of Hindutva" (2015). When NDTV was banned from screening the documentary, it staged a protest, declining to fill the TV hour with alternative programming apart from a screen grab of the film's title sequence.[13]

Others feel more ambivalent than straightforward supporters or opponents of the documentary. This has led to a sophisticated and worthwhile disagreement in the nation's vibrant public sphere. For Piyasree Dasgupta, the film's problems derive from its "Bollywood potboiler" narrative trajectory of equilibrium (the fateful day begins), disequilibrium (the heinous crime is committed), and equilibrium (the victim dies and the accused are tried), complete with manipulative music. All this is told with the documentarist herself rendered inaudible and invisible – we have no idea of the questions posed to the interviewees as they weep, protest, narrate, and so on (Dasgupta, 2015).

Then there is the question of due process under the law. At the time of the scheduled screening, India's Supreme Court had not concluded its deliberations on the appeal by those convicted against their death sentences. This raised significant matters: should a film address these matters prior to that decision, potentially prejudicing the final hearing? And what of the legitimacy of death sentences and the means of execution? Lastly, we must consider the defense counsels' misogyny and the film's amplification of their abhorrent contempt for legal equality and human rights, as the notable attorney Vrinda Grover explains.[14] Brinda Karat (2015) tells us that the All India Democratic Women's Association called for prosecution of the defense attorneys for their statements in the movie. Similar groups protest the way that the police discourage rape complaints, and Members of Parliament caution parents to restrict their daughter's autonomy of dress and movement.

We must also consider the question of privacy for vulnerable subjects, whether victims, assailants, or families, and what constitutes informed consent to appear in documentaries – less important, of course, than consent to sex, but still an issue in law for half a century, since *Titicut Follies* (Frederick Wiseman, 1966) filmed inmates in a prison for the criminally insane, including a convicted child rapist (Miller, 1998). In the Indian instance, the victim's father and mother both participated in the film, and the family later spoke out against the ban. Her father defended the value of *India's Daughter* as a means of shedding light on the brazenly misogynistic attitudes revealed by this crisis, opening them up to public criticism (D. Ghosh, 2015).

These struggles over the production, meaning, and distribution of *India's Daughter* are inevitably and inexorably overdetermined – perhaps most importantly by the general history of rape and the more specific one of claims from beyond to free South Asian women from their supposed oppression.

In terms of what the principal institutional actors ought to do, the right way to act should be obvious: the BBC should show greater political awareness of the people whose lives it depicts and the people whom they choose to interpret those lives. The Corporation should commission a series by Indian women documentarists of short films about life there and elsewhere, such as the United Kingdom. The Modi government should not censor. And children should learn that violence of all kinds is unacceptable.

"The Most Famous Soldier in the War"

Our next textual analysis case study is about a name and body – the Yanqui sports star and soldier Pat Tillman.[15] As per the cinema, a man becomes a sports star when his off-track lifestyle and personality merge with his sporting achievements in amalgams of training, playing, and the self. While bodies may be caked in mud or uniforms, their names, numbers, sponsors, case histories, and smiles can all be retrieved and replayed by the electronic brush of history under the sign of nationalistic fervor, and their dedication metaphorized to humanize and endorse imperialism. The internal ideological work of nationalism and the external violent work of imperialism meet neatly under the rubric of the US National Football League (NFL) with its efforts to generate a global hypermasculinist demesne that symbolizes brutality and produces revenue.

It comes as no surprise that studies of US TV sports fans indicate high correlations with support for imperialist warmongering, principally among white men (Stempel, 2006). Sporting allegory has traditionally reinforced masculinism and patriotism, especially at times of great conflict or formal celebration. To cite some prominent US instances: Andrew Johnson hosted the New York Mutuals baseball club at the White House in 1867; Theodore Roosevelt indexed his manliness by riding horses; opening day Major League baseball pitches have regularly been thrown by presidents since 1910; the first network TV broadcast in the United States was a 1945 football game with President Harry S. Truman in the stadium, binding sport, politics, and corporate power together in a symbolic whirl; Dwight D. Eisenhower played golf; and Ronald Reagan was carefully if comically depicted as a cowboy. Sport has also provided linguistic tropes of empire and masculinity: Richard M. Nixon's Secretary of Defense Melvin Laird euphemized the mining of Haiphong Harbor and increased bombing of North Vietnam as "an expansion ball club"; the Nixon White House staff called itself "operation linebacker"; and Tricky Dicky's own nickname was "quarterback." The oleaginous Reagan regularly cited the role he played as student "football" player George Gipp in the 1940 biopic of a Notre Dame football coach, *Knute Rockne, All American* (Lloyd Bacon and William K. Howard, 1940). Reagan repeatedly quoted Gipp's dying words that had inspired his side to new heights – "win one for the Gipper": in a 1981 Commencement address at the university commemorated in the film, when opening the 1984 LA Olympics, as a rallying cry during the Nevada Senate race in 1986, and at George H. W. Bush's nomination two years later. Reagan also trivialized his 1984 presidential opponent Walter Mondale as "Coach tax-hike." In 2000, Senator Bill Bradley's campaign for the Democratic nomination played on his Olympic gold medal in basketball and subsequent title-winning career with the New York Nicks. George W. Bush solidified his public image in the 1990s as owner of the Texas Rangers baseball franchise, and spent much of his presidency riding bikes and running trails when he wasn't sleeping or invading, while John Kerry fruitlessly countered with "I've been a hunter all my life" in 2004. During the 2008 presidential campaign, Barack Obama played basketball with soldiers in Iraq, John McCain appeared at National Association for Stock Car Racing events, and Sarah Palin announced that she enjoyed shooting caribou from planes (Miller, 2010a; Zirin, 2008).

Beyond presidential politics, militarists deploy this type of symbolism all the time: officers see themselves as all-rounders, as pentathletes (Keenan, 2006). "Football" has specialized in nationalistic fervor through coordination with the military since the American War in Vietnam, and there is now even an Armed Forces Bowl, in which college "football" is sponsored by Bell Helicopter-Textron, one of the vast array of "private enterprise" companies whose livelihoods rely on public sector welfare via the development and purchase of murderous technology. In this instance, promotional activities are not about selling products to fans, as per most sports underwriting. Instead, they are dedicated to creating goodwill toward corporate militaristic welfare through homologies between sport, nation, and *matériel*, via a contest that is televised – and owned – by ESPN, featuring ghoulish recruiters looking to prey on young spectators plus the presentation of a "Great American Patriot Award." For its part, baseball offers "Welcome Back Veterans" and "Military Appreciation" events (Butterworth and Moskal, 2009).

At both encoding and decoding levels, it seems as though sporting metaphors associate romantic male sacrifice with national glory through classic second-order meaning. The Gipp exemplar takes the mythic last words of an historical character as replayed in a film. Four decades later, the actor playing him redisposes the words for political purposes, cleaving to himself the persona of the original speaker. Enunciation loses historical specificity, banality benefits, and thought disorder reigns. And that is where the story of Pat Tillman begins.

Tillman was an Arizona State University (ASU) "football" player who joined the NFL's Arizona Cardinals, but turned down the opportunity to further his career through a US$3.6 million contract because of his ideological affinities with US imperialism: Tillman had interpreted the horrors of September 11, 2001 as justifications for military retribution – he enlisted. His decision became a crucial aspect of US propaganda, because of his status as a "football hero" (a bizarre Yanqui neologism). His prominence made him into individually symbolic, rather than lumpen, fodder, and he was sent a very public note of congratulation by the soon-to-be-disgraced Secretary of Defense, Rumsfeld.[16]

Why? Because Tillman's recruitment delivered a "testosterone cocktail" that "was impossible to resist" (Zirin, 2005): "Journalists simply could not write about Tillman without evoking his role as a protagonist of mythic proportions" (Chidester, 2009: 366). When he died in Afghanistan in 2004, Tillman was immediately hailed for his sacrifice by the state, academia, the NFL, and the bourgeois media, and was posthumously awarded a distinguished medal, the Silver Star, for "gallantry in action against an armed enemy" which he had supposedly pursued and "forced to withdraw" (Couric, 2008).

McCain (2004) gave a eulogy at Tillman's nationally televised (ESPN) funeral, quickly turning the occasion into a hymn to "our blessed and mostly peaceful society," supported of course by military service, where "the purpose of all good courage is love." McCain said that soldiers' "blood debts" and "goodness" would endure, and reassured Tillman's family as it waited "to see him again, when a loving god reunites us all." This courage and these debts had driven Tillman from football to fighting, according to this ideologue – who had never met him, and whose "thoughts" were immediately published by the far-right *National Review* magazine. Ann Coulter called Tillman "an American original – virtuous, pure and masculine like only an American male can be" (quoted in Collier, 2005). Why thank you, Ann. And the libertarian simpletons over at the Cato Institute took Tillman's volunteerism as a sign that a military draft was not necessary, so pure was the population's desire to serve the nation while sidestepping the state (Healy, 2004).

The White House hailed Tillman as "an inspiration on and off the football field ... who made the ultimate sacrifice in the war on terror" (quoted in Zirin, 2005). The Governor of Arizona ordered that flags at ASU be flown at half mast, and the university began to market match tickets under his name. There was even an embarrassingly performative, sentimental academic lament for him that fretted over the loss of US servicemen as if they were the central suffers of imperial overreach. The Cardinals divined that he "represented all that was good in sports" and placed his uniform in a glass case alongside bouquets and teddy bears. The NFL said Tillman "personified all the best values of his country and the NFL." Much was said of his non-stop energy and desire to hurt opponents in tackles (Lockford, 2008).[17] Thanks, then, to the NFL, that great source of US masculinity, complete with proletarian alibis avowing its importance for national identity.

The League's appalling record of metabolic syndrome and cardiovascular mortality amongst its "athletes" – much higher than ordinary people, let alone by comparison with authentic sporting stars – is matched by dreadful health reports in terms of their lack of fitness and chances of early death. The research points to an alarming, in fact astonishing, correlation with neurodegeneration (Selden et al., 2009; Wojtys, 2009). Tillman may have died on the field of adventurism, but his former colleagues were set to die less glamorous deaths as signs of empire's symbolic stars whose bodies were ultimately worth nothing.

But then Tillman's story became more complex and contradictory as time passed. He was an atheist, as his youngest brother Richard explained to McCain and ESPN at the funeral: "Pat isn't with God. He's fucking dead. He wasn't religious. So thank you for your thoughts, but he's fucking dead" (quoted in Tillman with Zacchino, 2008). And during his time abroad, Tillman had become anti-war and a fan of Noam Chomsky's – he was due to meet the veteran analyst of imperialism had he returned from theater (Zirin, 2005). Then it turned out that Tillman had been the victim of manslaughter by his colleagues, not murder by his enemies. In short, he failed the tasks laid down for him by history – he was not what he looked like, not what he had been built up to be, and not what the war machine had manufactured. He was a critic of US imperialism at the very moment that he was celebrated as its epigone and epitome. His movement into the NICL had gone from sporting recruit to nationalistic recruit to ideological recruit to dead refusenick. He was a countertext, open to varied readings.

General Stanley McChrystal is notorious for several things, foremost among them having been Obama's chief warmonger of Afghanistan and a key long-term operative in the empire's mistreatment of detainees. He was also a central player in the mendacious propaganda use of Tillman's name, service, and death. When McChrystal was appointed to run the empire in Afghanistan, Tillman's father accused him of having conducted "a falsified homicide investigation." Tillman's brother Kevin referred to him as a "fraud," because McChrystal had approved the award of a Silver Star to Pat despite the ranger's death at the hands of compatriots (which McChrystal admitted under oath that he had known, even though the citation referred to "devastating enemy fire"). In 2007, the Pentagon's Acting Inspector General held McChrystal "accountable for the inaccurate and misleading assertions" in the citation, but was overruled by the army (Lindlaw and Mendoza, 2007; Krakauer, 2009; Tillman with Zacchino, 2008).[18] The military later determined that the Silver Star citation was "based on what he [Tillman] intended to do" (White, 2005). Got it. Having been disgraced by a magazine story covering his time commanding allied forces in Afghanistan that exuded disrespect for civilian control of militarists, McChrystal has, needless to say, become a chorine for arms dealers, just like his colleagues whose "work" was discussed in the previous chapter (Hastings, 2010).

Tillman's family spent years trying to penetrate the Pentagon's obfuscation and propaganda simply to establish what had been known from the moment of his death – that he'd been killed by Yanquis, heroized by Yanquis, and used by Yanquis through their state, in a way that was first and foremost dedicated to lying to his family members as part of a massive cover-up of the kind that color Republican and Democrat administrations alike (Collier, 2005; Camacho and Hauser, 2007; Andrews, 2006). As second-order meaning, this bought into a long and disgraceful association of whiteness with sporting and military valor, versus an association of blackness with flashiness and selfishness (Kusz, 2007). As a white man, Tillman was fodder for this binary.

Tillman's brother and fellow-recruit Kevin testified before Congress that the impending disclosures about sexual torture by Yanqui soldiers at Abu Ghraib prison had driven the Pentagon to clutch at Pat and claim him for nationalism: "Revealing that Pat's death was a fratricide would have been a political disaster during a month already swollen with political disasters and a brutal truth that the American public would undoubtedly find unacceptable, so the facts needed to be suppressed. An alternative narrative had to be constructed."[19] Kevin Tillman (2006) went on to explain how repulsed the family was to learn that "our elected leaders were subverting international law and humanity" through the seizure and torture of people, because "suspension of Habeas Corpus is supposed to keep this country safe" and "reason is being discarded for faith, dogma, and nonsense." When the *San Francisco Chronicle* disclosed that Tillman had regarded the invasion of Iraq as "fucking illegal" (Collier, 2005), Coulter thundered: "I don't believe it" (quoted in Zirin, 2005).

As Kevin Tillman noted to Congress, querying the official rendition of his brother's death was equated with "casting doubt on Pat's bravery and sacrifice." It was nothing of the sort. Rather, once the nature of the scandal was exposed, "Pat was no longer of use as a sales asset." Needless to say, the accused war criminal Rumsfeld did not contact the family once this "asset" had been compromised – but did take time to deny there had been a cover-up. His typically torturous prose found that the story had been "handled in a way that was unsatisfactory." This was an oblique reference to the fact that Tillman's mother learnt her son was the victim of fratricide from the *Arizona Republic*, not an Arizona Republican. For questioning the Pentagon, she and her surviving sons were routinely derided by the right (Fish, 2006; Goff, 2006; Breslau, 2008; Couric, 2008).[20]

Any attempt to rearticulate Tillman's death and its faux heroization led to immediate and maddened calumny from conservatives. When ASU art professor John Leaños generated a poster of Tillman entitled "Friendly Fire," which questioned these militaristic distortions "and the quasi-religious and dogmatic adherence to Tillman's mythological heroic image by mainly conservative male Americans," he was immediately subjected to scrutiny by CBS, CNN, and ABC. That produced angry outbursts by viewers, hundreds of violent, splenetic emails and threats, and an inquiry into Leaños by ASU and denunciations of him by the school's bureaucrats (Leaños, 2005).

One of the army's principal investigators, and a recommender of the Silver Star award, Tillman's commander Ralph Kauzlarich, suggested to ESPN that the Tillman family had been unable to accept that this was "an unfortunate accident" because they were not religious (i.e., superstitious) and hence saw Pat's fate as to become "worm dirt." (This "reasoning" was also evident in an internal military memo – Breslau, 2008). At least Tillman's worm-afterlife had a name – the Afghan soldier killed alongside him was left unidentified for years (Greenwald, 2007; Goff, 2006).

But many did question the administration's propaganda. The TV drama series *Bones* (2005–) offered a thinly veiled fictionalization of the cover-up (Takacs, 2009). Once the Republicans lost their congressional majority in 2006, the House of Representatives committee system mounted inquiries, albeit ineffectual ones (Greenwald, 2007; Tillman with Zacchino, 2008). ESPN undertook very thorough investigative journalism, extremely rare in the fandom that characterizes the US sporting press. It essentially showed that everyone in the chain of command understood this was a fratricide within hours of the event (Fish, 2006). The depth and breadth of ESPN's research may be taken as one of those fissures that occur when the empire is viewed as a compromised bureaucratic thicket rather than a pure national *esprit de corps* – when the state overdetermines the nation, and reflexive Yanqui dislike of government overtakes the association of military command with, to cite McCain, "love."

But a decade after Tillman's death, many news media and public and private organizations continued to use him as an inspiration to militaristic propaganda in an uncritical, credulous, ahistorical way.[21] The polysemic, contradictory, tragic career of this man's body is a text laden with media signification and power, like the body in our previous case study and the one below.

Feminist nudity? Video consent? Moral panic?

Until the end of July 2012, Karina Bolaños was a vice-minister in the government of Laura Chinchilla Miranda, then President of Costa Rica. Bolaños's portfolio covered culture and young people.[22] She can be heard on a YouTube clip, during her term as vice-minister, talking about reproductive knowledge and rights as key questions for the young.[23]

Our next text (if by now we can even use the term in its single form) began life as another video featuring Bolaños. In this case, she was forced out of her job because of a private home video that appeared without her knowledge on YouTube. She had filmed it in 2007 (according to her) or 2009 (according to the government) as an erotic video letter to a boyfriend she was involved with during (or after) a separation in her marriage (which was later briefly reconciled). Bolaños wasn't naked in the text. In fact, she was wearing what might be described as "sensible" underwear, while delivering her private message of longing. The man who was allegedly her lover copied the file, blackmailed her, then posted it.[24]

President Chinchilla Miranda, a social conservative, wouldn't stand for the scandal, and immediately removed Bolaños from office. Feminists across the country and the region, such as Gloria Valerín, organized in support of Bolaños,[25] while Costa Rica's opposition pointed out that major ethical scandals had left other Cabinet members unscathed. Julia Ardón started the Facebook page "Todos somos Karina"[26] which quickly drew adherents, admirers, and media attention. It featured photos of women and children looking angry and holding up signs with the three words.

They were protesting an all-too typical moral panic, where female sexuality is used to question fitness for public life as moral panics index ideological contradictions about social, economic, and cultural inequality (Miller, 2013a). In this instance, a woman is labeled as dangerous to the social order because she differs from stereotypes of acceptable femininity. Open female desires supposedly compromise civic leadership, while male conflicts of interest do not; an intimate video letter is unacceptable, whereas unauthorized publication of it is whistleblowing; a bra is a problem, but misogyny – not so much.

During the Egyptian revolution of 2011, a young woman, Aliaa al-Mahdy, a student at the American University of Cairo – a communication major! – posted a picture of herself on a blog in full-frontal nudity, except for such accessories as ballerina flats and a red flower, alongside a political manifesto blasting power-holders for censorship, misogyny, and the oppression of women and other subalterns. In the polemic that ensued, some people went as far as threatening al-Mahdy with death. She left Egypt, was granted political asylum in Sweden, and started demonstrating naked, under the aegis of the sextremist – a self-description – group Femen in front of Egyptian embassies in Europe.[27] She became a global media sensation (Kraidy, 2012). In 2014, al-Mahdy posted a photograph on Facebook of herself and another woman menstruating and defecating on a banner that read "There is no God but Allah."[28]

Unlike al-Mahdy, who in spite of her middle-class identity was hounded out of Egypt, Bolaños was able to counter this scapegoating because of her social position: a politician with the reactionary Partido Liberación Nacional, the daughter of a mayor, the then-wife of a powerful man, and a public idolator of John Paul II. She had resources that few victims of moral panic possess. Bolaños told her story to CNN Mexico in a telephone interview.[29] During the 10-minute segment, the network clouded part of her body as seen in the notorious YouTube clip. Bolaños's voice trembles on the recording as she speaks of extortion and victimhood. The interviewer calls her "Karina" in a very intimate way, perhaps licensed by this outpouring of emotion and vulnerability. The politician apologizes to her family, her husband, and the people of Costa Rica. And insists on the unfairness of what has happened. Throughout, the ex-minister makes perfect sense, even as the feeling embodied in her speech is overwhelming. It's a classic case of body and brain registering and performing reason and emotion simultaneously, and all done with a CNN map of Central America that shows where she is and stands in for her otherwise overly viewable body.

Following that appearance, both middle-aged and new media criticized the administration for peremptorily firing Bolaños. The government responded that she had made the tape while on official business abroad, used a state-funded computer, and neglected to inform her colleagues that she was a target of blackmail, hence breaching administrative codes and becoming a security liability. This reversed its original reason for the sacking, which was to do with personal morality in the public realm.

As the case evolved, its rights and wrongs continued to touch on a hardy feminist perennial: how, whether, where, and when to distinguish the public from the private. And it was further complicated a few weeks later when Bolaños posed semi-naked and in a sexualized way in *Interviú*, a Spanish magazine, reportedly receiving €20,000 for her time. She informed readers and Costa Rican television that the President was a queen of *machismo* and protected corrupt politicians (Barrio, 2012; Díaz, 2012).[30] Three years after Bolaños's video became public, the blackmailer's trial was finally under way, and the bourgeois media continued to deliver the video to online readers.[31]

Even as the Bolaños issue erupted, related scandals emerged across the region. One concerned Elianis Garrido, a Colombian lawyer who worked as a dancer and had recently been expelled from the reality show *Protagonistas de Nuestra Tele* (2010–13) for fighting with a housemate.[32] Based on a Puerto Rican format, the program's participants compete to act in a *telenovela* and are judged by professors. *Protagonistas de Nuestra Tele* was so popular that it rated well against *Pablo Escobar: El Patrón del Mal* (2012), a series about the nation's most notorious cocaine kingpin that proceeded to draw more than two million viewers to its US premiere (Romero, 2012).

Like other residents in *Protagonistas de Nuestra Tele*'s Casa de Estudio, Garrido was filmed while using the toilet. In all cases, though, primary and secondary sexual organs were shielded from view. Prior to her expulsion, Garrido's increasingly iconic status on the show had fed rumors that she was transsexual. One media outlet dispatched an investigative team to determine her gender (Pink Sauce, 2012). Then a still photograph of her in the bathroom, minus shields, appeared across the internet. This time, a working-class man employed on the show was identified as the perpetrator. Again, discussion proliferated, as did reproduction of the image. And when it was announced that Garrido would be posing naked for a magazine and signing on for another TV program, counter-rumors circulated that this had all been a publicity stunt.

Meanwhile, in Brazil, lawyer Denise Rocha Leitao was fired from the Senate by the conservative Partido Progresista because a 2005 video of her having sex was published online. As she left the building, Leitao told journalists she was a victim of *machismo*: "If I'd been a man, nothing would have happened." Unlike the *Tica* and the *Barranquillera*, she declined to pose for men's magazines and made a successful appearance on the reality show *A Fazenda* (2009–).[33]

These women have attracted a wide range of commentators, from teen bloggers to concerned feminists, from stern politicians to anxious editorialists. And us. We like (some) gossip. We are fascinated by scandal as it indexes cultural politics. And we want to understand what captures the public imagination. We also want to see privacy rights amplified and enforced, especially over sexual pleasure, which is used so frequently against women and minorities.

When the nineteenth-century British courtesan Harriet Wilson threatened to circulate love letters from the Duke of Wellington, victorious general at the Battle of Waterloo and later Prime Minister, he supposedly replied "Publish and be damned!"

(quoted in Johnson, n.d.). And got away with it. For women, the reality remains very different. So how should professors, journalists, writers, and politicians deal with new ways of sharing intimacy via contemporary communication technologies that blur the distinction between public and private culture? Does academic freedom extend to spreading information about the intimate moments of simultaneously strong and vulnerable women? And how many of our readers didn't visit the Bolaños video?

Greenpeace, Shell, Lego: three multinationals

Our next case study also involves the intersection of the conventional and newer media. In this case, it concerns a core aspect of children's popular culture, a wildly successful Hollywood film, and their appropriation and critique by an environmental nongovernment organization. This was done in the name of the public (though enabled by a corporate advertising agency) as part of a campaign against oil exploration.

October 9, 2014 was a big day in eco-activism: Lego announced that it would not renew a product placement deal with Shell, following concerted pressure from Greenpeace as part of a campaign to ban Arctic oil exploration by attacking firms associated with such activities. Greenpeace and a tame advertising agency had made two very smart, ingenious videos attacking Lego's collaboration with Shell. The first and most popular took music, words, images, and logos from one of the most successful films of the year, *The Lego Movie* (Chris Miller and Phil Lord, 2014)[34] plus *Halo 3* (2007) and *Game of Thrones* (2011–), to create a postmodern pastiche aimed at the heartstrings of all.[35] The second, artier and less direct, was targeted at parents and sought to use the world's two other principal languages, Spanish and Putonghua, spoken by young people.[36] The idea was to broaden appeal and use the Edenic notion of childhood against Lego and Shell, both practiced at exactly this form of exploitation.

The first text, a brilliant video trope, worked magnificently and has become a market leader for advertising agencies in what are known as "attack ads," whose primary *raison d'être* is belittling others. As the industry Bible *AdWeek* put it, Greenpeace took "a page from Chipotle's marketing playbook – haunting animation plus a distressing cover of a well-known song" (Nudd, 2013, 2014).[37]

Corporate polluters engage in collaborations with companies like Lego as part of their quest to obtain what they call "a social license to operate." This surprisingly overt term has been adopted with relish by miners to explain their plans for winning over local, national, and international communities (Thomson and Boutilier, 2011; Prno and Slocombe, 2012).[38] *Forbes* magazine suggests that 2013 was *the* year of such licenses for the extractive sector (Klein, 2012). The International Energy Agency includes them among its ominously titled *Golden Rules for a Golden Age of Gas* (2012).

The social license to operate seeks to elude state regulation by appealing to the material or affective interests of communities through a complicated melange of consumerist self-interest and civic pride. This is especially troublesome because the national boundaries and interests that typically define and engage citizens are brought into question by the border-crossing impact of environmental despoliation (Dean, 2001).

In this case, the firm was Greenpeace's sworn enemy, Shell, which is always on the lookout for social licenses to operate. For its part, Lego benefited from the money that came with product placement by Shell: like a James Bond movie, producers could defray their costs well in advance of sales to customers by accepting funding from firms that want to be associated with a happy, friendly, child-oriented, trustworthy image. As a subplot, Lego boasted of its green credentials, claiming it was becoming carbon-neutral.

On July 1, 2014, just after the first video had emerged, a statement from Lego announced: "A co-promotion contract like the one with Shell is one of many ways we are able to bring LEGO˚ bricks into the hands of more children." It went on: "The Greenpeace campaign focuses on how Shell operates in a specific part of the world. We firmly believe that this matter must be handled between Shell and Greenpeace. We are saddened when the LEGO brand is used as a tool in any dispute between organisations."[39] A few months later, the company's tune was significantly different:

> We continuously consider many different ways of how to deliver on our promise of bringing creative play to more children. We want to clarify that as things currently stand we will not renew the co-promotion contract with Shell when the present contract ends.
>
> We do not want to be part of Greenpeace's campaign and we will not comment any further on the campaign. We will continue to deliver creative and inspiring LEGO play experiences to children all over the world.[40]

This is, surely, one of those moments when a big but pusillanimous multinational corporation withers in the face of critique from a gallant but small nongovernment organization – when activism trumps business, ethics triumphs over size, and scale is hapless in the face of righteousness. It has been hailed by Greenpeace true believers as "one of the most high-profile victories in its history" thanks to "guerrilla tactics" (Bermingham, 2014). The organization immodestly announced: "Today was a great day for the Arctic, and for people power" (Greenpeace email to supporters, October 9, 2014). The prevailing assumption was that the counter-advertisements produced by Greenpeace had gathered together an organically grassroots coalition of ordinary people against corporate power and won a significant victory. The organization argued that its grassroots campaign and direct action pranks were crucial.[41]

But these other actions, such as a few children building anti-oil Lego figures in central London, some adults climbing models at a theme park, and fun Lego figures placed in protests across major world cities, were minor irritants at best, drawing predictably minimal press coverage. They incarnated a grassroots legitimacy that appeals to donors and old-fashioned activists from pre-social media eras. The real success derived from smart, sophisticated, well-heeled multinational marketing campaigns, undertaken via a vast network, using the services of advertising agencies, and borrowing trademarks and copyrights to drag their owners down. In other words, these texts were part of an orchestrated, centralized campaign by full-time professional operatives and account managers that reused others' ideas and property to mock similarly powerful actors, while pretending to do so from an outsider's perspective. And their principal target was cultural elites, people like the Greenpeace employees and ad-agency apparatchiks inside Lego, who would be shocked by the campaign and influence their corporate masters. This was the triumph of a wealthy worldwide organization aided by sympathetic businesses – and it had no impact of any discernible kind on Arctic drilling. This story is really about what happens when multinationals fall out, when two vast companies (Shell and Lego) are separated by another powerful, albeit not-for-profit, multinational (Greenpeace) reveling in the fantasy that it is David taking on Goliath. Greenpeace had not achieved very much in its critiques of Shell, so it went after a soft target. Lego caved in, the victim of a form of secondary boycott. But even as the triumph occurred, Shell was luxuriating in Pele's endorsement for providing "the world's first player-powered community football pitch in the centre of Rio Di Janeiro's favela" (McCarthy, 2014).

It will take more than a sophisticated stunt by vanguardist apparatchiks to answer Pele. And it won't be the action of a brave wee David against a big nasty Goliath – more a contest between rivals for multinational space and control. Greenpeace is well placed to try – but thanks to its vast resources and smart links to advertising agencies, not some phantasmatic link to world opinion.

From soap operas to telenovelas

The period 2013–14 saw an immense impact of Turkish *telenovelas* in Chile. They provided a huge boost to the local Mega TV network, to the point of a shift in ratings so stark that it imperiled the future of other Chilean stations. This development reversed the longstanding tendency for Turkey to import Latin American *novelas* – a South-South counterflow (Zalewski, 2013; Yesil, 2015).[42]

Since 2008, Turkish *telenovelas* have been wildly popular across North Africa, the Balkans, and the Arab world (Al-Ghazzi and Kraidy, 2013). Turkish government figures boast that soap opera exports doubled in value in 2012 to US$130 million at a time when overall economic growth was stalling. The export price per episode had swollen in some cases from US$4,000 to US$150,000 in five years, depending on the series and territory. A nice externality has been boosts for tourism and the fashion trade. Huge increases in visitors were reported from Israel, Yemen, Saudi Arabia, and Qatar, along with consumer fascination for Turkish toupées for men (Candemir, 2013). Turkish soaps have even appeared on Swedish TV (Clarke, 2012).

The 2014 documentary *Kismet* covers the impact of these *novelas* in terms of the way they free viewers to share romantic, social, and legal frustrations with others and take power over their lives (Paschalidou, 2014).[43] In typically orientalist fashion, filmmaker Nina Maria Paschalidou argues that the mostly female screenwriters enchant women across the Arab world who must deal with sexual violence. In this view, soaps offer up male actors for display and pleasure who are more glamorous and less vile than those that these women generally encounter. But, as Christa Salamandra (2012) has demonstrated, good old-fashioned feminine desire, focused on an objectified male body, is at play – something that occurs over the world and is not atypical of "Islamic" or "Arab" culture (Kraidy and Al-Ghazzi, 2013a).[44]

Starting in 2008, *Gümüs*, a rag-to-riches story that would be perfectly at home in a Mexican or Brazilian *telenovela*, dominated discussions of Turkish television exports, particularly but not uniquely in the Arab world (Kraidy and Al-Ghazzi, 2013a, 2013b). A few years later, *Muhteşem Yüzyil* (*Suleiman the Magnificent*, or *Magnificent Century*, 2011–14), became a global sensation. It was broadcast to more than 200 million viewers in 2012 (Gutiérrez, 2014) and sold to Chile's Mega for around US$2,000 per episode (Almutawa, 2014).[45]

National Public Radio in the United States called *Muhteşem Yüzyil* "bodice-ripping" (Kenyon, 2013). The Turkish government criticized the program for displaying the "successful, expansionist Ottoman Sultan Suleiman as a leader who never leaves the palace or his harem (Sultan's family, concubines and children)" (Algan, 2012). Prime Minister Recep Tayyip Erdogan denounced both the director of the series and the proprietor of the broadcast network. He called for legislation proscribing the "humiliation of historical figures or perversion of real facts" (Rohde, 2012). Turkish Airlines reacted by removing the show from its in-flight entertainment options. The Emirates' equivalent immediately bought 12 episodes for travelers, its first purchase of Turkish material.[46]

Local officials were not the only outraged viewers. Macedonia's Minister of Information Society, Ivo Ivanoski, mused that "to stay under Turkish servitude for 500 years is enough." Saudi clerics issued fatwa ordering the execution of those responsible for a series that they claimed depicted debauchery and encouraged divorce amongst audiences. In Greece, anti-Turkish sentiment saw demonstrations outside the channel that screened it. And some Turkish women were not keen on the genre's female sexual empowerment; they petitioned for the deportation of Wilma Elles, the German actress who played a seductress in *Öyle Bir Geçer Zaman Ki* (*As Time Goes By*, 2010–13) (Zalewski, 2013). Ece Algan wrote to us that:

> The petition had nothing to do with Wilma's character being sexually empowered or the traditional Turkish women not being able to handle it. The TV series opened up a big wound among women whose husbands left home due to the Turkish state allowing a huge influx of Russian women, who wanted a better life and to make some money through prostitution, through its borders in the 1980s. Many Turkish men left their wives and married Russian women or spent their savings on those sex workers, bringing lots of STDs to their wives and/or abandoning them. There was quite a bit of drama as sleeping w beautiful blonde sexy "Natasha"s became a fashionable things to do among Turkish men. Those who didn't were considered old-fashioned.

As NICL talk renews of a "Hollywood on the Bosphorous" with investment from Los Angeles, a part will be played in any such boom by the popularity of these series in the Cordilleras and the Scandes; and perhaps the United States: *Suleiman: El Gran Sultán* began on Mundo Fox (now Mundo Max) in 2014 and drew more than 1,300 comments on its home page within six months (Candemir, 2013). Meanwhile, the next big Turkish hit to be sold, *Binbir Gece* (*Las mil y una noches/One Thousand and One Nights*, 2006–9; 2014–15 in Latin America) drew huge audiences in Chile, Argentina, Bolivia, Colombia, Uruguay, and Perú. Parents in Argentina and Colombia were naming their newborns after characters, notably Sherezade and Onur (Saucedo Añez, 2015).

Conclusion

Tracking the material life of a program such as *Muhteşem Yüzyil* and these other popular series and narratives is part of what global media studies and 3.0 must do. We have seen how the infrastructural elements of the media are organized, how the texts they make circulate, and what they signify. The next chapter engages more fully with a particular genre – reality television – in greater depth, drawing on the methods exhibited above.

8 Reality Television

Picking up on the previous chapter's discussion of genre and its exemplification of textual analysis, we turn here to reality television. It has spread like wildfire across the world since the beginning of the century, occupying a seemingly ever-increasing share of prime time television in many countries across the world. The reality genre is a strange hybrid of cost-cutting devices, game shows taken into the community, *cinéma-vérité* conceits, scripts written in postproduction, social Darwinist ideology, surveillance, and gossip. From the first, it has embodied the principle of customization through format sales. Globalization is at its heart. For example, a key function of BBC America, a cable network on the air since 1998, is to showcase reality programs that might then be sold as formats to US stations (Steemers, 2004: 142–3; Gray, 2009). An examination of reality television enables a unique vista into the ways in which contemporary global media depend on specific configurations of labor, capital, and meaning.

Michael Grade, head of Britain's ITV, claims that drama fails to match reality TV's "emotional drain" (quoted in Billington and Hare, 2009) and John Birt, the BBC's former director-general, says it has "liberated Britons to express themselves imaginatively and individually" (2005). Neoliberal chief executives can be relied upon to say such things. If they knew some history, their Olympian pronouncements might have more shades of meaning.

The origins of reality television lie in the propaganda ministry of the Nazi Party in the 1930s. *Die Kriminalpolizei Warnt!* (*The Criminal Investigation Department Warns!*) was the party's centerpiece of TV programming. Fritz Schiegk spoke live with police officers about unsolved cases and invited audiences to cooperate in catching opponents of the state. When television returned to Germany after the war, the genre quickly became popular. For 50 years, that show's successor, *Aktenzeichen XY . . . ungelöst* (*File Sign XY . . . Unsolved*, 1967–), has been a model for police–civilian collaboration series around the world, such as *Crimewatch* (1984–) and *America's Most Wanted* (1988–2012). The key contemporary source of the reality TV phenomenon has been Italy, where public television pioneered the modern genre due to competition from new private concerns (Bourdon *et al.* 2008: 113–20).

It also has origins in post-World War II US radio series and serials that dealt with the massive dislocation occasioned by that conflict. Soap operas emerged to index these radical shifts and domesticate them within manageable worlds (Zafra Zafra, 2012). Then came reality programming. During the 1930s, the psychology department at Columbia University had hired Allen Funt as a research assistant. Funt drew on the psy-function sadisms he learnt there to create a radio show called *Candid Microphone* (1947–48, 1950), which migrated to television in 1947 as *Candid Camera* and traversed five decades of television history (1948–53, 1960–7, 1974–9, 1991–2,

1998-2001). *Candid Camera* pioneered the notion of surveillance as a source of fun, information, and narcissism – Funt would hail his audience with "You are the star!" (Simon 2005: 180-81).

The genre also has something in common with melodrama, a genre that was damned from its origins in eighteenth-century Europe by contrast with naturalism and realism because of its high-intensity emotionalism, but can also be read as a site that tested out new social identities in times of intense disruption, when religious and monarchical power were being challenged by urbanizing capitalism and secular democracy (Merritt, 1983). One could say similar things about the neoliberal era, when reality TV and *telenovelas* alike offer testing grounds for new subjectivities in an era of apparent choice but also widening inequality (Abu-Lughod, 2005). The genre speaks to the supposed responsibility of all people to master their drives and harness their energies to get better jobs, homes, looks, and families. That said, it can also be very inclusive: US reality TV has featured queer characters on more than a dozen shows as part of this class-blind but inclusive push to appeal to all identities (Miller, 2008).

The genre is suffused with neoliberal deregulatory nostrums: individual responsibility, avarice, possessive individualism, hyper-competitiveness, and commodification, played out in the domestic sphere rather than the public world. For example, makeover programs take economically underprivileged people and offer them a lifestyle they cannot afford to sustain. The makeover varietal focuses on dramatic aesthetic transformations (Heyes, 2007). Its emphasis on spectacle and cost – transformations are very personal and hence cheap for broadcasters – has proven to be very appealing.

A Kaiser Foundation study of US reality television drew on encounters with TV producers and health care critics and professionals to get at the dynamics of how the genre represents medicine and related topics. The research found that, for all its populist alibis, reality television constructs professional medical expertise as a kind of magic beyond the ken of ordinary people – and certainly beyond their informed critique. Again and again, whether it's plastic surgeons or pediatricians, miraculous feats are achieved by heroic men who deliver ignorant and ugly people from the dross of the everyday, transcending what off-screen primary care physicians have been able to do for them. For all the world channeling *Ben Casey* (1961-6), these daring young men make astonishing breakthroughs. The Foundation's study could find nothing in the genre even remotely critical of this model of what "*they* can do": the representation of medical expertise deemed it ungovernable other than by its own caste (Christenson and Ivancin, 2006). The use of the commodity form to promise transcendence through the national health care system, as embodied in patriarchal medicine, is sickening. And as with makeovers of houses and personal style, it offers a transcendence of the putatively grubby working and lower-middle classes that viewers cannot afford to emulate. Helpless and ugly, patient bodies testify to the surgeons' skill just as fashion consultants might confront a lack of savoir-faire (Heyes 2007: 19).

And there are clear ties between the ideology of the texts we see and the public policies and investment patterns that govern them. The contemporary prominence of reality television derives from transformations in the political economy of TV, specifically deregulation. In place of the universalism of the old networks, where sport, weather, news, lifestyle, and drama programming had a comfortable and appropriate

frottage, highly centralized but profoundly targeted consumer stations emerged globally in the 1990s. They fetishized lifestyle and consumption *tout court* over a blend
of purchase and politics, of fun and foreign policy. Reality television, fixed upon by
cultural critics who either mourn it as representative of a decline in journalistic standards or celebrate it as the sign of a new public sphere, should frankly be understood as
a cost-cutting measure and an instance of niche marketing – but also and equally as a
fascinating instance of fantasy and hope, of social criticism and aspiration.

Consider *Undercover Boss* (2010–15) on CBS, which was nominated for an Emmy
as "Outstanding Reality Program" in 2010 and 2011 and won the following year.[1] It
accompanies corporate executives as they venture *incognito* into factories to experience grassroots life in their companies. This smacks of unreconstructed Maoism. It's
all rather reminiscent of Deng Xiaoping being sent off to the Xinjian County Tractor
Factory during the Cultural Revolution for some political re-education courtesy of
participant observation of the working class (Wang, 2003). On the other hand, it's
not – the corporations involved are guaranteed that nothing on the screen will reflect
negatively on them (York, 2010).

Timothy White, the then Chancellor of the University of California, Riverside, who
went on to run the California State University system, appeared on *Undercover Boss*
in 2011.[2] It began and ended in tears. He cried about personal loss. He cried about
student debt. He almost cried about putting in false teeth and wearing a Groucho
mustache as part of his thrilling disguise. He looked very miserable as he tried to
function as an athletic coach, a library assistant, a science adjunct – you name it.
But then Tim White removed the disguise. He came out, out of the closet of the faux
proletariat. And his young mentors in these various failed real jobs were rewarded.
Student loans? Forgiven. Poor athletic facilities? Sorted (a promise of US$2 million for
capital improvements). Untenured junior faculty? Supported. It was magic, provided
by unnamed benefactors.

What an absurd moment – but a teachable one, as we Socratic folks like to say.
It cloaked the horrors of a system that puts children of the working class into gen-
erational debt and wastes millions of dollars on anti-educational sports programs.
The cloak was one-off charity, made available to those lucky enough to be subject to
childish deceit by a media corporation and a public servant.

Both the program itself and White's conduct were of course betrayed by the title
– this was part of a wider trend toward scholarly surveillance. Regional accrediting
institutions that vouch for the quality of US degrees have been in place for well over
a century. But since the 1970s, there have been vast increases in auditing work: from
outside the university, on the campus itself, within departments, and in how faculty
members see themselves. For example, we have seen more and more performance-
based evaluations of teaching at departmental and Decanal levels, rather than in
terms of the standard of an overall school. Such methods are used by 95 percent of
departments (for the impact on feminist professors and faculty of color, see Valdivia,
2001).

Grants and commodification are valorized over publication, and administrators
refer to "change" as an unproblematic good that they adore and admire. This means
more obedience, more external review, more metrification of tasks, more forms, less
autonomy, and less time to research. "Change" refers, really, to managerial mistrust
of academics. It is a new kind of conformity, to national and international governmen-

talization and commodification. The picture is starkly sketched in Gaye Tuchman's telling ethnography *Wannabe U* (2009).

So White's seemingly solitary life at the top is actually quite sociable. Non-teaching, non-researching managers have increased their proportion from a tenth to a fifth of employees across US schools in the last three decades. The upshot of such ecstatically parthenogenetic managerialism is that more and more senior and junior administrative positions are created. Universities have added so many managers (a 240 percent increase from 1976 to 2001) that faculty amount to just a third of campus workers. And whereas senior faculty members are frequently replaced by assistant professors or adjuncts, senior managers tend to be replaced by those of equivalent rank (Deresiewicz, 2011; Martin, 2011). Reach out and feel the love. *Apparatchiks* are just a coquettish glance away for this subject of *Undercover Boss*. Makeover TV is neoliberalism at play, and it is deadly serious. But like melodrama, it references massive changes in autonomy and authority in a way that can open those transformations up for inspection. What have such investigations discovered?

As it developed during the last decade, scholarship on reality television has mostly focused on Europe, particularly the United Kingdom, and on one program, *Big Brother* (1999–). The topic has elicited a steady stream of studies concerned with issues of privacy, surveillance, and authenticity. *Big Brother UK 1* (2000) contestant "Nasty Nick," whose eviction from the show made the front pages of most British newspapers, is an extreme case of the boorish characters contrived by reality TV in order to dispense rudeness and animosity under the gaze of several cameras, in an effort to lure and hold viewers.

Until recently, the focus on *Big Brother* in the Anglo-American world was persistent. Even an explicitly comparative attempt to understand reality television as a global phenomenon was nonetheless undercut by a single-text focus on *Big Brother* (Mathjis and Jones, 2004), with three chapters dedicated to the British version of the show. Interesting accounts of the reality television phenomenon in France stayed for the most part outside the trans-Atlantic conversation on reality television, because they were written in French (for example, Macé, 2003). When scholarship sailed past the US–UK nexus, it washed up on the shores of Northern Europe, especially Belgium, the Netherlands, and the Nordic countries.

A decade after it started, the study of reality television is finally expanding beyond the customary North Atlantic cradle. The importance of this development does not reside merely in an expanded geographic scope, but also in terms of socially and politically contextualizing reality TV. As Minna Aslama and Mervi Pantti argued in their work on reality television and national identity in Finland:

> relatively little attention has been given to how the phenomenon may be nationally specific . . . the questions of how and to what extent the phenomenon of reality television is local as opposed to global and what kinds of mechanisms of nation building it may entail become both of great interest and of great relevance. (2007: 50).

An expanded geographical scope is a necessary, though insufficient, condition for a truly comparative perspective of these texts, in order to comprehend the nuanced but important differences between the social and political meaning and uptake of reality television in the Anglo-American North Atlantic world, on the one hand, and less powerful European countries (for example Finland and the Balkans), the Arab world,

Latin America, Asia, and Africa, on the other. There are also important differences between and within these regions, which we identify by considering reality television as a formation articulating site, genre, and technology. Ultimately, the significance of global analysis resides in decentering European and North American optics on texts. In doing so, we hope to compel scholars of reality television in the Anglo world to contextualize their work, rather than taking it as normative and universal.

To accomplish that goal, this chapter utilizes multilingual scholarship to understand reality television on a global scale. We shall see that in many parts of the world, nationalism emerges as a dominant trope related to reality television. The question arises whether the nationalism associated with reality television shows is qualitatively different from other kinds of nationalism, and what tensions are exhibited between liberalism, neoliberalism, and nationalism. Another, paradoxical, question we address concerns the extent to which the nation-state should be displaced as the locus of reality television shows. Given the importance of nationalism textually, it is reasonable to apply it contextually. But given the similarities and differences we can discern across territories and times, essentializing about reality TV as a whole, and extrapolating from one country or one language in a universalizing way, are insupportable.

These questions are triggered by the increasingly transnational and often global scope of media operations in much of the world. Whereas in Europe, each nation-state had a tailored version of *Big Brother*, reality shows in other parts of the world addressed a transnational audience. The continental *Big Brother Africa* (2003, 2007–) and pan-Arab *Star Academy* (2003–14) are two examples. As popular and controversial transnational phenomena, they activated social and political debates within and between nations. In the countries of the former Yugoslavia, the show *To Sam Ja* (*That's Me*, 2004–5), designed to make Bosnians, Croats, Macedonians, Montenegrans, Serbs, and Slovenes achieve a measure of reconciliation, ended up inciting sectarian tensions between those groups (Volcic and Andrejevic, 2009). In other cases, as we shall see, the intranational scale is the most interesting. For example, *Indian Idol* (2004–) rearticulated how the northwest Indian states of Meghalaya and Assam, politically and economically marginalized from national life, related to the nation more broadly (Punathambekar, 2010).

By operating worldwide, on sub- and supranational scales, reality television shows invite us to rethink venerable shibboleths about what counts as knowledge of a genre. The African, Arab, Indian, and ex-Yugoslav cases also raise questions about connections between mass mediation and nationalism that have been largely smothered during the last decade by international communication scholars' focus on media and cultural globalization.

Reality television reflects, perhaps more conspicuously than other genres, the convergence between "old" and "new" media in the culture industries. In a global context of privatized state assets and liberalized trade between nations and their media and telecommunications industries, a comparative examination of the genre enables a renewed appreciation of the complicated economic implications of convergent media industries across the local-to-global spectrum. For example, as Sean Jacobs (2007) convincingly argues, *Big Brother Africa* is best understood in the context of post-Apartheid South Africa's economic domination and cultural hegemony of sub-Saharan Africa. Adding a level of complication, South African companies have recently had to contend with the Chinese corporate and diplomatic offensive sweeping the continent. As Chinese businesses move to wrest control of key sectors of the African economy from South African firms – especially in mining – the latter redouble their efforts to maintain market power by exploiting other sectors. South Africa-based, transcontinental reality television shows operate as marketing platforms. They are all the more potent because they attract young people – emerging consumers – and stir controversy, which engenders visibility.

Big Brother Africa's first two seasons, in 2001 and 2002, were South African, broadcast by M-Net. For the 2003 season, M-Net made the show pan-African under its channel name MultiChoice Africa. The show was hugely successful; its final episode was "broadcast from Johannesburg to an estimated television audience of 30 million people in 46 countries on the continent" (Jacobs, 2007: 851). Showcasing a group of young, well-educated, well-off Africans leading a sequestered life of interpersonal and sexual tension, the program attracted strong criticism from some African intellectuals, clerics, and politicians. Other leaders praised it and sought photo opportunities with the show's contestants.

In the Arab world, where corporate audience research remains under a cloud for favoring certain media companies over others, the popularity of reality TV has enabled a new political economy predicated on viewer interactivity across cell phones, the internet, and television, increasing profits while multimedia applications spread the wealth to telecommunications companies. At the same time, interactive shows also herald new audience-measurement practices. The pan-Arab media industries, including reality television, are driven by a convergence of Saudi capital and Lebanese cultural labor, with the infrastructure – most centrally though not exclusively in DMC – made possible by migrant manual labor from Southeast Asia. In the cases of Africa, the Arab world, and elsewhere, the economic implications of reality television contribute to wide-ranging controversies over the NICL.

If in the Global South reality television articulates politics, understood as contesting for power in public discourse, then in the United States and the United Kingdom, reality television is seen as the harbinger of the "new" – i.e. the digital – economy, defining the political in terms of corporate surveillance and the micropolitics of confessional, self-revealing behavior. As Mark Andrejevic argues, reality television programs "help to define a particular form of subjectivity consonant with an emerging online economy: one which equates submission to comprehensive surveillance with self-expression and self-knowledge." He contends that by making celebrity appear to be accessible for everyone, reality TV promotes the notion that "a surveillance-based society can overcome the hierarchies of mass society." Andrejevic concludes that the subject positions promoted by reality shows programs bolster "the promise of the interactive economy to democratize production by relinquishing control to consumers and viewers" (2002: 253, 251).

Once we consider reality television globally, the question arises: to what extent is such an analysis helpful when we know that many countries that we discuss do not have basic internet infrastructure? In places where satellite television channels are substitutes for web streaming reality television, because most viewers do not have access to broadband, what are we to make of the following claim?

> [T]he online economy ... depends on the de-differentiation of the spheres of consumption, production, and leisure that coincided with the rise of mass production

> . . . the online economy achieves this de-differentiation, at least in part, through tech-
> niques of surveillance that allow leisure time and consumption time to participate in
> the creation of surplus value through the generation of information commodities.
> (Andrejevic, 2002: 259)

For several reasons, the advent of the digitally interactive economy is not yet a wholly
global factor. But although many countries in the Global South lack mass or affordable broadband internet access, as we saw in chapter 5, cell phones have become
ubiquitous. With the pan-Arab *Star Academy*, the pan-African *Big Brother Africa*, and
Indian Idol, cell phones are the dominant platform for interactivity, mainly through
text messaging. At the same time, mobile devices are not equally distributed. During
field research on reality television in the wealthy Gulf petro-monarchies, Marwan
heard many stories about upper-class women in Kuwait and Saudi Arabia "teaching"
their Filipina or Pakistani domestic workers to vote via text messages for particular
contestants (Kraidy, 2009). While the upper crust in these rentier states can afford
to vote early and often, in fact hundreds of times, for a compatriot contesting a
pan-Arab reality show, numerous Arabs from the popular classes carry inoperative
phones because they cannot afford calling time. This exposes the risibility of claims
that reality television "promotes democracy," unless by "democracy" we mean the
lopsided process in which a select group of deep-pocketed individuals exercise multiple "votes," while the vast majority cannot afford to use a cell phone. This is better
described as plutocracy.

Nonetheless, even without the infrastructure of digital enclosure, mobile telephony
enables the media industries to pinpoint attractive consumers and sell that information to advertisers in addition to peddling various gizmos – ringtones, wallpapers,
etc. – to consumers neatly organized in market niches as per "mass customization"
(Andrejevic, 2002: 256).

In the same vein, the notion of surveillance, which pervades most studies of reality television in Anglo-only contexts, requires qualification. In the post-9/11 world,
Western societies enacted laws that expanded their ability to surveil, harass, and
arrest segments of their population – i.e., Muslims and Arabs – making these groups
feel they live in police states, with the US media in lockstep, as we showed in chapter
6. We need to ask, without conceding ideological ground, what to make of the notion
of such surveillance when many people worldwide still live in actual police states.
For example, Syria, a country long ruled by a dictatorship and now seemingly fatally
fractured, is still in the early stages of shifting from a centrally planned economy to
a market-friendly system. Studying surveillance there would mean primarily analyzing the workings of the secret police in monitoring citizens, not the ways in which
the corporate world collects information about consumers. Nationalism, rather than
surveillance, emerges as a major issue when we look at the social and political impact
of reality television there. Though Syria itself has no reality TV industry, the transnational structure of satellite television made the genre an issue. The Syrian elite
and populace alike were shaken when their contestants in Lebanese reality shows
like *Star Academy* and *Superstar* (2003–8), the Arabic version of *Idol*, available on
satellite from the Beirut-based Future TV, were evicted in spectacularly politicized
episodes. Nonetheless, because of dismal infrastructure and limited internet access,
there were no cyber-battles like the ones spawned by reality shows in the former

Yugoslavia, which we discuss below. Also, though Syrian merchants tried to channel patriotic fervor around reality shows to peddle their wares, these businesses used old-fashioned advertising billboards on thoroughfares; they did not promise inter-activity and peddle the new economy. These options were simply not possible – and knowing the fact and taking it into account seems equally impossible for cybertarians and monolingual analysts.

We need to expand our analysis beyond the framework of neoliberalism in order to understand global reality television's articulation of politics and economics. Neoliberalism has emerged as a dominant approach in Western scholarship on the toopic, as per our pitiless account of *Undercover Boss*. Laurie Ouellette's argument that reality television "gained cultural presence . . . alongside the neoliberal poli-cies and discourses of the 1990s," and contributed to changing democratic ideals by establishing novel "templates for citizenship that complement the privatization of public life" (2004: 17), is certainly applicable to the United States and the United Kingdom. So is James Hay's remark that the neoliberal trope applies to television more broadly, since the medium enables "a kind of state control that values self-sufficiency and a kind of personal freedom that requires self-discipline" (2000: 56). But attempting to globalize reality television gives rise to the question: is neoliberal-ism a valid universal framework for reality television, or does it reflect North Atlantic premises that all nation-states share similar political-economic arrangements?

Though neoliberalism frequently functions on a global scale, various political and economic policies and forces mediate and mitigate its impact. As pan-Arab, pan-African, and Indian contexts demonstrate, ideological contests animated by reality television in many parts of the world embody progressive social and political values – gender equality, citizenship, and political pluralism. Sometimes, as we shall see, neoliberal concerns mix with such values. In many cases, however, neoliberal prem-ises are not important components of reality television's contentious global politics.

Expanding the theoretical repertoire beyond the narrow prism of neoliberalism – by, for example, considering it in conjunction with nationalism and examining the ensuing tensions – is therefore crucial to globalizing media studies and transcend-ing media studies 1.0 and 2.0. That said, lest the temptation strikes us to divide the world into two neat compartments, of a North Atlantic dominated by the question of neoliberalism, and a Global South consumed by the fight over progressive values, numerous examples puncture this binary *ballon d'essai*. *Star Academy* was called "moral terrorism" in Saudi Arabia, while, of the customized versions of *Big Brother*, *Gran Hermano* (2000–) in Spain was described as a "cultural Auschwitz" and *Loft Story* (2001–2), the French version, inspired a rich repertoire of scornful epithets. In fact, the French case reflects how reality television articulates an intriguing debate between the neoliberal ethos of the French commercial media and progressive argu-ments from the country's intellectual and (until Sarkozy's election to the presidency) political elites, in the name of French republicanism.

The French debate over reality television consumed the intellectual class, whose members dueled over the social implications of *Loft Story* and *La Ferme Célébrités* (2004–10) in the pages of newspapers like *Le Monde*, which published a "dossier spécial" in 2002 under the telling title "Télé-réalité, les nouveaux maîtres de l'écran" ("Reality television, the new masters of the screen"). For the most part, the French cultural establishment had a predictably visceral reaction against the phenomenon, with Jérôme Clément, then president of the Franco-German channel Arte, modestly terming reality television "rampant fascism" (quoted in Le Guay, 2005: 42). Less than a year later, the then Minister of Culture, Jean-Jacques Aillagon, summed up the view of the French intelligentsia in an interview with the conservative Catholic newspaper *La Croix*: that reality television programs "pose a threat to the equilibrium of our society" (quoted in Le Guay, 2005: 12). Similarly bizarre, Olympian diagnoses can be found all over the world, localized much like the very series they claim to denounce.

The notion of authenticity is another central concern in reality television studies. The argument can be summarized as follows: by subjecting participants to unrelenting surveillance for several months at a time, reality television elicits seemingly unvarnished behavior and expression from them – sincere, confessional, noncontrived. But everyone involved, from producers to viewers, knows that these shows stage individual performances. As Aslama and Pantti put it, "the participants and viewers are involved in and move skillfully from one reality to another, forming a continuous play between authenticity/reality and staged role playing/staged reality" (2006: 171). Paddy Scannell captured this dilemma when he wrote: "[I]f a person's behavior is perceived by others as a performance, it will be judged to be insincere, for sincerity presupposes, as its general condition, the absence of performance" (1996: 58).

The French philosopher Damien Le Guay, who entered public polemics over media influence in a book about how the celebration of Halloween has become endemic in France (2002), argues that reality television brings with it three postulates. The "rejection of mediation" promises access to the real by revealing the process of production; the "dictatorship of transparency" adds qualities of "direct democracy" and surveillance; and the "dictatorship of interiority" foregrounds emotional selves as key subject position (2005: 73).

The connections between claims and counterclaims of immediacy, transparency, surveillance, and interiority are clearly on display. Consider, for example, the monologue, a staple of much reality television. Contestants, usually isolated in a separate room, engage publicly in soul-searching, trying to make sense of what is happening to them, ascertain the success or lack thereof of their conduct, comment on other competitors, etc. The performance "contains an ambiguous interplay of the prescripted and non-scripted, individual and collective, performed and non-performed and fake and real" (Aslama and Pantii, 2006: 181). Highlighting the link between authenticity and surveillance,

> [the monologue] serves the purpose of giving the viewers the ultimate opportunity to assess the key characteristic of authenticity: the participant's integrity and credibility when it comes down to feelings. The paradox of an individualized society is that while one is talking alone about one's deepest emotions, at the same time one is selling one's authenticity to viewers. (Aslama and Pantti 2006: 181)

Andrejevic puts it explicitly:

> Being "real" is a proof of honesty, and the persistent gaze of the camera provides one way of guaranteeing that "realness" ... Submission to comprehensive surveillance is a kind of institutionally ratified individuation: it provides the guarantee of the authenticity of one's individuality. (2002: 266)

The question driving this chapter returns: does the connection between surveillance and authenticity emerge with the same force in the Global South?

In India, the popularity of *Kaun Banega Crorepati* (2000–), a localized version of *Who Wants to Be a Millionaire?*, now immortalized in the award-winning film *Slumdog Millionaire* (Danny Boyle, 2008), and the success of *Indian Idol*, raise several questions about the applicability of Western reality television studies to the Indian subcontinent. We can see traces of the theories and experiences of the Anglo sphere, but inflected in different ways. Its most prominent host is a fading star of Indian film, Amitabh Bhachan, remaking his image from an icon of socialism to a harbinger of risk-taking individualism. In that context, *Crorepati* can be understood as an important episode in Indian television's migration since its advent in 1959 from a developmentalist Nehruvian instrument in the hand of the state, to a private, commercial sector compatible with the deregulation and privatization of the Indian economy in the context of globalization (Ganguly and Kraidy, 2004; Kumar, 2005a, 2005b; Mankekar, 1999; Rajagopal, 2001; Mitra, 2012). For its part, *Slumdog* has been celebrated by Western critics as a triumph of personal transcendence; it might also be regarded as Dickensian porn blended with global neoliberalism (Ghosh, 2015).

The first success story of Indian commercial television was the soap opera *Hum Log* (*We, People*), which was broadcast in 1984 to popular success, one year after state-owned Doordashan allowed corporate sponsorship of programs (Ganguly and Kraidy, 2004; Punathambekar, 2010). By the late 1980s, neoliberal discourse was in the ascendant and developmentalism had receded in importance (Rajagopal, 2001). At the same time, because of the sizeable Indian populations in the countries of the Persian Gulf, the 1991 Gulf War created a spike in demand for satellite dishes in India from viewers who wanted to follow what was happening on CNN. In the 1990s, the advent of private channels like Zee TV and StarPlus reflected and reinforced a shift toward a consumer economy in which middle-class viewers became prime targets for advertisers. By 1996, India had 50 television channels.

Kaun Banega Crorepati went on the air in 2000 after Star TV purchased the format from the UK format house Celador, at a time when Indian ratings and advertising rates were low. By the time it launched, 200,000 Indians each day were calling to one of the 570 telephone lines made available by the producers, hoping to participate in the show (Punathambekar, 2010). *Kaun Banega Crorepati-2* (2005–6) attracted 130 million text messages, at costs of between two and three rupees (Chaudhuri, 2010). The numbers exploded again when the series was glossily relaunched by Sony in 2010 (Mitra, 2012).

Kaun Banega Crorepati brought in rural audiences who had never been taken into account before by commercial television. It also broke ratings records and became a signature moment in the history of Indian television. In addition to signaling a new era of commercialism in the country, the emergence of News Corporation's Star TV triggered debates about national identity and the role of the state – and how to succeed in television production and management. Studies indicated that while audiences still preferred cinema to television, *Crorepati* was more popular than other genres, notably soap operas. The Indian press was critical of Star TV's token domestic productions, which supposedly concealed its foreign ownership and a Western ethos. In response, the company invoked *Kaun Banega Crorepati* as the channel's contribution to livelier and more interesting programs for Indian viewers, in addition to claiming that the show's use of Hindi signaled a commitment to domestic culture and national identity (Ganguly and Kraidy, 2004; Mukherjee and Roy, 2006; Kumar and Chaudhary, 2013).

In a market of 80 million television homes, powerful commercial agendas under-girded these social and political debates. In effect, format adaptation was a perfect strategy for Star TV to "Indianize" its programs while remaining firmly embedded in the global media. *Kaun Banega Crorepati* allowed the company to move ahead of its main competitor Zee TV to the top of the ratings. At the same time, the show's ethos reflected the newly liberalized Indian economy, where individual initiative and risk-taking were awesomely rewarded. It had several other effects, stimulating the rise of similar programs, highlighting Tamil identity as cosmopolitan (Moorti, 2004).

If *Kaun Banega Crorepati* articulated a consummation of the transition from developmentalism to neoliberalism, lubricating the fraught boundaries between the nation and the global economy, a few years later *Indian Idol* would render problem-atic the Indian nation's relation to some of its provinces. In 2007, when Amit Paul, a young man from the impoverished northeastern state of Meghalaya, became a finalist in *Indian Idol 3*, popular mobilization around him redefined how people in a (subnational) state related to the Indian nation-state. In all, 70 million voters partici-pated (Punathambekar, 2010).

Historically, northeast Indian states have been politically and economically mar-ginalized, leading to the emergence of separatist movements. Tribal groups living in the region, like the Khasis, who are designated by the Indian state as one of the Scheduled Tribes of Meghalaya, have experienced tensions with people from other parts of the country who have migrated into the region, leading to a divisive public discourse of inclusion and exclusion. The national media rarely paid much attention to the region – in 1995, Doordashan's station in Shillong, Meghalaya's capital, pro-duced a meager 75 minutes of programs per day, and not in the local language. The national broadcaster had only a couple of correspondents, with coverage restricted to the large cities. The privately owned media paid scant attention to the region in the 1990s, because their viewers were of no interest to advertisers (Punathambekar, 2010; Ganguly, 2010).

Then rival organizations and parties coalesced around Paul, "a middle-class, Bengali, non-Khasi, [who] had become a catalyst for changing relations in Meghalaya," raising funds to distribute mobile prepaid calling cards, and mobilizing voters to ensure their favorite contestant moved forward in the show (Punathambekar, 2010). He afforded Meghalaya recognition from the rest of the country, as a consequence of this admittedly fleeting context.

Coming a couple of years after text messaging had become common, *Indian Idol* enabled wide participation and a realignment away from traditional animosities within Meghalaya. It also offered clear opportunities to advertisers, showcasing pow-erful overlaps of the popular, the political, and the economic as per reality television worldwide.

The global reality television wave hit China in 2000, beginning with outdoor sur-vival productions inspired by *Survivor* (2000–), whose popularity faded after a few years. In 2004 the studio contest genre of *Idol* became the dominant subgenre. Since 2006, a wide variety of formats has proliferated. Reality TV is seen as responding to the twin objectives of simultaneously satisfying the authoritarian state's propaganda agenda and consumer society's business imperatives. The propaganda is obvious; as Yuezhi Zhao and Zhenzhi Guo argue, television in China is "the most powerful site for the construction of an official discourse on nationalism and the mobilization of patriotism" (2005: 531). Business imperatives are less explicit, but have become increasingly important as the state has withdrawn its subsidies to the media industries over the last decade. To rehearse a cliché, reality television provided auspicious grounds for the party line to meet the bottom line.

That the agendas of the Chinese state apparatus and the for-profit media industry have increasingly converged was in plain view with *The Great Survival Challenge: Retracing the Long March* (2001) (*Shegcun da tiazhoan: Chongzou changzhenglu*), which was among a slew of programs celebrating the 65th anniversary of the Chinese Red Army's Long March. It showed 20 ordinary Chinese retracing the arduous revolutionary, 6,000-kilometer path. The failure of *Survivor: China* to attract a significant following the previous year prompted the producers of *The Great Survival Challenge* to lift key formal elements from *Survivor* and to embed them in a framework of historically resonant Chinese elements. The program's debt to *Survivor* was clear in the competition it staged between two teams, regular eliminations of contestants, and the staging of so-called "tribal councils." However, the production crew hesitated to implement the backstabbing and regular expulsion logic of *Survivor*. Instead, they suffused the text with what Luo Wei (2010) calls "propaganda gestures" about the Long March. This strategy, Wei argued,

> [was] not only beneficial for legitimizing the state-employed producer's attempt to localize the *Survivor* format in a government-censored domestic television market, but also for potentially minimizing the 'unfavorable' Western cultural influence (i.e. gambling, voyeurism, individualism, excessive consumption . . .) introduced by the ethically controversial global reality trend into an ideologically-controlled public space.

But viewers soon lost interest. As a result, the director was replaced and the program adjusted to highlight survival and de-emphasize revolutionary history. Crucially, the regular elimination process was implemented. Ratings improved dramatically.

In the Arab world, reality television caused major controversy. Coming in a context polarized by the US–UK invasion of Iraq and a slew of global scandals connected to Islam, from Guantánamo Bay to Danish cartooning, reality television lit a firestorm of sexuality, politics, business, and religion. The polemics started in 2003 when Arab Radio and Television, a subsidiary of the Saudi conglomerate Dalla al-Baraka, aired *al-Hawa Sawa*, a matchmaking reality show in which female contestants vie to win a husband from among viewers of the show. That same year, the Middle East Broadcasting Center (MBC), another Saudi company, launched the Arabic version of *Who Wants to Be a Millionaire?*, which was an enormous commercial success and generated only minor criticism. Simultaneously, *Superstar*, the Arabic version of *Idol*, triggered heated arguments in Kuwait after it was aired by the Beirut-based Future TV (Kraidy, 2010). As part of the international influences on this new sexual discourse, *La Malinche*, a complex female icon of Latin American sexual conquest and collaboration implicated with the Spanish invasion, appeared in struggles over *ikhtilat*, the concept of illicit sex in Arab reality TV (Glantz, 1992; Kraidy, 2009).

When MBC launched *al-Ra'is* (2004), the Arabic version of *Big Brother*, an intense controversy ensued that reflected the pitfalls of an increasingly transnational Arab television industry. Owned by the brother-in-law of Saudi Arabia's former king, MBC is considered liberal by Saudi standards – i.e., pro-royal family, pro-business, pro-US Middle-East policy, and not explicitly promoting *Wahhabiya*. In order to escape the influence of the conservative Saudi clerical-political establishment, MBC was initially launched in London in 1991. A decade later, it moved to Dubai, where the then newly established DMC offered relative autonomy and business opportunities that arose from a dense cluster of Arab and Western media institutions spanning market research, satellite television, advertising, and printing. Like other pan-Arab satellite channels, MBC considered oil-wealthy Saudi Arabia its most important market, but Saudi authorities prohibited the shooting of *al-Ra'is* there. As a result, the show was produced in the minuscule neighboring island of Bahrain, where Saudi men, crossing a long bridge on Thursday evenings, spend week-ends drinking and carousing in a comparatively liberal social atmosphere.

The Arabic version of *Big Brother* lasted just one week. A few days after it went to air on MBC4, a channel devoted to youth that latterly targeted women, there were street demonstrations in Manama, Bahrain's capital, and condemnations in the Bahraini and Saudi press. MBC decided to "make a sacrifice," as it argued in its press release, and canceled the show because it risked damaging the station's reputation as a "family" channel (Kraidy, 2009).

Whereas *Big Brother* briefly spurred controversy, *Star Academy*, a Lebanese adaptation of the Endemol format *Fame Academy* (2002–3), spawned an impassioned transnational upheaval that involved journalists, media moguls, clerics, and politicians in many Arab countries, most notably Algeria, Kuwait, and Saudi Arabia. In Algeria, the government first relayed *Star Academy* on the state channel, but after a fight with Islamist parliamentarians, the president sacrificed the program in exchange for concessions on other domestic policies. In Kuwait, the matter was instrumentalized by the "Salafi bloc" in the Kuwaiti parliament, whose 18 members (a large number considering that the entire legislature has 60 seats) succeeded in forcing the Information Minister to resign for allowing "immoral" programs into the country. The Kuwaiti episode also witnessed heated rhetorical skirmishes between liberals (typically women, small business owners, and secular lawyers) and conservatives over reality television and Arab–Western relations. In Saudi Arabia, liberals, conservatives, and (right-wing religious) radicals had heated exchanges over reality television in general, and *Star Academy* more specifically, for several years (Kraidy, 2009).

Reality TV in the African and Arab worlds provides interesting comparisons. There are several similarities between *Big Brother Africa* and the pan-Arab *Star Academy*. Both were available on satellite from nationally based channels with significant transnational markets. The South African channel M-Net launched *Big Brother Africa* on the transnational MultiChoice Africa; in the Arab world, LBC made major inroads in the pan-Arab market with al-Fada'iyya al-Lubnaniyya, its transitional satellite arm. Both institutions established separate satellite stations dedicated to flagship reality shows, a necessary substitute to continuous web streaming in parts of the world with limited and weak internet access but plenty of television sets. The shows were ratings sensations for the three (*Big Brother Africa*) or four (*Star Academy*) months they were on the air, emptying streets and filling public discourse with chatter. Both were hailed as unifying vast populations strewn across multiple nation-states: Arab and African media quipped that these shows accomplished in a few weeks what had eluded the League of Arab States and the Organization of African Unity over decades.

Both *Big Brother Africa* and *Star Academy* were condemned by intellectual, social, and religious elites. Wole Soyinka dismissed *Big Brother Africa* as inferior even to the creations of Nollywood, the Nigerian video industry despised by much of the African intelligentsia for its low-brow style (Michael, 2015; Jacobs, 2007). In the Arab world, *Star Academy* was criticized by secular writers for promoting consumerism and globalization, and by religious critics (Muslim, and in the case of Lebanon, Christian clerics) for inciting/exciting casual sexuality. In newspaper opinion pages, on talk show screens, and in the street, the two programs triggered discussion about changing identities. Their contestants were seen as reflecting a young cosmopolitan, socially liberal generation that indexed the fruitlessness of arguments about cultural authenticity when African and Arab societies had embraced commercial and cultural globalization (Jacobs, 2007; Kraidy, 2009).

There are other similarities between the social and political lives of reality television in Arab and African societies, where the shows spawned fights between various branches of national governments and polarized public opinion. The situation in Malawi was akin to what happened in Bahrain and Kuwait. The Malawian president Sam Nujoma had failed to have the show banned for indecent material in 2003. After segments of *Big Brother Africa* were shown on the national television channel TVM, irate legislators enacted a temporary ban. This was reversed by the High Court, in part due to public opinion. Viewers were avidly following the progress of a Malawian contestant. The Information Minister supported the court's ruling and accused MPs of having reacted emotionally to the show. In Nigeria, terrestrial television stations simply ignored an order from the Director General of the Nigerian Broadcasting commission to cease broadcasting it (Jacobs, 2007).

Comparisons of the African and Arab situations illustrate how reality television relates to social and political-economic conditions. To be young in both regions today entails being politically disenfranchised, economically precarious, and socially vulnerable (Kraidy and Khalil, 2008; Jacobs, 2007: 864). In this sense then, reality television obfuscates social reality, a process to which the commercial African and Arab media industries contribute by using the term "aspirational" and showcasing a small minority of relatively affluent, educated, successful youth as a model for the vast majority of poorer young men and women – who lead more precarious lives. This strategy is motivated not only by advertising calculations, but by cell phone companies that are far more interested in wealthy customers who purchase the latest devices with expensive plans and "value-added services" that come with them than the huddled masses with basic plans, old devices, or empty accounts.

Jacobs's conclusion about *Big Brother Africa* applies to the pan-Arab *Star Academy*, and more broadly to how format-adapted television shows are engaged by many societies:

> [They] shed light on a range of complex issues all too often cast aside or altogether ignored in discussions of cultural phenomena south of the Sahara: economic relations between countries, issues of race and class, and perceptions of self and other, among others. At the same time, they significantly complicate mainstream, primarily US- and Western Europe-centered, analyses of the reality TV phenomenon. Most

importantly, they bring into focus debates within Africa concerning processes of globalization. (2007: 852)

As we have seen in earlier chapters, there are also cultural imperialist elements to the genre. According to H. Leslie Steeves, US reality television shows "support Africa's colonization via commodification" (2008: 418). Such programs as *Survivor* and *The Amazing Race* (2001–), some seasons of which are shot in Africa, operate through what can perhaps be called "reverse neocolonial mimicry," with US contestants imitating African traditions "as observed in colonial narratives and tourism" (Steeves, 2008: 25). They include various "pseudotribal props" such as political councils and tiki torches that essentialize and exoticize the region. Different seasons of *Survivor* seasons are named for the country, island, or locality where the shooting occurs (Borneo, Marquesas, Thailand, Vanuatu); the third season in the only one to be called the much broader, vaguer, and exotic, *Survivor Africa*.

Jennifer Bowering Delisle (2003) and Laura Hubbard and Kathryn Mathers (2004) argue that *Survivor* casts participants as a mixture of gazing tourists, humanitarians, and colonialists:

> *Survivor Africa* combines nostalgic colonial flair with critical plots that turn on notions of a future of constant surveillance and a form of life conducive to an empire for a post-imperial age . . . It is no accident that it is Americans that are playing this game so successfully. It is America that needs to learn how to "be" in relation to a world that it increasingly dominates . . . *Survivor* is, thus, a primer for the subjects of this new empire, one that depends heavily on notions of the free market, human rights and what makes up the modern. (Hubbard and Mathers, 2004: 444)

As such, "*Survivor Africa* places an imagined Africa as central to an emerging discourse of a humanitarian American empire," enacting an "emaciated modernity" (Hubbard and Mathers, 2004: 444–5). Instead of undermining the premise of the show – primitive isolation – scenes with hospitals, sport utility vehicles, and other trappings of modernity typify Africa as a hopeless case, a last redoubt that stubbornly resists being transformed by global capitalism. The ensuing sympathy for ordinary people "gives rise to a form of care that rides on the belief that America can save Africa, that within the realm of responsibility for freedom is the need to care about Africa" (Hubbard and Mathers, 2004: 454).

If neocolonialism is for the most part the province of Western powers, nationalism seems universal. In Finland, for example, Aslama and Pantti (2007) argue for a consideration of reality television in the context of Michael Billig's (1995) notion of "banal nationalism." The Finnish program *Suuri Seikkailu* (*Extreme Escapades*, 2002–3) is part of the growth of domestically produced television since the 1990s: "the most watched programs have a distinctive national character" (Aslama and Pantti, 2007: 51). Not only did the producers embed explicitly nationalistic rhetoric in the show's production and promotion; they also intentionally stirred nationalistic sentiments, "flagging" Finnishness. This was achieved through a relationship between technology and nature (Nokia Nation within a Nordic backwoods landscape), the circulation of mythologies of Finnishness, the construction of competitors whose rivalry was cool and dispassionate (confrontation is supposedly alien to local culture), and the "quiet Finn" stereotype, which the show tried unsuccessfully to break for dramatic purposes. *Extreme Escapades'* "construction of national identity," the authors conclude, "can be interpreted as calculated intentionality," which is necessary for the survival of Finnish television production (2007: 63). As we shall see, nationalism and commercialism often work hand-in-hand in reality television worldwide.

In the Balkans, the pan-Yugoslav reality television show *To Sam Ja* promoted what Zala Volčič and Mark Andrejevic (2009) call "commercial nationalism . . . the way in which nationalist appeals migrate from the realm of political propaganda to commercial appeal." As the nations resulting from the break-up of Yugoslavia (Bosnia-Herzegovina, Croatia, Kosovo, Macedonia, Montenegro, Serbia, and Slovenia) attempt to forge collective identities, yet fit in with an emergent pan-Europeanism, their television systems have become increasingly commercialized. In the new media environment, reality TV has emerged as a pervasive genre. As in the Arab world (Kraidy, 2009), the initial trend was to adapt formats that had been successful elsewhere – *Big Brother, Who Wants to Be a Millionaire?*, etc. Then non-format-adapted local productions emerged. In Slovenia alone, seven local reality shows appeared between 2003 and 2007 (Volčič and Andrejevic, 2009). Reality television again promised a new economic model, integrating TV, the internet, and cell phones.

This multiplatform model is based on compelling viewers to nominate, vote, and purchase various related devices and applications, such as ringtones and propaganda: the US State Department has attempted to finance reality television shows to promote tolerance and "democracy" in the Balkans and the Middle East. The 1990s in the Balkans witnessed the establishment of neoliberalism as a triumphant ideology, leading to a focus on individuals at the expense of community or society. That fitted the new economy propounded by reality television. Interactivity was a natural tool of self-propaganda.

To Sam Ja promised reconciliation between the different nationalities spawned by the break-up of Yugoslavia. This inevitably involved what Volčič (2007) and others have called "yugonostalgia," a phenomenon whereby "events, spaces, identities and media representations . . . consumer goods and tourist travel . . . that invoke fond memories of the Yugoslav era" (Volčič and Andrejevic, 2009). Because it was available globally via satellite, the show attracted viewers across the vast post-Yugoslav diaspora. Its producers claimed that one and a half million people visited the program's website to post comments, follow developments, etc. In the process, the nations emerging from the former Yugoslavia were discursively pitted against each other, undermining the producers' soothing postnational pretensions and expressing stereotypes held by new nations about one other. This degenerated into offensive behavior and hateful rhetoric, including threats of stabbing, accusations of terrorism against a Bosnian Muslim contestant, and flare-ups inspired by a clash-of-civilizations discourse. Instead of a return to traditional notions of national identity, reality television had given rise to a nationalism imbricated with neoliberalism (Volčič and Andrejevic, 2009).

Thriving on a contrived dramatic conflict that is made all the more unavoidable by the seclusion and control that contestants are subjected to, it is no wonder that reality television's plebiscitary ethos makes it an arena for more or less overt expressions of racism and ethnocentrism. For example, *Extreme Escapades* underplayed Finland's ethnic diversity. It never addressed the fact that one of the participants, a "well-educated black computer engineer," was clearly not of Finnish "origin." More explicit were the chat rooms discussing the show, where people were "hateful and racist," which led the producers to shut them down (Aslama and Pantti, 2007: 56). Contestants in and fans of *To Sam Ja* in the ex-Yugoslavia used hateful language as the show devolved from a contrived attempt at (post-?)national reconciliation to a free-for-all barrage of mutual recrimination.

In Israeli reality programs like *Wanted: A Leader* (2005) and *The Ambassador* (2005), manifold processes of Othering reaffirmed Israeli nationalism at the expense of Arab Israelis and immigrants (Jamal et al., 2011). *Wanted: A Leader* consisted of searching for someone to supervise a social project. The single Arab contestant was subjected to various mechanisms of exclusion and struggled to belong in the group. *The Ambassador*, which sought to find an Israeli who would represent the country overseas and assist its propaganda efforts, did not include a single Arab-Israeli contestant. On *Big Brother Africa*, where most contestants hailed from the socio-economic elite, South African clichés about other Africans were perceptible. Most remarkable, however, was the fact that in the third season, Ludik, a white Namibian, received votes en masse from whites in Namibia and South Africa, while Platje, a colored South African woman, was victimized because she straddled faultlines of race, class, and gender (Jacobs, 2007).

Conclusion

Globalizing reality television studies requires an adjustment of the theoretical frameworks and analytical foci that have dominated its early, predominantly Anglo-US phase. Yuko Kawai (2009) argues that in the case of Japan, reality television stimulates a nationalism superficially redefined to fit globalization, but in its aspirational discourse rather than its cosmopolitan one. Intellectual space must be made for studies not solely framed by neoliberalism to allow for emerging emphases that are distinct from surveillance, authenticity, and self-confessional behavior. Pan-African, pan-Arab, Chinese, Indian, and ex-Yugoslav contexts show that nationalism is a recurring theme of reality shows, which questions the universal applicability of neoliberalism to the genre.

We are not advocating a wholesale rejection of neoliberalism as a tool for understanding reality television. For all we know, as telecommunications infrastructure grows in the Global South, issues of surveillance, interactivity, and digital enclosure may become salient, though probably in ways that are different from *Big Brother UK* or *American Idol*.

We *do* advocate pitting neoliberal forces of globalization against nationalism in reality TV worldwide. As Kawai puts it, "neoliberalism is in an ambivalent relationship with nationalism. Neoliberalism undermines nationalism because in the world as market, national boundaries that nationalisms attempt to establish and maintain become more fragile due to the increase of people and goods crossing borders" (2009: 17). In addition to bringing the nation-state back to the center of global media studies, the neoliberalism–nationalism dialectic enables us to focus on the controversies spawned by nationalism's treatment of internal difference, a fraught issue that is made visible by the social and political energy spawned by reality shows. Neoliberalism assumes that "the world is the market in which people – atomized individuals who are detached from historical and socioeconomic contexts – have the "freedom" to engage in various activities, whereas social problems are "personal" issues for which each individual is responsible . . . Put simply, neoliberalism individualizes human beings, [and] decontextualizes human relations (Kawai, 2009: 17).

Rather than promoting the privatization of social life and its separation from government, throwing it into the hands of the market, reality television in many parts of the world has brought government into cultural and social life. In African and Arab countries, some politicians intervened to ban, censor, or simply attack reality shows, while others craved a boost in their own popularity. In some countries, national legislatures debated the impact of reality shows and sought to prohibit or restrict their broadcasts. In both Africa and the Arab world, reality programs spawned broad debates about globalization's impact on society. Though these shows were rarely shut down, *al-Ra'is* being an exception, they created a space where facets of neoliberalism came under systematic attack – from reactionary forces.

Perhaps capitalism has not achieved full hegemony in these societies. Instead of neoliberal common sense, reality television worldwide generated controversies about progressive values like individual emancipation, political pluralism, and women's rights, at the same time as they unleashed nationalistic sentiments that both pushed in the direction of liberalism and unleashed illiberal speech.

While some reality shows have contributed to the decontextualization of human relations that is symptomatic of neoliberalism, others recontextualize human and social relations, wresting agency from global formats to imbue them with local cultural resonance. This was clearly the case in China, where producers resignified fledgling reality shows and saw them rise in the ratings (Wei, 2010). In the Arab world, the number of locally created reality formats grew as imported formats decreased between 2000 and 2006. Some locally produced shows staged competitions to accomplish good deeds as prescribed by Muslim tradition. Others pitted budding poets against each others, leading a revival of poetry, the greatest and quintessentially Arab art and performative form (Kraidy, 2010).

We hope that this final example makes the point that denouncing or celebrating a genre such as reality TV for being trivial, popular, or neoliberal misses the point. Closer inspection is required of the infrastructures of production and meaning that both bind it together and differentiate it as a concept. Realty television is thus a particularly mercurial and polysemic genre. Analysis of it as a worldwide phenomenon needs to focus on the interplay between global formats and local adaptations. In our last chapter, we consider just such binding and differentiation, this time of audiences.

9 Audiences

Having looked into how the media are organized, shaped, operated, and instrumentalized and what they produce, it is time to address in greater detail how people receive the output of global media, and what they do with it – how audiences "read," "consume," or "interpret" media texts. This chapter offers a metacritical survey of media effects, summarizes various forms of audience research, and engages the active audience tradition. We offer case studies of audience surveillance and spectators to US sport on television.

Understanding audiences is a necessary step to complete the circuit of communication that constitutes the social life of the media. After all, without the audience, it would make no sense to speak of political economy, governance, or textuality. To help us understand this crucial aspect of global media studies, we draw on Michel Foucault's concept of the psy-function to describe the shifting field of knowledge and power over the body. As mentioned in chapter 1, the "psy-function" comprises psychoanalysis, psychology, psychotherapy, psychiatry, social psychology, criminology, and psycho-pharmacology, and their success in various disciplinary sites – educational, military, industrial, and carceral (2006: 85–6, 189–90), deployed on this occasion for the purposes of media research and public order.

The psy-function is particularly powerful in the home of audience research, the United States, where effects studies work on behalf of reactionary politics to explain how a wealthy country can produce unprecedentedly high levels of violence and poor ones of public education. This explanation generally declines to account for economic, social, and cultural inequality as causes of violence and ignorance, so wedded is it to the behavioral *données* of the psy-function rather than questioning masculinity, the availability of firearms, and the redistribution of income upwards as causes of violence and educational failure.

Media Effects

Much contemporary media studies 1.0 effects research unselfconsciously incarnates conservative desires to maintain the status quo. These concerns arch over millennia. Drama, for example, has long been plagued with the reputation of being an ungodly public sphere of make-believe that dupes its audience. Writing in the first century AD, Plutarch recounts the following story about Solon. Having enjoyed what later became known as a tragedy, Solon asked the play's author, Thespis,

> whether he was not ashamed to tell such lies in front of so many people. When Thespis replied that there was no harm in speaking or acting in this way in make-believe, Solon struck the ground angrily with his staff and exclaimed, "Yes, but if we

allow ourselves to praise and honour make-believe like this, the next thing will be to find it creeping into our serious business." (Plutarch, 1976: 73)

Is this so different from today's panics over the media? We think not. And there are other harbingers of the "modern" effects tradition. The emergence of private, silent reading in the ninth century, which ended religion's monopoly on textuality, was criticized as an invitation to idleness. And in the twelfth century, John of Salisbury warned of the negative impact of juggling, mime, and acting on "unoccupied minds . . . pampered by the solace of some pleasure . . . to their greater harm" (quoted in Zyvatkauskas, 2007).

As printed books began to proliferate in the early eighteenth century, critics feared a return to the "barbarism" of the post-Roman Empire; erudition would be over-whelmed by popular texts, just as it had been by war (Chartier, 2004). When Goethe's *The Sorrows of Young Man Werther* was published in 1774, its hero was deemed to have caused numerous mimetic suicides among readers, and the book was banned in many cities (Stack, 2003).

The extension through societies of the capacity to read had as its corollary the pos-sibility of a public that transcended people physically gathered together. The obvious implication was that mass literacy could inform industrial and political turmoil. When unionists in the Cuban cigar industry organized readings of news and cur-rent affairs to workers on the line, management and the state responded brutally. In the United States, slave-owners terrorized African Americans who taught themselves and their colleagues to read; Nat Turner's 1831 rebellion was attributed by many to his literacy (Manguel, 1996).

The advent of reading outdoors and the arrival of the train as a new site of public culture generated anxieties about open knowledge and debate. The telegraph's capac-ity to spread information from the eastern states to nineteenth-century Californians before they had finished breakfast was accused of exhausting emotional energies at the wrong time of day, while its presence in saloons expanded working-class bet-ting on sporting events. Neurological experts attributed their increased business to telegraphy, alongside the expansion of steam, periodical literature, science, and edu-cated women. Nineteenth-century US society saw spirited debates over whether new popular media and genres, such as newspapers, crime stories, and novels, would breed anarchic readers lacking respect for the traditionally literate classes. The media posed a threat to established elites, because they enabled working people to become independently minded and informed, distracting them from servitude (Miller, 1998).

Gendered reactions against mass literacy became the heart of numerous cam-paigns against public sex and its representation, most notably the Comstock Law, which policed US sex from the late nineteenth century. The law was named after the founder of the New York Society for the Suppression of Vice, the noted post office moralist Anthony Comstock. Much exercised by "evil reading," Comstock avowed that, before Adam and Eve, reading was unknown. In the early twentieth century, opera, Shakespeare, and romance fiction were censored for their immodest impact on the young. Many effects studies since that time have been colored by their links to governments and courts policing sexual material because of its alleged impact on young people, all the way from the uptake of Britain's 1868 *Regina v. Hicklin* decision and its anxieties about vulnerable youth through to the US Supreme Court's 1978

Federal Communications Commission v. Pacifica (Heins, 2002: 9, 29-32, 23; Manguel, 1996: 110-11, 141, 280, 284; Stearns, 2006: 65).

The Industrial Revolution brought new communications technologies, new democratic urges, new class anxieties, and new knowledges. By the early twentieth century, academic experts had decreed media audiences to be passive consumers, thanks to the missions of literary criticism (distinguishing the cultivated from others) and the psy-function (distinguishing the competent from others) (Butsch, 2000: 3). The origins of social psychology can be traced to anxieties about "the crowd" in suddenly urbanized and educated countries that raised the prospect of a long-feared "ochlocracy" of "the worthless mob" (Pufendorf, 2000: 144) able to share popular texts.

Elite theorists emerged from both right and left, notably Vilfredo Pareto (1976), Gaetano Mosca (1939), Gustave Le Bon (1899), and Robert Michels (1915), arguing that newly literate publics were vulnerable to manipulation by demagogues. James Truslow Adams, the Latino founder of the "American Dream," saw "[t]he mob mentality of the city crowd" as "one of the menaces to modern civilization." He was especially exercised by "the prostitution of the moving-picture industry" (1941: 404, 413).

These critics were frightened of socialism, democracy, and popular reason (Wallas 1967: 137). With civil society growing restive, the wealth of radical civic associations was explained away in social-psychological terms rather than political-economic ones, thanks to "new" scholarship (media studies 1.0). The psy-function warmed itself by campus fires in departments of psychology, sociology, education, and communication. Scholars at Harvard took charge of the theory; faculty at Chicago the task of meeting and greeting the great unwashed; and those at Columbia and the Midwest the statistical manipulation (Staiger 2005: 21-22).

Such tendencies moved into high gear with the Payne Fund studies of the 1930s, which birthed the media-effects research we know today. They juxtaposed the impact of films on "'superior" adults – young college professors, graduate students, and their wives – with children in juvenile correction centers. Such scholarship inaugurated mass social science panic about young people at the cinema by collecting "authoritative and impersonal data which would make possible a more complete evaluation of motion pictures and their social potentialities" to answer "what effect do motion pictures have upon children of different ages?" Pioneering scholars set out to see whether "the onset of puberty is or is not affected by motion pictures." The researchers asked their subjects whether "all, most, many, some, few, or no Chinese are cunning and underhand" and investigated cinematic "demonstrations of satisfying love techniques" to establish whether "[s]exual passions are aroused and amateur prostitution . . . aggravated." Laboratory techniques used psychogalvanometers and wired beds with hypnographs and polygraphs (Charters, 1933: 8, iv–v, 12–13, 314, 10, 15, 25, 32, 49, 54, 60; Wartella, 1996: 173).

The example of the Payne Fund studies, the development of communication studies, and the massive growth of the psy-function have led to seven more decades of attempts to correlate youthful consumption of popular culture with anti-social conduct. Worries over the media's indexical and incarnate power underpin a wealth of research that questions, tests, and measures people and their texts. Not all this work assumes a strong relationship between social conduct and audience conduct, but that premise underpins it nevertheless.

Here are some concerned Australian pundits pondering what the new arrival, television, might do to 1950s adolescents:

> In September 1956 many Sydney residents had their first opportunity to experience first-hand contact with the new mechanical "monster" – TV – that had for the last seven or eight years been dominating the lounges of English and American homes. Speculation on its effects had run high. On the one hand it was claimed: it would eventually destroy the human race since young couples would prefer viewing to good honest courting; children would arrive at school and either go to sleep or disgorge half-baked concepts about the Wild West and the "gals" who inspired or confused the upholders of law; it would breed a generation of youngsters with curved spines, defective eyesight, American vocabulary but no initiative; it would result in a fragmentation of life whereby contact among, and even within, families would be reduced to the barest minimum. (Campbell assisted by Keogh, 1962: 9)

Television and the Australian Adolescent, the source of this quotation, finds its authors worried about the "habits of passivity" that TV might induce, and the power of particular genres to "instil certain emotions, attitudes and values." The upshot of all this, they feared, might be "a generation of people who are content to be fed by others" (Campbell assisted by Keogh, 1962: 23).

The audience as consumer, student, felon, voter, and idiot engages these institutional actors. Moral panics and the psy-function combine to create what Harold Garfinkel, writing in the 1960s, named a "cultural dope," a mythic figure who "produces the stable features of the society by acting in compliance with pre-established and legitimate alternatives of action that the common culture provides." The "common sense rationalities ... of here and now situations" used by ordinary people are obscured and derided by such categorizations (1992/1967: 68).

The pattern is that whenever new communications technologies emerge, young audiences in particular are immediately identified as both pioneers and victims, simultaneously endowed by manufacturers and critics with immense power and immense vulnerability – early adopters/early *naïfs*. They are held to be the first to know and the last to understand the media – the grand paradox of youth, latterly on display in the "digital sublime" of technological determinism, as always with the super-added valence of a future citizenship in peril (Mosco, 2004: 80).

As we noted in our chapter on textual analysis, new technologies and genres have brought with them marketing techniques focused on young people, even as concerns about supposedly unprecedented and unholy new risks also recur: cheap novels during the 1900s; silent then sound film during the 1920s; radio in the 1930s; comic books of the 1940s and '50s; pop music and television from the 1950s and '60s; satanic rock as per the 1970s and '80s; video cassette recorders in the 1980s; and rap music, video games, and the internet since the 1990s. Recent studies totalize 8–18-year-olds as "Generation M" (for media). The satirical paper *The Onion* cleverly mocked the interdependent phenomena of the psy-function, panic, and commodification via a faux 2005 study of the impact on US youth of seeing Janet Jackson's breast in a Super Bowl broadcast the year before (Kline 1993: 57; Mazzarella 2003: 228; Roberts *et al.*, 2005).[1]

Effects research suffers the disadvantages of ideal-typical psychological reasoning. Scholars rely on methodological individualism, failing to account for cultural norms and politics, let alone the arcs of history and waves of geography that situate texts and responses to them inside politics, war, ideology, and discourse. Abundant tests of media effects are based on, as the refrain goes, "undergraduates at a large university in the Midwest." As politicians, grant-givers, and pundits call for more and more research to prove that the media make you stupid, violent, and apathetic (or the opposite), the psy-function responds, rarely if ever interrogating its own conditions of existence – namely, that governments, religious groups, and the media themselves use it to account for social problems and engage in surveillance of popular culture.

Effects research is frequently complicit with what it professes to investigate. As jobs emerged from the 1950s for US marketers trained in the psy-function, it even infiltrated the very genres it drew strength from denouncing. Since that time, while some parts of the psy-function have aided consumer targeting, others feed anxieties about lost innocence via a raft of literature denouncing child commerce, promoted by media-panickers like Action for Children's Television (Cook, 2007; Cook and Kaiser 2004: 215; DeFao, 2006).[2] Right-wing front organizations such as the Parents Television Council adore such analyses: the Council's Entertainment Tracking System (2005) is designed to "ensure that children are not constantly assaulted by sex, violence and profanity on television and in other media . . . along with stories and dialogue that create disdain for authority figures, patriotism, and religion." This complex mosaic of effects-research fandom encompasses state, church, commerce, and academia, which may simultaneously governmentalize, demonize, and commodify youth culture (Hartley, 1998: 14).

Effects research continues to have considerable traction across the human sciences, thanks to media studies 1.0 true believers, self-loathing journalists, and research grant incentives. Materialist, embedded methods, rather than psychological and experimental ones, have shown that communities frequently create syncretic cultures of reception – and that audiences themselves become objects of control and sale. But despite its focus on structural power, political economy does not view spectators as naive viewers who are seamlessly and irrevocably stitched into the stories presented to them via an inexorable process of identification. For example, although Adorno (1981–2) thought popular cinema's "infantile character, regression manufactured on an industrial scale" diminished audiences' capacities for social critique, he acknowledged that Hollywood's factory-like norms could never entirely control the camera's tendency to reference what actually lay before it: the art of filmmaking was unable to suppress the power of objects and practices to express themselves and their histories.

Active Audiences

Of course, there have always been counters to the notion that audiences are influenced by the media. In the fifth century BC, Socrates may have been the first to argue that what we'd now call media effects could only occur by touching on already-extant proclivities in audiences. In the eighteenth century, Denis Diderot asked "who shall be the master? The writer or the reader?" Up to the early nineteenth century, it was mostly taken for granted that audiences were active interpreters, given their unruly and overtly engaged conduct at cultural events (Kline, 1993: 52–3, 55; Manguel, 1996: 51, 63, 71, 86). And within the effects tradition itself, some powerful tendencies have argued against the media's impact (Lewis, 2008).

By contrast with psy-function attempts to corral or control spectators, more populist, qualitative theories – articulated to progressive social change based on the insights of ordinary people – have fed into cultural and media studies (see Miller, 2006). This perspective has offered a way in to research via media studies 2.0's love affair with the audience as an all-powerful interpreter and ultimate arbiter of meaning. These scholars use ethnographies of audiences and studies of cultural memory, focusing on resistance to dominant norms and expressions of cultural politics rather than the bourgeois-individualist norms of the psy-function's investment in "behavior," which is as much about ideological *idées fixes* as aggression or learning.[3]

Dick Hebdige's *Subculture* (1979) is a foundational work within this tradition. A pathbreaking tour of the depressed, recessed, repressed Britain of the 1970s, *Subculture* focuses on resistance and reaction to workaday norms and cultures enacted by marginalized youth through the use of spectacle – audiences who have turned effects and reception into refusal and re-signification. Hebdige shows that subordinate groups adopt and adapt signs and objects of the dominant culture, reorganizing them to manufacture new meanings. He demonstrates how their *bricolage* subverts achievement-oriented, materialistic corporate and state culture. Paradoxically, consumption reverses the status of such consumers: the oppressed become producers of new fashions, inscribing alienation, difference, and powerlessness on their bodies, be it via punk dress or Rasta dreads.

In the case of children and television – one of the most politically charged areas of audience study – anxieties from the effects tradition about turning Edenic innocents into rabid monsters are challenged by research into children distinguishing between fact and fiction; the generic features and intertexts of children's news, drama, action adventure, education, cartooning, and play; and how talking about TV makes for social interaction (Hodge and Tripp, 1986; Buckingham, 2005). Against claims that soap operas see women identify with maternal, policing functions, active-audience advocates suggest that female viewers may empathize with villainous characters because of their power and that the genre appeals because it offers a world of glamour and joy in contradistinction to the workaday suburban ennui of patriarchy (Ang, 1982; Seiter et al., 1989). Similar findings have emerged from observing romance-fiction readers (Radway, 1991).

Lesley Johnson's (1988) detailed account of Australian radio between the 1920s and 1940s poses a number of policy and everyday queries from the time that resonate today with regulators, marketers, and critics: how are we to conceptualize the relationship of stations and listeners, whether at the hearth or in the kitchen? What is the appropriate division of public and private in broadcasting? How can ownership be regulated? And what has changed from the days when merely setting a receiver up that worked was a true sign of consumer mastery, to the sealed-set efficiencies and deskilling of the war years? The mostly male operators of the 1920s battled technological difficulties on a daily basis, exemplifying self-reliance and innovation. As one of these self-styled "radio maniacs" put it, the search for perfect reception was a struggle against "the endless perversity of the elements" (quoted in Douglas, 1987: 308). Before the advent of the sealed set (Apple's model for its hermetic paranoia today), both Germany and Australia saw union-owned stations pioneering choral response via two-way radio, a dream of worker–actor collaboration across the ether. This history shows that both the technical achievement of listening and the initial multipoint distribution of radio involved active audiences – a group that has been prized since as a kind of avant garde.

That "proper" life of initiative was replaced in the 1930s by the supposedly lazy, dependent listenership of women, because the proliferation of broadcast towers and loudspeakers made radio an effortless listening medium at the same moment as the advent of sealed sets made it a one-way device, with transmission centralized and only reception diversified. Now an apparatus of consumption rather than mastery, it had been feminized, with the will to buy advertised goods its defining quality. Noting this trend in a more positive vein, the Television Broadcasters Association in 1944 stressed the desire that TV avoid "any repetition of the errors that marked radio's beginnings" (Stavitsky, 1995: 81; Association quoted in Boddy, 1994: 114): those errors had situated the audience as a participant, not just a recipient.

Female viewers were central to corporate calculations about US television from the very first, because they were expected to spend more time in the home than other potential spectators. In the early days of tuning sets, it was thought that women would be unable to cope with the technical challenges of reception. Then there was the question of their unpaid domestic labor: how could this crucial economic and social service be safeguarded while they fulfilled their other useful role as captives of commercials? The US strategy, which became orthodoxy elsewhere, was to drop initial plans for reconstructing cinema in the home via this new, exciting apparatus: assumptions about seeking to repeat the immersive experience of movies – lights off, full attention, and immobile – were rejected in favor of a distracted experience. Like radio, TV would be just one aspect of home life, alongside demanding children, husbands, animals, and tasks. Its visuals would reinforce a message that could be understood in another room or while doing chores – the volume would go up when the commercials came on (Morley 2007: 277).

But the "mistakes" of early radio may in fact be inevitable – facts of culture. In accounting for cult cinema, Umberto Eco suggests fans can "own" a text, psychologically if not legally, by quoting and imitating characters' escapades and proclivities. References to segments of an episode or the typical behavior of an actant may catalyze collective memory, regardless of their significance for individual plot lines (1987: 198). Marie Gillespie (1995) illustrates how elderly Punjabi expatriates in London take the viewing of Hindi films with their children and grandchildren as opportunities to reminisce and educate family members about India. There was controversy and even violence among exiled Iranian audiences in Los Angeles in 1990 when their image of "home" was challenged during a film festival devoted to post-revolutionary cinema (Naficy, 1993). Right-wing diasporic Vietnamese picketed a Los Angeles video store for 53 days in 1999 because its owner had displayed a picture of Ho Chi Minh (Shore, 2004). Gay Asian-Caribbean-Canadian video-maker Richard Fung (1991) talks about "searching" for Asian genitals in the much-demonized genre of pornography; an account not available in conventional denunciations of porn and its impact on minorities.

When JoEllen Shively (2009) returned to the reservation where she grew up, her fellow Native Americans were reading Western films as they had done during her childhood, in an actantial rather than a political way that found them cheering for cowboys over Indians, because heroic narrativization had overdetermined racial identification. This may explain the Vietnamese audiences who applauded the former US soldier mowing down their people in the *Rambo* cycle (Sylvester Stallone, George P. Cosmatos, Ted Kotcheff, and Peter MacDonald, 1982–2008) (Iyer, 1989). Jacqueline Bobo's analysis of black US women viewers of *The Color Purple* (Steven Spielberg, 1985) shows that watching the movie and discussing it drew them back to Alice Walker's novel, with all three processes invoking personal experience (1995: 3).

Mexican women living in the United States enjoy watching exported Mexican *telenovelas*, because they actualize affective and symbolic ties, whereas many men dislike the genre's representation of their homeland. Differences abound: Argentine Armenians protest at the very idea of imported Turkish *novelas*, given Ankara's failure to acknowledge their genocide of a century before. But for other Latin American audiences, what matters is not geopolitics, but a mixture of exoticism and repetition, a blend of new scenery with familiar sexual relationships (Uribe, 2009; Concept Media, n.d.).[4]

In Taiwan, 智者生存 (2001–3), the supposedly localized version of *The Weakest Link*, an almost absurdly popular show of systematic, ritualized humiliation that was successful in dozens of countries and especially among self-loathing Britons (2000–12) was a failure. Its strategy of demeaning others from a position of authority alienated viewers (Wang, 2009). We see similar findings about aberrant TV decoding in the work of Karen Riggs (1998) on elderly US audiences, Purnima Mankekar (1999) on South Asian women viewers, and Eric Kit-Wai Ma (1999) on Hong Kong focus groups.

In such research, the audience seizes control of the media, regardless of factory norms or hegemonic meanings. This capacity is supposedly observable through the sinews of audience reactions, the materiality of their intersections with texts – the work they do. It is interesting that, despite the shibboleths adored in the West, Sovietism specialized in – and blatantly desired – active audiences, because the oscillation between control and participation governed its contradictory media policy (Mihelj, 2015).

In the early days of the web, one of us used a snowball method to mobilize these insights to identify and contact latter-day followers of the 1960s British television program *The Avengers* from across the world to juxtapose popular memories of the program with the cultural politics of the time, especially gender relations and the Cold War (Miller, 1997). This was in keeping with studies undertaken in Latin America under the aegis of García Canclini and his collaborators, which disclose that the interrelationship between audiences and reality must be understood as a "process by which subjects construct and undergo the facts, transform them, and experience the resistance provided by the real" (2001: 62).

This idea that the audience is active and powerful has been elevated to a virtual nostrum in some research into fans, who are thought to construct parasocial or imagined social connections to celebrities and actants in ways that fulfill the function of friendship and make sense of human interaction. Picking up on Garfinkel's (1992/1967) "cultural dope" insight to counter the psy-function, active-audience mavens claim that the public is so active that it makes its own meanings, outwitting institutions of the state, academia, and capitalism that seek to measure and control it. This critique asserts that media audiences routinely subvert patriarchy, capitalism, and other forms of oppression because they decode texts in keeping with their social situations. The audience is said to be weak at the level of cultural production, but strong as an interpretative community, especially via imagined links to stars. All this is supposedly evident to scholars from their perusal of audience conventions, web pages, discussion groups, quizzes, and rankings, or by watching television with their children (Baym, 2000; Fiske, 1987; Jenkins, 1992).

Surveillance

On the other hand, the drive to know about audiences is frequently about the desire to govern them, as we saw in the previous chapter. Surveillance has long been a central strut of modernity, allegedly to make populations secure, content, and productive. With the expansion of state authority into the everyday, into all corners of life, the quid pro quo for the security afforded by governments became knowing everyone's identities and practices. The equivalent expansion of corporations into the everyday, into the same corners of life, had as *its* quid pro quo for the provision of goods and services that they, too, know more and more about us. The proliferation of methods for studying how people interact with the media may even infringe privacy and free speech, given the proprietorial methods used by corporations to undermine autonomous reading. Corporate concoctions like affective economics and sentiment research reflect the ongoing development and sharpening of ever more precise and pernicious tools to harvest, predict, and control the conduct of media users (Turow, 2005; Andrejevic, 2006; Baruh, 2004; Gandy, 1989).

For whether we see audiences in accordance with either media studies 1.0 or media studies 2.0 – as knowledgeable, ignorant, passive, active, powerful, weak, intelligent, idiotic – or none, all, or some of the above – their principal role for the media industries is to be known, to be investigated. Active participation in watching texts or creating paratexts offers corporations greater surveillance of audiences' attention. Their mental and emotional labor makes them valuable. The more visible that labor becomes – the more that is known about the audience's composition and conduct – the better for corporate capital (Wasko et al., 2001). The media therefore position themselves "at the intersection of time and real estate" (Maggio, 2008).

Three basic fantasies about media audiences dominate marketing: the individual, the regional, and the global. The first is animated by classifications of race, class, gender, age, and psyche; the second by geopolitical clusters; and the third by a growing cosmopolitanism. Audience surveillance starts before television programs have even been made, via focus groups, which scrutinize small numbers of people whose identities represent the social formations desired by advertisers. They are shown pilots of programs to judge the likelihood that people like them will watch shows that are picked up by networks. These groups are crucial to the arrival and departure of US TV texts. The firms that undertake such research frequently work for both producers and networks, thereby creating a conflict of interest, and are rarely multilingual, unlike their equivalents in public relations or advertising (Miller, 2010a).

Online sites such as Hulu replay television programs and films, using "geofiltered access logs" to identify audiences. These are measured each day, alongside confessional testimonies by potential viewers – if you tell us about your life and practices of consumption, we'll tell you about programs that may interest you. YouTube's video identification software, developed with Disney and Time Warner, is a surveillance device for tracking copyrighted materials on the site that follows the history of each uploaded frame, spying on users to disclose their internet protocols, aliases, and practices to corporations. The software permits these companies to block or enable reuse of texts, depending on their marketing and surveillance needs of the moment. YouTube has thus become middle-aged media's valued ally, tracking intellectual property and realizing the culture industries' paradoxical dream of engaging in product placement each time copyright is infringed on line, while learning more and more about their audiences (Miller, 2010a).

Can audiences be said to resist labor exploitation, patriarchy, racism, and US neo-imperialism, or in some specifiable way make a difference to politics beyond their own selves when they interpret texts unusually, dress up in public as men from outer space, or chat about their romantic frustrations? Why have such practices become popular in the Global North at the very moment when media policy fetishizes deregulation and consumer sovereignty? And are media studies 2.0's favored methods and samples so self-directed and self-regarding that they amount to narcissography? The *Wall Street Journal* welcomes such work as "deeply threatening to traditional leftist views of commerce." The *Journal* suggests that "cultural-studies mavens are betraying the leftist cause, lending support to the corporate enemy and even training graduate students who wind up doing market research" (Postrel, 1999).

Marketing likes nothing better than active audiences who are bursting with knowledge about media texts; nothing better than diverse groups with easily identified cultural politics and practices; nothing better than fine-grained ethnographic and focus-group work to supplement large-scale surveys and demographic data. For instance, interactive digital television is a key innovation for spying on the US public via set-top boxes that provide information about viewers to marketers and advertisers, from their use of mute buttons to their psychographic profiles. This "research" can be done at the behest of the state, which has already ordered such firms to share their data (Chmielewski, 2002). And PriceWaterhouse (2015) offers specialist advice on how to exploit the "super-fan," who invests time and money on global media like no one else. "[I]ncremental revenue" can be generated by "[h]arnessing the most passionate advocates" via forms of participation that make them feel special in their roles as unpaid marketers.

The internet also provides cheap market testing. TV producers leak information or request audience input about planned changes to programming to capture opinion without paying for it, keeping their attention on such noted TV critic websites as *Television Without Pity, TV Squad,* and *Futon Critic. Television Without Pity* is even owned by NBC Universal (Kushner, 2007).

Once a series is on the air, ratings and subscriptions are the keys to determining their success. They have become of increasing importance as the audience for single media platforms has fractured. The English-language US TV broadcast networks attained their peak viewing numbers in 1976, with 92 percent of the national audience; by 2005, they had 45 percent of it. US cable programming thrived at their expense with the deregulation of the 1980s and '90s, which permitted cable networks to start their own stations and make their own programs. Today's highly targeted cable networks offer original programming. They seek a signature in the public mind and correlate consumption with viewing. The upshot? Perhaps most spectacularly, more people watched CNN than any broadcast network on election night in 2008, and no fewer than 37 cable stations that carry commercials reported their best prime time viewing figures that year, while audience numbers for US broadcast networks dropped by an average of 11 percent (Attallah, 2007: 330; Flaherty, 2008; Richardson and Figueroa, 2005; Collins, 2009; Hassan et al., 2003: 446f.; Morris, 2007).

Companies like MTV attract young audiences who are less inclined to sit through commercials than their elders. Some research suggests they customize TV schedules to suit their diaries, not to avoid advertising. So now there are more and more ideas about interactive commercials, where viewers use remote controls to respond to pitches – and disclose data about themselves (Helm, 2007; Downey, 2007; Reynolds, 2008; Edgecliffe-Johnson, 2007).

A US network drama like *Alias* (2001–6), which did not rate well, remained on the air for five years because of the youthfulness of its fans and its successful promotion of DVD sales. Low-rating situation comedies for and about elites, like *30 Rock* (2006–13) and *The Office* (2005–13), kept their places on the schedule as a consequence of being much loved by affluent viewers. Such qualities can enable unpopular series to survive, because advertisers of costly merchandise are promised ruling-class audiences by networks. With overall declines in ratings, the broadcast networks are sometimes forced to offer commercial time free to advertisers who have paid for programs that do not attract the "right" people. Then there is very specific, local targeting, where broadcast stations follow the lead of radio and the airlines, via credit and debit cards articulated to frequent viewing and rewards systems with local advertisers (Downey, 2007; Consoli, 2008; Greenwald, 2009).

Youthful audiences are of particular concern to the media in terms of surveillance, because the young are thought to be still deciding on their favorite commodities – toothpaste, transport, tutus, and so on. To quote 1970s ABC TV executive Leonard Goldstein, they are "the most curious" viewers, the likeliest to "seek out the new." The success of *Friends* (1994–2004) encouraged US broadcast networks to schedule comedies that would appeal to people in their 20s and 30s. Other age groups got the message that they were not a priority and did the sensible thing of turning to cable stations. Ironically, when CBS reverted to the idea of addressing a mass audience in 2008, it won the ratings both overall *and* among young people (Collins, 2009).

The media are forever announcing new, failsafe schemes for captivating and capturing the audience. In 2006, NBC unveiled "Television 2.0," which was meant to be the end of drama in prime time. In 2008, it declared the return of the "8 o'clock Family Hour" with serial drama throughout the year – this was called "The New Paradigm." Then 2009 ushered in "The NBCUniversal2.0," a "New, New Paradigm" with less original programming and more reality and talk shows, described in the idiotic vocabulary of managerialism as a "margin enhancer." Consider this embarrassing quotation from the head of NBC-Universal's TV and movie interests in 2009: "We have a sniper focus on 8 p.m. to 10 p.m. to drive a power audience flow" (de Moraes, 2008; Friedman, 2009a). It is hard to believe that these people inhabit the world of English when they use such laughably inelegant and aggressive metaphors to describe the surveillance and management of viewers. The translation is that the network had given up on creating high-quality drama other than during those two hours. The media turn the manifold, manifest failures of these manager-warlocks into assertions that audiences are their masters.

We do not suggest that the practice of surveillance is omniscient and omnipotent. Audience numbers and practices have massive effects, but they are not pure, unvarnished accounts of popularity and conduct. For example, ratings apartheid was practiced for decades in the United States until 2007, initially because Spanish-language networks thought their viewers were being lost in the Anglo-Yanqui mass. When Spanish-language networks were finally measured alongside their English-language equivalents, Univision won the ratings amongst advertising's most desired age group, 18–49, no fewer than 14 times in 2008, because Latin@s were not departing network TV for cable or the internet, due to their economic situation (Bauder, 2008). This prompted one more tedious but nasty turn in a national debate over assimilation that saw ludicrous accusations to the effect that young Latin@s were not learning English or patriotism because they were watching shows in another tongue (Arnoldy, 2007).

Empirical studies of minority groups using TV to solidify their culture and remain in touch with places of origin, such as Turks in Greece or Arabs in the United States, counter the notion that this precludes integration, and Latin@s move easily between languages, code-switching both intersententially and between phrases, in keeping with their use of both Anglo and Spanish television channels (Madianou, 2005: 55; Rizkallah and Razzouk, 2006; Loechner, 2009).

The belated recognition of Univision's importance emphasizes the limitations of ratings. The measurement of bilingual audiences to Anglo networks was so incompetent that it was wrongly used to downplay the appeal of ethnically inclusive English-language material, misreading viewers' desires and hence diminishing work prospects for minority talent. Numerous multicultural shows were prematurely cancelled, such as *Greetings from Tucson* (2002–3), *Kingpin* (2003), and *Luis* (2003), because their audiences were underestimated – in every sense. What else were Spanish speakers to do but turn to Univision, when Anglo networks systematically ignored, distorted, or misunderstood them, as decades of content analysis in the *National Brownout Report* have illustrated (National Association of Hispanic Journalists, 2006; Rincón & Associates, 2004; James, 2007)? This connects to the intellectual narrowness of Anglo executives and attempts by traditional networks to minimize the power of cable stations by stressing prime time as the centerpiece of measuring audience size, which suited their heavy investments in marquee programming at that time, and their cozy relationship with the companies that research viewers.

To repeat, the elemental desire that drives advertisers is not absolute numbers of readers, listeners, or viewers. They want to know about those audiences in terms of identity, wealth, and taste. Ratings firms have developed ever more impressive-sounding methods of investigating audiences – 10,000 US TV viewers (and more in dozens of other countries) are under surveillance through People Meters nowadays, to add to the 15,000 examined by other means, such as Anytime Anywhere Media Measurement (Mermigas, 2008).[5] This is the future of "TV Everywhere" initiatives, for example.

This passion for knowing customers at the same time as claiming to serve them explains the advent of firms such as Phorm and FrontPorch.[6] Corporate consultant Openwave's *Privacy Primer* says it protects consumers from an *Era of Behavioral Marketing*. But the *Primer* gleefully avows that "[o]n the internet, customer feedback isn't requested so much as it's collected, like a digital trail of breadcrumbs. Mobile technology only sharpens the focus on user behavior by bringing location and contextual information into play" (Openwave, 2009).

US TV and Sport

Some telling examples of audience targeting and surveillance come from sporting TV. For marketers in the Global North, young affluent men are the most desirable spectators. By contrast with other segments of the population, they have protean preferences for brands, earn sizeable incomes, and often love TV sport, which makes their interest in it disproportionately influential on programming (Commission on the Future of Women's Sport, 2010: 7).

At the height of the contemporary Great Recession, the premium cable television network HBO had 41 million US subscribers paying US$3.84 billion a year. Their social identities and viewing interests are very precisely calibrated. For example, visitors to HBO's website on boxing encounter a section titled "TALK," which invites them to participate in polls, sign up for a newsletter, and write on bulletin boards.[7] "TALK" is also and equally a system of surveillance that allows the network to monitor viewers' tastes and ideas without paying them for their intellectual property. Disney's sports network ESPN uses interactive TV forums such as "My Vote" and "My Bottom Line" to uncover audience drives in the name of enabling participation and pleasure in watching. It has also purchased broadband portals that ensure global dominance, including Cricinfo, Scrum.com, and Racing-Live, which provide two-way exchanges with audiences to build loyalty and deliver intelligence to advertisers (Miller, 2010a).

Until 2013, when it lost key contracts covering football to NBC, the US cable and satellite network, Fox Soccer, targeted men aged 18–34 with annual household incomes of US$75,000 and above; it also undertook surveillance of viewers on the web. The station boasted that three-quarters of its audience was male and half owned their own homes.[8] Its biggest-ever rating, for a 2011 English Premier League game, drew 418,000 average viewers and 285,000 households.[9] That may not seem significant in a country of more than 350 million people, but with a highly targeted demographic strategy, such numbers can produce profitable outcomes. Commercials provided textual hints about the network's plan for matching viewers to advertisers: its advertisements concentrated remorselessly on regaining and sustaining hair-growth and hard-ons, losing and hiding pimples and pounds, and becoming and adoring soldiers and sailors (Miller, 2010a).

Who is the implied spectator to the bourgeois media's coverage of sport? Newsrooms are largely male-run and coverage of sport focuses predominantly on men. But women viewers, readers, and listeners are active and numerous – and have been from the first. After explaining this contradictory story, we examine the rise, fall, and televisualization of the football hooligan and wrestling fan. They represent breach moments, occasions when cultures recalibrate due to gender issues expressed through spectatorship and the sporting media.

The vast majority of scholarship on this topic is beholden to the psy-function, whose authors imagine the space inside people's heads to account for gender, spectatorship, and sport. There is a fascination with relaxation, relief, arousal, aggression, entertainment, and identification – Aristotelian categories about drama endowed with the marvel of modern, scientific labels. A personal favorite is the "Sport Fan Motivation Scale" (later contested by the "Motivation Scale for Sport Consumption"). Such research typically finds that men watch more media sport than women, are more animated by it, and are likelier to define themselves through it. The experience is deemed to be a means of experiencing closeness without profound intimacy (Sloan, 1989; Wann, 1995; Trail and James, 2001; Tang and Cooper, 2012; Arehart-Treichel, 2012). There are culturalist as well as scientist versions of this mythology (Earnheardt et al., 2012; Markovits and Albertson, 2012; Weed, 2008; Benkwitz and Molnar, 2012). The media themselves indulge in it, as in the film *Diner* (Barry Levinson, 1982) (Haspel, 2009), or the preposterous, childlike hypermasculinity that pervades sports radio and TV self-promotions.

As in the case of reality television, such nostrums generally extrapolate from English-speaking research undertaken in the Global North. They essentialize spectatorship via an account of male sports fans as immature or at least biologically determined, driven by testosterone levels that shift with team success and failure on TV (Bernhardt et al., 1998).

The sociologist Norbert Elias borrows such psy-*données*, but he also accounts for time and space in his history of the European ruling classes and other imperialist adventurers beginning the globalization of sport in the sixteenth century (Elias, 1978; Elias and Dunning, 1986). His followers argue that today's sporting body sends messages to viewers about discipline, mirroring, dominance, and communication (Maguire, 1993). The disciplined body is remodeled through diet and training. The mirroring body functions as a machine of desire, encouraging mimetic conduct via the purchase of commodities. The dominating body exercises power through physical force. The communicative body is an expressive totality, balletic and beautiful, wracked and wrecked. Fans invest in these bodies as extensions of themselves and sites where repressed desire can be played out. Consider the fury unleashed on an Australian Olympian who engaged in antinationalistic refusal by ceasing to perform toward the end of a rowing race. The media found her wanting and public grief and anger erupted in the wake of such "un-Australian" conduct (McKay and Roderick, 2010).

The US Armed Forces Bowl, a college American football event sponsored by Bell Helicopter-Textron, is designed to create goodwill toward corporate military welfare through broad-brush suburbanite homologies constructed between sport, nation, and *matériel*. The contest is televised – and owned – by ESPN, which is available in 194 countries and 15 languages. It features ghoulish military recruiters preying on young spectators and the creepy "Great American Patriot Award" (Butterworth and Moskal, 2009; Miller, 2010a). Such events manufacture ideological links between nationalism, violence, and sacrifice. As we saw in examining the case of Pat Tillman, studies of US TV sports fans indicate white men's support for such imperialist warmongering (Stempel, 2006).

Sponsors pay sizeable sums to associate their products with sporting stars. By 2005, these endorsements were estimated at over a billion dollars in US corporate expenditure, based on a wager about fan interest in lifestyle that contractually favors athletic reliability and decency, but finds those qualities hard to separate from surprise headlines and excess. This credulous investment assumes that audiences seek to gain stars' fetishized qualities by purchasing commodities associated with them. Marketing mavens call this "associative learning" (Till et al., 2008; Thrall et al., 2008). The tabloid media subsidize these transmogrifications in search of celebration and condemnation, as photo shoots of big weddings are displaced by paparazzi shots of big waistlines. Conversely, the psy-function derides cathectic responses onto celebrity athletes by media audiences as evidence of pathological erotomania (McCutcheon et al., 2002).

In early 1990s Canada, the beer company that owned The Sports Network (TSN) adopted "We deliver the male" as its cable motto. As late as 1998, an advertisement for ESPN promised "More tackles, less tutus" (TSN, quoted in Sparks, 1992: 330, 334).[10] And at the same moment, women spectators felt excluded from TV's "discourse of [Australian] football" in their pleasurable voyeurism (Poynton and Hartley, 1990: 144).

But commercial and cultural changes have exerted tremendous pressure on the gendered norms of sport, weakening the seemingly rock-solid maleness at its core. Female US spectators tune to the Olympics in large numbers. The 1992 Winter Games drew 57 percent of its US TV audience from women. Women's figure skating out-rated that year's men's baseball World Series and National Collegiate Athletic Association basketball championship game. And the women's technical skating program at the 1994 Winter Games drew the fourth-highest ratings of any program in US history. In 1995, more women than men in Britain watched Wimbledon tennis on television, and the numbers were nearly equal for boxing. In the 1998 National Basketball Association play-offs, more women were drawn to Game Seven of the Bulls-Pacers series than *Veronica's Closet* (1997–2000) or *ER* (1994–2009). Every major professional men's league in the United States has a women's media marketing plan. Male spectatorship of TV sport in the United States is in serious decline, as more and more viewers turn to the History and Discovery Channels. The perennial savior of network sportscasters, the NFL, saw 1998-9 and 1999-2000 ratings for *Monday Night Football* at record lows – and a third of its audience was female. In 1999, more men aged 18–34 watched professional women's softball on ESPN2 than Arena football, the National Hockey League, or Major League Soccer. The NFL suffered a 13 percent decrease in TV ratings in the five seasons from 1997 and Disney exiled *Monday Night Football* from its broadcast network ABC to ESPN in 2006. The sport increasingly relied for survival on women viewers, who made up perhaps 40 percent of the audience by 2012 (Wenner and Gantz, 1998; Daddario, 1997; Miller, 2001, 2010a, 2010b; Oates, 2012).

Something is happening. A further clue comes from ABC's coverage of Super Bowl 2000, which featured Giants cornerback Jason Seahorn in uniform pants during a pregame show and reporter Meredith Vieira offering that the sport is "all about the butt." This is not to say that the objectification of the male body is universally welcome or relevant (Nelson, 2002; Weissman, 2010). But it compromises the hitherto powerful assumption of male spectatorship to sport.

Women comprise half of ESPN's US viewers (McBride, 2011). And TSN, which undertook to "deliver the male" 20 years ago, now promises that "sponsorship programs on TSN.ca can be tailored to your target audience."[11] The failure of *Sports Illustrated for Women*, which ran from 2000 to 2002, was attributed to the first George W. Bush recession, which affected advertising budgets first, in keeping with Republican-curated economic downturns. In 2010, ESPN launched espnW, a website targeting female fans that followed on a thrice-yearly magazine for women (Hueter, 2010).[12] *The Onion* grotesquely but tellingly satirized the stereotyped reaction by suggesting what the site would concentrate on:

> Highlights that feature an explanation of the rules, what's happening, and who everyone is . . . Team-by-team sensitivity ratings . . . Message boards where a bunch

of chicks can dyke it out like crazy ... Community feature where site users can discuss goings-on, share stories, and then secretly trash on each other in private chats ... [and] Somewhat less male-on-male eroticism.[13]

Gender distinctions and inequalities of course remain at play. US TV assumes women are attracted to biographical narratives about stars rather than statistics. So NBC initiated "a female-inclusive sports subgenre" at the 1992 Summer Games, offering "private-life" histories of selected contestants. It targeted women and families in 1996 to such effect that 50 percent of the Olympic audience was adult women and 35 percent men, with women's gymnastics one of the most popular events and male boxing and wrestling edged out of prime time (though there remained a disproportionate address of men's sport). The network reported an increase of 26 percent in the number of women viewers aged 25–54 by comparison with the 1992 Games (Miller, 2001).

Moving forward two decades, Summer Games coverage on TV and the web attracted 80 percent of the US population, without significant social divisions, other than those following online, which largely remained the province of the young (a billion worldwide). TV rules the roost in sport compared to the internet, though they sometimes work in tandem, and this situation may change if screening rights shift media. Already, well over half the US population connected with broadband uses it to follow sport, but a much higher proportion of women than men follow sport on TV as opposed to online. Male fans prefer cell phones and tablets to laptops or desktops (Pew Research Center for the People and the Press, 2012; Burst, 2012).

In 2009, the million people viewing England's Football Association Women's Cup Final out-rated numerous men's cricket, rugby, and football fixtures, and the British Women's Open Golf drew larger audiences than the men's Ryder Cup contest between the United States and Europe. Interestingly, the vast majority of people watching women's sport on UK TV are men (Commission on the Future of Women's Sport, 2010: 6–8).

The hypermasculinity characteristic of newsrooms and the specific biases of sporting departments remain issues, however. In the United States, there are 48 male sportscasters for every female and 94 percent of sports editors are men, as are 90 percent of their assistants. The corollaries of inattention to female fans are clear (Schreiber, 2012; Adams and Tuggle, 2004). And the Australian bourgeois media continue to discriminate: in 2008–9, just 9 percent of non-news TV was dedicated to women's sport. The figure for men was 86 percent (Australian Sports Commission, 2009: v).

In addition, the functionalist sociological and psy-function accounts explained earlier have encountered some problems since the 1970s. In Western Europe, live football became the crucible of their anxieties, often impelled by concerns about nationalistic, racist, misogynistic, and hypermasculinist conduct as unemployment spiraled, the welfare state was compromised, and immigration became a tinderbox with the arrival of people from former colonies (in small numbers) to a deindustrializing metropole.

In Britain, many football grounds became places to enact these tensions through white male heterosexual violence. Countermeasures included all-seat stadiums, individual profiling, life bans, Interpol information exchange, high ticket prices, checks on alcohol, separation of rival fans, ground security, banning clubs for poor crowd control, and scheduling matches between local teams at lunchtime to reduce drunkenness beforehand.

The media both played out and resolved this gendered audience problem. They provided sites for pundits and politicians to deride football fans as male monsters. Then as new media technologies, most importantly satellite, came into play, proprietors sought to corral male audiences by purchasing the rights to cover football on TV. More and more matches became available to watch, but in pubs and homes rather than in person, thereby simultaneously pricing out the problem and diffusing it (Pope, 2011).

Liz Moor (2007) claims that these developments should not be regarded as simply excluding people on a class basis through commodification. They have also stimulated new forms of gendered spectatorship, as pubs and sports bars have become crucial sites for collective, deterritorialized viewing (Eastman and Land, 1997; Wenner, 1998; McCarthy, 1995). So a Dominican-dominated bar in New York during summer may see immigrant men viewing baseball games involving their countrymen on various television sets (Cooper, 1999). A visit to a Santa Monica British-style bar may offer football and rugby union on different walls at the same time, while, in London, a Clerkenwell gastro pub provides one television set dedicated to La Liga and another to the English Premier League.

Such viewing practices can be understood through three lenses. As we saw in chapter 2, globalization also deglobalizes, in that it is not only about mobility and exchange, but also disconnectedness and exclusion; cultural groups frequently emerge transnationally, due to migration by people who continue to communicate, work, and consume through their languages of origin; and demographic minorities within sovereign-states may form textually specific rather than profound minorities on their adopted terrain (García Canclini, 2004). These mobile subject positions are ambivalently received by the psy-function. On the one hand, public viewing is welcomed because it may diminish domestic struggles over attention and media access. On the other, it could reduce industrial productivity (Gantz, 2012).

Hooligans and dawdlers are not the only sports spectators who provoke distrust. In the United States, the long capitalist crisis has found expression in the controlled chaos of televised wrestling, which occupies a liminal status between sport and scripted entertainment. Wrestling is an exemplary site for the evaluation of male bodies reshaped by training, medication, and display – and for the derision of its fans by the psy-function. These antique stories come from the archive of Mass-Observation, a strange blend of British surrealism and empiricism that gathered a vast array of data about ordinary life in the late 1930s and early 1940s. They illustrate that the sexualized gaze was alive in the earliest moments of media wrestling:

> No other sport has such fine husky specimens of manhood as wrestling. I find it such a change to see real he men after the spineless and insipid men one meets ordinarily – "A woman," 1938.

> I love it because it brings back to me, I am 67 years of age, my young days when men were men and not the namby pamby, simpering, artificial, hair curling variety – "A man," 1938. (Quoted in Mass-Observation, 1939: 133)

After great successes with women viewers of 1940s and '50s French and US television, the sport's popularity with commercial networks fell away, a victim of their decision to neglect general audiences in favor of male spectators and their disposable incomes. The US reintroduced wrestling on cable in the 1980s, when deregulation amidst the long crisis enabled genre-based channels and encouraged lawless forms of representation. Sport morphed into fiction (Geurens, 1989; Sammond, 2005).

Wrestling's return involved a new address of women and revised rules. Quick falls, tightly circumscribed moves, and rigorous refereeing were forsaken. In their stead came a circus-like activity, dominated by absurd persons in silly costumes adopting exotic personae and acrobatic show as means of success (Mazer, 1998). Utopic critics celebrated this as a carnivalesque play with gendered hierarchy that engaged mock hysteria amongst fans (Fiske, 1987; Sammond, 2005; Schimmel et al., 2007). The psy-function worried that the genre's lawlessness had a deleterious effect on young audiences (Waxmonsky and Beresin, 2001).

Of course, the female gaze had been at work and play for a long time – in 1869, the Cincinnati Red Stockings baseball team song addressed it like this:

> The ladies want to know
> Who are those gallant men in
> Stockings red, they'd like to know. (quoted in Schreier, 1989: 104)

The Reds were on the money. Whenever the sporting body is exposed to view in its bloodied, bowed, and beaten form, or its triumphant, tall, and talented one, anxieties and hopes about audience await. A century and a half later, the internet has seen an efflorescence of women's sports writing. Sites run by and for female fans are impressive in their blend of organic interest and professional whimsy. *HerGameLife*, for instance, has more than 200 female bloggers[14] (Maria, 2012). Of course, the web is no utopic media site: for instance, in December 2012, Google offered 409,00 hits for "soccer is gay," a homophobic US remark about anything that escapes popular ken.[15] Many of these sites attack the sexuality of football's players and followers (Mercado, 2008) even though they include *The Onion*'s parody of soccer coming out.[16]

And none of the above means there is equality in the media's coverage of sport or their valuation of men and women as subjects and objects of the gaze or address. Despite the fascination of women as well as men with sport, and repeated evidence that women's sport appeals to viewers at profound levels and across social categories, the resources dedicated by the bourgeois media to such tastes remain structured in dominance. Men remain privileged as performers, commentators, sponsors, and spectators (Commission on the Future of Women's Sport, 2010).

Because sport and gender jumble together in a complex weave of commodification, they cannot be kept apart. They live cheek by capital, torso by Totti, boot by Beckham. The paradox of sport, its simultaneously transcendent and imprisoning qualities and capacity to allegorize, is most obvious, most dangerous, and perhaps most transformative when it comes to sex. With the advent of consumer capitalism and postmodern culture, the body has become an increasingly visible locus of desire. It's not just women who are objects of this gaze, not just women who are physically damaged in the interests of social expectations, and not just men who inspect the bodies of others for foibles and follicles.

Across the past three decades, sport has transformed itself through the media into an internationalist capitalist project   and new pressures accompany the spoils. As part of the desire to address media spectators and capture their attention for advertisers, the body has become an object of lyrical rhapsody and gendered money. It is up for grabs as a sexual icon. Sculpted features, chiseled waistlines, well-appointed curves, dreamy eyes, administered hair, and an air of casual threat are the currency of the day. Like beauty and fitness of all kinds, the years will attenuate them and the media will identify new names, new bodies, new Eros, new Euros.

Conclusion

The direct opposition that is frequently drawn between active-audience theory (interpretation matters) and political economy (production matters) assumes that the variety of audience niches and responses nullifies the concentration and reach of economic power in mass culture – that pluralism ensures diversity (Schiller, 1989: 147–8, 153). Political-economic/cultural approaches that track the material lives of commodity signs bring attention to the fact that cultural texts change their meaning and value depending on where, when, and how they are experienced.

It is often alleged that political economists have not accounted for the ability of audiences to interpret what they receive. But if we look back at the scholars who created that tradition, it is evident that they were well aware of this capacity. In the 1950s, Smythe wrote that "audience members act on the program content. They take it and mold it in the image of their individual needs and values." He took it as read that soap-opera *habituées* sometimes viewed the genre as fictional and sometimes as a guide for dealing with problems (1954: 143, 148). At the height of his 1970s policy interventions in revolutionary societies, from Latin America to Africa, Armand Mattelart recognized the relative autonomy of audiences and their capacity and desire to generate cultural meanings (1980: 111). And in the classic 1960s text *Mass Communications and American Empire*, Herb Schiller (1992/1969) stressed the need to build on the creativity of audiences by offering them entertaining and informative media. Their example resonates in the best global media studies.

At a policy level, Stuart Cunningham (1992) had an impact on Australian public inquiries into the representation of violence and the impact of commercials with his survey of political-economic and cultural-studies approaches to television audiences, and Justin Lewis's (2001) study of US public opinion was a significant intervention. Rosalía Winocur (2002) produced a major account of the part played by audiences to talk-back radio in Latin American democracies newly freed from US-backed dictators, while Ellen Seiter's (2005) ethnography of young Californians and new media is compelling. García Canclini and his associates (2001) have mobilized a melange of field observations, interviews, surveys, and textual analyses to examine the reception of cultural events in Mexico. At a conceptual level, several theorists have explained the essentially constructed nature of the audience, its ontology forever scarred by the way it is brought into being through the psy-function to perform specific tasks of surveillance and sales (Ang, 1991; Hartley, 1987; Lewis, 1991; Maxwell, 1991, 1996a, 1996b, 2000).

Future research can follow their fine examples and articulate scholarship on media audiences with work on activist and social movement media to theorize and explore John D. H. Downing's (2003) argument that what used to be called alternative media is the locus of the "real active" audience – another way to combine the study of media structure and representation.

Marketers avow their powerlessness over audiences when challenged in the public sphere, but boast omnipotence over them in the private world: the essay that won the oleaginous "Best New Thinking Award" at the 2003 Market Research Society Conference acknowledged that successful marketing does not "view . . . the consumer as an individual" but "part of the herd" (Earls, 2003).

Such corporate awareness enables, for instance, the successful marketing of the *Pearl Harbor* film (Michael Bay, 2001) in Japan, via a poster and trailer that framed it as primarily a love story, with war, violence, and US–Japanese enmity a backdrop. Such methods are available to capital, which understands that audiences are not already-extant entities participating in the neoliberal wet dream of supply and demand. Most of the time, the media are not directly selling to their audience, and their audience is not buying from them.

The task for those of us who want the media to be more entertaining, informative, inclusive, and democratic is to alert our fellow-audience members about the ways in which their labor is exploited, their environment is polluted, and their viewing and social identities are governed and commodified by the media.

Conclusion

Throughout *Global Media Studies*, we have tried to strike a balance between broad-brush theorizing and attention to specific examples. Chapters 1 and 2 explained the terms "media" and "global," their contemporary manifestations, and how the two have come to be interlaced. The next two chapters presented two approaches and bodies of literature, political economy and governance policy, to the understanding of the structural features of global media – their material manifestations and social impact. Chapters 5 and 6 narrowed our focus down to two phenomena, mobile telephony and the United States as a global media behemoth. Subsequent chapters illustrated how to analyze media content, focused on the global genre of reality television, and concluded with an analysis of audiences. We hope that by going through processes of production, distribution, reception, and social reproduction on an international scale, this book has provided an introductory tour of the global media and how to study them.

Driven by free market fundamentalism and the forced weakening of national policy and cultural boundaries, the contemporary hypercommercial media environment knows few boundaries. Ancient ways of life on territories at the margin of the global system are incorporated into reality television tribal councils (*Survivor*) and myths, legends, and stories of the marginalized are appropriated by Hollywood blockbusters (from Aladdin to Pocahontas). Places at the extremeties of the global economy function as playgrounds for action heroes who demolish structures, annihilate men, and seduce women to entertain the privileged quarter of humankind with reliable access to food, shelter, electricity, and disposable income. At this juncture, the study of media should therefore signify the study of global media.

Several factors drive the convergence of "media" and "global." The first is technology. Though ascribed magical powers and fetishized beyond measure, undersea cables, communication satellites, and interlinked computers have expanded the scale of communication to encompass the whole world. This infrastructure is a necessary but insufficient element in the global media sphere. Here we come to the second factor, the economic order; for capitalism never ceases to seek, create, even extract by force, new markets.

The dominant political economy of newspapers, television, film, "social" media, mobile telephony, games, etc., is advertising and data-mining supported. In other words, it is driven by the imperative to turn users and consumers into commodities. Both the media themselves and the study of the media must scale up to the global scope of humanity. Enabled by technology and driven by economics, global media industries adapt, borrow, or steal from the literature, stories, myths, legends, flora, fauna, and labor of the whole world, which these industries cook up and serve as monetary bait. Culture, in other words, is increasingly becoming raw material for the planetary makers, distributors, and sellers of texts and images and sounds, as the NICL becomes a key player in our ecological peril.

In the new era, readers become writers, listeners transform into speakers, viewers emerge as stars, fans are academics, and vice versa. Think of the job prospects that follow! Bloggers are copywriters. Children are columnists. Bus riders are journalists. Coca-Cola hires African Americans to drive through the inner city selling soda and playing hip-hop. AT&T pays San Francisco buskers to mention the company in their songs. Urban performance poets rhyme about Nissan cars for cash, simultaneously hawking, entertaining, and researching. Subway's sandwich commercials are marketed as made by teenagers. Cultural studies majors become designers. Unpaid interns to public relations firms post putatively organic desires for products and services on social media as part of lucrative contracts for their elders and betters in PR and marketing.

Is that the best we can do? What should be done to ameliorate this situation? Clearly, casualized labor suits some people in particular places at certain moments in their lives; but to make it a requirement, a norm, means that there must be accompanying programs to ameliorate the inequalities and poverty it can cause through the consolidation of primary and secondary labor markets, which segregate societies by power and money.

The answer lies in environmental justice and welfare tailored to patterns of employment (Murray and Gollmitzer, 2011). This also necessitates global solidarity with workers at the sharpest end of the NICL – those who make and recycle media devices under oppressive, dangerous circumstances, and struggle for political rights (Chan et al., 2013). The NICL has become a model for exploitation across territories, industries, and occupations, so thinking about it critically remains vital. Analytically, we need to focus on the division of labor as a theoretical, empirical, and organizational tool if we are to understand everyday work in a way that can enrich and liberate it in accord with ecological and employee experiences and necessities. Labor and environmental justice are intimately implicated with the increasingly worldwide power of culture – and the means of powering it. The theory of the NICL can contribute to those goals once it accounts for the entire life of the commodity sign, from conception to manufacture to distribution to use – and finally, recycling.

We began in the Introduction with the Olsen twins. As we were finishing this Conclusion, work had begun on a sequel to their first series. *Fuller House* was to be on Netflix rather than a free-to-air channel, and minus its original mega-stars. This was announced via a series of rather bitter interviews, tweets, and Facebook posts by those involved (Rosen, 2015). All good publicity. Meanwhile, they won an award as "Top Womenswear Designers" from the Council of Fashion Designers of America awards and faced a class-action lawsuit by dozens of interns in protest at unpaid exploitation (Fearn, 2015; Marsh and Fenton, 2015). The names of the workers making their lines remained unknown, while the flailing about over the remake of their TV series continued to inscribe their origins. The way in which the Olsens were indistinct, as two people playing the same character for eight years, still haunted their media coverage – how were they differentiating themselves from one another and their past, and should they? And questions about gender and health continued to swirl around them.

We almost forgot this tidbit: the *New York Times* listed one of the twins as among the world's top nine icons who had published with the paper. Others included John F. Kennedy and Kurt Vonnegut.[1] Mary-Kate's article was about "a large, red quilted Chanel bag that I borrowed from my sister Ashley. I wore it to an event and never gave it back. Luckily, she's moved on to another bag, so I'm safe for now" (Olsen, 2007). Meanwhile, the cult intertextual film *You're Invited – The Olsen Twins Movie* (2012), which interlaced scenes from their commercials and other texts with a young man's imagined interactions with them, continued to garner viewers.[2]

And Clare of Assisi? Her canonization had been "part of a creative trawl through medieval hagiography to find old saints to guard and protect the inventions of modern times" (Pattenden, 2008: 226). The Catholic Church soon arched even further back in history to identify a patron saint of the internet: Isidore of Seville was proposed by John Paul II because of his multivolume encyclopedia.[3]

Minus such quasi-divine guidance, we have tried in this book to offer as wide a view as possible of the intersection of the media and the globe. Though necessarily selective – a representative narrative of all of the world's texts, cultures, technologies, and politics and their intersection would be beyond us – we have presented a range of cases, forces, and outcomes related to the topic as we reached for media studies 3.0.

As stated in the Introduction, we have been both hobbled and aided by our own linguistic abilities and intellectual predilections. We hope that our efforts have at least provoked a dose, however minute, of skepticism toward the conventional wisdoms that rule the global media and how to study them. Perhaps we have sparked some ideas that will help our readers understand and democratize the global media today.

Notes

Introduction

1 See also "The Surprise Luxury Label," *The Wall Street Journal* (May 14, 2014): http://www.wsj.com/articles/SB10001424052702303627504579558221512719340.
2 See: http://www.globallabourrights.org/press/maternity-leave-campaign-mary-kate-and-ashley-olsen; *Times of India*, "Ashley and Mary-Kate's Sisterly Bond" (August 11, 2007): https://web.archive.org/web/20071217163654/http://timesofindia.indiatimes.com/Entertainment/International_Buzz/Ashley_and_Mary-Kates_sisterly_bond/articleshow/2273415.cms.
3 See also: www.catholic.org/saints/saint.php?saint_id=215#wiki.

Chapter 1 Media Studies

1 In Chapter 2, we'll explain the meaning of "global," the first word in our title. In this chapter we focus on the media, the second word – English syntax does not favor our logic!
2 *Television Advertising Bureau*, "What Topped TV's Holiday List? Tablets!" (December 21, 2012): http://www.tvb.org/4685/about_tvb/commentary/commentary_article/1339337.
3 See: http://downloads.bbc.co.uk/historyofthebbc/1920s.pdf.
4 In the US, the challenge from the left was more muted, with disciplines dedicated to the industry and normal science.
5 See: http://www.aejmc.org/; http://www.natcom.org/about/.
6 See: http://www.beaweb.org/wp/.
7 See: http://www.cmstudies.org/.
8 See: http://www.icahdq.org/about_ica/mission.asp.
9 See: http://www.meccsa.org.uk/.
10 See: http://iamcr.org/iamcr-profile.
11 See: http://www.democraticcommunications.net/about.
12 Political science (http://www.politicalcommunication.org/); anthropology (http://www.societyforvisualanthropology.org/); sociology (http://www.asanet.org/sections/CIT.cfm); education (http://www.aera.net/DivisionC/CommunicationandSocialMedia/tabid/15413/Default.aspx); law (http://www.lawandsociety.org/crn.html); pediatrics (http://www.aap.org/en-us/about-the-aap/Committees-Councils-Sections/Council-on-Communications-Media/Pages/default.aspx); psychology (http://www.apa.org/about/division/div46.aspx).
13 Perhaps there should be more of a focus on the material dangers posed to children by TVs: well over 385,000 young people have been admitted to US emergency rooms in the last two decades due to physical injuries caused by sets (De Roo et al., 2013).
14 See: http://www.theguardian.com/media/2013/sep/01/you-them-mediaguardian-100-2013.
15 See: http://maleyinvestigations.com/child-custody.asp?tip=45.
16 As Harvard long hosted a journal of media studies (the ungainly titled *Harvard International Journal of Press/Politics*, now thankfully free of its oxymoronic Yanqui moniker) and a New Approaches to International Law colloquium that engaged with cultural studies, and MIT has held major conferences called "Media In Transition" to trope its acronym, Hoggart's dismissiveness was ill-informed – but quite representative.
17 See: http://www.meccsa.org.uk/.
18 Calm down, Kevin. Women continue to be excluded from key positions in TV newsrooms around the globe in favor of people like you (Byerly, 2013). In any event, once you lost your job in 2014 as Fox ratings descended into the mire, perhaps you found more time to appreciate NBC (James, 2014).

19 "The Surprise Luxury Label," *The Wall Street Journal* (May 14, 2014): http://www.wsj.com/arti
    cles/SB10001424052702303627504579558221512719340.

Chapter 2 Global Studies

1 We both frequently review manuscripts for journals about sections of the non-English-speaking
   world in which all the knowledge drawn upon is in one language. The same tendency is alive in omnibus survey volumes of global media – no knowledge of any kind in any other language is deemed
   citable (e.g., Flew, 2013 – a useful volume for its engagement with the Anglosphere's debates).
2 This tradition's founding texts included: in the US, Schiller's *Mass Communication and American
   Empire* (1971) and *Communication and Cultural Domination* (1976); in the UK, Tunstall's *The
   Media are American* (1977) and Oliver Boyd-Barrett's "Media Imperialism" (1977); in Chile, Ariel
   Dorfman and Mattelart's *Para Leer al Pato Donald* [*How to Read Donald Duck*] (1971); in France,
   Mattelart's *Multinational Corporations and the Control of Culture* (1979); and in Norway, Johann
   Galtung's "A Structural Theory of Imperialism" (1971).
3 See: http://blogs.ft.com/beyond-brics/.
4 That said, most published scholarly knowledge is available in English, because of its publishing
   hegemony. This is clear from our bibliography.
5 "A Cyber-House Divided," *The Economist* (September 4, 2010): 61.

Chapter 3 Political Economy

1 This chapter draws on Maxwell and Miller, 2012; Miller, 2014b.
2 A handful of examples amongst dozens, covering classical Hollywood to the end of the last century, might include Perretti and Negro, 2007; Cattani et al., 2008; Shamsie et al., 2009; Simonton,
   2009; Hadida, 2010; Hsu et al., 2012; Cattani et al., 2013.
3 Distinguished examples from the political economy of the media and culture more broadly
   include Schiller, 1989; Maxwell, 2001; Meehan and Riordan, 2001; Ruccio and Amariglio, 2003;
   Wayne, 2003; Mosco, 2004; Chakravartty and Zhao, 2007; McKercher and Mosco, 2007; Schiller,
   2007; Mosco and McKercher, 2008; Amariglio et al., 2009; Mosco et al., 2010; Wasko et al., 2011;
   McChesney, 2013.
4 See: http://www.blueadvertising.com/#/american-petroleum-institute/.
5 See: http://www.api.org/policy-and-issues/policy-items/environment/climate_change.
6 See also: http://www.edelman.com/p/6-a-m/edelmans-position-climate-change/; http://www.
   holmesreport.com/latest/article/edelman's-american-petroleum-institute-assignment-set-to-
   end.
7 See: http://www.greenpeace.org/international/en/publications/reports/dealing-in-doubt/.
8 See: https://assets.documentcloud.org/documents/1362369/tc-energy-east-grassroots-advo
   cacy-vision-document.pdf.
9 See: http://www.prsa.org/aboutprsa/ethics/codeenglish/#.VOrW-VOUf7c.
10 See: http://www.womma.org/ethics/womma-code-of-ethics.
11 See: http://www.corporatewatch.org/company-profiles/edelman.
12 See: http://www.greenpeace.org/canada/Global/canada/file/2014/11/Astroturf-backgrounder.
    pdf.
13 See: http://www.edelman.com/insights/intellectual-property/2015-edelman-trust-barometer/.
14 See: http://www.prsa.org/aboutprsa/ethics/codeenglish/#.VOrW-VOUf7c.
15 See also: *In the Matter of Facebook, Inc.*, Federal Trade Commission File No. 092 3184 (November
    2011): http://www.ftc.gov/enforcement/cases-proceedings/092-3184/facebook-inc.
16 See also: http://www.mindworksglobal.com/.
17 See also: http://www.poptent.net/.
18 See: "DiCaprio Calls on Yingluck to Ban Ivory Trade," *The Nation* (February 22, 2013): http://www.
    nationmultimedia.com/national/DiCaprio-calls-on-Yingluck-to-ban-ivory-trade-30200375.
    html.
19 See also: "Supreme Court Ruling: Filming 'Damaged Beach'," *The Nation* (December 1, 2006):
    http://www.nationmultimedia.com/2006/12/01/national/national_30020443.php.
20 See also: "World Television Market," *IDATE NEWS* (January 14, 2009): 452.
21 See: "Deutsche Welle to Launch Second Asian Channel," *Indiantelevision* (January 7, 2009):
    http://www.indiantelevision.com/headlines/y2k9/jan/jan36.php.

22 See: https://www.frapa.org/.
23 Viacom et al. v. YouTube et al. 07 Civ. 2103.
24 See also: "Listen to the Music," *The Economist* (November 22, 2008): 78; "Job 1 at Viacom: Fix MTV's Image," *Marketwatch* (February 12, 2009): http://www.marketwatch.com/story/job-1-viacom-fix-mtvs-image; "2008: The Top Ten Happenings in Indian TV," *Indiantelevision* (December 27, 2008): http://www.indiantelevision.com/node/102741.
25 See also: "CSI the Most Watched Show in the World," *Mail Online India* (June 15, 2012): http://www.dailymail.co.uk/indiahome/indianews/article-2160093/CSI-watched-world.html.
26 See: "World Television Market," *IDATE NEWS* (January 14, 2009): 452.
27 See: https://twitter.com/DrodriguezMinci.
28 See: http://www.tntdrama.com/shows/legends.html.
29 See: "Venezuela investiga a TNT por serie que dice Maduro compra armas químicas," *El Nuevo Herald* (September 4, 2014): http://www.elnuevoherald.com/noticias/mundo/america-latina/venezuela-es/article2040752.html; "Serie Legends de TNT acusa al president Maduro de comprar armas biológicas para usarlas contra manifestantes," *Correo del Orinoco* (September 1, 2014): http://www.correodelorinoco.gob.ve/politica/nueva-serie-tnt-acusa-al-presiente-maduro-comprar-una-bomba-biologica-para-usarla-contra-manifestantes/; "Venezuela Outcry as US Drama Legends Maligns President Nicolás Maduro;" *Guardian* (September 3, 2014): http://www.theguardian.com/world/2014/sep/03/venezuelan-government-denounces-us-spy-show-legends.

Chapter 4 Policy and Governance

1 This chapter borrows extensively from Kraidy, 2011; Miller, 2014a.
2 See: https://www.youtube.com/watch?v=aWAxbq3qbJc.
3 See: http://archive.org/stream/baudelairehispro00baudiala/baudelairehispro00baudiala_djvu.txt.
4 See: "Saudi 'Ulemas Demand the Total Prohibition of Women Appearing in the Mass Media," *Al-Quds al-Arabi* (March 25, 2009): http://www.alquds.co.uk.
5 See: http://www.dubaimediacity.com/media-centre/press-releases/280-tecom-s-media-cluster-grows-to-2-000-companies-during-2013.
6 See: "Arab Satellite TV Channels: The Future is Promising but . . . ," *Arab Ad* (May 2005): 12.
7 See: "About Dubai Holding," *Dubai Holding* (2008): http://dubaiholding.com/en/about-dubai-holding.
8 See: "The Next Generation," *Gulf Business* (April 2002): 22–3.
9 See: "Dubai Shuts Down Independent Pakistan TV Station Under Pressure," *Associated Press* (November 17, 2007): http://www.foxnews.com/story/2007/11/17/dubai-shuts-down-independent-pakistan-tv-station-under-pressure/.

Chapter 5 Mobile Telephony

1 See: http://mobiforge.com/research-analysis/global-mobile-statistics-2014-part-a-mobile-subscribers-handset-market-share-mobile-operators#subscribers; "U.S. Smartphone Penetration Reaches 75 Percent," *Comscore* (February 9, 2015): http://www.comscore.com/Insights/Market-Rankings/comScore-Reports-December-2014-US-Smartphone-Subscriber-Market-Share; "Mobile-Broadband Penetration Approaching 32 per cent," International Telecommunication Union (2014, May 5): https://www.itu.int/net/pressoffice/press_releases/2014/23.aspx.
2 See: http://www.alcatel-lucent.com/bell-labs/GWATT.
3 See: "*L'Express* Interview with Marshall McLuhan," *E-Compós: Revista da Associação Nacional dos Programas de Pós-Graduação em Comunicação* 14/3 (2011): http://compos.org.br/seer/index.php/e-compos/article/viewFile/845/610.
4 We note that in 2014, there were 629 million mobile phone subscriptions in Africa and 742 million people had access to potable water, out of a population of well over a billion (http://mobiforge.com/research-analysis/global-mobile-statistics-2014-part-a-mobile-subscribers-handset-market-share-mobile-operators#subscribers).
5 See: "The Revolution That Wasn't," *The Economist* (April 25, 2009): 68, 70.
6 See: http://blog.nielsen.com/nielsenwire/media_entertainment/tv-usage-trends-q3-and-q4-2010.

7   See also: "The Revolution That Wasn't."

8   See "How Smartphones Are on the Verge of Taking Over the World," *Daily News* (March 22, 2013): http://www.nydailynews.com/life-style/smartphones-world-article-1.1295927.

9   See: http://www.hedonometer.org/index.html.

10 See: https://support.google.com/legal/contact/lr_eudpa?product=websearch.

11 See: "AT&T Mobility to Pay $105 Million to Settle Wireless and Truth-In-Billing," *Federal Communications Commission* (October 8, 2014): http://www.fcc.gov/document/att-pay-105-million-resolve-wireless-cramming-investigation-0.

12 See: "AT&T to Pay Almost $52M for Environmental Violations, Cleanup," *Environmental Leader* (November 24, 2014): http://www.environmentalleader.com/2014/11/24/att-to-pay-almost-52m-for-environmental-violations-cleanup/.

13 See: http://www.naaaom.com/.

14 See "I'm a Mac. And I'm Un-PC," *Mother Jones* (March/April 2010): 51.

15 See: http://topdocumentaryfilms.com/blood-coltan; http://bloodinthemobile.org/categories/p/videos; http://www.guardian.co.uk/world/video/2011/sep/02/congo-blood-gold-mobile-phones-video.

16 See also: "Light and Death," *The Economist* (May 29, 2010,): 67; "Union Leaders and Workers Remain in Jail in Foxconn Dispute in India," International Metalworkers' Federation (October 18, 2010): http://www.industriall-union.org/archive/imf/union-leaders-and-workers-remain-in-jail-in-foxconn-dispute-in-india; "Massive Protest in Chennai in Support of Foxconn Workers," International Metalworkers' Federation (October 22, 2010): http://www.industriall-union.org/archive/imf/massive-protest-in-chennai-in-support-of-foxconn-workers.

17 See: http://wb.sznews.com/page/1721/2014-10/10/A18/20141010A18_pdf.pdf.

18 See: "Apple is Like Hitler, Says Chinese Billionaire," *The Register* (March 30, 2015): http://www.theregister.co.uk/2015/03/30/apple_is_like_hitler_says_chinese_billionaire/.

19 See: http://gwatt.net/.

20 See: http://www.verizon.com/about/news/ge-and-verizon-take-energy-efficiency-and-sustainability/.

21 See also: "Italy Court Ruling Links Mobile Phone Use to Tumor," *Reuters* (October 19, 2012): http://www.reuters.com/article/2012/10/19/us-italy-phones-idUSBRE89I0V320121019.

22 See: http://news.bbc.co.uk/panorama/hi/front_page/newsid_9481000/9481923.stm; http://www.cbsnews.com/stories/2008/11/06/60minutes/main4579229.shtml.

23 We do not suggest it is wrong for the Global South to participate in the same plenitude as the Global North. Rather, we wish to highlight the unsustainability of consumer practices pioneered by the latter and turbocharged by the former.

24 See also: "Avian/Communication Tower Collisions," Federal Communications Commission (September 30, 2004), . West Chester, PA: Avatar Environmental, Llc; Center for Responsible Nanotechnology: http://crnano.org/; "Deadly Spires in The Night: The Impact of Communications Towers on Migratory Birds," *Issue Brief from the Ornithological Council* 1/8 (1999): http://nmnh.si.edu/BIRDNET/OC/issues/OCBv1n8.html. This may look like a domestic US matter, but birds are the most experienced and determined of globalizers, with boundaries set by geography rather than sovereignty.

25 See: https://www.youtube.com/watch?v=y0CRWAz09r8.

Chapter 6   The United States of America as Global Media Behemoth

1   Some sections of this chapter derive from Miller, 2012c, and Miller et al., 2005, and forthcoming work between Toby and Bill Grantham.

2   See: "A Tale of Two Tinsel Towns," *The Economist* (February 23, 2013): http://www.economist.com/news/business/21572218-tale-two-tinseltowns-split-screens.

3   See: "A Tale of Two Tinsel Towns."

4   See: http://www.statista.com/statistics/224676/export-value-of-chinese-tv-programs-by-world-region/.

5   See: *National Review* Online, October 13, 2001.

6   This is no surprise, given the cohort's laughable predictions about the Shiite rising against the Ba'th, resistance from the Special Republican Guard and security agencies, and the deployment of gas and other mass destruction weaponry by the Iraqi military. The list of failed assessments

goes on and on, in keeping with the errors many such pundits had made in the 1980s, when they welcomed the Iraqi regime as an ally.

7 See "APME Requests Pentagon Halt Harassment of Media in Iraq," *Associated Press* (November 12, 2003): http://www.monabaker.com/pMachine/more.php?id=1485_0_1_36_M20.

8 See also: "New Wargames for Sir Bono's Profit," *The Phoenix* (April 6, 2007): 4.

9 See also: "AA:SF Tops 9 Million User Mark!" (February 10, 2008): http://news.americasarmy.com/aasf-tops-9-million-user-mark/.

10 See also: http://ict.usc.edu/news/item/usc_institute_for_creative_technologies_receives_135_million_contract_exten. We should note that there is skepticism about the efficacy of such work as military training (Newsome and Lewis, 2011).

11 See: http://www.unr.edu/art/DELAPPE/DeLappe%20Main%20Page/DeLappe%20Online%20MAIN.html.

12 See: http://www.producersguild.org/?page=history.

13 We recommend http://meninblack3sunglasses.com/ for those blinded by the light.

14 See: "Sony's Loss Grows as Company Cuts Earnings Forecast," *Guardian* (August 2, 2012): http://www.theguardian.com/technology/2012/aug/02/sony-loss-grows-cuts-earnings-forecast.

15 How do we know these numbers? Hollywood accounting is notoriously opaque even as it is indiscreet: we learn a great deal about the cost of movies, especially blockbusters, in the bourgeois press, but the information frequently comes from publicity departments. Getting "real" figures on costs and revenue through the forms mentioned above is notoriously difficult. The one reliable, opportunistic avenue is a lawsuit where a blockbuster's accounts are subpoenaed. That rarely happens.

16 For folks keen on contemporary stories of that ilk, listen to podcasts with Jonathan Taplin: http://culturalstudies.podbean.com/2013/09/09/jonathan-taplin/; http://culturalstudies.podbean.com/2013/09/09/jonathan-taplin/; Lloyd Segan: http://culturalstudies.podbean.com/2011/05/18/a-conversation-with-lloyd-segan-hollywood-producer-about-the-bachelor-boondock-saints-dead-zone/; and Bill Grantham: http://culturalstudies.podbean.com/2011/05/15/a-conversation-with-bill-grantham-on-hollywood-and-the-law/.

17 It borrows from Maxwell and Miller, 2011.

18 See: "'Wolf of Wall Street' Won Oscar for Best Tax Break," *Manhattan Institute* (January 17, 2014): http://www.economics21.org/commentary/%E2%80%9Cwolf-wall-street%E2%80%9D-won-oscar-best-tax-break.

19 See also: "The Money Shot," *The Economist* (August 15, 2009): 57.

20 See: http://www.peta.org/blog/bob-barker-hollywood-must-protect-animals/.

Chapter 7 Textual Analysis

1 See: "Anglo-American Film Agreement," *The Times* (July 11, 1938): http://the.hitchcock.zone/wiki/The_Times_(11/Jul/1938)_-_Anglo-American_film_agreement.

2 See: "Film Studio Strike: Cinemas Open as Usual," *The Times* (April 20, 1938).

3 See: "New Films in London: *The Lady Vanishes*," *The Times* (October 10, 1938): http://the.hitchcock.zone/wiki/The_Times_(10/Oct/1938)_-_New_films_in_London:_The_Lady_Vanishes.

4 This analysis draws on King and Miller, 2011.

5 See: "First 100 Days: Margaret Thatcher," *BBC News* (March 16, 2006): http://news.bbc.co.uk/2/hi/uk_news/politics/4809830.stm.

6 See: "The Lady Vanishes," *The Economist* (June 7, 2003): http://www.economist.com/node/1826785.

7 See: "How '24' and Keifer Sutherland's Morally Compromised Hero Jack Bauer Changed TV Forever," *Huffington Post* (February 5, 2015): http://www.huffingtonpost.co.uk/2015/02/05/how-jack-bauer-24-changed-tv-boxsets-10-seasons_n_6620730.html.

8 See also: "How '24'."

9 See also: "Torture Spreading as 'Glorified' by TV Series Like '24': Amnesty," *Jakarta Globe* (May 13, 2014): http://www.thejakartaglobe.com/international/torture-spreading-glorified-television-series-like-24-amnesty-intl/.

10 See: www.theguardian.com/media/video/2009/mar/23/stella-artois-viral-ad.

11 See: "Indians React to Delhi Bus Rape Documentary," *BBC News* (March 5, 2015): http://www.bbc.co.uk/news/world-south-asia-31749524.

12 See: "How Indians Are Evading Ban on Rape Documentary," *BBC News* (March 6, 2015): http://www.bbc.co.uk/news/world-asia-india-31761632.

13 See: https://twitter.com/soniandtv/status/574604884609122305.

14 See: https://www.facebook.com/vrinda.grover.56/posts/10153086086286358?fref=nf.

15 This analysis draws on Miller, 2013c.

16 See: "Mary Tillman, Mother of Slain Army Ranger and Former NFL Star Pat Tillman, on Her Four-Year Quest to Expose the Military Cover-Up of Her Son's Death by Members of His Own Unit," *Democracy Now!* (May 22, 2008): http://www.democracynow.org/2008/5/22/mary_tillman_mother_of_slain_nfl.

17 See also: "Tillman Killed in Afghanistan," *Sports Illustrated* (April 23, 2004): 1.

18 See also: "Parents of Slain Army Ranger Tillman: McChrystal Shouldn't Get Top Afghanistan Post," *Foxnews* (May 13, 2009): http://www.foxnews.com/story/2009/05/13/parents-slain-army-ranger-tillman-mcchrystal-shouldnt-get-top-afghanistan-post.html; "Mary Tillman, Mother of Slain Army Ranger."

19 Quoted in "Mary Tillman, Mother of Slain Army Ranger."

20 See also: "Mary Tillman, Mother of Slain Army Ranger."

21 See: "10 Years Later, Pat Tillman's Death, Service Still Inspiring Students at Leland High School," (April 22, 2014): *NBC Bay Area* http://www.nbcbayarea.com/news/local/10-Years-Later-Pat-Tillman-Death-Still-Inspiring-Students-at-Leland-High-School-256263721.html.

22 This analysis draws on Miller, 2012b.

23 See: http://www.youtube.com/watch?v=T891ogg7QKo.

24 See: "Audiencia preliminar del caso de video érotico de exviceministra de Costa Rica," *La Jornada* (April 21, 2015): http://www.lajornadanet.com/diario/archivo/2015/abril/21/9.php.

25 See: https://www.youtube.com/watch?v=jd8wYSWeEHY.

26 See: http://www.facebook.com/TodosSomosKarina.

27 See: http://femen.org/.

28 See: "Egypt Feminist Defecates on ISIS Flag in the Nude," *Times of Israel* (August 24, 2014): http://www.timesofisrael.com/egypt-feminist-defecates-on-is-flag-in-the-nude/.

29 See: http://mexico.cnn.com/videos/2012/07/31/destituyen-a-viceministra-de-costa-rica.

30 See also: http://www.canal9.cr/hoy/2012/09/10/karina-bolanos-critica-al-gobierno-tras-posar-semidesnuda-en-revista-espanola/.

31 See: "Audiencia preliminar del caso de video érotico."

32 See: "'Me arrepiento de haber agredido a Óscar': Elainis Garrido, Protagonistas de Nuestra Tele," *El País* (July 25, 2012): http://www.elpais.com.co/elpais/entretenimiento/noticias/entrevista-con-elianis-garrido-ex-protagonista-nuestra-tele.

33 See: "Abogada despedida por video se niega a posar desnuda," *La Prensa* (August 15, 2013): http://www.laprensa.hn/csp/mediapool/sites/LaPrensa/Mundo/Noticiasinsolitas/story.csp?cid=364529&sid=287&fid=98#.UCVHTmOe6oc.

34 See: http://www.boxofficemojo.com/movies/?id=lego.htm.

35 See: http://www.youtube.com/watch?v=qhbliUq0_r4&list=UUTDTSx8kbxGECZJxOa9mIKA.

36 See: http://www.youtube.com/watch?v=Ci4I-VK9jew&list=UUTDTSx8kbxGECZJxOa9mIKA.

37 Chipotle's notorious critique of industrialized food production was a remarkable indictment that deeply troubled the right (http://www.wsj.com/video/chipotle-ad-named-one-of-2013-worst/9DC4D7E8-11CB-48DD-834C-380BEC238833.html).

38 See also: "Social License to Operate," *International Journal of Mining, Reclamation and Environment* 20/3 (2006), special issue.

39 See: http://aboutus.lego.com/en-us/news-room/2014/july/lego-group-comment-on-greenpeace-campaign.

40 See: http://aboutus.lego.com/en-us/news-room/2014/october/comment-on-the-greenpeace-campaign-and-the-lego-brand.

41 See: http://www.greenpeace.org.uk/blog/climate/how-lego-got-awesome-savethearctic-2014 1009.

42 See also: "Turquía estrena con éxito su primera telenovela en Latinoamérica: 'Las mil y una noches'," *Hispanatolia* (September 3, 2014): http://www.hispanatolia.com/seccion/2/id,20032/turquia-estrena-con-exito-su-primera-telenovela-en-latinoamerica-las-mil-y-una-noches-.

43 See also: https://www.youtube.com/watch?v=NX8Un4nneXg.

44 See also: http://www.dailymotion.com/video/x17qv49_witness-kismet-how-soap-operas-chan ged-the-world_news.
45 Dubbing costs were a significant addition given the premium on Turkish-Spanish translators.
46 See: "Emirates Pick Up Ottoman Show After Turkish Airlines Blocks in on Flights," *Hurriyet Daily News* (December 19, 2012): http://www.hurriyetdailynews.com/emirates-pick-up-ottoman-show-after-turkish-airlines-blocks-it-on-flights.aspx?pageID=238&nid=37179.

Chapter 8 Reality Television

1 See: "Undercover Boss: Awards and Nominations," *Emmys* (2012): http://www.emmys.com/shows/undercover-boss.
2 See: http://www.cbs.com/shows/undercover_boss/bios/67722/.

Chapter 9 Audiences

1 See also: "US Children Still Traumatized One Year After Seeing Partially Exposed Breast on TV," *The Onion* (January 26, 2005): http://www.theonion.com/articles/us-children-still-traumatized-one-year-after-seein-1285/.
2 See also: "Children's Television: Too Much of a Good Thing?" *The Economist* (December 18, 2004): 97–8.
3 This borrows from Miller, 2009. Some materials have been transliterated and translated from Arabic.
4 See also: "Comunidad armenia insiste para que saquen del aire 'Las mil y una noches'," *Diario26* (January 30, 2015): http://www.diario26.com/comunidad-armenia-insiste-para-que-saquen-del-aire-las-mil-y-una-noches-202981.html.
5 See also: "Nielsen Media Research Reports Television's Popularity is Still Growing," *Nielsen Media Research* (September 21, 2006): http://www.thinktv.com.au/media/.../Nielsen_Media_Reports_TV's_Popularity_Is_Still_Growing.pdf.
6 See: "Watching While You Surf," *The Economist* (June 7, 2008): 3–4.
7 See: http://www.hbo.com/boxing/index.html#/boxing/talk/index.html.
8 See: http://surveys.researchresults.com/mrIWeb/mrIWeb.dll; http://www.cvadsales.com/network_fox_soccer.html.
9 See: http://www.epltalk.com/fox-soccer-channel-sets-new-record-for-chelsea-vs-liverpool-telecast-29232.
10 See also: "There's Life Outside Sports. There's Also Ballet," *Broadcasting and Cable* (May 11, 1998): 24–5.
11 See: http://www.tsn.ca/contact/#advertsing_contact.
12 See also: http://espn.go.com/espnw/.
13 See: "Features of the New espnW.com," *The Onion* (December 10, 2010): http://www.theonion.com/articles/features-of-the-new-espnwcom,18642/.
14 See also: http://www.hergamelife.com/about-her-game-life/.
15 See: http://www.google.com.mx/search?q=%22soccer+is+gay%22&oq=%22soccer+is+gay%22&sugexp=chrome,mod=3&sourceid=chrome&ie=UTF-8.
16 See: http://www.theonion.com/video/soccer-officially-announces-it-is-gay,17603/.

Conclusion

1 See: "9 Cultural Icons Who Have Written for 'The New York Times'," *New York Times*: http://mashable.com/2014/09/05/new-york-times-writers-brandspeak/.
2 See: https://www.youtube.com/watch?v=_PUNRd_OqDE.
3 See: http://www.americancatholic.org/features/saints/saint.aspx?id=1343.

References

Abrahamian, Ervand. (2003). "The US Media, Huntington and September 11," *Third World Quarterly* 24/3: 529–44.

Abramson, Bram Dov. (2001). "Media Policy After Regulation?" *International Journal of Cultural Studies* 4/3: 301–26.

Abu-Lughod, Lila. (2005). *Dramas of Nationhood: The Politics of Television in Egypt*. Chicago: University of Chicago Press.

Adams, James Truslow. (1941). *The Epic of America*. New York: Triangle Books.

Adams, Richard. (2014). "Home Economics GCE Set to Be Scrapped," *Guardian* (June 4). http://www.theguardian.com/education/2014/jun/04/home-economics-gcse-scrapped-a-levels.

Adams, Terry, and Charles A. Tuggle. (2004). "ESPN's SportsCenter and Coverage of Women's Athletics: 'It's a Boys' Club'," *Mass Communication & Society* 7/2: 237–48.

Addington, Tim. (2005). "2005: A Year to Remember," *Campaign Middle East* (December 25). http://m.arabianbusiness.com/2005--year-remember-60697.html.

Addington, Tim. (2006). "Media Tribunal Awaits First Case," *Campaign Middle East* (March 26). http://www.arabianbusiness.com/media-tribunal-awaits-first-case-63263.html.

Adorno, Theodor W. (1981–2). "Transparencies on Film," trans. Thomas Y. Levin. *New German Critique* 24–25: 199–205.

Adorno, Theodor W. (2009). "*Kultur* and Culture," trans. Mark Kalbus. *Social Text* 99: 145–58.

Adorno, Theodor W., and Max Horkheimer. (1977). "The Culture Industry: Enlightenment as Mass Deception," in *Mass Communication and Society*, ed. James Curran, Michael Gurevitch, and Janet Woollacott. London: Edward Arnold, 349–83.

Advisory Committee on Cultural Diplomacy. (2005). *Cultural Diplomacy: The Linchpin of Public Diplomacy*. US Department of State. http://www.state.gov/documents/organization/54374.pdf.

Agha, Laith. (2009). "The Lady Vanishes," *Monterey County Herald* (April 2). http://www.monterey herald.com/general-news/20090402/the-lady-vanishes.

Aguilar, Miguel Ángel, Eduardo Nivón, María Ana Portal, and Rosalía Winocur, eds. (2009). *Pensar lo Contemporáneo: De la cultura situada a la convergencia tecnológica*. Barcelona/Ciudad de México: Anthropos/Universidad Autónoma Metropolitana.

Agur, Colin. (2015). "Second-Order Networks, Gambling, and Corruption on Indian Mobile Phone Networks," *Media, Culture & Society*. http://mcs.sagepub.com/content/early/2015/05/28/0163443715587873.full.pdf+html.

Aitkenhead, Decca. (2009). "One Hour with Kiefer Sutherland," *Guardian* (February 2). http://www.theguardian.com/lifeandstyle/2009/feb/02/kiefer-sutherland-interview-tv-film.

Al Abed, Ibrahim. (2009). "Facts About the New UAE Media Law," *Gulf Times* (April 19).

Algan, Ece. (2012). "Dreaming of a Horse with a Bigger Role: Television and Erdogan's Quest for Soft Power in the Middle East," *On Media and Cultural Politics in Turkey* (November 28). https://ecealgan.wordpress.com/2012/11/28/dreams-of-a-horse-with-a-bigger-role-in-the-middle-east-erdogans-quest-for-soft-power-and-tv/.

Al-Ghazzi, Omar, and Marwan M. Kraidy. (2013). "Neo-Ottoman Cool 2: Turkish Nation Branding and Arabic-Language Transnational Broadcasting," *International Journal of Communication* 7: 2341–360.

Almutawa, Shatha. (2014). "Magnificent Century: Historical Turkish Soap Opera Finds a Global Audience," *AHA Today* (July 29). http://blog.historians.org/2014/07/magnificent-century-historical-turkish-soap-opera-finds-global-audience/.

Al-Saggaf, Yeslam, and Sharon Nielsen. (2014). "Self-Disclosure on Facebook Among Female Users and its Relationship to Feelings of Loneliness," *Computers in Human Behavior* 36: 460–68.

Alterman, Eric. (2003). *What Liberal Media? The Truth about Bias and the News*. New York: Basic Books.

Althusser, Louis. (1969). *For Marx*, trans. Ben Brewster. Harmondsworth: Penguin.

Amariglio, Jack, Joseph Childers, and Stephen Cullenberg, eds. (2009). *Sublime Economy: On the Intersection of Art and Economics*. New York: Routledge.

Andersen, Robin. (2006). *A Century of Media, A Century of War*. New York: Peter Lang.

Andersen, Robin. (2007). "Bush's Fantasy Budget and the Military/Entertainment Complex," *PRWatch* (February 12). http://www.prwatch.org/news/2007/02/5742/bushs-fantasy-budget-and-militaryentertainment-complex.

Anderson, Christopher, and Michael Wolff. (2010). "The Web is Dead: Long Live the Internet," *Wired* (August 17). http://www.wired.com/magazine/2010/08/ff_webrip/all/1.

Anderson, Elisabeth. (2013). "Media Studies "The UK's Second-Most Employable Degree"," *Management Today* (November 19). http://www.managementtoday.co.uk/news/1221489/.

Anderson, Jon R. (2013). "'America's Army: Probing Grounds' Out Today," *Army Times* (August 29). http://www.armytimes.com/article/20130829/OFFDUTY02/308290054.

Andrejevic, Mark. (2002). "The Kinder, Gentler Gaze of *Big Brother*: Reality TV in the Era of Digital Capitalism," *New Media & Society* 4/2: 251–70.

Andrejevic, Mark. (2006). "Total Information Awareness: The Media Version," *Flow* 4/8. http://flowtv.org/2006/07/total-information-awareness-the-media-version.

Andrews, David L. (2006). "Introduction: Playing with the Pleasure Principle," *South Atlantic Quarterly* 105/2: 269–76.

Ang, Ien. (1982). *Het geval Dallas*. Amsterdam: Uitgeverij SUA.

Ang, Ien. (1991). *Desperately Seeking the Audience*. London: Routledge.

Appadurai, Arjun. (1994). "Disjuncture and Difference in the Global Cultural Economy," in *Global Culture*, ed. Mike Featherstone. London: Sage, 295–310.

Arab Advisors Group. (2004). *Media Cities in the Arab World*. Amman: Arab Advisors Group.

Arehart-Treichel, Joan. (2012). "Why Sports Evoke Passion, for Better or Worse," *Psychiatric News* 47/9: 13.

Armbrust, Walter. (2011). "The Revolution Against Neoliberalism," *Jadaliyya* (February). http://www.jadaliyya.com/pages/index/717/the-revolution-against-neoliberalism-.

Arnheim, Rudolf. (1969). *Film as Art*. London: Faber and Faber.

Arnold, Matthew. (1875). *Essays in Criticism*, 3rd edn. London: Macmillan.

Arnoldy, Ben. (2007). "Among Networks, Spanish-Language Univision is now a Top Contender," *Christian Science Monitor* (September 17). http://www.csmonitor.com/2007/0917/p01s03-ussc.html.

Arrighi, Giovanni. (2007). "States, Markets, and Capitalism, East and West," *positions* 15/2: 251–84.

Aslama, Minna, and Mervi Pantti. (2006). "Talking Alone: Reality TV, Emotions and Authenticity," *European Journal of Cultural Studies* 9/2: 167–84.

Aslama, Minna, and Mervi Pantti. (2007). "Flagging Finnishness: Reproducing National Identity in Reality Television," *Television & New Media* 8/1: 49–67.

Asma, Stephen T. (2007, October 12). "Looking Up From the Gutter: Philosophy and Popular Culture," *Chronicle of Higher Education*. http://www.chronicle.com/article/Looking-Up-From-the-Gutter-/13840.

Attali, Jacques. (2008). "This Is Not America's final Crisis," *New Perspectives Quarterly* 29/2: 31–3.

Attali, Jacques, and Yves Stourdze. (1977). "The Birth of the Telephone and Economic Crisis: The Slow Death of Monologue in French Society," in *The Social Impact of the Telephone*, ed. Ithiel de Sola Pool. Cambridge, MA: MIT Press, 97–111.

Attallah, Paul. (2006). Review. *Canadian Journal of Communication* 31/4. http://www.cjc-online.ca/index.php/journal/article/view/1706/1826.

Attallah, Paul. (2007). "A Usable History for the Study of Television," *Canadian Review of American Studies/Revue canadienne d'études américaines* 37/3: 325–49.

Australian Sports Commission. (2009). *Towards a Level Playing Field: Sport and Gender in Australian Media January 2008–July 2009.* Canberra: Australian Sports Commission.

Balfour, Fredrik, and Tim Culpan. (2010). "The Man Who Makes Your iPhone," *Bloomberg Business Week* (September 9). http://www.bloomberg.com/bw/magazine/content/10_38/b4195058423479.htm.

Balmori, Alfonso. (2009). "Electromagnetic Pollution from Phone Masts. Effects on Wildlife," *Pathophysiology* 16/2–3: 191–9.

Bar, François, with Caroline Simard. (2006). "From Hierarchies to Network Firms," in *The Handbook of New Media: Updated Students Edition*, ed. Leah Lievrouw and Sonia Livingstone. Thousand Oaks, CA: Sage, 350–63.

Barboza, David. (2011). "Workers Sickened at Apple Supplier Chain in China," *New York Times* (February 23). http://www.nytimes.com/2011/02/23/technology/23apple.html?pagewanted=all.

Barkin, Gareth. (2014). "Commercial Islam in Indonesia: How Television Producers Mediate Religiosity Among National Audiences," *International Journal of Asian Studies* 11/1: 1–24.

Barrett, Steve. (2015). "Edelman Boots 2014 Global Revenues 8.2% to $812 Million," *PR Week* (February 17). http://www.prweek.com/article/1334277/edelman-boosts-2014-global-revenues-82-812-million.

Barrio, Carlos. (2012). "Karina Bolaños: 'La presidenta de mi país protégé a los corruptos'," *Interviú* (September 7). http://www.interviu.es/entrevistas/articulos/karina-bolanos-la-presidenta-de-mi-pais-solo-protege-a-los-corruptos.

Baruh, Lemi. (2004). "Anonymous Reading in Interactive Media," *Knowledge, Technology, & Policy* 17/1: 59–73.

Bauder, David. (2008). "Univision Takes 18-49 Demo Crown," *TVNewsday* (December 31). http://www.tvnewscheck.com/article/2008/12/31/28301/univision-takes-1849-demo-crown.

Baudrillard, Jean. (1988). *Selected Writings*, ed. Mark Poster. Stanford, CA: Stanford University Press.

Baym, Nancy K. (2000). *Tune In, Log On: Soaps, Fandom, and Online Community.* Thousand Oaks, CA: Sage.

Beck, Ulrich. (1999). *World Risk Society.* Cambridge: Polity.

Beck, Ulrich. (2002). "The Cosmopolitan Society," *Theory, Culture & Society* 19/1–2: 17–44.

Beck, Ulrich, Anthony Giddens, and Scott Lash. (1994). *Reflexive Modernization: Politics, Tradition and Aesthetics in the Modern Social Order.* Stanford, CA: Stanford University Press.

Becker, Amy B. (2013). "Star Power? Advocacy, Receptivity, and Viewpoints on Celebrity Involvement in Issue Politics," *Atlantic Journal of Communication* 21/1: 1–16.

Becker, Gary S., Dennis W. Carlton, and Hal S. Sider. (2010). "Net Neutrality and Consumer Welfare," *Journal of Competition Law & Economics* 6/3: 497–519.

Beckman, Karen. (2003). *Vanishing Women: Magic, Film, and Feminism.* Durham, NC: Duke University Press.

Beder, Sharon. (1998). "Public Relations' Role in Manufacturing Artificial Grass Roots Coalitions," *Public Relations Quarterly* 43/2: 20.

Behnke, Andreas. (2006). "The Re-Enchantment of War in Popular Culture," *Millennium: Journal of International Studies* 34/3: 937–49.

Bell, Daniel. (1977). "The Future World Disorder: The Structural Context of Crises," *Foreign Policy* 27: 109–35.

Bellah, Robert N., Richard Madsen, William M. Sullivan, Ann Swidler, and Steven M. Tipton. (1992). *The Good Society.* New York: Alfred A Knopf.

Beltrán, Luis Ramiro. (1978). "Communication and Cultural Domination: US–Latin America Case," *Media Asia* 5: 183–92.

Beltrán, Luis Ramiro, and Elizabeth Fox de Cardona. (1980). *Communicacíon dominada: Estados Unidos en los medios de América Latina.* Mexico City: Instituto Latinoamericano de Estudios Transnacionales/Editorial Nueva Imagen.

Ben Block, Alex. (2015). "LA Screenings Preview: TV Niche Viewing Goes Global," *Hollywood Reporter* (May 11). http://www.hollywoodreporter.com/news/la-screenings-preview-tv-niche-794421.

Ben Block, Alex, and Scott Roxborough. (2014). "US Sellers Say LA Screenings Market is International

TV's 'Most Important Event'," *Hollywood Reporter* (May 15). http://www.hollywoodreporter.com/news/us-sellers-say-la-screenings-704228.

Benaim, Daniel, Visesh Kumar, and Priyanka Motaparthy. (2003). "TV's Conflicted Experts," *The Nation* (April 21): 6–7.

Benhabib, Seyla. (2002). *The Claims of Culture: Equality and Diversity in the Global Era*. Princeton, NJ: Princeton University Press.

Benjamin, Walter. (1985). "Central Park," trans. Lloyd Spencer with Mark Harrington. *New German Critique* 34: 48.

Benjamin, Walter. (1992). *Illumination*, trans. Harry Zohn, ed. Hannah Arendt. London: Fontana.

Benkwitz, Adam, and Gyozo Molnar. (2012). "Interpreting and Exploring Football Fan Rivalries: An Overview," *Soccer & Society* 13/4: 479–94.

Bennett, Tony, and Janet Woollacott. (1987). *Bond and Beyond: The Political Career of a Popular Hero*. Basingstoke: Macmillan.

Bermingham, Finbarr. (2014,). "Greenpeace's Biggest Victories Against Corporations and Politicians," *International Business Times* (October 9). http://www.ibtimes.co.uk/greenpeaces-biggest-victories-against-corporations-politicians-1469239.

Bernhardt, Paul C., James M. Dabbs, Jr., Julie A. Fielden, and Candice D. Lutter. (1998). "Testosterone Changes During Vicarious Experiences of Winning and Losing Among Fans at Sporting Events," *Physiology & Behavior* 65/1: 59–62.

Bernstein, Paula. (2001). "Hardest-Working Actor of the Season: The CIA," *New York Times* (September 2). http://www.nytimes.com/2001/09/02/arts/television-radio-hardest-working-actor-of-the-season-the-cia.html.

Besio, Cristina, Ruth Hungerbühler, Luca Morici, and Benedetta Prario. (2008). "The Implementation of the Quota Requirements of the Directive 'Television Without Frontiers': The Broadcasters' Perspective," *International Communication Gazette* 70/2: 175–91.

Bianchi, Matías. (2015). "Digital Age Inequality In Latin America," *democracia Abierta* (June 24). https://www.opendemocracy.net/democraciaabierta/mat%C3%ADas-bianchi/digital-age-inequality-in-latin-america.

Best, Steve, Richard Kahn, Anthony Nocella II, and Peter McLaren, eds. (2011). *The Global Industrial Complex: Systems of Domination*. Lanham, MD: Lexington Books.

Bielby, Denise D., and C. Lee Harrington. (2008). *Global TV: Exporting Television and Culture in the World Market*. New York: New York University Press.

Bignell, Jonathan, and Andreas Fickers. (2008). "Introduction: Comparative European Perspectives on Television History," in *A European Television History*, ed. Jonathan Bignell and Andreas Fickers. Malden: Wiley-Blackwell, 1–54.

Bignell, Jonathan, Stephen Lacey, and Madeleine Macmurraugh-Kavanagh, eds. (2000). *British Television Drama: Past, Present and Future*. Houndmills: Palgrave.

Billig, Michael. (1995). *Banal Nationalism*. London: Sage.

Billington, Michael, and David Hare. (2009). "The Lame, the Weak and the Godawful," *Guardian* (January 19). http://www.theguardian.com/stage/2009/jan/19/david-hare-television.

Birt, John. (2005). "TV Needs More Truth and Beauty." *Guardian* (August 27). http://www.theguardian.com/politics/2005/aug/27/media.publicservices.

Boateng, Boatema. (2008). "Local and Global Sites of Power in the Circulation of Ghanaian Adinkra," in *Global Communications: Toward a Transcultural Political Economy*, ed. Paula Chakravartty and Yuezhi Zhao. Lanham, MD: Rowman & Littlefield, 163–88.

Bobo, Jacqueline. (1995). *Black Women as Cultural Readers*. New York: Columbia University Press.

Boddy, William. (1994). "Archaeologies of Electronic Vision and the Gendered Spectator," *Screen* 35/2: 105–22.

Boddy, William. (2005). "In Focus: The Place of Television Studies," *Cinema Journal* 45/1: 79–82.

Boellstorff, Tom. (2003). "I Knew It was Me: Mass Media, 'Globalization,' and Lesbian and Gay Indonesians," *Mobile Cultures: New Media in Queer Asia*, ed. Chris Berry, Fran Martin, and Audrey Yue. Durham, NC: Duke University Press. 21–51.

Bolaño, César, ed. (2009). *Comunicação e a Crítica da Economia Política: Perspectivas Teóricas e Epistemológicas*. São Cristovão: Editora-UFS.

Bolaño, César, ed. (2012). *Comunicación y la crítica de la economía política*. Quito: CIESPAL.

Bolas, Terry. (2009). *Screen Education: From Film Appreciation to Media Studies*. Bristol: Intellect.

Bolton, Sharon C. (2009). "The Lady Vanishes: Women's Work and Affective Labour," *International Journal of Work Organisation and Emotion* 3/1: 72–80.

Boney, Jeffrey L. (2015,). "Race in America: The Ultimate 'Tipping Point'," *Forward Times* (June 10). http://forwardtimesonline.com/2013/index.php/editorial/jboney-speaks/item/2733-race-in-america-the-ultimate-%E2%80%98tipping-point%E2%80%99.

Bormann, Ernest G. (1985). "Symbolic Convergence Theory: A Communication Formulation," *Journal of Communication* 35/4: 128–38.

Bourdieu, Pierre. (1984). *Distinction: A Social Critique of the Judgement of Taste*, trans. Richard Nice. Cambridge, MA: Harvard University Press.

Bourdon, Jérôme, with Juan Carlos Ibáñez, Catherine Johnson, and Eggo Müller. (2008). "Searching for an Identity for Television: Programmes, Genres, Formats," in *A European Television History*, ed. Jonathan Bignell and Andreas Fickers. Malden, MA: Wiley-Blackwell, 101–26.

Boyd, Douglas A. (1991). "Lebanese Broadcasting: Unofficial Electronic Media During a Prolonged Civil War," *Journal of Broadcasting & Electronic Media* 35/3: 269–87.

Boyd, Douglas A. (1999). *Broadcasting in the Arab World: A Survey of the Electronic Media in the Middle East*, 2nd edn. Ames: Iowa State University Press.

Boyd-Barrett, Oliver, ed. (2006). *Communications Media, Globalization and Empire*. Eastleigh: John Libbey Publishing.

Boyd-Barrett, Oliver. (1977). "Media Imperialism: Towards an International Framework for the Analysis of Media Systems," in *Mass Communication and Society*, ed. James Curran, Michael Gurevitch, and Janet Woollacott. London: Edward Arnold, 116–35.

Boyd-Barrett, Oliver. (1998). "Media Imperialism Reformulated," in *Electronic Empires: Global Media and Local Resistance*, ed. Daya Kishan Thussu. London: Arnold, 57–76.

Bragazzi, Nicola Luigi, and Giovanni Del Puente. (2014). "A Proposal for Including Nomophobia in the New DSM-V," *Psychology Research and Behavior Management* 7: 155–60.

Braman, Sandra. (2002). "A Pandemonic Age: The Future of International Communication Theory and Research," *Handbook of International and Intercultural Communication*, 2nd edn., ed. William B. Gudykunst and Bella Mody. London: Sage, 399–413.

Braman, Sandra. (2004a). "Where has Media Policy Gone? Defining the Field in the Twenty-First Century," *Communications Law and Policy* 9/2: 153–82.

Braman, Sandra. (2004b). "The Emergent Global Information Policy Regime," *The Emergent Global Information Policy Regime*, ed. Sandra Braman. Houndsmills: Palgrave Macmillan. 12-37.

Brecht, Bertolt. (1935). "Questions from a Worker Who Reads." https://www.marxists.org/subject/art/literature/brecht/.

Breslau, Karen. (2008). "Pat Tillman's Mother on His Friendly-Fire Death," *Newsweek* (May 5). http://www.newsweek.com/pat-tillmans-mother-his-friendly-fire-death-89777.

Brewer, Stephanie M., Jason M. Kelley, and James J. Jozefowicz. (2009). "A Blueprint for Success in the US Film Industry," *Applied Economics* 41/5: 589–606.

Briggs, Asa, and Peter Burke. (2003). *A Social History of the Media: From Gutenberg to the Internet*. Cambridge: Polity.

Broad, William J. (2007). "NASA Forced to Steer Clear of Junk in Cluttered Space," *New York Times* (July 31): F4.

Brown, John. (2004). "Changing Minds, Winning Peace: Reconsidering the Djerejian Report," *American Diplomacy*. http://www.unc.edu/depts/diplomat/archives_roll/2004_07-09/brown_djerejian/brown_djerejian.html.

Brzezinski, Zbigniew. (1969). *Between Two Ages: America's Role in the Technotronic Era*. New York: Viking Press.

Buckingham, David. (2005). "A Special Audience? Children and Television," in *A Companion to Television*, ed. Janet Wasko. Malden, MA: Blackwell, 468–86.

Bueno, Gustavo. (2002). "La canonización de Marilyn Monroe," *El Catoblepas* 9: 2.

Burrell, Ian. (2008). "Greg Dyke's Back: The Former BBC Director General on His New Job – And What's Wrong with Britain's Media," *Independent* (March 17). http://www.independent.co.uk/news/media/greg-dykersquos-back-the-former-bbc-director-general-on-his-new-job-ndash-and-whatrsquos-wrong-with-britainrsquos-media-796749.html.

Burri-Nenova, Mira. (2007). "The New Audiovisual Media Services Directive: Television without Frontiers, Television without Cultural Diversity," *Common Market Law Review* 44/6: 1689–725.

Burst Media. (2012). *Sports Fans and Digital Media: A Scorecard on Preferences and Behaviors.* Boston, MA: Burst Media.

Burston, Jonathan. (2003). "War and the Entertainment Industries: New Research Priorities in an Era of Cyber-Patriotism," in *War and the Media: Reporting Conflict 24/7*, ed. Daya Kishan Thussu and Des Freedman. London: Sage, 163–75.

Burton, Bob, and Andy Rowell. (2003). "Unhealthy Spin," *British Medical Journal* 326: 1205.

Butsch, Richard. (2000). *The Making of American Audiences: From Stage to Television, 1750–1990.* Cambridge: Cambridge University Press.

Butterworth, Michael L., and Stormi D. Moskal. (2009). "American Football, Flags, and 'Fun': The Bell Helicopter Armed Forces Bowl and the Rhetorical Production of Militarism," *Communication, Culture & Critique* 2/4: 411–33.

Bycroft, Michael. (2011). *Energy for Radio: A Guide for Practitioners.* CAMECO Practice Series 2. Aachen: Catholic Media Council.

Byerly, Carolyn L. (2013). *Global Report on the Status of Women in News Media.* Washington, DC: International Women's Media Foundation.

Cain, Rob. (2015). "China's Pivotal Role in Hollywood's Billion Dollar Movie Club," *Forbes* (May 17). http://www.forbes.com/sites/robcain/2015/05/17/chinas-pivotal-role-in-hollywoods-billion-dollar-movie-club/.

Cairns, Richard. (2013). "Gloomy Times are Pushing Today's Pupils in Right Direction," *Telegraph* (August 16). http://www.telegraph.co.uk/education/universityeducation/10247291/Gloomy-times-are-pushing-todays-pupils-in-right-direction.html.

Cajueiro, Marcelo. (2009). "TV Globo Telenova Heads to India," *Variety* (January 16). http://variety.com/2009/scene/markets-festivals/tv-globo-telenova-heads-to-india-1117998720/.

Caldwell, John T. (2013). "Para-Industry: Researching Hollywood's Backwaters," *Cinema Journal* 52/3: 157–65.

Camacho, Paul R., and William Locke Hauser. (2007). "Civil-Military Relations – Who Are the Real Principals? A Response to 'Courage in the Service of Virtue: The Case of General Shinseki's Testimony Before the Iraq War'," *Armed Forces & Society* 34/1: 122–37.

Campbell, W. J. assisted by Rosemary Keogh. (1962). *Television and the Australian Adolescent: A Sydney Survey.* Sydney: Angus and Robertson.

Candemir, Yeliz. (2013). "Turkish Soap Operas: The Unstoppable Boom," *Wall Street Journal* (April 29). http://blogs.wsj.com/middleeast/2013/04/29/turkish-soap-operas-the-unstoppable-boom/.

Caplan-Bricker, Nora. (2013). "Hollywood's Animal Cruelty Problem Must Look Familiar to the NFL and Military," *New Republic* (November 25). http://www.newrepublic.com/article/115740/hollywoods-animal-cruelty-pitfalls-self-regulation.

Cardoso, Fernado Henrique. (2009). "New Paths: Globalization in Historical Perspective," *Studies in Comparative International Development* 44/4: 296–317.

Carey, James W. (2005). "Historical Pragmatism and the Internet," *New Media & Society* 7/4: 443–55.

Carley, Kathleen, Il-Chul Moon, Mike Schneider, and Oleg Shigiltchoff. (2005). *Detailed Analysis of Factors Affecting Team Success and Failure in the America's Army Game.* CASOS Technical Report http://www.casos.cs.cmu.edu/publications/papers/CMU-ISRI-05-120.pdf.

Carlson, Matt. (2006). "Tapping into TiVo: Digital Video Recorders and the Transition from Schedules to Surveillance in Television," *New Media & Society* 8/1: 97-115.

Castells, Manuel. (2007). "Communication, Power and Counter-Power in the Network Society," *International Journal of Communication* 1: 238-66.

Castells, Manuel, Mireia Fernández-Ardèvol, Jack Linchuan Qiu, and Arab Sey. (2007). *Mobile Communication and Society: A Global Perspective.* Cambridge, MA: MIT Press.

Cattani, Gino, Simone Ferriani, Giacomo Negro, and Fabrizio Perretti. (2008). "The Structure of Consensus: Network Ties, Legitimation, and Exit Rates of US Feature Film Producer Organizations," *Administrative Science Quarterly* 53/1: 145–82.

Cattani, Gino, Simone Ferriani, Marcello M. Mariani, and Stefano Mengoli. (2013). "Tackling the 'Galácticos' Effect: Team Familiarity and the Performance of Star-Studded Projects," *Industrial and Corporate Change* 22/6: 1629–662.

Celot, Paolo and Fausto Gualtieri. (2007). "TV Viewers' Rights in the European Union," in *Broadcasters and Citizens in Europe: Trends in Media Accountability and Viewer Participation*, ed. Paolo Baldi and Uwe Hasebrink. Bristol: Intellect.

Centre for Energy-Efficient Telecommunications, Bell Labs, and University of Melbourne. (2013). *The Power of Wireless Cloud: An Analysis of the Impact on Energy Consumption of the Growing Popularity of Accessing Cloud Services Via Wirless Services* (June). http://www.ceet.unimelb.edu.au/publications/downloads/ceet-white-paper-wireless-cloud.pdf.

Centro de Reflexión y Acción Laboral. (2006). *New Technology Workers: Report on Working Conditions in the Mexican Electronics Industry.* http://business-humanrights.org/en/mexico-sexual-harassment-anti-union-activities-persist-among-major-electronics-suppliers#c42521.

Chadha, Kalyani, and Anandam Kavoori. (2000). "Media Imperialism Revisited: Some Findings from the Asian Case," *Media, Culture & Society* 22/4: 415–16.

Chadha, Kalyani, and Anandam Kavoori. (2015). "The New Normal: From Media Imperialism to Market Liberalization – Asia's Shifting Television Landscapes," *Media, Culture & Society* 37/3: 479–92.

Chakravartty, Paula, and Katherina Sarikakis. (2006). *Media Policy and Globalization*, Edinburgh: Edinburgh University Press.

Chakravartty, Paula, and Yuezhi Zhao, eds. (2007). *Global Communications: Toward a Transcultural Political Economy.* Lanham, MD: Rowman & Littlefield.

Chalmers, Robert. (2008). "The Lady Vanishes: Whatever Happened to Fenella Fielding?" *Independent* (February 24). http://www.independent.co.uk/arts-entertainment/films/features/the-lady-vanishes-what-ever-happened-to-fenella-fielding-785265.html.

Chan, Debby. (2010). *Apple Owes Workers and Public a Response over the Poisonings.* Students and Scholars Against Corporate Misbehaviour. http://csr-asia.com/download/SACOM_apple_20100505.pdf.

Chan, Jenny and Charles Ho. (2008). *The Dark Side of Cyberspace.* Berlin: World Economy, Ecology & Development.

Chan, Jenny, Ngai Pun, and Mark Selden. (2013). "The Politics of Global Production: Apple, Foxconn and China's New Working Class," *New Technology, Work and Employment* 28/2: 100–15.

Chandler, Raymond. (1945). "Writers in Hollywood," *The Atlantic* (November 1). http://www.theatlantic.com/magazine/archive/1945/11/writers-in-hollywood/306454/.

Chandler, Raymond. (2001). "Hollywood's Big Sleep," *The Nation* (March 15). http://www.thenation.com/article/hollywoods-big-sleep.

Charters, W. W. (1933). *Motion Pictures and Youth: A Summary.* New York: Macmillan.

Chartier, Roger. (1989). "Texts, Printings, Readings," in *The New Cultural History*, ed. Lynn Hunt. Berkeley: University of California Press, 154–75.

Chartier, Roger. (2004). "Languages, Books and Reading from the Printed Word to the Digital Text," trans. T. L. Fagan. *Critical Inquiry* 31/1: 133–52.

Chartier, Roger. (2005a). "Crossing Borders in Early Modern Europe: Sociology of Texts and Literature," trans. Maurice Elton. *Book History* 8: 37–50.

Chartier, Roger. (2005b,). "Le Droit d'auteur est-il une parenthèse dans l'histoire?" *Le Monde* (December 17). http://www.lemonde.fr/societe/article/2005/12/17/roger-chartier-le-droit-d-auteur-est-il-une-parenthese-dans-l-histoire_722516_3224.html.

Chatterjee, Bela Bonita. (2008). "The Lady Vanishes: Gender, Law and the (Virtual) Body," *Australian Law Journal* 29: 13–30.

Chaudhuri, Maitrayee. (2010). "Indian Media and its Transformed Public," *Contributions to Indian Sociology* 44/1-2: 57–78.

Chidester, Phillip J. (2009). "'The Toy Story of Life': Myth, Sport and the Mediated Reconstruction of the American Hero in the Shadow of the September 11th Terrorist Attacks," *Southern Communication Journal* 74/4: 352–72.

Chmielewiski, Dawn C. (2002). "SonicBlue Ordered to Track Digital Video Recorder Users," *Chicago Tribune* (May 6). http://articles.chicagotribune.com/2002-05-06/business/0205060017_1_son icblue-high-speed-internet-port-video-tape.

Chmielewski, Dawn C. (2012,). "Poptent's Amateurs Sell Cheap Commercials to Big Brands," *Los Angeles Times* (May 8). http://articles.latimes.com/2012/may/08/business/la-fi-ct-pop tent-20120508.

Christenson, Peter and Maria Ivancin. (2006). *The "Reality" of Health: Reality Television and the Public Health.* Henry J Kaiser Foundation. https://kaiserfamilyfoundation.files.wordpress.com/2013/01/7567.pdf.

Christopherson, Susan. (2013). "Hollywood in Decline? US Film and Television Producers Beyond the Era of Fiscal Crisis," *Cambridge Journal of Regions, Economy and Society* 6/1: 141–57.

Clark, Danae. (1995). *Negotiating Hollywood: The Cultural Politics of Actors' Labor.* Minneapolis: University of Minnesota Press.

Clark, Elizabeth A. (1998). "The Lady Vanishes: Dilemmas of a Feminist Historian after the 'Linguistic Turn'," *Church History* 67/1: 1–31.

Clarke, Stewart. (2012). "Sweden's SVT Buys Hit Turkish Drama," *TBI Vision* (September 27). http://tbivision.com/news/2012/09/swedens-svt-buys-hit-turkish-drama/16804/.

Clifford, Reginald. (2005). "Engaging the Audience: The Social Imaginary of the *Novela*," *Television & New Media* 6/4: 360–9.

Climate Group. (2008). *Smart2020: Enabling the Low Carbon Economy in the Information Age.* London: Global Sustainability Initiative.

Cloud, Dana. (2004). "'To Veil the Threat of Terror': Afghan Women and the *Clash of Civilizations* in the Imagery of the US War on Terrorism," *Quarterly Journal of Speech* 90/3: 285–306.

Cochrane, Laura. (2015). "How the Olsen Twins Won Over the Fashion World," *Guardian* (March 19). http://www.theguardian.com/fashion/2015/mar/19/how-the-olsen-twins-won-over-the-fas hion-world.

Cohan, Steven. (2008). *CSI: Crime Scene Investigation.* Houndmills: BFI/Palgrave Macmillan.

Cohen, Jeff. (2001). "The CIA Goes Primetime," *FAIR* (September 4). http://fair.org/article/the-cia-goes-primetime/.

Cohen, Karl. (2003). "The Cartoon That Came in from the Cold," *Guardian* (March 7). http://www.theguardian.com/culture/2003/mar/07/artsfeatures.georgeorwell.

Colla, Elliott. (2012). "Roundtable on Language of Revolution: The Revolution Continues (Present Continuous) (Colla)," *Jadaliyya* (August 12). http://www.jadaliyya.com/pages/index/6829/roundtable-on-language-of-revolution_the-revolutio.

Collier, Robert. (2005). "Family Demands the Truth," *San Francisco Chronicle* (September 25). http://www.sfgate.com/news/article/FAMILY-DEMANDS-THE-TRUTH-New-inquiry-may-expose-2567400.php.

Collins, Richard. (1994). *Broadcasting and Audio-Visual Policy in the European Single Market.* Eastleigh: John Libbey Publishing.

Collins, Scott. (2009). "TV Starts to Notice Others in the Room," *Los Angeles Times* (January 11). http://articles.latimes.com/2009/jan/11/entertainment/et-demographic11.

Commission on the Future of Women's Sport. (2010). *Prime Time: The Case for Commercial Investment in Women's Sport.* London: Women's Sport and Fitness Foundation.

Concept Media S. A. (n.d.). *Las Mil y Una Noches: Cuales son las claves de esye éxito y cómo son sus televidentes.* http://www.conceptmedia.com.ar/notas_mail/las_mil_y_una_noches.html.

Connell, Raewyn. (2014). "Rethinking Gender from the South," *Feminist Studies* 40/3: 518–39.

Connelly, Michael. (2009). *Nine Dragons: A Novel.* New York: Little, Brown and Company.

Consoli, John. (2008). "TV Retains Marketing Dollars in Hard Times," *New York Times* (December 30). http://www.nytimes.com/2008/12/30/business/media/30adco.html.

Cook, Daniel Thomas. (2007). "Children's Consumer Culture," in *Encyclopedia of Sociology*, ed. George Ritzer. Malden, MA: Blackwell http://www.blackwellreference.com/public/tocnode?id=g9781405124331_chunk_g97814051243319_ss1-100.

Cook, Daniel Thomas, and Susan B. Kaiser. (2004). "Betwixt and be Tween: Age Ambiguity and the Sexualization of the Female Consuming Subject," *Journal of Consumer Culture* 4/2: 203-27.

Cook, Tim. (2015). "Pro-Discrimination 'Religious Freedom' Laws Are Dangerous," *Washington Post* (March 29). http://www.washingtonpost.com/opinions/pro-discrimination-religious-freedom-laws-are-dangerous-to-america/2015/03/29/bdb4ce9e-d66d-11e4-ba28-f2a685dc7f89_story.html.

Cooper, Michael. (1999). "2-TV Béisbol: Ramirez and Sosa," *New York Times* (September 18): B1, B6. http://www.nytimes.com/1999/09/18/nyregion/2-tv-beisbol-ramirez-sosa-dominican-fans-washington-hts-love-their-star-problems.html?pagewanted=all.

Copeland, Larry. (2013). "Crashes Caused by Drivers on Cellphones Underreported," *USA Today* (May 8). http://www.usatoday.com/story/news/nation/2013/05/07/car-crashes-cell-phones-distracted-driving/2142157/.

Corbett, Charles J., and Richard P. Turco. (2006). *Sustainability in the Motion Picture Industry*. Report prepared for the Integrated Waste Management Board of the State of California. http://personal.anderson.ucla.edu/charles.corbett/papers/mpis_report.pdf.

Council on Foreign Relations. (2003). *Finding America's Voice: A Strategy for Reinvigorating U.S. Public Diplomacy*. New York: Council on Foreign Relations.

Couric, Katie. (2008). "What Really Happened to Pat Tillman?" *CBSNews* (May 4). http://www.cbsnews.com/news/what-really-happened-to-pat-tillman/.

Court of Justice of the European Union (2011). *Judgment in Cases C-403/08 and C-429/08 Football Association Premier League and Others v QC Leisure and Others Karen Murphy v Media Protection Services Ltd.* (October 4). http://curia.europa.eu/jcms/upload/docs/application/pdf/2011-10/cp110102en.pdf.

Cox, Stan. (2009). "Cell Phones Generate Particularly Dangerous E-Waste," in *What Is the Impact of E-Waste?*, ed. Cynthia A. Bily. Detroit, MI: Greenhaven Press, 18-26.

Craig, Kathleen. (2006). "Dead in Iraq: It's No Game," *Wired* (June 6). http://archive.wired.com/gaming/gamingreviews/news/2006/06/71052.

Cristiani, Mathilde and Jean-Louis Missika. (2007). "Internet ne fait pas disparaître le lien social, il donne aux individus la possibilité de le maîtriser davantage," *L'Atelier* (April 12). http://www.atelier.net/fr/node/180667/summary/227764.

Crosby, Jackie. (2007). "The Mania Over Apple's Latest Product Could Translate into an Avalanche of Electronic Waste," *Star Tribune* (June 29): 1D.

Crusafon, Carmina. (2009). "La política audiovisual del MERCOSUR y la influencia del modelo europeo," *Cuadernos de Información* 25: 93-104.

Cunningham, Stuart. (1992). *Framing Culture: Criticism and Policy in Australia*. Sydney: Allen & Unwin.

Cunningham, Stuart and John Sinclair. (2000). *Floating Lives: The Media and Asian Diasporas*. Brisbane: University of Queensland Press.

Curran, James and Myung-Jin Park, eds. (2000). *De-Westernizing Media Studies*. London: Routledge.

Curtin, Michael. (2007). *Playing to the World's Biggest Audience: The Globalization of Chinese Film and Television*. Berkeley: University of California Press.

Dabashi, Hamid. (2013). "Can Non-Europeans Think?" *Aljazeera* (January 15). http://www.aljazeera.com/indepth/opinion/2013/01/2013114142638797542.html.

D'Addario, Daniel. (2013). "Hollywood Memoirist Lynda Obst: "Women Make Wonderful Producers"," *Salon* (June 14). http://www.salon.com/2013/06/14/hollywoodmemoiristlyndaobstwomenmakewonderfulproducers/.

Daddario, Gina. (1997). "Gendered Sports Programming: 1992 Summer Olympic Coverage and the Feminine Narrative Form," *Sociology of Sport Journal* 14/2: 103-20.

Dasgupta, Piyasree. (2015,). "Here's Why I Wish I Hadn't Watched Leslee Udwin's BBC Documentary 'India's Daughter'," *First Post India* (March 7). http://www.firstpost.com/india/man-raped-indias-daughter-heres-wish-hadnt-watched-bbc-documentary-2137299.html.

Dave, Paresh. (2015). "Army to station Up to 70 Researchers at USC's Institute for Creative Technologies," *Los Angeles Times* (November 3). http://www.latimes.com/business/technology/la-fi-tn-usc-ict-army-open-campus-20151103-story.html.

Davidson, Adam. (2012). "How Does the Film Industry Actually Make Money?" *New York Times* (June 26). http://www.nytimes.com/2012/07/01/magazine/how-does-the-film-industry-actually-make-money.html?r=0.

Davis, Devra. (2013). "War-Gaming Cell Phone Science Protects Neither Brains Nor Private Parts," *Huffington Post* (May 21). http://www.huffingtonpost.com/devra-davis-phd/cell-phones-brain-cancer_b_3232534.html.

Dean Hartley. (2001). "Green Citizenship," *Social Policy & Administration* 35/5: 490–505.

de Carvalho, Angela Maria Grossi, and Juliano Maurício de Carvalho. (2014). "Televisão digital terrestre na agenda do Mercosul," *Tram[p]as de la Comunicación y la Cultura* 77. http://www.revistatrampas.com.ar/2014/10/televisao-digital-terrestre-na-agenda.html.

Deck, Andy. (2004). "Demilitarizing the Playground," *Art Context*. http://artcontext.com/crit/essays/noQuarter/.

DeFao, Janine. (2006). "TV Channel for Babies? Pediatricians Say Turn it Off," *San Francisco Chronicle* (September 11). http://www.sfgate.com/health/article/TV-channel-for-babies-Pediatricians-say-turn-it-2552399.php.

Delisle, Jennifer Bowering. (2003). "Surviving American Cultural Imperialism: *Survivor* and Traditions of Nineteenth-Century Colonial Fiction," *Journal of American Culture* 26/1: 42–55.

della Cava, Marco R. (2003). "Iraq Gets Sympathetic Press Around the World," *USA Today* (April 2): 1D.

de Moraes, Lisa. (2008). "At NBC, There is no Script for Success," *Washington Post* (December 30): C1.

Der Derian, James. (1992). *Antidiplomacy: Spies, Terror, Speed, and War*. Cambridge, MA: Blackwell.

Der Derian, James. (2003). "War as Game," *Brown Journal of World Affairs* 10/1: 37–48.

Der Derian, James. (2005). "Imaging Terror: Logos, Pathos and Ethos," *Third World Quarterly* 26/1: 23–37.

Deresiewicz, William. (2011,). "Faulty Towers: The Crisis in Higher Education," *The Nation* (April 2). http://www.thenation.com/article/160410/faulty-towers-crisis-higher-education.

De Roo, Ana C., Thiphalak Chounthirath, and Gary A. Smith. (2013). "Television-Related Injuries to Children in the United States, 1990–2011," *Pediatrics* 132/2: 267–74.

De Santis, Saimar. (2014). "Caso 'Legends' y otras series que nombran a Venezuela," *2001* (September 2). http://www.2001.com.ve/en-la-agenda/caso--legends--y-otras-series-que-nombran-a-venezuela.html.

de Sola Pool, Ithiel. (1980). "Communications Technology and Land Use," *Annals of the American Academy of Political and Social Science* 451: 1–12.

de Sola Pool, Ithiel. (1983). *Technologies of Freedom*. Cambridge, MA: Harvard University Press.

De Vany, Arthur S. (2003). *Hollywood Economics: How Extreme Uncertainty Shapes the Film Industry*. New York: Routledge.

Díaz, Doriam. (2012). "Karina Bolaños," *La Nación* (December 2). http://www.nacion.com/archivo/Karina-Bolanos_0_1308869237.html.

Dickenson, Donna L. (2006). "The Lady Vanishes: What's Missing from the Stem Cell Debate," *Journal of Bioethical Inquiry* 3/1–2: 43–54.

Directors Guild of America. (2000). "DGA Commends Action by Governor Gray Davis to Fight Runaway Production," Press release (May 18).

Dixon, Pam. (2010). *The One-Way Mirror Society: Privacy Implications of the New Digital Signage Networks*. World Privacy Forum. https://www.worldprivacyforum.org/2010/01/report-one-way-mirror-society/.

Dorfman, Ariel, and Armand Mattelart. (1971). *Para leer el pato Donald*. Santiago de Chile: Ediciones Universitarias de Valparaíso.

Dou, Eva. (2014). "After Suicide, Foxconn Worker's Poems Strike a Chord," *Wall Street Journal* (November 7). http://blogs.wsj.com/chinarealtime/2014/11/07/after-suicide-foxconn-workers-poems-strike-a-chord/.

Douglas, Hilary. (2011). "3000% Increase in "Worthless" Subjects," *Daily Express* (March 13). http://www.express.co.uk/news/uk/234186/3000-increase-in-worthless-subjects.

Douglas, Susan J. (1987). *Inventing American Broadcasting 1899–1922*. Baltimore, MD: Johns Hopkins University Press.

Douthat, Ross. (2008). "The Return of the Paranoid Style," *Atlantic Monthly* (April). http://www.theatlantic.com/magazine/archive/2008/04/the-return-of-the-paranoid-style/306733/.

Downey, Kevin. (2007). "In Their TV Tastes, the Rich are Different," *Media Life* (March 5). http://www.medialifemagazine.com/artman/publish/article_10573.asp.

Downing, John D. H. (2003). "Audiences and Readers of Alternative Media: The Absent Lure of the Virtually Unknown," *Media, Culture, & Society* 25/5: 625–45.

Downing, John D. H. (2007). "Terrorism, Torture, and Television: *24* in its Context," *Democratic Communiqué* 21/2: 62–82.

Dugan, Emily. (2014). "'Soft GCSEs" Could Face Axe from Exam Watchdog Ofqal," *Independent* (May 25). http://www.independent.co.uk/news/education/education-news/soft-gcses-could-face-the-axe-from-exam-watchdog-ofqual-9433736.html.

Duhig, Charles. (2012). "Psst, You in Aisle 5," *New York Times* (February 19): MM30.

Duncan, Andy. (2009). "Britain's Media Needs Radical Change to Stay on Top," *Telegraph* (January 16). http://www.telegraph.co.uk/finance/newsbysector/mediatechnologyandtelecoms/4247084/Britains-media-needs-radical-change-to-stay-on-top.html.

Dutton, William H., and Malcolm Peltu. (2007). "The Emerging Internet Governance Mosaic: Connecting the Pieces," *Information Polity* 12/1–2: 63–81.

Dyer, Richard. (1986). *Heavenly Bodies: Film Stars and Society*. New York: St. Martin's Press.

Dyson, Esther, George Gilder, George Keyworth, and Alvin Toffler. (1994). *Cyberspace and the American Dream: A Magna Carta for the Knowledge Age*. Version 1.2 Progress and Freedom Foundation. http://www.pff.org/issues-pubs/futureinsights/fi1.2magnacarta.html.

Eagleton, Terry. (1982). "The Revolt of the Reader," *New Literary History* 13/3: 449–52.

Earls, Mark. (2003). "Advertising to the Herd: How Understanding Our True Nature Challenges the Ways We Think about Advertising and Market Research," *International Journal of Market Research* 45/3: 311–37.

Earnheardt, Adam C., Paul M. Haridakis, and Barbara S. Hugenberg, eds. (2012). *Sports Fans, Identity, and Socialization: Exploring the Fandemonium*. Lanham, MD: Lexington Books.

Eastman, Susan Tyler, and Arthur M. Land. (1997). "The Best of Both Worlds: Sports Fans Find Good Seats at the Bar," *Journal of Sport & Social Issues* 21/2: 156–78.

Eco, Umberto. (1972). "Towards a Semiotic Inquiry into the Television Message," trans. Paolo Splendore. *Working Papers in Cultural Studies* 3: 103–21.

Eco, Umberto. (1987). *Travels in Hyperreality: Essays*, trans. William Weaver. London: Picador.

Edelman, Daniel J. (1983). "Managing the Public Relations Firm in the 21st Century," *Public Relations Review* 9/3: 3–10.

Edgecliffe-Johnson, Andrew. (2007). "Targeted Television Ads Three Years Away," *Financial Times* (October 30). http://www.ft.com/cms/s/0/587c32c2-868b-11dc-b00e-0000779fd2ac.html#axzz1GLfDgcZl.

Edgeworth, Matt. (2010). "Beyond Human Proportions: Archaeology of the Mega and the Nano," *Archaeologies: Journal of the World Archaeological Congress* 6/1: 138–49.

Editor. (2014). "What's Keeping Some Graduates from Getting Hired?" *KUOW* (June 4). http://www.kuow.org/post/whats-keeping-some-graduates-getting-hired.

Edwards, Katie M., Jessica A. Turchik, Christina M. Dardis, Nicole Reynolds, and Christine A. Gidyez. (2015). "Rape Myths: History, Individual and Institutional-Level Presence, and Implications for Change," *Sex Roles* 65/11–12: 761–73.

Eilperin, Juliet. (2013). "Outdoor Cats Kill Between 1.4 Billion and 3.7 Billion Birds a Year, Study Says," *Washington Post* (January 31). http://www.washingtonpost.com/national/health-sci

ence/outdoor-cats-kill-between-14-billion-and-37-billion-birds-a-year-study-says/2013/01/31/
2504f744-6bbe-11e2-ada0-5ca5fa7ebe79_story.html.

Elias, Norbert, and Eric Dunning. (1986). *Quest for Excitement: Sport and Leisure in the Civilizing Process*. Oxford: Basil Blackwell.

Elias, Norbert. (1978). "On Transformations of Aggressiveness," *Theory and Society* 5/2: 229–42.

Elliott, Larry. (2013). "Europe and US Launch Plans for Ambitious Transatlantic Deal," *Guardian* (June 17). http://www.theguardian.com/business/2013/jun/17/europe-us-transatlantic-trade-deal.

Elliott, Stuart. (2014). "Edelman P. R. Firm Acts to Correct Faux Pas," *New York Times* (August 17). http://www.nytimes.com/2014/08/18/business/media/edelman-pr-firm-is-taking-steps-to-address-faux-pas-.html?_r=1.

el-Nawawy, Mohammed, and Leo A. Gher. (2003). "Al Jazeera: Bridging the East-West Gap Through Public Discourse and Media Diplomacy," *Transnational Broadcasting Studies* 10. http://tbsjournal.arabmediasociety.com/Archives/Spring03/nawawy.html.

Environmental Working Group. (2009). *Cell Phone Radiation: Science Review on Cancer Risks and Children's Health*. http://ewg.org/cellphoneradiation/fullreport.

European Commission. (2014). *State Aid SA.38373 (2014/C) (ex 2014/NN) (ex 2014/CP) – Ireland: Alleged Aid to Apple*. C(2014) 3606 Final. http://ec.europa.eu/competition/state_aid/cases/253200/253200_1582634_87_2.pdf.

Evens, Tom, Katrien Lefever, Peggy Valcke, Dimitri Schuurman, and Lieven De Marez. (2011). "Access to Premium Content on Mobile Television Platforms: The Case of Mobile Sports," *Telematics and Informatics* 28/1: 32–9.

Evusa, Juliet. (2008). "Children's Television in Kenya: The Need for a Comprehensive Media Policy Regulating Children's Content," *African Media, African Children*, ed. Norma Pecora, Enyonam Osei-Hwere, and Ulla Carlsson. Gothenburg: NORDICOM. 207-18.

Fair, Jo Ellen, and Hemant Shah. (1997). "Continuities and Discontinuities in Communication and Development Research Since 1958," *Journal of International Communication* 4/2: 3–23.

FAIR. (2003a). "Do Media Know That War Kills?" (March 14). http://fair.org/take-action/action-alerts/do-media-know-that-war-kills/.

FAIR. (2003). "In Iraq Crisis, Networks Are Megaphones for Official Views" (March 18). http://fair.org/article/in-iraq-crisis-networks-are-megaphones-for-official-views/.

FAIR. (2005). "*Time* Covers Coulter" (April 21). http://fair.org/take-action/action-alerts/time-covers-coulter/.

FAIR. (2008). "The 'Great Mystery' of Iraq's WMDs? CBS Ignores Evidence from its Own Show" (February 1). http://fair.org/take-action/action-alerts/the-great-mystery-of-iraqs-wmds/.

Fearn, Rebecca. (2015). "Olsen Twins Win the Big Award at the CFDAs," *Glamour News* (June 2). http://www.glamourmagazine.co.uk/news/celebrity/2015/06/02/olsen-twins-win-the-big-award-at-the-cfdas.

Federal Trade Commission. (2012). *Protecting Consumer Privacy in an Era of Rapid Change: Recommendations for Businesses and Policymakers*. http://www.ftc.gov/sites/default/files/documents/reports/federal-trade-commission-report-protecting-consumer-privacy-era-rapid-change-recommendations/120326privacyreport.pdf.

Feifei, Fan. (2014). "Adding to the Drama Across Region," *Asia Weekly* (October 17). http://epaper.chinadailyasia.com/asia-weekly/article-3454.html.

Ferriani, Simone, Gino Cattani, and Charles Baden-Fuller. (2009). "The Relational Antecedents of Project-Entrepreneurship: Network Centrality, Team Composition and Project Performance," *Research Policy* 38/10: 1545–558.

Film L.A. Research. (2014). *Filming On Location Los Angeles 1993–2013*. Los Angeles: Film LA Inc.

Fischer, Lucy. (1979). "The Lady Vanishes: Women, Magic and the Movies," *Film Quarterly* 33/1: 30–40.

Fish, Mike. (2006). "E-Ticket: An Un-American Tragedy." http://espn.go.com/espn/eticket/story?page=tillmanpart1.

Fiske, John. (1987). *Television Culture*. London: Routledge.

Fiske, John. (1989). *Understanding Popular Culture*. London: Unwin Hyman.

Flaherty, Mike. (2008). "Turner Unveils Television Statistics," *Variety* (December 10). http://www.variety.com/article/VR1117997186?refCatId=18.

Flanders, Laura. (2001). "Media Criticism in Mono," *WorkingForChange* (November 9).

Flew, Terry. (2013). *Global Creative Industries*. Cambridge: Polity.

Florida, Richard. (2002). *The Rise of the Creative Class: And How it's Transforming Work, Leisure, Community and Everyday Life*. New York: Basic Books.

Ford, Henry. (1929). *My Philosophy of Industry: An Authorized Interview by Ray Leone Faurote*. New York: Coward-McCann.

Forsyth, Tim. (2002). "What Happened on 'The Beach'? Social Movements and Governance of Tourism in Thailand," *International Journal of Sustainable Development* 5/3: 326-37.

Foster, Pacey, Stephan Manning, and David Terkla. (2013). "The Rise of Hollywood East: Regional Film Offices as Intermediaries in Film and Television Production Clusters," *Regional Studies* 49/3: 433-50.

Foucault, Michel. (2006). *Psychiatric Power: Lectures at the Collège de France, 1973-74*, trans. Graham Burchell, ed. Jacques Lagrange. Basingstoke: Palgrave Macmillan.

Foucault, Michel. (2008). *The Birth of Biopolitics: Lectures at the Collège de France, 1978-79*, trans. Graham Burchell, ed. Michel Senellart. Houndmills: Palgrave Macmillan.

Fox, Adam. (2003). "Talking About My Generation," *Guardian* (May 23). http://www.theguardian.com/education/2003/may/23/highereducation.comment.

Fox, Jonathan. (2002). "Ethnic Minorities and the Clash of Civilizations: A Quantitative Analysis of Huntington's Thesis," *British Journal of Political Science* 32/3: 415-35.

Frazier, Mya. (2006). "Edelman Eats Humble Pie," *AdAge* (October 19). http://adage.com/article/news/edelman-eats-humble-pie/112588/.

Freedland, Jonathan. (2013). "Danny Boyle: Champion of the People," *Guardian* (March 9). http://www.guardian.co.uk/film/2013/mar/09/danny-boyle-queen-olympics-film.

Freedman, Des. (2008). *The Politics of Media Policy*. Cambridge: Polity.

Friedman, Wayne. (2009a,). "NATPE Executives Call for Risk-Taking with 'Laser Focus'," *MediaPost's TV Watch* (January 28). http://www.mediapost.com/publications/?fa=Articles.showArticle&art_aid=99270.

Friedman, Wayne. (2009b). "Study: Teens Love Live TV," *MediaDailyNews* (April 21). http://www.mediapost.com/publications/?fa=Articles.showArticle&art_aid=104573.

Frith, Simon. (1991). "The Good, the Bad, and the Indifferent: Defending Popular Culture from the Populists," *diacritics* 21/4: 102-15.

Fröbel, Friedrich, Jürgen Heinrichs, and Otto Kreye. (1980). *The New International Division of Labor: Structural Unemployment in Industrialised Countries and Industrialisation in Developing Countries*, trans. Peter Burgess: Cambridge: Cambridge University Press; Paris: Éditions de la Maison des Sciences de l'Homme.

Fuchs, Christian. (2014). *Digital Labour and Karl Marx*. New York: Routledge.

Fung, Anthony. (2008). *Global Capital, Local Culture: Transnational Media Corporations in China*. New York: Peter Lang.

Fung, Richard. (1991). "Looking for My Penis: The Eroticized Asian in Gay Video Porn," in *How Do I Look? Queer Film and Video*, ed. Bad Object-Choices. Seattle, WA: Bay Press, 145-68.

Galbraith, J. K. (1967). *The New Industrial State*. Boston, MA: Houghton Mifflin.

Galperin, Herman. (1999). "Cultural Industries Policy in Regional Trade Agreements: The Case of NAFTA, the European Union and MERCOSUR," *Media, Culture, & Society* 21: 627-648.

Galtung, Johan. (1971). "A Structural Theory of Imperialism," *Journal of Peace Research* 2: 81-117.

Gandy, Oscar H., Jr. (1989). "The Surveillance Society: Information Technology and Bureaucratic Control," *Journal of Communication* 39/3: 61-76.

Ganguly, Lauhona. (2010). "Reality TV Shows, Private Television Networks and Social Change in India," in *International Cultural Policies and Power*, ed. J. P. Singh. Basingstoke: Palgrave, 181-93.

Ganguly, Lauhona, and Marwan M. Kraidy. (2004). Crorepati and Hybridity: Indian Television and Globalization (May). Competitive paper, Intercultural and Development Communication Division, International Communication Association, New Orleans.

Ganti, Tejaswini. (2012). "No Longer a Frivolous Singing and Dancing Nation of Movie-Makers: The Hindi Film Industry and its Quest for Global Distinction," *Visual Anthropology* 25/4: 340–65.

Gantz, Walter. (2012). "Reflections on Communication and Sport: On Fanship and Social Relationships," *Communication and Sport* 1/1–2: 176–87.

García Canclini, Néstor. (1995). *Hybrid Cultures: Strategies for Entering and Leaving Modernity*, trans. Christopher L. Chiappari and Silvia L. López. Minneapolis: University of Minnesota Press.

García Canclini, Néstor. (2001). *Consumers and Citizens: Multicultural Conflicts in the Process of Globalization*, trans. George Yúdice. Minneapolis: University of Minnesota Press.

García Canclini, Néstor. (2002). *Latinoamericanos buscando lugar en este siglo*. Buenos Aires: Paidós.

García Canclini, Néstor. (2004). *Diferentes, desiguales y desconectados: Mapas de la interculturalidad*. Barcelona: Editorial Gedisa.

García Canclini, Néstor. (2008). "Interview for the 9th Spanish Sociology Conference, 2007," trans. Toby Miller. *Social Identities* 14/3: 389–94.

García Canclini, Néstor. (2014). "Epilogue: Social and Imaginary Changes in Globalization Today: Conversation Between Néstor García Canclini and Toby Miller, Autumn 2011," in Néstor García Canclini, *Imagined Globalization*, trans. George Yúdice. Durham, NC: Duke University Press, 201–15.

Garfinkel, Harold. (1992/1967). *Studies in Ethnomethodology*. Cambridge: Polity.

Garnham, Nicholas. (1987). "Concepts of Culture: Public Policy and the Cultural Industries," *Cultural Studies* 1/1: 23–37.

Gaudiosi, John. (2005, July 13). "PLAY," *Wired*. http://archive.wired.com/wired/archive/13.07/play. html.

Gerbner, George. (1994). "Unesco in the US Press," in *The Global Media Debate: Its Rise, Fall, and Renewal*, ed. George Gerbner, Hamid Mowlana, and Kaarle Nordenstreng. Norwood, NJ: Ablex, 111–21.

Gerbner, George, Hamid Mowlana, and Kaarle Nordenstreng, eds. (1994). *The Global Media Debate: Its Rise, Fall and Renewal*. Norwood, NJ: Ablex.

Geurens, Jean-Pierre. (1989). "The Brainbusters: The Upside Down World of Television Wrestling," *Spectator* 9/2: 56–67.

Ghosh, Deepshikha. (2015). "Everyone Must See 'India's Daughter,' Says Nirbhaya's Father After Ban in India" (March 5). *NDTV* http://www.ndtv.com/india-news/everyone-must-see-indias-daughter-says-nirbhayas-father-after-ban-in-india-744411.

Ghosh, Tanushree. (2015). "'Yet We Believe His Triumph Must Surely Be Ours': The Dickensian Liberalism of *Slumdog Millionaire*," *Neo-Victorian Studies* 8/1: 77–106.

Gibson, William. (2010). *Zero History*. London: Viking.

Giddens, Anthony. (1990). *The Consequences of Modernity*. Palo Alto, CA: Stanford University Press.

Gilboa, Eytan. (1998). "Media Diplomacy: Conceptual Divergence and Applications," *Harvard Journal of Press/Politics* 3/3: 56–75.

Gillespie, Marie. (1995). *Television, Ethnicity and Cultural Change*. London: Routledge.

Giuliani, Livio, and Morando Soffritti, with Marne Glaser and Francesca Romana Orlando. (2012). *ICEMS Position Paper on the Cerebral Tumor Court Case Final Paper*. http://icems.eu/docs/ICEMS_Position_paper.pdf?f=/c/a/2009/12/15/MNHJ1B49KH.DTL.

Glantz, Margo. (1992). "Las hijas de la Malinche," *Debate Feminista* 6: 161–79.

Glenn, Ian. (2008). "Cryptic Rhetoric: The ANC and Anti-Americanization," *Safundi: The Journal of South African and American Studies* 9/1: 69–79.

Glez, Damien. (2014). "L'Oeil de Glez: Jack Bauer vs Amnesty," *Jeune Afrique* (May 14). http://www.jeuneafrique.com/Article/ARTJAWEB20140514115527/.

Global Witness. (2009). *"Faced with a Gun, What Can You Do?": War and the Militarisation of Mining in Eastern Congo*. London: Global Witness.

Goff, Stan. (2006). "Playing the Atheism Card Against Pat Tillman's Family," *Truthdig* (July 28). http://www.truthdig.com/report/item/20060728_worm_dirt.

Goldenberg, Suzanne. (2013). "Daryl Hannah Leads Celebrity Keystone XL Protest at White House Gates," *Guardian* (February 13). http://www.guardian.co.uk/environment/2013/feb/13/daryl-hannah-keystone-xl-protest-obama.

Goldenberg, Suzanne. (2014). "Edelman Formally Declares it Will not Accept Climate Denial Campaigns," *Guardian* (August 7). http://www.theguardian.com/environment/2014/aug/07/edelman-pr-climate-change-denial-campaigns.

Golding, Peter. (1974). "The Communication Paradox: Inequality at the National and International Levels," *Media Development* 4: 7–9.

Golding, Peter, and Phil Harris, eds. (1997). *Beyond Cultural Imperialism: Globalization, Communication and the New International Order.* London: Sage.

Gómez, Rodrigo. (2007). "El impacto del Tratado de Libre Comercio de América del Norte (TLCAN) en la industria audiovisual mexicana (1994–2002)." PhD thesis, Universidad Autónoma de Barcelona.

Goode, Ian. (2007). *"CSI: Crime Scene Investigation*: Quality, the Fifth Channel and 'America's Finest'," in *Quality TV: Contemporary American Television and Beyond*, ed. Janet McCabe and Kim Akass. London: IB Tauris, 118–28.

GoodElectronics, Paula Overeem, and CSR Platform (MVO Platform). (2009). *Reset: Corporate Social Responsibility in the Global Electronics Supply Chain.* Amsterdam: GoodElectronics.

Goodwin, Christopher. (2009). "Latino TV Station Tops US Ratings," *Observer* (January 18). http://www.theguardian.com/world/2009/jan/18/usa-television.

Gopnik, Adam. (1994). "Read All About It," *New Yorker* 70/41: 84–102.

Götz, M., O. Hoffmann, H.-B. Brosius, C. Carter, K. Chan, St. H. Donald, . . . and H. Zang. (2008). "Gender in Children's Television Worldwide," *Televizion* 21: 4–9.

Government Accountability Office. (2007). *US Public Diplomacy: Actions Needed to Improve Strategic Use and Coordination of Research.* http://www.gao.gov/new.items/d07904.pdf.

Graham, Mark. (2008). "Warped Geographies of Development: The Internet and Theories of Economic Development," *Geography Compass* 2/3: 771–89.

Graham, Mark. (2015). "The Geography of Academic Knowledge," *Geonet: Investigating the Changing Connectivities and Potentials of Sub-Saharan Africa's Knowledge Economy* (September 22). http://geonet.oii.ox.ac.uk/blog/the-geography-of-academic-knowledge/.

Gramsci, Antonio. (1978). *Selections from the Prison Notebooks of Antonio Gramsci*, trans. Quentin Hoare and Geoffrey Nowell-Smith. New York: International Publishers.

Grand Rapids Institute for Information Democracy. (2005). *Violence, Soldier Deaths and Omissions.*

Grantham, Bill. (1998). "America the Menace: France's Feud with Hollywood," *World Policy Journal* 15/2. http://www.worldpolicy.newschool.edu/wpi/journal/grantham.html.

Grantham, Bill. (2000). *"Some Big Bourgeois Brothel": Contexts for France's Culture Wars With France.* Luton: University of Luton Press.

Gray, Laura Craig. (2009). "Media Revolution: Tomorrow's TV," *BBC News* (February 18). http://www.bbc.co.uk/programmes/b00hs97g.

Greenberg, David. (2003). "We Don't Even Agree on What's Newsworthy," *Washington Post* (March 16): B1.

Greenpeace. (2012). *How Clean is Your Cloud?* (April 17). http://www.greenpeace.org/international/Global/international/publications/climate/2012/iCoal/HowCleanisYourCloud.pdf.

Greenwald, Arthur. (2009). "KVVU Rewards Build Ratings, Revenue," *TVNewscheck* (March 2). http://www.tvnewscheck.com/article/2009/03/02/30005/kvvu-rewards-build-ratings-revenue.

Greenwald, Glenn. (2007). "The Pat Tillman and Jessica Lynch Frauds," *Salon* (April 25). http://www.salon.com/2007/04/25/tillman_lynch/.

Grossman, Elizabeth. (2006). *High Tech Trash: Digital Devices, Hidden Toxics, and Human Health.* Washington, DC: Island Press.

Grossman, Lev. (2006). *"Time's* Person of the Year: You," *Time* (December 13). http://content.time.com/time/magazine/article/0,9171,1570810,00.html.

Gryta, Thomas, and Tess Stynes. (2014). "AT&T Reports Profit Decline," *Wall Street Journal* (July 23). http://www.wsj.com/articles/at-t-reports-profit-decline-1406147443.

Gunther, Marc. (2014). "Climate Changeable: Waffling Lands PR Firm Edelman in Hot Water,"

Guardian (August 19). http://www.theguardian.com/sustainable-business/2014/aug/19/climate-change-denial-flip-flop-public-relations-firm-edelman.

Gutiérrez, Cecilia. (2014). "Teleseries turcas: Canal 13 se suma al fenómeno de Las mil y una noche," *Entretención* (May 6). http://www.latercera.com/noticia/entretencion/2014/06/661-581102-9-teleseries-turcas-canal-13-se-suma-al-fenomeno-de-las-mil-y-una-noche.shtml.

Ha, Vinh Hung, Jae-Chun Lee, Jinki Jeong, Huynh Trung Hai, and Manis K. Jha. (2010). "Thiosulfate Leaching of Gold from Waste Mobile Phones," *Journal of Hazardous Materials* 178/2–3: 1115–19.

Hadida, Allègre L. (2010). "Commercial Success and Artistic Recognition of Motion Picture Projects," *Journal of Cultural Economics* 34/1: 45–80.

Hafez, Kai. (2002). "Al Jazeera Meets CNN," *The Big Story* (June 4). http://thebigstory.org/int/int-aljazeera.html.

Hall, Karen J. (2006). "Shooters to the Left of Us, Shooters to the Right: First Person Arcade Shooter Games, the Violence Debate, and the Legacy of Militarism," *Reconstruction: Studies in Contemporary Culture* 6/1. http://reconstruction.eserver.org/Issues/061/hall.shtml.

Hall, Stuart. (1980). "Encoding/Decoding," in *Culture, Media, Language*, ed. Stuart Hall, Dorothy Hobson, Andrew Lowe, and Paul Willis. London: Hutchinson, 128–39.

Hall, Stuart, and Tony Jefferson, eds. (1976). *Resistance Through Rituals: Youth Subcultures in Post-War Britain*. London: Hutchinson.

Hallin, Dan, and Paolo Mancini. (2004). *Comparing Media Systems: Three Models of Media and Politics*. Cambridge: Cambridge University Press.

Halloran, James. (1997). "International Communication Research: Opportunities and Obstacles," in *International Communication and Globalization: A Critical Introduction*, ed. Ali Mohammadi. London: Sage, 27–47.

Halse, Rolf. (2015). "Counter-Stereotypical Images of Muslim Characters in the Television Serial *24*: A Difference that Makes no Difference?" *Critical Studies in Television: The International Journal of Television Studies* 10/1: 54–72.

Halter, Ed. (2006). *From Sun Tzu to Xbox: War and Video Games*. New York: Thunder's Mouth Press.

Hamelink, Cees, and Karle Nordenstreng. (2007). "Towards Democratic Media Governance," in *Media Between Culture and Commerce: An Introduction*, ed. Els De Bens. Bristol: Intellect, 225–40.

Hancock, Simon. (2009). "Iceland New Home of Server Farms?" *BBC News* (October 10). http://news.bbc.co.uk/go/pr/fr/-/2/hi/programmes/click_online/8297237.stm.

Hanna, Nagy K., and Christine Zhen-Wei Qiang. (2010). "China's Emerging Informatization Strategy," *Journal of the Knowledge Economy* 1/2: 128–64.

Hannerz, Ulf. (1989). "Notes on the Global Ecumene," *Public Culture* 1/2: 66–75.

Hardell, Lennart, Michael Carlberg, and Kjell Hansson Mild. (2009). "Epidemiological Evidence for an Association Between Use of Wireless Phones and Tumor Diseases," *Pathophysiology* 16/2–3: 113–22.

Hardt, Hanno. (1984). "Comparative Media Research: The World According to America," *Critical Studies in Mass Communication* 5/2: 129–46.

Harmon, Amy. (2003). "More Than Just a Game, But How Close to Reality?" *New York Times* (April 3). http://www.nytimes.com/2003/04/03/technology/more-than-just-a-game-but-how-close-to-reality.html.

Harris, Daisy. (2014). "Bonfire of "Soft" GCSEs: Media Studies, Astronomy and Tourism Could be Axed in a Bid to Make Qualification More Rigorous," *Daily Mail* (June 1). http://www.dailymail.co.uk/news/article-2645486/Michael-Gove-set-axe-soft-GCSEs-including-media-studies-astronomy-tourism-bid-make-qualification-rigorous.html?ITO=1490&ns_mchannel=rss&ns_campaign=1490.

Hartley, John. (1987). "Invisible Fictions: Television Audiences, Paedocracy, Pleasure," *Textual Practice* 1/2: 121–38.

Hartley, John. (1992). *The Politics of Pictures: The Creation of the Public in the Age of Popular Media*. London: Routledge.

Hartley, John. (1998). "When Your Child Grows Up Too Fast: Juvenation and the Boundaries of the Social in the News Media," *Continuum: Journal of Media & Cultural Studies* 12/1: 9–30.

Hartley, John, ed. (2005). *Creative Industries*. Malden, MA: Blackwell.

Hartley, John. (2008). *Television Truths*. Malden, MA: Blackwell.

Haspel, Paul. (2009). "Baltimore Colts and Diner Guys: Pro Sports Fandom and Social Identity in Barry Levinson's *Diner*," *Aethlon* 26/2: 59–73.

Hassan, Salah S., Stephen Craft, and Wael Kortam. (2003). "Understanding the New Bases for Global Market Segmentation," *Journal of Consumer Marketing* 20/5: 446–62.

Hastings, Michael. (2010). "The Runaway General," *Rolling Stone* (June 22). http://www.rollingstone.com/politics/news/the-runaway-general-20100622.

Havens, Timothy. (2005). "Globalization and the Generic Transformation of Telenovelas," in *Thinking Outside the Box: A Contemporary Television Genre Reader*, ed. Gary R. Edgerton and Brian G. Rose. Lexington: University Press of Kentucky, 271–92.

Hay, James. (2000). "Unaided Virtues: The Neo-Liberalization of the Domestic Sphere," *Television & New Media* 1/1: 53–73.

Hays, Will. (1927). "Supervision from Within," in *The Story of the Films as Told by Leaders of the Industry to the Students of the Graduate School of Business Administration George F. Baker Foundation Harvard University*, ed. Joseph P. Kennedy. Chicago: AW Shaw Company, 29–54.

Healy, Gene. (2004). "You Gotta Serve Somebody," *Cato.org* (May 7). http://www.cato.org/publications/commentary/you-gotta-serve-somebody.

Hearon, Fanning. (1938). "The Motion-Picture Program and Policy of the United States Government," *Journal of Educational Sociology* 12/3: 147–62.

Hebdige, Dick. (1979). *Subculture: The Meaning of Style*. London: Methuen.

Heilemann, John. "A Survey of Television: Feeling for the Future," *The Economist* 330/7850 (1994): SURVEY 1–18.

Heins, Marjorie. (2002). *Not in Front of the Children: "Indecency," Censorship, and the Innocence of Youth*. New York: Hill and Wang.

Helm, Burt. (2007). "Cable Takes a Rating Hit," *Business Week* (September 23). http://www.bloomberg.com/bw/stories/2007-09-23/cable-takes-a-ratings-hit.

Henchman, Joseph. (2008). "Film Tax Credits: Lower Taxes for Celebrities, Higher Taxes for You," *Tax Policy Blog* (May 30). http://taxfoundation.org/blog/film-tax-credits-lower-taxes-celebrities-higher-taxes-you.

Hennigan, W. J. (2010). "Computer Simulation is a Growing Reality for Instruction," *Los Angeles Times* (November 2). http://articles.latimes.com/2010/nov/02/business/la-fi-virtual-reality-20101102.

Hennig-Thurau, Thorsten, André Marchand, and Barbara Hiller. (2012). "The Relationship Between Reviewer Judgements and Motion Picture Success: Re-Analysis and Extension," *Journal of Cultural Economics* 36/3: 249–83.

Herold, Marc W. (2001). "Who Will Count the Dead?" *Media File* 21/1, http://www.media-alliance.org/article.php?id=432.

Heyes, Cressida J. (2007). "Cosmetic Surgery and the Televisual Makeover: A Foucauldian Feminist Reading," *Feminist Media Studies* 7/1: 17–32.

Higgott, Richard. (1993). *Political Development Theory: The Contemporary Debate*. London: Routledge.

Higgott, Richard and Richard Robison, eds. (1985). *Southeast Asia: Essays in the Political Economy of Structural Change*. London: Routledge & Kegan Paul.

High, Peter B. (2003). *The Imperial Screen: Japanese Film Culture in the Fifteen Years' War, 1931–1945*. Madison: University of Wisconsin Press.

Hiley, Nicholas. (1991). "Decoding German Spies: British Spy Fiction 1908–18," in *Spy Fiction, Spy Films, and Real Intelligence*, ed. Wesley K. Wark. London: Frank Cass, 55–79.

Hilmes, Michele. (2005). "The Bad Object: Television in the American Academy," *Cinema Journal* 45/1: 111–17.

Hjort, Mette, ed. (2013). *The Education of the Filmmaker in Africa, the Middle East, and the Americas*. New York: Palgrave Macmillan.

Hobbes, Thomas. (n.d.). *Of Man, Being the First Part of Leviathan*. http://www.bartleby.com/34/5/13.html.

Hochschild, Arlie R. (1983). *The Managed Heart: Commercialization of Human Feeling.* Berkeley: University of California Press.

Hodge, Bob and David Tripp. (1986). *Children and Television.* Cambridge: Polity.

Hogan, Phil. (2004). "Television Studies," *Observer* (February 1). http://www.theguardian.com/life-andstyle/2004/feb/01/features.familyandrelationships.

Holmwood, Leigh. (2008). "Don't Steal TV Formats, ABC is Warned," *Guardian* (August 15). http://www.theguardian.com/media/2008/aug/15/television.usa.

Höpfl, Heather, and Sumohon Matilal. (2007). "'The Lady Vanishes': Some Thoughts on Women and Leadership," *Journal of Organizational Change Management* 20/2: 198–208.

Hozic, Aida A. (2001). *Hollyworld: Space, Power, and Fantasy in the American Economy.* Ithaca, NY: Cornell University Press.

Hsu, Greta, Giacomo Negro, and Fabrizio Perretti. (2012). "Hybrids in Hollywood: A Study of the Production and Performance of Genre-Spanning Films," *Industrial and Corporate Change* 21/6: 1427–50.

Hubbard, Laura, and Kathryn Mathers. (2004). "Surviving American Empire in Africa: The Anthropology of Reality Television," *International Journal of Cultural Studies* 7: 441–59.

Hueter, Megan. (2010). "espnW: A Brand for Female Athletes," *Blogs with Balls* (October 4). http://blogswithballs.com/2010/10/espnw-a-brand-for-female-athletes/.

Human Rights Watch. (2009). *Just the Good News, Please: New UAE Media Law Continues to Stifle Press* (April). http://www.hrw.org/sites/default/files/related_material/uae0409.pdf.

Hunter, Ian. (1988). "Providence and Profit: Speculations in the Genre Market," *Southern Review* 22/3: 211–23.

Hunter, Ian. (2008). "Critical Response II: Talking About My Generation," *Critical Inquiry* 34/3: 583–600.

Huntington, Samuel. (1993). "The Clash of Civilizations?" *Foreign Affairs* 72/3: 22–8.

Hutton, Jan. (2011). "Mobile Phones Dominate in South Africa," *Nielsen Wire* (September 30). http://blog.nielsen.com/nielsenwire/global/mobile-phones-dominate-in-south-africa.

Huxley, Aldous. (1932). *Brave New World.* London: Chatto & Windus.

Imre, Aniko. (2009). *Identity Games.* Cambridge, MA: MIT Press.

Inform. (2008). *The Secret Life of Cell Phones.* http://www.informinc.org/pages/media/the-secret-life-series/the-secret-life-of-cell-phones.html.

Innis, Harold A. (1991). *The Bias of Communication.* Toronto: University of Toronto Press.

Instrell, Rick. (2014). "Media Studies Course is Gaining in Value," *Scotsman* (May 13). www.scotsman.com/news/media-studies-course-is-gaining-in-value-1-3408501.

Institute of Public and Environmental Affairs. (2011). *The Other Side of Apple: Investigative Report into Heavy Metal Pollution in the IT Industry.* http://www.ipe.org.cn/en/about/report.aspx.

International Energy Agency. (2009). *Gadgets and Gigawatts: Policies for Energy Efficient Electronics – Executive Summary.* Paris: Organization for Economic Cooperation and Development.

International Energy Agency. (2012). *Golden Rules for a Golden Age of Gas: World Energy Outlook Special Report on Unconventional Gas.* Paris: International Energy Agency.

International Energy Agency. (2014). *More Data, Less Energy: Making Network Standby More Efficient in Billions of Connected Devices.* http://www.iea.org/publications/freepublications/publication/MoreData_LessEnergy.pdf.

International Federation of Journalists. (2001). *Les Journalistes du Monde Entier Produisent un Rapport sur les Médias, la Guerre et le Terrorisme* (October 23).

International Telecommunication Union. (2008). *ICTs for Environment: Guidelines for Developing Countries, with a Focus on Climate Change.* Geneva: ICT Applications and Cybersecurity Division Policies and Strategies Department International Telecommunication Union Telecommunication Development Sector.

International Telecommunication Union. (2009). *ITU Symposium on ICTs and Climate Change Hosted by CTIC, Quito, Ecuador, 8–10 July 2009: ITU Background Report.* Geneva: International Telecommunication Union.

International Telecommunication Union. (2012). *Measuring the Information Society: Executive Summary.* Geneva: International Telecommunication Union.

Irwin, William, Mark T. Conard, and Aeon J. Skoble, eds. (2001). *The Simpsons and Philosophy*. Chicago, IL: Open Court.

Ishak, Siti Zanariah Ahmad. (2011). "Cultural Hybridity: Adapting and Filtering Popular Culture in Malaysian Television Programmes," *Jurnal Pengajian Media Malaysia/Malaysian Journal of Media Studies* 13/1: 1–15.

Iyer, Pico. (1989). *Video Nights in Kathmandu: And Other Reports From the Not-so-Far-East*. New York: Vintage.

Jacobs, Sean. (2007). "*Big Brother*, Africa is Watching," *Media, Culture & Society* 29/6: 851–68.

Jacobson, Brad. (2013) "What the Cellphone Industry Doesn't Want You to Know About Radiation," *AlterNet* (June 7). http://www.alternet.org/personal-health/radiation-concerns-about-cellphones?paging=off.

Jamal, Amal, Nelly Elias, and Orly Soker. (2011). "Cultural Encoding and Fake Equality in Popular Reality Shows: Lessons from Israel," *Journal of Ethnic and Migration Studies* 37/9: 1349–66.

James, Meg. (2007). "Nielsen Ends Separate Latino TV Survey," *Los Angeles Times* (August 27): C1, C4.

James, Meg. (2009). "Univision, Televisa Settle High-Stakes Lawsuit," *Los Angeles Times* (January 23). http://articles.latimes.com/2009/jan/23/business/fi-televisa23.

James, Meg. (2014). "Kevin Reilly to Step Down as Fox Entertainment Chairman," *Los Angeles Times* (May 29). http://www.latimes.com/entertainment/envelope/cotown/la-et-ct-fox-entertainment-kevin-reilly-steps-down-20140529-story.html.

Jameson, Fredric. (1998). "Globalization as a Philosophical Issue," in *The Cultures of Globalization*, ed. Fredric Jameson and Masao Miyoshi. Durham, NC: Duke University Press, 54–80.

Jasperson, Amy E., and Mansour O. El-Kikhia. (2003). "CNN and al Jazeera's Media Coverage of America's War in Afghanistan," in *Framing Terrorism: The News Media, the Government, and the Public*, ed. Pippa Norris, Montague Kern, and Marion Just. New York: Routledge, 113–32.

Jenkins, Henry. (1992). *Textual Poachers: Television Fans & Participatory Culture*. New York: Routledge.

Jenkins, Henry. (2006). *Fans, Bloggers, and Gamers: Exploring Participatory Culture*. New York: New York University Press.

Jenkins, Tricia. (2009). "Get Smart: A Look at the Current Relationship Between Hollywood and the CIA," *Historical Journal of Film, Radio and Television* 29/2: 229–43.

Jensen, Elizabeth. (2003). "Network's War Strategy: Enlist Armies of Experts," *Los Angeles Times* (March 18). http://articles.latimes.com/2003/mar/18/entertainment/et-jensen18.

Jensen, Robert. (2007). "The Digital Provide: Information Technology, Market Performance, and Welfare in the South Indian Fisheries Sector," *Quarterly Journal of Economics* 122/3: 879–924.

Johnson, Ben. (n.d.) "Duke of Wellington," *Historic UK*. http://www.historic-uk.com/HistoryUK/HistoryofBritain/Duke-of-Wellington/.

Johnson, Lesley. (1988). *The Unseen Voice: A Cultural Study of Early Australian Radio*. London: Routledge.

Johnston, Eric. (1950). "Messengers from a Free Country," *Saturday Review of Literature* (March 4): 9–12.

Jones, Van. (2008). *The Green-Collar Economy: How One Solution Can Fix Our Two Biggest Problems*. New York: HarperOne.

Kahn, E. J., Jr. (1981). *Jock: The Life and Times of John Hay Whitney*. Garden City, NY: Doubleday.

Kant, Immanuel. (1987). *Critique of Judgment*, trans. Werner S. Pluhar. New York: Hackett Publishing.

Kant, Immanuel. (1991). *Groundworks of the Metaphysics of Morals*, trans. Mary J. Gregor. Cambridge: Cambridge University Press.

Kaplan, Fred. (2009). "Hillary Clinton, Watch These Movies! High Noon, Godfather II, Grand Illusion, and 22 Other Indispensable Movies for Understanding War and Diplomacy," *Slate* (May 4). http://www.slate.com/articles/news_and_politics/war_stories/2009/05/hillary_clinton_watch_these_movies.html.

Kapur, Jyotsna, and Keith B. Wagner, eds. (2011). *Neoliberalism and Global Cinema: Capital, Culture, and Marxist Critique*. New York: Routledge.

Karat, Brinda. (2015). "Face the Truth," *Indian Express* (March 6). http://indianexpress.com/article/opinion/columns/face-the-truth/.

Kaufman, Leslie. (2009). "Car Crashes to Please Mother Nature," *New York Times* (March 2): C3.

Kavoori, Anandam, and Kalyani Chadha. (2009). "The Cultural Turn in International Communication," *Journal of Broadcasting & Electronic Media* 53/2: 336–46.

Kawai, Yuko. (2009). "Neoliberalism, Nationalism, and Intercultural Communication: A Critical Analysis of Japan's Neoliberal Nationalism Discourse Under Globalization," *Journal of International and Intercultural Communication* 2/1: 16–43.

Keen, Andrew. (2007). *The Cult of the Amateur: How Today's Internet is Killing Our Culture and Assaulting Our Economy.* London: Nicholas Brealey Publishing.

Keenan, Jimmie. (2006). *Developing the Pentathlete: The Army Congressional Fellowship Experience.* Masters of Strategic Studies, Carlisle Barracks: United States Army War College.

Kellner, Douglas. (2003). *From 9/11 to Terror War: The Dangers of the Bush Legacy.* Lanham, MD: Rowman & Littlefield.

Kellner, Douglas. (2004). "Media Propaganda and Spectacle in the War on Iraq: A Critique of US Broadcasting Networks," *Cultural Studies↔Critical Methodologies* 4/3: 329–38.

Kent, Sidney R. (1927). "Distributing the Product," in *The Story of the Films as Told by Leaders of the Industry to the Students of the Graduate School of Business Administration George F. Baker Foundation Harvard University,* ed. Joseph P. Kennedy. Chicago, IL: AW Shaw Company, 203–32.

Kenyon, Peter. (2013). "Prime Minister Finds Soap Opera's Turkish Delights in Bad Taste," *NPR* (January 3). http://www.npr.org/2013/01/03/167981036/prime-minister-finds-soap-operas-turkish-delights-in-bad-taste.

Kerr, Paul. (1981). "Watching the Detectives," *Primetime* 1/1: 2–6.

Keynes, John Maynard. (1963). *Essays in Persuasion.* New York: WW Norton.

Khalili, Laleh. (2011). "Gendered Practices of Counterinsurgency," *Review of International Studies* 37/4: 1471–91.

King, Noel, and Toby Miller. (2011). "*The Lady Vanishes,* But She Won't Go Away," in *Hitchcock at the Source: The Auteur as Adaptor,* ed. R. Barton Palmer and David Boyd. Albany: State University of New York Press. 103–16.

Kissinger, Henry. (1999). "Globalization and World Order," Independent Newspapers Annual Lecture (October 12), Trinity College Dublin.

Kittross, John Michael. (1999). "A History of the BEA," *Feedback* 40/2 http://www.beaweb.org/pdfs/beahistory.pdf.

Klein, Paul. (2012). "Three Ways to Secure Your Social License to Operate in 2013," *Forbes* (December 28). http://www.forbes.com/sites/csr/2012/12/28/three-ways-to-secure-your-social-license-to-operate-in-2013/.

Kleinwachter, Wolfgang. (1994). "Three Waves of the Debate," in *The Global Media Debate: Its Rise, Fall, and Renewal,* ed. George Gerbner, Hamid Mowlana, and Kaarle Nordenstreng. Norwood: Ablex, 13–20.

Kline, Stephen. (1993). *Out of the Garden: Toys, TV, and Children's Culture in the Age of Marketing.* London: Verso.

Klos, Diana Mitsu. (2013). *The Status of Women in the US Media 2013.* Women's Media Centre. http://www.womensmediacenter.com/pages/statistics.

Kolar-Panov, Dona. (1996). "Video and the Diasporic Imagination of Selfhood: A Case Study of the Croatians in Australia," *Cultural Studies* 10/2: 288–314.

Kolbert, Elizabeth. (2007). "The Lady Vanishes," *New Yorker* (June 11). http://www.newyorker.com/magazine/2007/06/11/the-lady-vanishes-2.

Kosinski, Michal, David Stillwell, and Thore Graepel. (2013). "Private Traits and Attributes are Predictable from Digital Records of Human Behavior," *Proceedings of the National Academy of Sciences of the United States of America* 110/15: 5802–5. http://www.pnas.org/content/110/15/5802.full.

Kraidy, Marwan M. (1998). "Broadcasting Regulation and Civil Society in Post-War Lebanon," *Journal of Broadcasting & Electronic Media* 42/3: 387–400.

Kraidy, Marwan M. (1999). "State Control of Television News in 1990s Lebanon," *Journalism and Mass Communication Quarterly* 76/3: 485–98.

Kraidy, Marwan M. (2002). "Ferment in Global Media Studies," *Journal of Broadcasting & Electronic Media* 46/4: 630–40.

Kraidy, Marwan M. (2003). "The Shutdown of Lebanon's MTV: National and Regional Factors," unpublished ms.

Kraidy, Marwan M. (2005). *Hybridity, or the Cultural Logic of Globalization.* Philadelphia, PA: Temple University Press.

Kraidy, Marwan M. (2006). "Governance and Hypermedia in Saudi Arabia," *First Monday.* 11/9 http://firstmonday.org/issues/special11_9/kraidy/index.html.

Kraidy, Marwan M. (2007). "Saudi Arabia, Lebanon, and the Changing Arab Information Order," *International Journal of Communication* 1/1: 139–56.

Kraidy, Marwan M. (2008). "Arab States: Emerging Consensus to Muzzle Media?" *Arab Reform Bulletin* 6/2 (March). http://www.carnegieendowment.org/publications/.

Kraidy, Marwan M. (2009). "Reality TV, Gender and Authenticity in Saudi Arabia," *Journal of Communication* 59: 345–66.

Kraidy, Marwan M. (2010). *Reality Television and Arab Politics: Contention in Public Life.* Cambridge: Cambridge University Press.

Kraidy, Marwan M. (2011). "The Emergent Supranational Arab Media Policy," in *The Handbook of Global Media and Communication Policy,* ed. Robin Mansell and Marc Raboy. London: Blackwell, 293–305.

Kraidy, Marwan M. (2012). "The Revolutionary Body Politic: Preliminary Thoughts on a Neglected Medium in the Arab Uprisings," *Middle East Journal of Culture and Communication* 5: 68–76.

Kraidy, Marwan M., and Omar Al-Ghazzi. (2013a). "Neo-Ottoman Cool: Turkish Popular Culture in the Arab Public Sphere," *Popular Communication* 11/1: 17–29.

Kraidy, Marwan M., and Omar Al-Ghazzi. (2013b). "'Turkish Rambo': Geopolitical Drama as Narrative Counter-Hegemony," *Flow.* http://flowtv.org/2013/11/%E2%80%9Cturkish-rambo%E2%80%9D-geopolitical-drama-as-narrative-counter-hegemony-marwan-m-kraidy-university-of-pennsylvania-omar-al-ghazzi-university-of-pennsylvania/.

Kraidy, Marwan M., and Joe F. Khalil. (2008). "Youth, Media, and Culture in the Arab World," in *International Handbook of Children, Media and Culture,* ed. Sonia Livingstone and Kirsten Drotner. London: Sage, 330–44.

Kraidy, Marwan M., and Joe F. Khalil. (2009). *Arab Television Industries.* London: British Film Institute/Palgrave Macmillan.

Krakauer, Jon. (2009). *When Men Win Glory: The Odyssey of Pat Tillman.* Garden City, NY: Doubleday.

Krasnow, Erwin G., and Henry A. Solomon. (2008). "Communication Towers: Increased Demand Coupled with Increased Regulation," *Media Law & Policy* 18/1: 45–68.

Kroll, Jack. (1988). "The Lady Vanishes," *Newsweek* (March 7): 68.

Kross, Ethan, Philippe Verduyn, Emre Demiralp, Jiyoung Park, David Seungjae Lee, Natalie Lin, Holly Shablack, John Jonides, and Oscar Ybarra. (2013). "Facebook Use Predicts Declines in Subjective Well-Being in Young Adults," *PLoS ONE* 8/8. http://journals.plos.org/plosone/article?id=10.1371/journal.pone.0069841.

Kumar, Arun, and Nanda Kumar. (2010, October 25). "Government Seeks to Crush Strike of Foxconn Workers in India," *World Socialist Web Site.* http://www.wsws.org/en/articles/2010/10/foxc-o25.html.

Kumar, Satinder, and Sonika Chaudhary. (2013). "Indian Reality TV Shows: An Empirical Study on Perceptions," *Srusti Management Review* 6/1: 31–5.

Kumar, Shanti. (2005a). "Innovation, Imitation, and Hybridity in Indian Television," in *Thinking Outside the Box: A Contemporary Television Genre Reader,* ed. Gary R. Edgerton. Lexington: University of Kentucky Press, 314–35.

Kumar, Shanti. (2005b). *Gandhi Meets Primetime: Globalization and Nationalism in Indian Television.* Urbana: University of Illinois Press.

Kundnani, Arun. (2004). "Wired for War: Military Technology and the Politics of Fear," *Race & Class* 46/1: 116–25.

Kushner, David. (2007). "TV Enters the Blog World," *Rolling Stone* (September 20): 48.

Kusz, Kyle W. (2007). "From NASCAR Nation to Pat Tillman: Notes on Sport and the Politics of White Cultural Nationalism in Post-9/11 America," *Journal of Sport & Social Issues* 31/1: 77–88.

La Ferla, Ruth. (2005). "Mary-Kate, Fashion Star," *New York Times* (March 6). http://query.nytimes.com/gst/fullpage.html?res=9C06EFD81E3DF935A35750C0A9639C8B63.

Lakshman, Nandini. (2008). "Copyediting? Ship the Work Out to India," *Business Week* (July 8). http://www.businessweek.com/globalbiz/content/jul2008/gb2008078_678274.htm.

Lasén, Amparo. (2004). "Affective Technologies – Emotions and Mobile Phones," *Receiver* 11. http://www.receiver.vodafone.com/11/articles/index03.html.

Latour, Bruno. (1993). *We Have Never Been Modern*, trans. Catherine Porter. Cambridge, MA: Harvard University Press.

Latour, Bruno. (2004). *The Politics of Nature*, trans. Catherine Porter. Cambridge, MA: Harvard University Press.

Lauzen, Martha M. (2013). *The Celluloid Ceiling: Behind-the-Scenes Employment of Women in the Top 250 Films of 2012*. http://womenintvfilm.sdsu.edu/files/2011CelluloidCeilingExecSumm.pdf.

Lazarsfeld, Paul F. (1950). "Foreword," in *Hollywood Looks at its Audience*, Leo A. Handel. Urbana: University of Illinois Press, ix–xiv.

Lazonick, William, Mariana Mazzucato, and Öner Tulum. (2013). "Apple's Changing Business Model: What Should the World's Richest Company Do With All These Profits?" *Accounting Forum* 37/4: 249–67.

Lean, Geoffrey. (2008). "Mobile Phones 'More Dangerous Than Smoking'," *Independent* (March 30). http://independent.co.uk/life-style/health-and-wellbeing/health-news.

Leaños, John. (2005). "Intellectual Freedom and Pat Tillman," *Bad Subjects*. http://bad.eserver.org/reviews/2005/leanosstatement.html.

Le Bon, Gustav. (1899). *Psychologie des foules*. Paris: Alcan.

Le Borgne, Florence. (2014). "TV & Video Services: Can Anyone Compete Against American On-Demand Vendors?" *Digiworld* (October 16). http://blog.idate.fr/tv-video-services-can-anyone-compete-against-american-on-demand-vendors/?/lang-pref/en/.

Lee, Chin-Chuan. (1980). *Media Imperialism Reconsidered: The Homogenizing of Television Culture*. Beverly Hills: Sage.

Legislative Research Service, Library of Congress. (1964). *The US Ideological Effort: Government Agencies and Programs: Study Prepared for the Subcommittee on International Organizations and Movements of the Committee on Foreign Affairs*. Washington, DC: Legislative Research Service, Library of Congress.

Le Guay, Damien. (2002). *La Face cachée d'Halloween*. Paris: Editions du Cerf.

Le Guay, Damien. (2005). *L'Empire de la télé-réalité*. Paris: Presses de la Renaissance.

Lenhart, Amanda, Rich Ling, Scott Campbell, and Kristen Purcell. (2010). *Teens and Mobile Phones*. Pew Internet & American Life Project (April 20). http://pewinternet.org/Reports/2010/Teens-and-Mobile-Phones.aspx.

Lenoir, Timothy. (2003). "Programming Theaters of War: Gamemakers as Soldiers," in *Bombs and Bandwidth: The Emerging Relationship Between Information Technology and Security*, ed. Robert Latham. New York: New Press, 175–98.

Leong, Laurence Wei-Teng. (1992). "Cultural Resistance: The Cultural Terrorism of British Male Working-Class Youth," *Current Perspectives in Social Theory* 12: 29–58.

Lerner, Daniel. (1958). *The Passing of Traditional Society: Modernizing the Middle East*. New York: Free Press.

Leung, Anna O. W., Nurdan S. Duzgoren-Aydin, K. C. Cheung, and Ming H. Wong. (2008). "Heavy Metals Concentrations of Surface Dust from E-Waste Recycling and its Human Health Implications in Southeast China," *Environmental Science and Technology* 42/7: 2674–80.

Lewis, Bernard. (1990). "The Roots of Muslim Rage: Why so Many Muslims Deeply Resent the West, and Why Their Bitterness Will Not be so Easily Mollified," *Atlantic Monthly* (September): 47–58.

Lewis, Gerry. (2001). "Think Local When Going Global," *Variety* (February 26–March 4): 7.

Lewis, Justin. (1991). *The Ideological Octopus: An Exploration of Television and its Audience*. New York: Routledge.

Lewis, Justin. (2001). *Constructing Public Opinion: How Political Elites do What They Like and Why We Seem to Go Along with it*. New York: Columbia University Press.

Lewis, Justin. (2008). "Thinking by Numbers: Cultural Analysis and the Use of Data," in *The SAGE Handbook of Cultural Analysis*, ed. Tony Bennett and John Frow. London: Sage, 654–73.

Lewis, Justin, Terry Threadgold, Rod Brookes, Nick Mosdell, Kirsten Brander, Sadie Clifford, Ehab Bessaiso, and Zahera Harb. (2004). *Too Close for Comfort? The Role of Embedded Reporting During the 2003 Iraq War: Summary Report*. London: British Broadcasting Corporation.

Lightfoot, Liz. (2005). "Students Mark Down Media and Tourism Degrees," *Telegraph* (September 8). http://www.telegraph.co.uk/news/uknews/1497885/Students-mark-down-media-and-tourism-degrees.html.

Lindblom, Charles E. (1977). *Politics and Markets: The World's Political-Economic Systems*. New York: Basic Books.

Lindlaw, Scott. and Martha Mendoza. (2007). "General Suspected Cause of Tillman Death," *Washington Post* (August 4). http://www.washingtonpost.com/wp-dyn/content/article/2007/08/03/AR2007080301868.html.

Lipczynska, Sonya. (2007). "Website Review," *Journal of Mental Health* 16/4: 545–8.

Lithwick, Dahlia. (2008). "The Bauer of Suggestion," *Slate* (July 26). http://www.slate.com/articles/news_and_politics/jurisprudence/2008/07/the_bauer_of_suggestion.html.

Lockford, Lesa. (2008). "Investing in the Political Beyond," *Qualitative Inquiry* 14/1: 3–12.

Lodhia, Sharmila. (2015). "From 'Living Corpse' to India's Daughter: Exploring the Social, Political and Legal Landcsape of the 2012 Delhi Gang Rape," *Women's Studies International Forum* 50: 89–101.

Loechner, Jack. (2007). "Multi-Tasking Sports Fans See More Ads," *MediaPost* (September 5). http://www.mediapost.com/publications/article/66798/multi-tasking-sports-fans-see-more-ads.html.

Loechner, Jack. (2009). "Bi-lingual Hispanics Live with Ease in Both Worlds," *MediaPost* (February 16). http://www.mediapost.com/publications/?fa=Articles.showArticle&art_aid=100359.

Lorenzen, Mark. (2007). "Internationalization vs. Globalization of the Film Industry," *Industry and Innovation* 14/4: 349–57.

Lotz, Amanda D. (2008). *The Television Will Be Revolutionized*. New York: New York University Press.

Ma, Eric Kit-Wai. (1999). *Culture, Politics, and Television in Hong Kong*. London: Routledge.

Ma, Tiffany. (2009). "China and Congo's Coltan Connection," Project 2049 Institute. http://project2049.net/documents/china_and_congos_coltan_connection.pdf.

Macé, Eric. (2003). "*Loft Story*: un Big Brother à la française," *Médiamorphoses*. http://documents.irevues.inist.fr/bitstream/handle/2042/22461/2003_HS_127.pdf?sequence=1&isAllowed=y.

Macedonia, Mike. (2002). "Games, Simulation, and the Military Education Dilemma," in *The Internet and the University: 2001 Forum*. Boulder: Educause, 157–67.

Macherey, Pierre. (1977). "Culture and Politics: Interview with Pierre Macherey," trans. and ed. Colin Mercer and Jean Radford. *Red Letters* 5: 3–9.

Macherey, Pierre. (2007). "The Literary Thing," trans. Audrey Wasser. *diacritics* 37/4: 21–30.

Machlup, Fritz. (1962). *The Production and Distribution of Knowledge in the United States*. Princeton, NJ: Princeton University Press.

Madden, Mary, Amanda Lenhart, Sandra Cortesi, Urs Gasser, Maeve Duggan, Aaron Smith, and Meredith Beaton. (2013). *Teens, Social Media, and Privacy*. Pew Research Center and Berkman Center for Internet & Society at Harvard University. http://www.pewinternet.org/2013/05/21/teens-social-media-and-privacy/.

Maddox, David. (2009). "The Lady Vanishes," *Scotsman* (September 25): 14.

Madianou, Mirca. (2005). *Mediating the Nation: News, Audiences and the Politics of Identity*. London: UCL Press.

Magder, Ted. (2003). "Watching What We Say: Global Communication in a Time of Fear," in *War and the Media: Reporting Conflict 24/7*, ed. Daya Kishan Thussu and Des Freedman. London: Sage Publications, 28–44.

Maggio, Frank. (2008). "The Forest from the TVs," *MediaPost's TVBoard* (December 12). http://www.mediapost.com/publications/article/96609/the-forest-from-the-tvs.html#axzz2TfzrZtjv.

Maguire, Joseph. (1993). "Bodies, Sportscultures and Societies: A Critical Review of Some Theories in the Sociology of the Body," *International Review for the Sociology of Sport* 28/1: 33–52.

Mahapatra, Bidhubhusan, Niranjan Saggurti, Shiva S. Halli, and Anrudh K. Jain. (2012). "HIV Risk Behaviors Among Female Sex Workers Using Cell Phone for Client Solicitation in India," *Journal of AIDS and Clinical Research* S1: 14.

Mandel, Ernest. (1984). *Delightful Murder: A Social History of the Crime Story*. London: Pluto Press.

Manguel, Alberto. (1996). *A History of Reading*. New York: Viking.

Mankekar, Purnima. (1999). *Screening Culture, Viewing Politics: An Ethnography of Television, Womanhood, and Nation in Postcolonial India*. Durham, NC: Duke University Press.

Manyozo, Linje. (2006). "Manifesto for Development Communication: Nora Quebral and the Los Baños School of Development Communication," *Asian Journal of Communication* 16/1: 79–99.

Marconi, Guglielmo. (1924). "Foreword," in *The Story of Broadcasting*, A. R. Burrows. London: Cassell, vii.

Maria. (2012). "A Conversation with Men: Can You Relate?" *HerGameLife* (November 25). http://www.hergamelife.com/2012/11/a-conversation-with-men-can-you-relate/.

Markovits, Andrei S., and Emily Albertson. (2012). *Sportista: Female Fandom in the United States*. Philadelphia, PA: Temple University Press.

Marks, Shula, and Dagmar Engels, eds. (1994). *Contesting Colonial Hegemony: State and Society in Africa and India*. New York: IB Tauris.

Marr, David. (2005). "The Lady Vanishes," *Age* (June 23). http://www.theage.com.au/news/immigration/the-lady-vanishes/2005/06/22/1119321797895.html.

Marsh, Julia, and Reuven Fenton. (2015). "Olsen Twins Made Us Work 50-Hour Weeks Without Pay: Interns," *New York Post* (August 11). http://pagesix.com/2015/08/11/olsen-twins-made-us-work-50-hour-weeks-without-pay-interns/.

Martín-Barbero, Jesús. (2003). "Proyectos de modernidad en América Latina," *Metapolítica* 29: 35–51.

Martín-Barbero, Jésus, and Germán Rey. (1999). *Los ejercicios del ver: Hegemonía audiovisual y ficción televisiva*. Barcelona: Gedisa Editorial.

Martin, Randy. (2011). "Taking an Administrative Turn: Derivative Logics for a Recharged Humanities," *Representations* 116/1: 156–76.

Marvin, Carolyn. (1988). *When Old Technologies Were New: Thinking About Electronic Communication in the Late Nineteenth Century*. New York: Oxford University Press.

Marx, Karl. (1906). *Capital: A Critique of Political Economy*, trans. Samuel Moore and Edward Aveling, ed. Frederick Engels. New York: Modern Library.

Masmoudi, Mustapha. (1979). "The New World Information Order," *Journal of Communication* 29/2: 172–9.

Massardo, Jaime. (1999). "La recepción de Gramsci en America Latina: Cuestiones de orden teórico y político," *International Gramsci Society Newsletter* 9: electronic supplement 3. http://www.internationalgramscisociety.org/igsn/articles/a09_s3.shtml.

Mass-Observation. (1939). *Britain*. Harmondsworth: Penguin.

Mathijs, Ernest, and Janet Jones, eds. (2004). *Big Brother International: Formats, Critics and Publics*. London: Wallflower Press.

Matsuura, Koichiro. (2001). "La riqueza cultural del mundo reside en su diversidad dialogante," *Déclaración Universal de la UNESCO Sobre la Diversidad Cultural*. United Nations Educational, Scientific and Cultural Organization. http://unesdoc.unesco.org/images/0012/001271/127162s.pdf.

Mattelart, Armand. (1979). *Multinational Corporations and the Control of Culture*. Atlantic Highlands, NJ: Humanities Press.

Mattelart, Armand. (1980). *Mass Media, Ideologies and the Revolutionary Movement*, trans. Malcolm Coad. Atlantic Highlands: Humanities Press.

Mattelart, Armand. (1994). *Mapping World Communication: War, Progress, Culture.* Minneapolis: University of Minnesota Press.

Mattelart, Armand. (2003). *The information Society: An Introduction,* trans. Susan G. Taponier and James A. Cohen. London: Sage.

Mattelart, Armand, and Michèle Mattelart. (1998). *Theories of Communication: A Short Introduction,* trans. Susan G. Taponier and James A. Cohen. London: Sage.

Maxwell, Richard. (1991). "The Image is Gold: Value, the Audience Commodity, and Fetishism," *Journal of Film and Video* 43/1–2: 29–45.

Maxwell, Richard. (1996a). "Ethics and Identity in Global Market Research," *Cultural Studies* 10/2: 218–36.

Maxwell, Richard. (1996b). "Out of Kindness and into Difference: The Values of Global Market Research," *Media, Culture & Society* 18/1: 105–26.

Maxwell, Richard. (2000). "Picturing the Audience," *Television & New Media* 1/2: 135–57.

Maxwell, Richard, ed. (2001). *Culture Works.* Minneapolis: University of Minnesota Press.

Maxwell, Richard, and Toby Miller. (2012). *Greening the Media.* New York: Oxford University Press.

Maxwell, Richard, and Toby Miller. (2013). "Learning from Luddites: Media Labour, Technology and Life Below the Line," in *Theorising Cultural Work: Labour, Continuity and Change in the Cultural and Creative Industries,* ed. Mark Banks, Rosalind Gill, and Stephanie Taylor. London: Routledge, 113–21.

May, Harvey, and Greg Hearn. (2005). "The Mobile Phone as Media," *International Journal of Cultural Studies* 8/2: 195–211.

Mayer, Vicki, and Tanya Goldman. (2010). "Hollywood Handouts: Tax Credits in the Age of Economic Crisis," *Jump Cut* 52. http://www.ejumpcut.org/archive/jc52.2010/mayerTax/.

Mazer, Sharon. (1998). *Professional Wrestling: Sport and Spectacle.* Jackson: University Press of Mississippi.

Mazzarella, Sharon R. (2003). "Constructing Youth: Media, Youth, and the Politics of Representation," in *A Companion to Media Studies,* ed. Angharad N. Valdivia. Malden: Blackwell. 227–46.

Mazziotti, Nora. (1996). *La industria de la telenovela: La producción de ficción en América latina.* Buenos Aires: Paidós.

Mazumdar, Ranjani. (2015). "'Invisible Work' in the Indian Media Industries," *Media Industries Journal* 1/3. http://www.mediaindustriesjournal.org/index.php/mij/article/view/102/140.

Mazzucato, Mariana. (2015). *The Entrepreneurial State: Debunking Public vs. Private Sector Myths,* rev. edn. New York: Public Affairs.

Mbembe, Achille, Nsizwa Dlamini, and Grace Khunou. (2004). "Soweto Now," *Public Culture* 16/3: 499–506.

McAnany, Emile G., and Kenton T. Wilkinson, eds. (1996). *Mass Media and Free Trade: NAFTA and the Cultural Industries.* Austin: University of Texas Press.

McBride, Kelly. (2011). "Can a Sports Network Known for its Male Brand Serve the Female Fan?" *Poynter* (December 26). http://www.poynter.org/latest-news/top-stories/157096/can-a-sports-network-known-for-its-male-brand-serve-the-female-fan/.

McCain, John. (2004). "Courage and Honor: Remembering Pat Tillman," *National Review* (May 4). http://www.nationalreview.com/document/mccain200405041412.asp.

McCarthy, Anna. (1995). "'The Front Row is Reserved for Scotch Drinkers': Early Television's Tavern Audiences," *Cinema Journal* 34/4: 31–49.

McCarthy, John. (2014). "Shell Enlists Pele to Open Kinetic Energy Favella Football Field," *The Drum* (September 11). http://www.thedrum.com/news/2014/09/11/shell-enlists-pele-open-kinetic-energy-favella-football-field.

McChesney, Robert W. (2007). *Communication Revolution: Critical Junctures and the Future of Media.* New York: New Press.

McChesney, Robert W. (2013). *Digital Disconnect: How Capitalism Is Turning the Internet Against Democracy.* New York: New Press.

McClintock, Anne. (1995). *Imperial Leather: Race, Gender and Sexuality in the Colonial Context.* London: Routledge.

McClintock, Pamela. (2012). "Box Office Report: 'Men in Black 3' Becomes Highest-Grossing Title in Franchise," *Hollywood Reporter.* http://www.hollywoodreporter.com/news/box-office-report-men-black-mib3-will-smith-tommy-lee-jones-josh-brolin-sony-343957.

McCutcheon, Lynne E., Rense Lange, and James Houran. (2002). "Conceptualization and Measurement of Celebrity Worship," *British Journal of Psychology* 93/1: 67–87.

McDonald, Kevin M. (1999). "How Would You Like Your Television: With or Without Borders and With or Without Culture – A New Approach to Media Regulation in the European Union," *Fordham International Law Journal* 22: 1991–2023.

McElwee, Patrick. (2008). "A Million Iraqi Dead? The U.S. Press Buries the Evidence," *Extra!* (January/February). http://fair.org/extra-online-articles/a-million-iraqi-dead/.

McGuigan, Jim. (1996). *Culture and the Public Sphere.* London: Routledge.

McHoul, Alec, and Tom O'Regan. (1992). "Towards a Paralogics of Textual Technologies: Batman, Glasnost and Relativism in Cultural Studies," *Southern Review* 25/1: 5–26.

McHugh, Jack P., and James M. Hohman. (2008). "Legislators' Hollywood Dreams Defy Economic Reality," *Mackinac Center for Public Policy* (April 10). http://mackinac.org/article.aspx?ID=9367.

McInerny, Thomas K. (2013). Letter (August 29). http://apps.fcc.gov/ecfs/document/view?id=7520941318.

McKay, Jim, and Martin Roderick. (2010). "'Lay Down Sally': Media Narratives of Failure in Australian Sport," *Journal of Australian Studies* 34/3: 295–315.

McKercher, Catherine, and Vincent Mosco, eds. (2007). *Knowledge Workers in the Information Society.* Lanham, MD: Lexington.

McMahon, Jennifer L. (2008). "*24* and the Existential Man of Revolt," in *The Philosophy of TV Noir*, ed. Steven M. Sanders and Aeon J. Skoble. Lexington: University Press of Kentucky, 115–29.

McPhail, Thomas L. (2009). "Introduction to Development Communication," in *Development Communication: Reframing the Role of the Media*, ed. Thomas L. McPhail. Malden, MA: Wiley-Blackwell, 1–20.

McPherson, Tara. (2008). "'The End of TV As We Know It": Convergence Anxiety, Generic Innovation, and the Case of *24*," in *The Oxford Handbook of Film and Media Studies*, ed. Robert Kolker. New York: Oxford University Press, 306–26.

Meehan, Eileen R., and Ellen Riordan, eds. (2001). *Sex and Work: Feminism and Political Economy in the Media.* Minneapolis: University of Minnesota Press.

Mehta, Nalin. (2015). "India and its Television: Ownership, Democracy, and the Media Business," *Emerging Economy Studies* 1/1: 50–63.

Meinrath, Sacha D., and Victor Pickard. (2008). "Transcending Net Neutrality: Ten Steps Toward an Open Internet," *Journal of Internet Law* 12/6: 12–21.

Melville, Herman. (1850). "Hawthorne and His Mosses," *The Literary World* (August 17 and 24). http://www.eldritchpress.org/nh/hahm.html.

Mensch, Nancy L. (2006). "Codes, Lawsuits or International Law: How Should the Multinational Corporation be Regulated with Respect to Human Rights?" *University of Miami International & Comparative Law Review* 14/2: 243–69.

Mercado, Marty. (2008). "Why America Hates Soccer," *Football* (March 25). http://www.football.co.uk/football_features/story_306.shtml.

Mermigas, Diane. (2008). "Hulu CEO: More Global Moves Planned for '09," *Media PostNews Online Media Daily* (December 29). http://www.mediapost.com/publications/index.cfm?fa=Articles.showArticle&art_aid=97283.

Merritt, Russell. (1983). "Melodrama: Postmortem for a Phantom Genre," *Wide Angle* 5/3: 24–31.

Michael. (2015, March 30). "'Nigerian Politicians Remind me of Nollywood' – Wole Soyinka Gives His Opinion on 2015 Elections," *Stargist.* http://stargist.com/news/nigerian-politicians-remind-me-of-nollywood-wole-soyinka-gives-his-opinion-on-2015-elections/.

Michels, Robert. (1915). *Political Parties: A Sociological Study of the Oligarchical Tendencies of Modern Democracy*, trans. and ed., Cedar Paul. London: Jarrold & Sons.

Mickiewicz, Ellen. (1999). *Changing Channels: Television and the Struggle for Power in Russia*, rev. ed,. Durham, NC: Duke University Press.

Mihelj, Sabina. (2015). "Audience History as a History of Ideas: Towards a Transnational History," *European Journal of Communication* 30/1: 22–35.

Miklos, David. (2008). "El império en peligro," *La Tempestad* 59: 78–79.

Mikulan, Steven. (2009). "The Lady Vanishes: Rachel Uchitel Press Conference Canceled," *The Wrap* (December 3). http://www.thewrap.com/deal-central/column-post/lady-vanishes-rachel-uchi tel-press-conference-canceled-11162/.

Miladi, Noureddine. (2003). "Mapping the Al-Jazeera Phenomenon," in *War and the Media: Reporting Conflict 24/7*, ed. Daya Kishan Thussu and Des Freedman. London: Sage Publications, 149–60.

Miller, Jade L. (2011). "Producing Quality: A Social Network Analysis of Coproduction Relationships in High Grossing Versus Highly Lauded Films in the U.S. Market," *International Journal of Communication* 5: 1014–33.

Miller, J. D. B. (1981). *The World of States: Connected Essays*. London: Croom Helm.

Miller, J. D. B. (1984). "The Sovereign State and its Future," *International Journal* 39/2: 284–301.

Miller, Martin. (2007). "'24' and 'Lost' Get Symposium on Torture," *Seattle Times* (February 14). http://seattletimes.com/html/entertainment/2003570697_tvtorture14.html.

Miller, Toby. (1993). *The Well-Tempered Self: Citizenship, Culture, and the Postmodern Subject*. Baltimore, MD: The Johns Hopkins University Press.

Miller, Toby. (1997). *The Avengers*. London: British Film Institute.

Miller, Toby. (1998). *Technologies of Truth: Cultural Citizenship and the Popular Media*. Minneapolis: University of Minnesota Press.

Miller, Toby. (2001). *SportSex*. Philadelphia, PA: Temple University Press.

Miller, Toby. (2005). "Hollywood, Cultural Policy Citadel," in *Understanding Film: Marxist Perspectives*, ed. Mike Wayne. London: Pluto Press, 182–93.

Miller, Toby, ed. (2006). *A Companion to Cultural Studies*. Oxford: Blackwell.

Miller, Toby. (2007). *Cultural Citizenship: Cosmopolitanism, Consumerism, and Television in a Neoliberal Age*. Philadelphia: Temple University Press.

Miller, Toby. (2008). *Makeover Nation: The United States of Reinvention*. Columbus: Ohio State University Press.

Miller, Toby. (2009). "Media Effects and Cultural Studies: A Contentious Relationship," in *The Sage Handbook of Media Processes and Effects*, ed. Robin L. Nabi and Mary Beth Oliver. Thousand Oaks: Sage Publications, 131–43.

Miller, Toby. (2010a). *Television Studies: The Basics*. London: Routledge.

Miller, Toby. (2010b). "Culture + Labour = Precariat," *Communication and Critical/Cultural Studies* 7/1: 96–9.

Miller, Toby. (2012a). *Blow Up the Humanities*. Philadelphia, PA: Temple University Press.

Miller, Toby. (2012b). "Feminist Nudity? Video Consent? Moral Panic?" *Los Angeles Review of Books* (August 23). http://lareviewofbooks.org/essay/feminist-nudity-video-consent-moral-panic.

Miller, Toby. (2012c). "The Shameful Trinity: Game Studies, Empire, and the Cognitariat," in *Guns, Grenades, and Grunts: First-Person Shooter Games*, ed. Gerald A. Voorhees, Josh Call, and Katie Whitlock. New York: Continuum, 113–30.

Miller, Toby. (2013a). "Tracking Moral Panic as a Concept," in *The Ashgate Research Companion to Moral Panics*, ed. Charles Krinsky. Farnham: Ashgate, 37–54.

Miller, Toby. (2013b). "If English Becomes the Only Linguistic Currency, the Global Academy Will be Debased," *Times Higher Education* (March 7). https://www.timeshighereducation. co.uk/if-english-becomes-the-only-linguistic-currency-the-global-academy-will-be-debased-argues-toby-miller/2002381.article.

Miller, Toby. (2013c). "US Imperialism, Sport, and 'the Most Famous Soldier in the War'," in *A Companion to Sport*, ed. David L. Andrews and Ben Carrington. Malden, MA: Blackwell, 229–45.

Miller, Toby. (2014a). "Before, During, and After the Neoliberal Moment: Media, Sports, Policy, Citizenship," in *Sport, Public Broadcasting, and Cultural Citizenship: Signal Lost?*, ed. Jay Scherer and David Rowe. New York: Routledge, 30–47.

Miller, Toby. (2014b). "The Political Economy of Media Work and Watching," in *Media Sociology: A Reappraisal*, ed. Silvio Waisbord. Cambridge: Polity, 114–29.

Miller, Toby, Geoffrey Lawrence, Jim McKay, and David Rowe. (2001a). *Globalization and Sport: Playing the World*. London: Sage.

Miller, Toby, Nitin Govil, John McMurria, and Richard Maxwell. (2001b). *Global Hollywood*. London: British Film Institute.

Miller, Toby, Nitin Govil, John McMurria, Richard Maxwell, and Ting Wang. (2005). *Global Hollywood 2*. London: British Film Institute.

Mills, Mark P. (2013). *The Cloud Begins with Coal: Big Data, Big Networks, Big Infrastucture, and Big Power*. National Mining Association and American Coalition for Clean Coal Electricity. http://www.tech-pundit.com/wp-content/uploads/2013/07/Cloud_Begins_With_Coal.pdf?c761ac.

Minogue, Kenneth. (1994). "Philosophy," *Times Literary Supplement* (November 25): 27–8.

Mitra, Sreya. (2012). "'The Show of the Millennium': Screening the Big-Money Quiz Show and the Bollywood Superstar," *South Asian History and Culture* 3/4: 566–82.

Mitra, Subrata K. (2000). "The Discourse Vanishes: Revolution and Resilience in Indian Politics," *Contemporary South Asia* 9/3: 355–65.

Mobil Oil. (1978). "Business and Pluralism," *New York Times* (February 9): A21.

Moguillanksy, Marina. (2009). "Cine, política y Mercosur: Un balance de los comienzos de una política cinematográfica regional," *Políticas Culturais em Revista* 2/2: 137–54.

Mokhiber, Russell, and Robert Weissman. (2003). "Christian Fundamentalists to Produce Iraqi News," *AlterNet* (May 2). http://www.alternet.org/story.html?StoryID=15801.

Montague, Dena. (2002). "Stolen Goods: Coltan and Conflict in the Democratic Republic of Congo," *SAIS Review* 22/1: 103–18.

Mooallem, Jon. (2008). "The Afterlife of Cellphones," *New York Times* (January 13): 38–43.

Moor, Liz. (2007). "Sport and Commodification: A Reflection on Key Concepts," *Journal of Sport & Social Issues* 31/2: 128–42.

Moore, Malcolm. (2010a). "Apple Admits Using Child Labour," *Daily Telegraph* (February 27). http://www.telegraph.co.uk/technology/apple/7330986/Apple-admits-using-child-labour.html.

Moore, Malcolm. (2010b). "Four Suicide Attempts in a Month at Foxconn, the Makers of the iPad," *Daily Telegraph* (April 7). http://www.blogs.telegraph.co.uk/news/malcolmmoore/100033036/four-suicide-attempts-in-a-month-at-foxconn-the-makers-of-the-ipad.

Moorti, Sujata. (2004). "Fashioning a Cosmopolitan Tamil Identity: Game Shows, Commodities and Cultural Identity," *Media, Culture & Society* 26/4: 549–67.

Moran, Albert, with Justin Malbon. (2006). *Understanding the Global TV Format*. Bristol: Intellect.

Morawetz, Norbert, Jane Hardy, Colin Haslam, and Keith Randle. (2007). "Finance, Policy and Industrial Dynamics – The Rise of Co-Productions in the Film Industry," *Industry and Innovation* 14/4: 421–43.

Morin, Edgar. (1999). *Seven Complex Lessons in Education for the Future*, trans. Nidra Poller. Paris: United Nations Educational, Scientific and Cultural Organisation.

Morley, David. (2007). *Media, Modernity and Technology: The Geography of the New*. London: Routledge.

Morris, Ben. (2012). "Blockbuster Economics: So You Want to Make a Movie?" *BBC News* (May 8). http://www.bbc.co.uk/news/business-17812247.

Morris, Jeremy. (2007). "Drinking to the Nation: Russian Television Advertising and Cultural Differentiation," *Europe-Asia Studies* 59/8: 1387–403.

Morris, Meaghan. (1990). "The Banality of Cultural Studies," in *Logics of Television: Essays in Cultural Criticism*, ed. Patricia Mellencamp. Bloomington: Indiana University Press, 14–43.

Morris, Nancy. (2003). "A Comparative Analysis of the Diffusion and Participatory Models in Development Communication," *Communication Theory* 13/2: 225–48.

Morris, Nancy, and Silvio Waisbord, eds. (2001). *Media and Globalization: Why the State Matters*. Lanham, MD: Rowman & Littlefield.

Morrison, Grant. (1990). "Un Monde de miraculeuses métamorphoses," trans. David Fakrikian and Bruno Billion, in *Chapeau Melon et Bottes de Cuir*, ed. Alain Carrazé and Jean-Luc Putheaud. Paris: Huitième Art, 21–2.

Mosca, Gaetano. (1939). *The Ruling Class*, trans. Hannah D. Kahn, ed. Arthur Livingston. New York: McGraw-Hill.

Mosco, Vincent. (2004). *The Digital Sublime.* Cambridge, MA: MIT Press.

Mosco, Vincent. (2014). *To the Cloud: Big Data in a Turbulent World.* Boulder, CO: Paradigm Publishers.

Mosco, Vincent and Dan Schiller, eds. (2001). *Continental Order? Integrating North America for Cybercapitalism.* Lanham, MD: Rowman and Littlefield.

Mosco, Vincent, and Catherine McKercher. (2008). *The Laboring of Communication: Will Knowledge Workers of the World Unite?* Lanham, MD: Lexington.

Mosco, Vincent, Catherine McKercher, and Ursula Huws, eds. (2010). *Getting the Message: Communications Workers and Global Value Chains.* London: Merlin Books.

Motion Picture Association of America. (2014). *Theatrical Market Statistics 2014.* http://www.mpaa.org/wp-content/uploads/2015/03/MPAA-Theatrical-Market-Statistics-2014.pdf.

Mouawad, Jad, and Kate Galbraith. (2009). "Plugged in Age Feeds Hunger for Electricity," *New York Times* (September 20): A1.

Mowlana, Hamid. (2000). "The Renewal of the Global Media Debate: Implications for the Relationship Between the West and the Islamic World," *Islam and the West in the Mass Media: Fragmented Images in a Globalizing World*, ed. Kai Hafez. Cresskill, NJ: Hampton Press. 105–18.

Moynihan, Ray, Iona Heath, and David Henry. (2002). "Selling Sickness: The Pharmaceutical Industry and Disease Mongering," *British Medical Journal* 324: 886.

Mukherjee, Avinandan, and Rahul Roy. (2006). "A System Dynamic Model of Management of a Televisión Show," *Journal of Modelling in Management* 1/2: 95–115.

Murdock, Graham. (2005). "Continental Shifts: Capitalism, Communications and Change in Europe," Comunicação e Sociedade 7: 11–23.

Murdock, Graham. (2014). "Digital Domesday: Saturation Surveillance and the New Serfdom," *Medianz* 14/2 https://medianz.otago.ac.nz/medianz/article/view/120.

Murphy, Patrick D., and Marwan M. Kraidy. (2003). *Global Media Studies: Ethnographic Perspectives.* London: Routledge.

Murray, Catherine, and Mirjam Gollmitzer. (2011). "Escaping the Precarity Trap: A Call for Creative Labour Policy," *International Journal of Cultural Policy* 18/4: 419–38.

Musso, Pierre. (2009). *Télé-Politique: le sarkoberlusconisme a l'écran.* Paris: Editions de l'Aube.

Naficy, Hamid. (1993). *The Making of Exile Cultures: Iranian Television in Los Angeles.* Minneapolis: University of Minnesota Press.

Nao. (2014). "The Poetry and Brief Life of a Foxconn Worker: Xu Lizhi (1990–2014)," *LibCom* (October 29). http://libcom.org/blog/xulizhi-foxconn-suicide-poetry.

Nasar, Jack L., and Derek Troyer. (2013). "Pedestrian Injuries Due to Mobile Phone Use in Public Places," *Accident Analysis & Prevention* 57: 91–5.

National Association of Hispanic Journalists. (2006). *Network Brownout Report: The Portrayal of Latinos and Latino Issues on Network Television News, 2005.* http://www.nahj.org/2006/10/network-brownout-reports.

Negri, Antonio. (2007). *Goodbye Mister Socialism.* Paris: Seuil.

Negrine, Ralph, and Stylianos Papathanassopoulos. (1990). *The Internationalization of Television.* London: Pinter.

Nelson, Kelly. (2002). "The Erotic Gaze and Sports: An Ethnographic Consideration," *Journal of Sport History* 29/3: 407–12.

Newcomb, Horace. (1996). "Other People's Fictions: Cultural Appropriation, Cultural Integrity, and International Media Strategies," in *Mass Media and Free Trade: NAFTA and the Cultural Industries*, ed. Emile McAnany and Kenton Wilkinson. Austin: University of Texas Press, 92–109.

Newsome, Bruce, and Matthew B. Lewis. (2011). "Rewarding the Cowboy, Punishing the Sniper: The Training Efficacy of Computer-Based Urban Combat Training Environments," *Defence Studies* 11/1: 120–44.

Nieborg, David B. (2004). "America's Army: More Than a Game," in *Transforming Knowledge into*

Action Through Gaming and Simulation, ed. Thomas Eberle and Willy Christian Kriz. Munich: SAGSAGA. CD-ROM.

NielsenWire. (2011). *Cellphones and Global Youth: Mobile Internet and Messaging Trends* (January 11). http://www.nielsen.com/us/en/insights/news/2011/cellphones-and-global-youth-mobile-internet-and-messaging-trends.html.

Norris, Pippa, and Ronald Inglehart. (2003). "Public Opinion Among Muslims and the West," in *Framing Terrorism: The News Media, the Government, and the Public*, ed. Pippa Norris, Montague Kern, and Marion Just. New York: Routledge, 203–28.

Northdurft, John. (2008). "Film Tax Credits: Do They Work?" *Heartland Institute* (November 21). http://heartland.org/policy-documents/film-tax-credits-do-they.work.

Nudd, Tim. (2013). "Ad of the Day: Chipotle Makes Magic Yet Again with Fiona Apple and a Dark Animated Film," *AdWeek* (September 12). http://www.adweek.com/news/advertising-branding/ad-day-chipotle-makes-magic-again-fiona-apple-and-dark-animated-film-152380.

Nudd, Tim. (2014). "Even if You Hate Greenpeace and Love Lego, You Have to Admire This Gorgeous Attack Ad," *Adweek* (July 9). http://www.adweek.com/adfreak/even-if-you-hate-greenpeace-and-love-lego-you-have-admire-gorgeous-attack-ad-158809.

Nye, Joseph S., Jr. (2002–3). "Limits of American Power," *Political Science Quarterly* 117/4: 545–59.

Ó Siochrú, Seán, and Bruce Girard, with Amy Mahan. (2002). *Global Media Governance: A Beginner's Guide*. Lanham, MD: Rowman & Littlefield.

Oates, Thomas P. (2012). "Representing the Audience: The Gendered Politics of Sport Media," *Feminist Media Studies* 12/4: 603–7.

Ofcom. (2007). *Public Service Broadcasting: Annual Report 2007*. http://stakeholders.ofcom.org.uk/broadcasting/reviews-investigations/public-service-broadcasting/annrep/psb07/.

Office for National Statistics. (2013). *Full Report – Graduates in the UK Labour Market. 2013* http://www.ons.gov.uk/ons/dcp171776_337841.pdf.

Ofqal. (2014). *Completing GCSE, AS and A Level Reform*. http://webarchive.nationalarchives.gov.uk/20141031163546/http://www.ofqual.gov.uk/news/gcse-level-reform-consultation/.

Ogan, Christine L., Manaf Bashir, Lindita Camaj, Yunjuan Luo, Brian Gaddie, Rosemary Pennington, Sonia Rana, and Mohammed Salih. (2009). "Development Communication: The State of Research in an Era of ICTs and Globalization," *Gazette* 71/8: 655–70.

Olsen, Mary-Kate. (2007). "Timeless: Brand Loyalty," *New York Times* (February 25). http://www.nytimes.com/2007/02/25/style/tmagazine/25ttimeless.html?WT.mc_id=E-MASHABLE-FAMOUSNYTBYLINES-OS-0814&WT.mc_ev=click&bicmp=AD&bicmlukp=WT.mc_id&bicmst=1408720476000&bicmet=1420038876000.

Open Society Institute EU Monitoring and Advocacy Program, Network Media Program. (2005). *Television Across Europe: Regulation, Policy and Independence*. Budapest: Open Society Institute.

Openwave. (2009). *Privacy Primer: Protecting the Consumer in an Era of Behavioral Marketing*. Redwood City, CA: Openwave.

Organisation for Economic Co-operation and Development. (2007). *Extended Producer Responsibility*. Paris: OECD.

Organisation for Economic Co-operation and Development. (2008). *Remaking the Movies: Digital Content and the Evolution of the Film and Video Industries*. Geneva: OECD.

Organisation for Economic Co-operation and Development. (2010). *Greener and Smarter: ICTs, the Environment and Climate Change*. Paris: OECD.

Orwell, George. (1944). "As I Please," *Tribune* (May 12). http://www.telelib.com/authors/O/OrwellGeorge/essay/tribune/AsIPlease19440512.html.

Orwell, George. (1949). *Nineteen Eighty-Four*. London: Secker & Warburg.

Osei-Hwere, Enyonam, and Norma Pecora. (2008). "Children's Media in Sub-Saharan Africa," in *African Media, African Children*, ed. Norma Pecora, Enyonam Osei-Hwere, and Ulla Carlsson. Gothenburg: NORDICOM, 15–27.

Ott, Brian L. (2007). *The Small Screen: How Television Equips Us to Live in the Information Age*. Malden: Blackwell.

Ouellette, Laurie. (2004). "Take Responsibility for Yourself: Judge Judy and the Neoliberal Citizen," in *Reality TV: Remaking Television Culture*, ed. Sue Murray and Laurie Ouellette. New York: New York University Press, 231–50.

Pahwa, Sonali, and Jessica Winegar. (2012). "Culture, State and Revolution," *Middle East Report* 42: 263.

Pardo, Alejandro. (2010). "The Film Producer as a Creative Force," *Wide Angle* 2/2: 1–23.

Parekh, Bhikhu. (2000). *Rethinking Multiculturalism: Cultural Diversity and Political Theory.* Basingstoke: Palgrave.

Pareto, Vilfredo. (1976). *Sociological Writings,* trans. Derick Mirfin, ed. Samuel E. Finer. Oxford: Basil Blackwell.

Park, Sang-Chul. (1997). "The Transformation of the South Korean Economy and International Economic Development in East and Southeast Asia," *International Planning Studies* 2/2: 241–55.

Parker, George, and Vanessa Houlder. (2013). "EU–US Trade Talks Launched Amid French Fury with Brussels," *Financial Times* (June 17). http://www.ft.com/cms/s/0/a785d93c-d73d-11e2-8279-00144feab7de.html#axzz2WPekxdVb.

Parkin, Frank. (1971). *Class Inequality and Political Order.* London: MacGibbon & Kee.

Paschalidou, Nina Maria. (2014). "Kismet: How Soap Operas Changed the World," *Al Jazeera* (January 15). http://www.aljazeera.com/programmes/witness/2013/11/kismet-how-soap-ope ras-changed-world-20131117152457476872.html.

Patnaik, Arun Kumar. (2004). "Gramsci Today," *Economic & Political Weekly* (March 13–19): 1120–3.

Paton, Graeme. (2007). "Media Studies Wastes Good Brains, Says Sugar," *Telegraph* (May 7). http://www.telegraph.co.uk/news/uknews/1550580/Media-studies-wastes-good-brains-says-Sugar.html.

Paton, Graeme. (2014). "Ofqal: Dozens of 'Soft' GCSEs and A-levels to be Axed," *Telegraph* (June 4). http://www.telegraph.co.uk/education/educationnews/10873368/Ofqual-dozens-of-soft-GCSEs-and-A-levels-to-be-axed.html.

Pattenden, Miles. (2008). "The Canonisation of Clare of Assisi and Early Franciscan History," *Journal of Ecclesiastical History* 59/2: 208–26.

Pauwels, Caroline, and Jan Loisen. (2003). "The WTO and the Audiovisual Sector: Economic Free Trade vs Cultural Horse Trading?" *European Journal of Communication* 18/3: 291–313.

Perretti, Fabrizio, and Giacomo Negro. (2007). "Mixing Genres and Matching People: A Study in Innovation and Team Composition in Hollywood," *Journal of Organizational Behavior* 28/5: 563–86.

Pew Research Center. (2004). *Trouble Behind, Trouble Ahead? A Year of Contention at Home and Abroad. 2003 Year-End Report.* Washington: Pew Research Center.

Pew Research Center. (2011). *Americans and Text Messaging* (September 19). http://pewresearch.org/databank/dailynumber/?NumberID=1324

Pew Research Center. (2012). *High Marks for NBC's Coverage: Eight-in-Ten Following Olympics on TV or Digitally* (August 6). http://www.people-press.org/2012/08/06/eight-in-ten-following-olympics-on-tv-or-digitally/.

Phalen, Patricia, and Julia Osellame. (2012). "Writing Hollywood: Rooms with a Point of View," *Journal of Broadcasting & Electronic Media* 56/1: 3–20.

Pilger, John. (2003). "We See Too Much. We Know Too Much. That's Our Best Defense," *Dissident Voice* (April 6). http://www.dissidentvoice.org/Articles3/Pilger_Iraq.htm.

Pink Sauce. (2012). "¿Es Elianis Garrido transsexual? Aquí la respuesta," *La Fiscalia* (June 28). http://www.lafiscalia.com/2012/06/28/es-elianis-garrido-transexual-aqui-la-respuesta/.

Piñón, Juan. (2011). "Estados Unidos: Crecimiento, reestructura y diversificación de la televisión hispana," in *OBITEL 2011: Calidad de la ficción televisiva y participación transmediática de las audiencias,* ed. Guillermo Orozco and I. Vasallo. Rio de Janeiro: Globo Universidade, 354–73.

Piore, Michael J., and Charles F. Sabel. (1984). *The Second Industrial Divide: Possibilities for Prosperity.* New York: BasicBooks.

Pius XII. (1958). "La Lettre Apostolique," *Acta Apostolica Sedis* 50 (August 21): 512–13.

Plumb, J. H. (1964). "Introduction," in *Crisis in the Humanities,* ed. J. H. Plumb. Harmondsworth: Penguin, 7–10.

Plutarch. (1976). *The Rise and Fall of Athens: Nine Greek Lives by Plutarch*, trans. Ian Scott-Kilvert. Harmondsworth: Penguin.

Poirier, Agnès Catherine. (2007). "Cécilia Sarkozy: The Lady Vanishes," *Independent on Sunday* (June 24). http://www.independent.co.uk/news/europe/article2695281.ece.

Polansky, Jonathan, and Stanton A. Glantz. (2009). *Taxpayer Subsidies for US Films with Tobacco Imagery*. San Francisco, CA: Center for Tobacco Control Research and Education.

Pope, Stacey. (2011). "'Like Pulling Down Durham Cathedral and Building a Brothel': Women as 'New Consumer' Fans?" *International Review for the Sociology of Sport* 46/4: 471–87.

Portella, Eduardo. (2000). "Cultural Cloning or Hybrid Cultures?" *UNESCO Courier* (April): 9.

Porter, Bernard. (1989). *Plots and Paranoia: A History of Political Espionage in Britain 1790-1988*. London: Unwin Hyman.

Postrel, Virginia. (1999,). "The Pleasures of Persuasion," *Wall Street Journal* (August 2): A18.

Potts, Jason, John Hartley, John Banks, Jean Burgess, Rachel Cobcroft, Stuart Cunningham, and Lucy Montgomery. (2008). "Consumer Co-Creation and Situated Creativity," *Industry & Innovation* 15/5: 459–74.

Pourlis, Aris F. (2009). "Reproductive and Developmental Effects of EMF in Vertebrate Animal Models," *Pathophysiology* 16/2-3: 179–89.

Powdermaker, Hortense. (1950). *Hollywood: The Dream Factory: An Anthropologist Looks at the Movie-Makers*. Boston, MA: Little, Brown and Company.

Power, Marcus. (2007). "Digitized Virtuosity: Video War Games and Post-9/11 Cyber-Deterrence," *Security Dialogue* 38/2: 271–88.

Poynton, Beverley, and John Hartley. (1990). "Male-Gazing: Australian Rules Football, Gender and Television," in *Television and Women's Culture: The Politics of the Popular*, ed. Mary Ellen Brown. Sydney: Currency Press. 144–57.

Prahalad, Coimbatore Krishnarao, and Stuart L. Hart. (2008). "The Fortune at the Bottom of the Pyramid," *Revista Electrônica de Estratégia & Negócios*. 1/2 http://portaldeperiodicos.unisul.br/index.php/EeN/article/viewArticle/39.

Prebisch, Raúl. (1982). *The Crisis of Capitalism and the Periphery: 1st Raúl Prebisch Lecture*. Geneva: United Nations Conference on Trade and Development.

Price, Monroe E. (2008, March). "A Charter of Contradictions," *Arab Media and Society*. http://www.arabmediasociety.com/?article=650.

Price, Monroe E. (2009). "Media Transitions in the Rear-View Mirror: Some Reflections," *International Journal of Politics, Culture and Society* 22/4: 485–96.

PriceWaterhouse. (2015). *Engaging with the Super-Fan: A Growing Source of Incremental Revenue*. http://www.pwc.com/gx/en/global-entertainment-media-outlook/assets/superfan.pdf.

Primo, Alex Fernando Teixeira. (1999). "The Paradoxical Brazilian Views Concerning American Media Products. *Images of the U.S. Around the World: A Multilateral Perspective*," ed. Yahya R. Kamalipour. Albany: State University of New York Press, 179–95.

Prno, Jason, and D. Scott Slocombe. (2012). "Exploring the Origins of 'Social License to Operate' in the Mining Sector: Perspectives from Governance and Sustainability Theories," *Resources Policy* 37/3: 346–57.

Probyn, Elspeth. (2008). "Troubling Safe Choices: Girls, Friendship, Constraint, and Freedom," *South Atlantic Quarterly* 107/2: 231–49.

Project for Excellence in Journalism. (2008). *The Media's Olympics* (August 22). http://www.journalism.org/node/12484/feed.

Protzel, Javier. (2005). "Changing Political Cultures and Media Under Globalism in Latin America," in *Democratizing Global Media: One World, Many Struggles*, ed. Robert A. Hackett and Yuezhi Zhao. Lanham, MD: Rowman & Littlefield, 101–20.

Pufendorf, Samuel. (2000). *On the Duty of Man and Citizen According to Natural Law*, trans. Michael Silverthorne, ed. James Tully. Cambridge: Cambridge University Press.

Punathambekar, Aswin. (2010). "Reality TV and Participatory Culture in India," *Popular Communication* 8/4: 241–55.

Puppis, Manuel. (2010). "Media Governance: A New Concept for the Analysis of Media Policy and Regulation," *Communication, Culture and Critique* 3/2: 134–49.

Puri, Jyoti. (2004). *Encountering Nationalism*. Malden, MA: Blackwell.

Pye, Lucien W., and Sidney Verba, eds. (1965). *Political Culture and Political Development*. Princeton, NJ Princeton University Press.

Quinn, Erin, and Chris Young. (2015). "DC Influencers Spend More in Advertising and PR Than Lobbying," *Time* (January 15). http://time.com/3668128/lobbying-advertising-public-relations/.

Qiu, Jack Linchuan. (2007). "Mobile Messaging Service as a Means of Control," *International Journal of Communication* 1: 74–91.

Raboy, Marc, and Cinzia Padovani. (2010). "Mapping Global Media Policy: Concepts, Frameworks, Methods," *Communication, Culture and Critique* 3/2: 150–69.

Raboy, Marc. (2007). "Global Media Policy – Defining the Field," *Global Media and Communication* 3/3: 343–61.

Radway, Janice. (1991). *Reading the Romance*. Chapel Hill: University of North Carolina Press.

Rajagopal, Arvind. (2001). *Politics After Television: Religious Nationalism and the Reshaping of the Indian Public*. New York: Cambridge University Press.

Rajagopal, Arvind. (2015). "The Reinvention of Hindutva," *The Hindu* (March 4). http://www.the-hindu.com/opinion/op-ed/the-reinvention-of-hindutva/article6955945.ece.

Rantanen, Terhi. (2002). *The Global and the National: Media and Communications in Post-Communist Russia*. Lanham, MD: Rowman & Littlefield.

Rasmussen, Terje. (2007). *Techno-Politics, Internet Governance and Some Challenges Facing the Internet*. Research Report 15 Oxford Internet Institute. www.oii.ox.ac.uk/research/publications/RR15.pdf.

Rasul, Azmat, and Jennifer M. Proffitt. (2012). "An Irresistible Market: A Critical Analysis of Hollywood-Bollywood Coproductions," *Communication, Culture & Critique* 5/4: 563–83.

Rawnsley, Andrew. (1999). "The Lady Vanishes," *Guardian* (April 25). http://www.theguardian.com/politics/1999/apr/25/thatcher.uk2.

Ray, Manas Ranjan, Gopeshwar Mukherjee, Sanghita Roychowdhury, and Twisha Lahiri. (2004). "Respiratory and General Health Impairments of Ragpickers in India: A Study in Delhi," *International Archives of Occupational and Environmental Health* 77/8: 595–8.

Reagan, Ronald. (1966). "The Creative Society" (April 19). http://www.freerepublic.com/focus/news/742041/posts.

Rendall, Steve, and Daniel Butterworth. (2004) "How Public is Public Radio?" *EXTRA!* (May/June): 16–19.

Reynolds, Mike. (2008). "Nielsen Log: Football, Holiday Fare Rule," *Multichannel News* (December 24). http://www.multichannel.com/article/161295-Nielsen_Log_Football_Holiday_Fare_Rule.php.

Ribeiro, John. (2010). "Foxconn Workers Exploited in India, Activists Say," *Computerworld* (October 27). http://www.computerworld.com/article/2513753/it-careers/foxconn-workers-exploited-in-india--activists-say.html.

Rydh, Carl Johan. (2003). *Environmental Assessment of Battery Systems: Critical Issues for Established and Emerging Technologies*. PhD, Department of Environmental Systems Analysis, Chalmers University of Technology. Göteborg.

Rich, Vera. (2003). "The Price of Return," *Index on Censorship* 32/3: 82–6.

Richardson, Damone, and Maria C. Figueroa. (2005). *Basic Cable Television Industry Research and Corporate Profiles*. Industrial & Labor Relations, Cornell University for the Writers Guild of America, East.

Riggs, Karen E. (1998). *Mature Audiences: Television in the Lives of Elders*. New Brunswick, NJ: Rutgers University Press.

Rincón & Associates. (2004). *Latino Television Study*. National Latino Media Coalition. http://www.rinconassoc.com/nbc4nielsen.pdf.

Ritman, Alex. (2015). "Aaron Sorkin Rips Apple's Tim Cook Over 'Steve Jobs' Critique: "You've Got a Lot of Nerve"," *Hollywood Reporter* (September 25). http://www.hollywoodreporter.com/news/aaron-sorkin-tim-cook-youve-827284.

Ritzer, George, and Nathan Jurgenson. (2010). "Production, Consumption, Prosumption: The Nature of Capitalism in the Age of the Digital 'Prosumer'," *Journal of Consumer Culture* 10/1: 13–36.

Rizkallah, Elias G., and Nabil Y. Razzouk. (2006). "TV Viewing Motivations of Arab American Households in the US: An Empirical Perspective," *International Business & Economics Research Journal* 5/1: 65–74.

Robb, David L. (2004). *Operation Hollywood: How the Pentagon Shapes and Censors the Movies.* Amherst, MA: Prometheus Books.

Roberts, Donald F., Ulla G. Foehr, and Victoria Rideout. (2005). *Generation M: Media in the Lives of 8–18-Year Olds.* Kaiser Family Foundation. https://kaiserfamilyfoundation.files.wordpress.com/2013/01/generation-m-media-in-the-lives-of-8-18-year-olds-report.pdf.

Roberts, Les, Riyadh Lafta, Richard Garfield, Jamal Khuhairi, and Gilbert Burnham. (2004). "Mortality Before and After the 2003 Invasion of Iraq: Cluster Sample Survey," *The Lancet* 364: 1857–64.

Robertson, Roland. (1992). *Globalization.* London: Sage.

Rogers, Everett. (1976). "Communication and Development: The Passing of the Dominant Paradigm," *Communication Research* 3/2: 121–33.

Rohde, David. (2012). "Why Turkey's Prime Minister Can't Stand His Country's Top Soap Opera," *The Atlantic* (December 14). http://www.theatlantic.com/international/archive/2012/12/why-turkeys-prime-minister-cant-stand-his-countrys-top-soap-opera/266274/.

Rollins Saas, Darcy. (2006). "Hollywood East? Film Tax Credits in New England," Policy Brief 06-3. *New England Public Policy Center* (October). http://www.bostonfed.org/economic/neppc/briefs/2006/briefs063.pdf.

Romero, Juan Moreno. (2012). "Serie de Pablo Escobar es éxito en Twitter y Telemundo," *VOA Noticias* (August 10). http://www.voanoticias.com/content/pablo-escobar-telemundo-caracol-serie-telenovela-controversia/1476384.html.

Romundstad, Pål, Aage Andersen, and Tor Haldorsen. (2001). "Cancer Incidence Among Workers in the Norwegian Silicon Carbide Industry," *American Journal of Epidemiology* 153/10: 978–86.

Rose, Marla Matzer. (2001). "Television Industry Profile," *Business.com.*

Rosen, Christopher. (2015). "John Stamos is 'Heartbroken' the Olsen Twins Won't be on 'Fuller House'," *Entertainment Weekly* (May 23). http://www.ew.com/article/2015/05/23/john-stamos-olsen-twins-fuller-house-heartbroken.

Rosenau, James N. (1992). "Governance, Order and Change in World Politics," in *Governance Without Government: Order and Change in World Politics*, ed. James N. Rosenau and Ernst-Otto Czempiel. New York: Cambridge University Press, 1–29.

Ross, Andrew. (2009). *Nice Work if You Can Get It: Life and Labor in Precarious Times.* New York: New York University Press.

Rothkopf, David. (1997). "In Praise of Cultural Imperialism," *Foreign Policy* 107: 38–53.

Rowlatt, Justin. (2009). "Justin Does Dallas!" *BBC News* (March 6). http://www.bbc.co.uk/blogs/ethicalman/2009/03/justin_does_dallas.html.

Roy, Arundhati. (2004). "Do Turkeys Enjoy Thanksgiving?" *OutlookIndia* (January 24). http://www.outlookindia.com/article/Do-Turkeys-Enjoy-Thanksgiving/222711.

Ruccio, David F., and Jack Amariglio. (2003). *Postmodern Moments in Modern Economics.* Princeton, NJ: Princeton University Press.

Rusciano, Frank. (2003). "Framing World Opinion in the Elite Press," in *Framing Terrorism: The News Media, the Government, and the Public*, ed. Pippa Norris, Montague Kern, and Marion Just. New York: Routledge, 159–79.

Sabry, Tarik. (2010). *Cultural Encounters in the Arab World: On Media, the Modern and the Everyday.* London: IB Tauris.

Sachs, Jeffrey. (2008). "The Digital War on Poverty," *Guardian* (August 21). http://www.theguardian.com/commentisfree/2008/aug/21/digitalmedia.mobilephone.

Sadetzki, Siegal, Angela Chetrit, Avital Jarus-Hakak, Elisabeth Cardis, Yonit Deutch, Shay Duvdevani, . . . and Michael Wolf. (2007). "Cellular Phone Use and Risk of Benign and Malignant Parotid Gland Tumors – A Nationwide Case-Control Study," *American Journal of Epidemiology* 167/4: 457–67.

Said, Edward. (1993). "An Interview with Edward Said," *boundary 2* 20/1: 1–25.

Said, Edward. (2001). "We All Swim Together," *New Statesman* (October 15): 20.

Said, Edward. (2003). "The Other America," *Al-Ahram* (March 20-6). http://weekly.ahram.org.eg/2003/630/focus.htm.

Sakr, Naomi, ed. (2004). *Women and Media in the Middle East: Power Through Self-Expression*. London: IB Tauris.

Salamandra, Christa. (2012). "The Muhannad Effect: Media Panic, Melodrama and the Arab Female Gaze," *Anthropological Quarterly* 85/1: 45-77.

Salwen, Michael B. (1991). "Cultural Imperialism: A Media Effects Approach," *Critical Studies in Mass Communication* 8/1: 29-38.

Sammond, Nicholas, ed. (2005). *Steel Chair to the Heap: The Pleasure and Pain of Professional Wrestling*. Durham, NC: Duke University Press.

Sarikakis, Katharine, and Sarah Ganter. (2014). "Priorities in Global Media Policy Transfer: Audiovisual and Digital Policy Mutations in the EU, MERCOSUR and US Triangle," *European Journal of Communication* 29/1: 17-33.

Sarnoff, David. (2004). "Our Next Frontier . . . Transoceanic TV," in *Mass Communication and American Social Thought: Key Texts, 1919-1968*, ed. John Durham Peters and Peter Simonson. Lanham, MD: Rowman & Littlefield. 309-10.

Saucedo Añez, Patricia Carolina. (2015). "Why Some Latin Americans Are Naming Their Children 'Onur' and 'Sherezade'," trans. Dominic Fernandez. *Public Radio International* (May 25). http://www.pri.org/stories/2015-05-25/why-some-latin-americans-are-naming-their-children-onur-and-sherezade.

Scannell, Paddy. (1996). *Radio, Television and Modern Life*. London: Blackwell.

Schäfer, Mike S. (2012). "Online Communication on Climate Change and Climate Politics: A Literature Review," *Wiley Interdisciplinary Reviews: Climate Change* 3/6: 527-43.

Schelling, Felix E. (1914). "New Humanities for Old," *Classical Weekly* 7/23: 179-84.

Schiller, Dan. (2007). *How to Think About Information*. Champaign: University of Illinois Press.

Schiller, Herbert I. (1971). *Mass Communication and American Empire*. New York: Beacon Press.

Schiller, Herbert I. (1974). "Freedom From the 'Free Flow'," *Journal of Communication* 24/1: 110-17.

Schiller, Herbert I. (1976). *Communication and Cultural Domination*. New York: International Arts and Sciences Press.

Schiller, Herbert I. (1989). *Culture Inc.: The Corporate Takeover of Public Expression*. Oxford: Oxford University Press.

Schiller, Herbert I. (1991a). "Not Yet the Post-Imperialist Era," *Critical Studies in Mass Communication* 8/1: 13-28.

Schiller, Herbert I. (1991b). "Corporate Sponsorship: Institutionalized Censorship of the Cultural Realm," *Art Journal* 50/3: 56-9.

Schiller, Herbert I. (1992/1969). *Mass Communications and American Empire*, 2nd edn. Boulder, CO: Westview Press.

Schimmel, Kimberly S., C. Lee Harrington, and Denise D. Bielby. (2007). "Keep Your Fans to Yourself: The Disjuncture between Sport Studies' and Pop Culture Studies' Perspectives on Fandom," *Sport in Society* 10/4: 580-600.

Schlesinger, Philip. (1991). *Media, State and Nation: Political Violence and Collective Identities*. London: Sage.

Schlichting, Inga. (2013). "Strategic Framing of Climate Change by Industry Actors: A Meta-Analysis," *Environmental Communication* 7/4: 493-511.

Schmitt, Eric. (2005). "New U.S. Commander Sees Shift in Military Role in Iraq," *New York Times* (January 16): 10.

Schoenfeld, Amy. (2007). "Everyday Items, Complex Chemistry," *New York Times* (December 22): C9.

Schramm, Wilbur. (1964). *Mass Media and National Development: The Role of Information in the Developing World*. Palo Alto, CA: Stanford University Press.

Schramm, Wilbur, Jack Lyle, and Edwin B. Parker. (1961). *Television in the Lives of Our Children*. Stanford, CA: Stanford University Press.

Schreiber, Katherine. (2012). "Why Don't We Watch More Women's Sports?" *Greatist* (August 2). http://greatist.com/fitness/women-sports-viewership-080212/.

Schreier, Barbara A. (1989). "Sporting Wear," in *Men and Women: Dressing the Part*, ed. Claudia Brush Kidwell and Valerie Steele. Washington: Smithsonian Institution Press, 92–123.

Schwartz, Herman M., and Aida Hozic. (2001). "Who Needs the New Economy?" *Salon* (March 16). http://www.salon.com/2001/03/16/schwartz_2/.

Sconce, Jeffrey. (2004). "What If? Charting Television's New Textual Boundaries," in *Television After TV: Essays on a Medium in Transition*, ed. Lynn Spigel and Jan Olsson. Durham, NC: Duke University Press. 93–112.

Secretaría Federal de Asuntos Económicos, Cámara Colombiana de Informática y Telecomunicaciones, Ministerio de Ambiente, Vivienda y Desarrollo Territorial, Computadores para Educar, Universidad de los Andes. (2008). *Gestión de Residuos Electrónicos en Colombia Diagnóstico de Computadores y Teléfonos Celulares Informe Final*. Bogotá: Secretaría Federal de Asuntos Económicos, Cámara Colombiana de Informática y Telecomunicaciones, Ministerio de Ambiente, Vivienda y Desarrollo Territorial, Computadores para Educar, Universidad de los Andes.

Segoviana García, Jenny. (2011). "Dialéctica de la ilustración y sus aportaciones al studio de los medios masivos," *Razón y Palabra* 75. http://www.razonypalabra.org.mx/N/N75/monotematico_75/34_Segoviano_M75.pdf.

Seiter, Ellen. (2005). *The Internet Playground: Children's Access, Entertainment, and Mis-Education*. New York: Peter Lang.

Seiter, Ellen, Hans Borchers, Gabriele Kreutzner, and Eva-Marie Wrath, eds. (1989). *Remote Control: Television, Audiences and Cultural Power*. London: Routledge.

Selden, M. A., Helzberg, J. H., Waeckerle, J. F., Browne, J. E., Brewer, J. H., Monaco, M. E., Tang, F., and O'Keefe, J. H. (2009). "Cardiometabolic Abnormalities in Current National Football League Players," *American Journal of Cardiology* 103/7: 969–71.

Semati, Mehdi. (2007). "Media, the State, and the Prodemocracy Movement in Iran," in *Negotiating Democracy: Media Transformations in Emerging Democracies*, ed. Isaac A. Blankson and Patrick D. Murphy. Albany: State University of New York Press, 143–60.

Sen, Amartya. (2009). *The Idea of Justice*. Cambridge, MA: The Belknap Press.

Sen, Sudhi Ranjan. (2015). "Government Serves Legal Notice to BBC, Asks YouTube to Remove Nirbhaya Documentary: 10 Developments," *NDTV* (March 6). http://www.ndtv.com/cheat-sheet/on-nirbhaya-documentary-its-the-government-vs-bbc-youtube-google-10-developments-744579?site=full.

Sénat français. (2009). *Projet de loi portant engagement national pour l'environnement*. Paris: Sénat français.

Shachtman, Noah. (2002). "Shoot 'Em Up and Join the Army," *Wired* (July 4). http://archive.wired.com/gaming/gamingreviews/news/2002/07/53663.

Shade, Leslie Regan, and Nikki Porter. (2008). "Empire and Sweatshop Girlhoods: The Two Faces of the Global Culture Industry," in *Feminist Interventions in International Communication: Minding the Gap*, ed. Katharine Sarikakis and Leslie Regan Shade. Lanham, MD: Rowman & Littlefield, 241–56.

Shamsie, Jamal, Xavier Martin, and Danny Miller. (2009). "In with the Old, In with the New: Capabilities, Strategies, and Performance: Among the Hollywood Studios," *Strategic Management Journal* 30/13: 1440–52.

Shapiro, Judy. (2010). "Why Mobile Technology is Still Going to Save the World," *Advertising Age* (July 26). http://adage.com/article/digitalnext/mobile-technology-save-world/145084/.

Shapiro, Michael J. (2004). *Methods and Nations: Cultural Governance and the Indigenous Subject*. New York: Routledge.

Shapiro, Michael J. (2007). "The New Violent Cartography," *Security Dialogue* 38/3: 291–313.

Sharkey, Jacqueline E. (2003). "The Television War." *American Journalism Review* 25/4 (May): 20.

Shepherd, Ben, and Susan Stone. (2013). "Global Production Networks and Employment: A Developing Country Perspective," *OECD Trade Policy Papers* 154. http://dx.doi.org/10.1787/5k46j0rjq9s8-en.

Shils, Edward. (1966). "Mass Society and its Culture," in *Reader in Public Opinion and Communication*, 2nd edn., ed. Bernard Berelson and Morris Janowitz. New York: Free Press, 505–28.

Shimpach, Shawn. (2010). *Television in Transition: The Life and Afterlife of the Narrative Action Hero*. Malden, MA: Blackwell.

Shively, JoEllen. (2009). "Cowboys and Indians: Perceptions of Western Films Among American Indians and Anglos," in *The Contemporary Hollywood Reader*, ed. Toby Miller. London: Routledge, 409–20.

Shor, Eran. (2010). "In Search of a Voice: Arab Soccer Players in the Israeli Media," *Viewpoints*: 7–10.

Shore, Elena. (2004). "Ho Chi Minh Protests," *Pacific News Service*. http://02e1137.netsolhost.com/villages/asian/politics_law/archives/pns_hochiminh_protests_0504.asp.

Siebert, Fred S., Theodore Peterson, and Wilbur Schramm. (1963/1956). *Four Theories of the Press*. Urbana: University of Illinois Press.

Silber, John R. (1968). "Television: A Personal View," in *The Meaning of Commercial Television: The Texas-Stanford Seminar*, ed. Stanley T. Donner. Austin: University of Texas Press, 113–39.

Silicon Valley Toxics Coalition. (n.d). *Electronic Industry Overview*. San Jose, CA: Silicon Valley Toxics Coalition.

Silver, David, and Alice Marwick. (2006). "Internet Studies in Times of Terror," in *Critical Cyberculture Studies*, ed. David Silver and Adrienne Massanari. New York: New York University Press, 47–54.

Simon, Ron. (2005). "The Changing Definition of Reality Television," in *Thinking Outside the Box: A Contemporary Television Genre Reader*, ed. Gary R. Edgerton and Brian G. Rose. Lexington: University Press of Kentucky, 179–200.

Simonton, Dean Keith. (2009). "Cinematic Success Criteria and Their Predictors: The Art and Business of the Film Industry," *Psychology & Marketing* 26/5: 400–20.

Sinclair, John. (1982). "From 'Modernization' to Cultural Dependence: Mass Communication Studies and the Third World," *Media Information Australia* 23: 5–11.

Sinclair, John. (1992). "The Decentering of Cultural Imperialism: Televisa-ion and Globo-ization in the Latin World," *Intercom* 16: 120–34.

Sisler, Vit. (2008). "Digital Arabs: Representation in Video Games," *European Journal of Cultural Studies* 11/2: 203–20.

Siwek, Stephen E. (2013). *Copyright Industries in the US Economy: The 2013 Report*. International Intellectual Property Alliance. http://www.iipa.com/pdf/2013_Copyright_Industries_Full_Report.PDF.

Skilton, Paul F. (2008). "Similarity, Familiarity and Access to Elite Work in Hollywood: Employer and Employee Characteristics in Breakthrough Employment," *Human Relations* 61/12: 1743–73.

Slade, Christina, and Annabel Beckenham. (2005). "Introduction: *Telenovelas* and Soap Operas: Negotiating Reality," *Television & New Media* 6/4: 337–41.

Sloan, L. R. (1989). "The Motives of Sports Fans," in *Sports, Games, and Play: Social and Psychological Motivations*, 2nd edn., ed. J. H. Goldstein. Hillsdale, NJ: Lawrence Erlbaum, 175–240.

Smith, Aaron. (2010). *Americans and Their Gadgets*. Pew Research Center (October 14). http://www.pewinternet.org/2010/10/14/americans-and-their-gadgets/.

Smith, Dorothy E. (1987). *The Everyday World as Problematic: A Feminist Sociology*. Boston, MA: Northeastern University Press.

Smith, Sydney. (1844). *The Works of the Rev. Sydney Smith*. Philadelphia, PA: Carey and Hart.

Smythe, Dallas. (1954). "Reality as Presented by Television," *Public Opinion Quarterly* 18/2: 143–56.

Smythe, Dallas. (2004). "The Consumer's Stake in Radio and Television," in *Mass Communication and American Social Thought: Key Texts, 1919-1968*, ed. John Durham Peters and Peter Simonson. Lanham, MD: Rowman & Littlefield, 318–28.

Snow, C. P. (1987). *The Two Cultures and a Second Look: An Expanded Version of the Two Cultures and the Scientific Revolution*. Cambridge: Cambridge University Press.

Solomon, Norman. (2001). "Media War Without End," *Z Magazine* (December). https://zcomm.org/zmagazine/media-war-without-end-by-norman-solomon/.

Song, Seagull Haiyan. (2011). "How Should China Respond to the Online Piracy of Live Sports

Telecasts? A Comparative Study of Chinese Copyright Legislation to US and European Legislation," *University of Denver Sports and Entertainment Law Journal* 9: 3–21.

Sparks, Robert. (1992). "'Delivering the Male": Sports, Canadian Television, and the Making of TSN," *Canadian Journal of Communication* 17/1: 319–42.

Spears, Nancy, Marla Royne, and Eric Van Steenburg. (2013). "Are Celebrity-Heroes Effective Endorsers? Exploring the Link Between Hero, Celebrity, and Advertising Response," *Journal of Promotion Management* 19/1: 17–37.

Spigel, Lynn. (2005). "TV's Next Season?" *Cinema Journal* 45/1: 83–90.

Spindler, Amy. (2001). "The Lady Vanishes," *New York Times* (January 21). http://www.nytimes.com/2001/01/21/magazine/style-the-lady-vanishes.html.

Sreberny-Mohammadi, Annabelle. (1997). "The Many Cultural Faces of Imperialism," in *Beyond Cultural Imperialism: Globalization, Communication and the New International Order*, ed. Peter Golding and Phil Harris. London: Sage, 49–68.

Stack, Steven. (2003). "Media Coverage as a Risk Factor in Suicide," *Journal of Epidemiology and Community Health* 57: 238–40.

Staiger, Janet. (2005). *Media Reception Studies*. New York: New York University Press.

Stam, Robertm, and Toby Miller, eds. (2000). *Film and Theory: An Anthology*. Oxford: Blackwell.

State Department. (2010). *Leading Through Civilian Power: The First Quadrennial Diplomacy and Development Review*. http://www.state.gov/s/dmr/qddr/.

State Department. (2011). "State Department on Palestinian Admission to UNESCO" (October 31). http://translations.state.gov/st/english/texttrans/2011/10/20111031170111su0.1734082.html#axzz3bX4xdZ4P.

Stavitsky, Al. (1995). "Ear on America," in *Radio – The Forgotten Medium*, ed, Edward C. Pease and Everett E. Dennis. New Brunswick, NJ: Transaction, 81–93.

Stearns, Peter N. (2006). *American Fear: The Causes and Consequences of High Anxiety*. New York: Routledge.

Steemers, Jeanette. (2004). *Selling Television: British Television in the Global Marketplace*. London: British Film Institute.

Steeves, H. Leslie. (2008). "Commodifying Africa on US Network Reality Television," *Communication, Culture & Critique* 1/4: 416–46.

Steinberg, Brian. (2009). "Is CBS's 'Harper's Island' a New Broadcast Model?" *AdvertisingAge* (February 20). http://adage.com/article/media/cbs-s-harper-s-island-a-broadcast-model/134739/.

Stempel, Carl. (2006). "Televised Sports, Masculinist Moral Capital, and Support for the US Invasion of Iraq," *Journal of Sport & Social Issues* 30/1: 79–106.

Stockwell, Stephen, and Adam Muir. (2003). "The Military-Entertainment Complex: A New Facet of Information Warfare," *Fibreculture* 1. http://one.fibreculturejournal.org/fcj-004-the-military-entertainment-complex-a-new-facet-of-information-warfare.

Stonor Saunders, Frances. (1999). *Cultural Cold War: The CIA and the World of Arts and Letters*. New York: New Press.

Strange, Susan. (1995). "The Defective State," *Daedalus* 124/2: 55–74.

Straubhaar, Joseph. (1991). "Beyond Media Imperialism: Asymmetrical Interdependence and Cultural Proximity," *Critical Studies in Mass Communication* 8/1: 29–38.

Straubhaar, Joseph. (2007). *World Television: From Local to Global*. London: Sage.

Students & Scholars Against Corporate Misbehaviour. (2010). *Workers as Machines: Military Management in Foxconn*. http://sacom.hk/wp-content/uploads/2010/11/report-on-foxconn-workers-as-machines_sacom.pdf.

Suckling, James, and Jacquetta Lee. (2015). "Redefining Scope: The True Environmental Impact of Smartphones?" *International Journal of Life Cycle Assessment* 10.1007/s11367-015-0909-4.

Sullivan, Margo. (2007). "Is There Hollywood Gold in Our Hills? Tax Incentives for Filmmakers Get Mixed Reviews," *Eagle-Tribune* (February 25). http://www.eagletribune.com/local/x1876328263/Is-there-Hollywood-gold-in-our-hills-Tax-incentives-for-filmmakers-get-mixed-reviews.

Sun, Wanning. (2010). "Mission Impossible? Soft Power, Communication Capacity, and the Globalization of Chinese Media," *International Journal of Communication* 4: 54–72.

Takacs, Stacy. (2009). "The Body of War and the Management of Imperial Anxiety on US Television," *International Journal of Contemporary Iraqi Studies* 3/1: 85–105.

Tang, Tang, and Roger Cooper. (2012). "Gender, Sports, and New Media: Predictors of Viewing During the 2008 Beijing Olympics," *Journal of Broadcasting & Electronic Media* 56/1: 75–91.

Tannenwald, Robert. (2010). *State Film Subsidies: Not Much Bang for Too Many Bucks.* Washington, DC: Center on Budget and Policy Priorities.

Taylor, Brendan. (2005). "Coral Bell's Contribution to Australian Foreign Policy," *Australian Journal of International Affairs* 59/3: 257–60.

Thompson, Clive. (2004). "The Making of an X Box Warrior," *New York Times Magazine* (August 22). http://www.nytimes.com/2004/08/22/magazine/22GAMES.html.

Thompson, Jon. (1993). *Fiction, Crime, and Empire: Clues to Modernity and Postmodernism.* Urbana: University of Illinois Press.

Thomson, Ian, and Robert G. Boutilier. (2011). "Social License to Operate," in *SME Mining Engineering Handbook*, ed. Peter Darling. Littleton, CO: Society for Mining, Metallurgy and Exploration, 1779–796.

Thrall, A. Trevor, Jaime Lollio-Fahkreddine, Jon Berent, Lana Donnelly, Wes Herrin, Zachary Paquette, Rebecca Wenglinski, and Amy Wyatt. (2008). "Star Power: Celebrity Advocacy and the Evolution of the Public Sphere," *International Journal of Press/Politics* 13/4: 362–85.

Thussu, Daya Kishan. (2004). "Media Plenty and the Poverty of News," in *International News in the 21st Century*, ed. Chris Paterson and Annabelle Sreberny. London: John Libbey Publishing, 47–61.

Till, Brian D., Sarah M. Stanley, and Randi Priluck. (2008). "Classical Conditioning and Celebrity Endorsers: An Examination of Belongingness and Resistance to Extinction," *Psychology & Marketing* 25/2: 179–96.

Tillman, Kevin. (2006). "After Pat's Birthday," *Truthdig* (October 19). http://www.truthdig.com/report/item/200601019_after_pats_birthday.

Tillman, Mary, with Narda Zacchino. (2008). *Boots on the Ground at Dusk: My Tribute to Pat Tillman.* New York: Modern Times.

Toffler, Alvin. (1983). *Previews and Premises.* New York: William Morrow.

Tomlinson, John. (1991). *Cultural Imperialism.* Baltimore, MD: Johns Hopkins University Press.

Toomer, Jessica. (2014). "Human Rights Group Skewers '24' for Graphic Torture Scenes," *Huffington Post* (May 16). http://www.huffingtonpost.com/2014/05/16/amnesty-international-24-torture_n_5337058.html.

Trail, Galen T. and Jeffrey D. James. (2001). "The Motivation Scale for Sport Consumption: Assessment of the Scale's Psychometric Properties," *Journal of Sport Behavior* 24/1: 108–27.

Trumpbour, John. (2002). *Selling Hollywood to the World: U.S. and European Struggles for Mastery of the Global Film Industry, 1920–1950.* Cambridge: Cambridge University Press.

Tuchman, Gaye. (2009). *Wannabe U: Inside the Corporate University.* Chicago, IL: University of Chicago Press.

Tunstall, Jeremy. (1977). *The Media Are American.* New York: Oxford University Press.

Turow, Joseph. (2005). "Audience Construction and Culture Production: Marketing Surveillance in the Digital Age," *Annals of the American Academy of Political and Social Science* 597: 103–21.

Turse, Nick. (2008). *The Complex: How the Military Invades Our Everyday Lives.* New York: Metropolitan Books.

Ulrich, Pamela Conley and Lance Simmers. (2001). "Motion Picture Production: To Run or Stay Made in the USA," *Loyola of Los Angeles Entertainment Law Review* 21: 357–70.

United Nations Conference on Trade and Development. (2013). "Trade in Creative Products Reached New Peak in 2011, UNCTAD Figures Show" (May 15). http://unctad.org/en/pages/newsdetails.aspx?OriginalVersionID=498&Sitemap_x0020_Taxonomy=UNCTAD%20Home.

United Nations Development Program. (2004). *Human Development Report 2004: Cultural Liberty in Today's Diverse World.* http://hdr.undp.org/en/content/human-development-report-2004.

United Nations Development Program. (2009). *Communication for Development: A Glimpse at UNDP's Practice.* http://www.undp.org/content/undp/en/home/librarypage/democratic-governance/civic_engagement/communication-for-development-a-glimpse-at-undps-practice-.html.

United Nations Panel of Experts on the Illegal Exploitation of Natural Resources and Other Forms of Wealth of the Democratic Republic of the Congo. (2002). *Final Report*. http://www.srwolf.com/reports/UNCONGO.pdf.

United States Fish and Wildlife Service. (1999). *Bird Kills at Towers and Other Human-Made Structures: An Annotated Partial Bibliography (1960–1998)*. Washington, DC: Office of Migratory Bird Management.

Uribe, Ana Berta. (2009). *Mi México imaginado: Televisión, telenovelas y migrantes*. Colima: Editorial Porrúa/El Colegio de la Frontera Norte/Universidad de Colima.

Valdivia, Angharad. (2001). "Rhythm Is Gonna Get You! Teaching Evaluations and the Feminist Multicultural Classroom," *Feminist Media Studies* 1/3: 387–9.

Varis, Tapio. (1974). "Global Traffic in Television," *Journal of Communication* 24/1: 102–9.

Varis, Tapio. (1984). "The International Flow of Television Programs," *Journal of Communication* 34/1: 143–52.

Verklin, David, and Bernice Kanner. (2007). "Why a Killer Videogame is the US Army's Best Recruitment Tool," *MarketingProfs* (May 29). http://www.marketingprofs.com/7/videogame-us-army-recruitment-tool-verklin-kanner.asp.

Verrier, Robert. (2013). "Hollywood's New Financiers Make Deals with State Tax Credits," *Los Angeles Times* (December 26). http://www.latimes.com/entertainment/envelope/cotown/la-et-ct-holly wood-financiers-20131226,0,5151886.story.

Verrier, Robert. (2014a). "Paramount Stops Releasing Major Movies on Film," *Los Angeles Times* (January 18). http://www.latimes.com/entertainment/envelope/cotown/la-et-ct-paramount-end-to-film-20140118,0,806855.story.

Verrier, Robert. (2014b). "Paramount to Make Some Exceptions to All-Digital Policy," *Los Angeles Times* (January 28). http://www.latimes.com/entertainment/envelope/cotown/la-et-ct-para mount-pictures-digital-20140128,0,276668.story#axzz2sLvViX9i.

Vincent, Norah. (2000). "Hop on Pop: Lear, Seinfeld, and the Dumbing Down of the Academy," *Village Voice* (February 2–8). http://www.villagevoice.com/2000-02-01/nyc-life/hop-on-pop/full/.

Virilio, Paul. (2004). *Art and Fear*, trans. Julie Rose. New York: Continuum.

Vohra, Paromita. (2015). "A Very Short but So Open Letter to White Feminist Filmmakers," *The Ladies Finger* (March 5). http://theladiesfinger.com/a-very-short-but-so-open-letter-to-white-feminist-filmmakers/.

Voigt, Kevin. (2011). "Mobile Phone: Weapon Against Global Poverty," *CNN* (October 9). http://www.cnn.com/2011/10/09/tech/mobile/mobile-phone-poverty/index.html.

Volčič, Zala, and Mark Andrejevic. (2009). "That's Me: Nationalism and Identity of Balkan Reality TV," *Canadian Journal of Communication* 34/1. http://www.cjc-online.ca/index.php/journal/article/view/2113.

Volčič, Zala. (2007). "Yugo-Nostalgia: Cultural Memory and Media in the Former Yugoslavia," *Critical Studies in Media Communication* 24/1: 21–38.

Volz, Dustin. (2014). "Sen. Levin Blasts Apple for Abusing 'Sweetheart' Tax Deal with Ireland," *National Journal* (October 1). http://www.nationaljournal.com/tech/sen-levin-blasts-apple-for-abusing-sweetheart-tax-deal-with-ireland-20140930.

von Rimscha, M. Bjørn. (2009). "Managing Risk in Motion Picture Project Development," *Journal of Media Business Studies* 6/4: 75–101.

Wallas, Graham. (1967). *The Great Society: A Psychological Analysis*. Lincoln: University of Nebraska Press.

Wallerstein, Immanuel. (1989). "Culture as the Ideological Battleground of the Modern World-System," *Hitotsubashi Journal of Social Studies* 21/1: 5–22.

Walsh, Michael. (1997). "Fighting the American Invasion with Cricket, Roses, and Marmalade for Breakfast," *Velvet Light Trap* 40: 3–17.

Wang, Georgette. (2009). "Going Beyond the Dualistic View of Culture and Market Economy: Learning from the Localization of Reality Television in Greater China," *Chinese Journal of Communication* 2/2: 127–39.

Wang, Yanlai. (2003). *China's Economic Development and Democratization*. Farnham: Ashgate.

Wanger, Walter. (1950). "Donald Duck and Diplomacy," *Public Opinion Quarterly* 14/3: 443–52.

Wann, Daniel L. (1995). "Preliminary Validation of the Sport Fan Motivation Scale," *Journal of Sport & Social Issues* 19/4: 377–96.

Wark, Wesley K. "The Intelligence Revolution and the Future," *Queen's Quarterly* 100/2 (1993): 273–87.

Warner, Michael. (2002). "Publics and Counterpublics," *Public Culture* 14/1: 49–90.

Wartella, Ellen. (1996). "The History Reconsidered," in *American Communication Research – The Remembered History*, ed. Everett E. Dennis and Ellen Wartella. Mahwah, NJ: Erlbaum, 169–80.

Wasko, Janet, ed. (2005). *A Companion to Television*. Malden, MA: Blackwell.

Wasko, Janet, Graham Murdock, and Helena Sousa, eds. (2011). *The Handbook of Political Economy of Communications*. Malden, MA: Blackwell.

Wasko, Janet, Mark Phillips, and Eileen R. Meehan, eds. (2001). *Dazzled by Disney: The Global Disney Audiences Project*. London: Leicester University Press.

Waters, Malcolm. (1996). *Globalization*. London: Routledge.

Waxmonsky, Jim, and Eugene V. Beresin. (2001). "Taking Professional Wrestling to the Mat: A Look at the Appeal and Potential Effects of Professional Wrestling on Children," *Academic Psychiatry* 25/2: 125–31.

Wayne, Mike. (2003). *Marxism and Media Studies: Key Concepts and Contemporary Trends*. London: Pluto Press.

Weber, Max. (2000). "Commerce on the Stock and Commodity Exchanges," trans. Steven Lestition. *Theory and Society* 29/3: 339–71.

Weber, Samuel. (2000). "The Future of the Humanities: Experimenting," *Culture Machine* 2. http://www.culturemachine.net/index.php/cm/article/viewArticle/311.

Webster, Wendy. (2009). "'Europe Against the Germans": The British Resistance Narrative, 1940–1950," *Journal of British Studies* 48: 958–82.

Weed, Mike. (2008). "Exploring the Sport Spectator Experience: Virtual Football Spectatorship in the Pub," *Soccer & Society* 9/2: 189–97.

Wei, Luo. (2010). "Chinese Reality TV and Politics: Entertainment vs. Socio-Political Responsibility," in *Reel Politics: Television as a Platform for Political Discourse*, ed. Lemi Baruh and Ji Hoon Park. Newcastle upon Tyne: Cambridge Scholars Publishing, 165–81.

Weissman, Nicole. (2010). "A Timely Message About Female Sports Fans," *Washington Post* (September 16). http://voices.washingtonpost.com/box-seats/2010/09/a_timely_message_about_female.html.

Wells, H. G. (1902). *Anticipations of the Reaction of Mechanical and Scientific Progress Upon Human Life and Thought*, 2nd edn. London: Chapman & Hall.

Wenner, Lawrence A. (1998). "In Search of the Sports Bar: Masculinity, Alcohol, Sports, and the Mediation of Public Space," *Sport and Postmodern Times*, ed. Geneviève Rail. Albany: State University of New York Press, 302–32.

Wenner, Lawrence A., and Walter Gantz. (1998). "Watching Sports on Television: Audience Experience, Gender, Fanship, and Marriage," in *MediaSport*, ed. Lawrence A. Wenner. London: Routledge. 233–51.

Wentz, Laurel. (2009). "Univision: YouTube's Most Pirated Broadcast TV Network," *AdvertisingAge* (February 12). http://adage.com/article/hispanic-marketing/univision-youtube-s-pirated-broadcast-tv-network/134572/.

Westlake, Mike. (1980). "The Classic TV Detective Genre," *Framework* 13: 37–8.

Weston, Kath. (2009). "The Lady Vanishes: On Never Knowing, Quite, Who is a Lesbian," *Journal of Lesbian Studies* 13: 136–48.

Wheeler, Mark. (2004). "Supranational Regulation: Television and the European Union," *European Journal of Communication* 19/3: 349–69.

White, E. B. (1997). *One Man's Meat*. Gardiner, ME: Tilbury House.

White, Josh. (2005). "Army Withheld Details About Tillman's Death," *Washington Post* (May 4): A3.

Whiten, Jon. (2004). "Bad News from Iraq?" *EXTRA!Update* (February): 3.

Whittam Smith, Andreas. (2008). "Media Studies is No Preparation for Journalism," *Independent*

(February 25). http://www.independent.co.uk/voices/commentators/andreas-whittam-smith/andreas-whittam-smith-media-studies-is-no-preparation-for-journalism-786785.html.

Wikle, Thomas A. (2002). "Cellular Tower Proliferation in the United States," *Geographical Review* 92/1: 45–62.

Wilkins, Karin. (1998). "Gender, Power and Development," *Journal of International Communication* 4/2: 102–20.

Williams, Raymond. (1977). *Marxism and Literature*. London: Oxford University Press.

Williams, Raymond. (1983). *Keywords: A Vocabulary of Culture and Society*, rev. edn. New York: Oxford University Press.

Wilson, Robert. (2004). *The Vanished Hands*. Orlando, FL: Harcourt, Inc.

Winocur, Rosalía. (2002). *Ciudadanos mediáticos: La construcción de lo publico en la radio*. Barcelona: Editorial Gedisa.

Wojtys, Edward M. (2009). "Big Hits," *Sports Health: A Multidisciplinary Approach* 1/6: 459.

Wong, Coby S. C., S. C. Wu, Nurdan S. Duzgoren-Aydin, Adnan Aydin, and Ming H. Wong. (2007). "Trace Metal Contamination of Sediments in an E-Waste Processing Village in China," *Environmental Pollution* 145/2: 434–42.

Wood, Gaby. (2009). "'I'm a Little Bit of a Nerd'," *Guardian* (June 7). http://www.guardian.co.uk/film/2009/jun/07/interview-daryl-hannah.

Woodhead, Chris. (2009). "Dive for Cover if You See 'Studies': It Means Bogus," *Times* (March 8): 9.

World Health Organization. (2011). *Smoke-Free Movies: From Evidence to Action*, 2nd ed. Geneva: WHO.

Yang, Guobin. (2009). *The Power of the Internet in China: Citizen Activism*. New York: Columbia University Press.

Yesil, Bilge. (2015). "Transnationalization of Turkish Dramas: Exploring the Convergence of Local and Global Market Imperatives," *Global Media and Communication* 11/1: 43–60.

Yildirim, Caglar, and Ana-Paula Correia. (2015). "Exploring the Dimensions of Nomophobia: Development and Validation of a Self-Reported Questionnaire," *Computers in Human Behavior* 49: 130–7.

York, Emily Bryson. (2010). "What it Takes to be an 'Undercover Boss'," *AdAge* (February 15). http://adage.com/article/news/7-eleven-hooters-risk-undercover-boss/142119/.

Yúdice, George. (2002). *El recurso de la cultura: Usos de la cultura en la era global*. Barcelona: Editorial Gedisa.

Zafra Zafra, Guillermo. (2012). *El reality en Colombia: Un género de telenovela*. Bogotá: Primera Edición.

Zalewski, Piotr. (2013). "As Turkey Turns," *Slate* (August 16). http://www.slate.com/articles/arts/roads/2013/08/turkish_soap_operas_go_global_turkey_s_homemade_melodramas_are_popular_across.html.

Zamyatin, Yevgeny. (1924). *We*, trans. Gregory Zillboorg. New York: E. P. Dutton.

Zassoursky, Yassen, and Sergei Losev. (1981). "Information in the Service of Progress," *Journal of Communication* 31/4: 118–121.

Zhao, Yuezhi, and Zhenzhi Guo. (2005). "Television in China: History, Political Economy, and Ideology," iin *A Companion to Television*, ed. Janet Wasko. London: Blackwell, 521–39.

Zhao, Yuezhi and Paula Chakravartty, eds. (2007). *Global Communications: Towards a Trascultural Political Economy*. Boulder, CO: Rowman and Littlefield.

Zirin, Dave. (2005). "Pat Tillman, Our Hero," *The Nation* (October 6). http://www.thenation.com/article/pat-tillman-our-hero.

Zirin, Dave. (2008). "Sarah Palin's Extreme Sports," *The Nation* (October 7). http://www.thenation.com/article/sarah-palins-extreme-sports.

Žižek, Slavoj. (2006,). "The Depraved Heroes of *24* are the Himmlers of Hollywood," *Guardian* (January 10). http://www.theguardian.com/media/2006/jan/10/usnews.comment/print.

Zuraik, Rami. (2011). *Food, Farming and Freedom: Sowing the Arab Spring*. Charlottesville, NC: Just World Books.

Zyvatkauskas, Caz. (2007). "Theatre Critic," *The Economist* (February 3): 18.

Index

ABC, 48–50, 102–3, 135, 170, 174
Abramson, Bram Dov, 62–3
academic disciplines, 9–10
Action for Children's Television, 164
activism, 17, 38, 46–7, 139
Adams, James Truslow, 162
Adorno, Theodor W., 7, 164
advertising, 8, 9, 29, 57, 180
  celebrity endorsements, 45, 173
  Saudi Arabia, 71
  sport, 172
  television, 170
aesthetics, 5, 18
Afghanistan, 103, 104, 129, 132,
  133–4
Africa
  cell phones, 85, 185n4
  class interests, 7
  emergence from imperial control,
    24
  e-waste, 94
  reality television, 145–6, 154–6, 158,
    159
African Americans, 161, 181
The Age, 124
Aillagon, Jean-Jacques, 150
Al Abed, Ibrahim, 76, 77
al-'Alam, 78, 80
al-Aqsa television, 77, 80
al-Arabiya, 69
Algan, Ece, 141
Algeria, 154
al-Hawa Sawa, 153
al-Hurra, 77–8
Alias, 170
al-Jazeera, 69, 70, 77, 103, 104
al-Mahdy, Aliaa, 136
al-Maktoum, Sheikh Mohammad bin
  Rashed, 75
al-Manar, 71, 77, 80
Almunia, Joaquín, 89
al-Qaeda, 26, 104, 108
al-Ra'is, 154, 159
The Amazing Race, 156
The Ambassador, 158

American Petroleum Institute (API), 38
America's Army, 98, 106–7
America's Most Wanted, 142
Amnesty International, 128
Andrejevic, Mark, 147–8, 150, 157
animal rights, 121
Anytime Anywhere Media Measurement,
  171
Appadurai, Arjun, 32
Apple, 89, 90, 91–2, 96
The Apprentice, 19, 48
Arab News, 26
Arab Radio and Television, 153
Arab Satellite Television Charter (ASTC),
  60, 69, 76–80
Arab states
  Arab Spring, 85
  policies, 60, 69–80
  reality television, 145–6, 147, 148, 153–5,
    159
Arabic TRT, 78
Ardón, Julia, 136
Argentina, 3, 68, 141
Aridi, Ghazi, 73
Arnheim, Rudolf, 35
Arnold, Matthew, 23
Asia
  Asian Tigers, 40
  audiences, 167
  class interests, 7
  emergence from imperial control, 24
  e-waste, 94
  reality television, 145–6
  rise of, 80
  television trade, 52, 54
  universities, 34
Aslama, Minna, 145, 150, 156
Associated Press, 104
Association for Education in Journalism
  and Mass Communication (AEJMC),
  11–12
astroturfing, 38
AT&T, 89, 181
Atari, 106
Attali, Jacques, 7